Shopify

by Paul Waddy

for dummies®
A Wiley Brand

Shopify For Dummies®

Published by

John Wiley & Sons Australia, Ltd

42 McDougall Street

Milton, Qld 4064

www.dummies.com

Copyright © 2022 John Wiley & Sons Australia, Ltd

The moral rights of the author have been asserted.

 A catalogue record for this book is available from the National Library of Australia

ISBN: 978-0-730-39445-7

Cover image: © AnnaStills/Shutterstock

Typeset by Straive
Printed and bound by CPI Group (UK) Ltd, Croydon, CR0 4YY

C9780730394457_280923

Contents at a Glance

Introduction 1

Part 1: Getting Started with Shopify 5

CHAPTER 1: Introducing the Ecommerce Essentials. 7
CHAPTER 2: Finding Your Way Around Shopify 15
CHAPTER 3: Sourcing Products and Identifying Sales Channels. 35

Part 2: Preparing Your Store for Launch 53

CHAPTER 4: Designing Your Shopify Store. 55
CHAPTER 5: Filling Your Virtual Shelves: Creating Products and Collections 81
CHAPTER 6: Setting Up Shipping and Receiving Payments 109

**Part 3: Curating the Customer Experience:
The Customer Is Always Right** 143

CHAPTER 7: What's the Difference? Customer Service and
Customer Experience. 145
CHAPTER 8: Reviews, Customer Loyalty and User-Generated Content 161
CHAPTER 9: Understanding the User Experience 189
CHAPTER 10: Getting Personal: Personalizing Your Website. 203

**Part 4: Taking Stock of the Situation: Inventory,
Logistics and Orders** 221

CHAPTER 11: Stocked Up: Buying, Receiving and Managing Inventory. 223
CHAPTER 12: So, You've Received an Order — Now What?. 247
CHAPTER 13: From Here to There: Fulfilling Your Orders 267

Part 5: Attracting Attention: Sales and Marketing 291

CHAPTER 14: Pricing, Discounts and Promotions: Creating Eye-Catching Offers . . . 293
CHAPTER 15: Getting Discovered: Finding New Customers 317
CHAPTER 16: Advertising and Promoting Your Online Store 333
CHAPTER 17: Getting Social: Using Social Media to Grow Your Business 363

Part 6: The Part of Tens 379

CHAPTER 18: Ten Helpful Apps for Your Shopify Store 381
CHAPTER 19: Ten Ways to Improve the Customer and User Experience 389
CHAPTER 20: Ten Ways to Prepare to Go Live 399

Index 409

Table of Contents

INTRODUCTION 1
  About This Book. 2
  Foolish Assumptions. 2
  Icons Used in This Book 3
  Where to Go from Here 4

PART 1: GETTING STARTED WITH SHOPIFY 5

CHAPTER 1: **Introducing the Ecommerce Essentials** 7
  Explaining Ecommerce 8
  Introducing Shopify. 9
  Planning for Ecommerce Success 10
  Getting Creative: Setting Up Your Shopify Store. 11
  Making Friends with Your Customers 12
  Taking Care of Business: Managing Stock Levels and Delivering
    Orders 12
  Growing Your Business through Marketing .13
  Going Live! 14

CHAPTER 2: **Finding Your Way Around Shopify** 15
  Choosing a Shopify Plan. 15
    Basic Shopify 16
    Shopify 16
    Advanced Shopify 17
    Shopify Plus 17
  Shopify's Support Services. 19
  Deciding on Your Domain Name. 21
  Where Am I? Signing Up with Shopify. 22
  Navigating the Shopify Admin Panel 25
    Home. 26
    Orders. 27
    Products 27
    Customers 27
    Analytics 27
    Marketing 30
    Discounts 30
    Apps. 30
    Sales channels 30
    Settings 32
  Using Shopify to Sell In-store and Digital Products 32
    Shopify POS 32
    Using Shopify to sell digital products 33

CHAPTER 3: Sourcing Products and Identifying Sales Channels 35

Sourcing the Right Products to Sell..36
    Locating products to sell 36
    Supply and demand: Tools to check for trending products 37
    Checking trending products in Shopify 40

Introducing Online Sales Channels...41
    D2C: Direct to consumer sales 41
    B2C: Business to Consumer sales............................42
    B2B: Business to Business sales 43

All about Dropshipping...44
    Comparing the different kinds of dropshipping...............45
    Considering the pros and cons of dropshipping 47
    Dropshipping on Shopify 47

Selling on Online Marketplaces..48

PART 2: PREPARING YOUR STORE FOR LAUNCH............ 53

CHAPTER 4: Designing Your Shopify Store 55

Coding, Web Developers and Shopify 56
Finding Your Way: Website Architecture 57
Team with the Theme: Exploring Shopify Themes....................59
    Choosing a theme 60
    Eureka! You've found your theme............................60
    Publishing your theme 61
    Customizing your theme 62

Designing Your Shop Window: The Homepage 62
    What's on the menu? 63
    Styling your homepage.......................................64
    Adjusting your theme's settings 74

Adding Menus and Pages..76
    Creating a page 77
    Creating a menu item..79

CHAPTER 5: Filling Your Virtual Shelves: Creating Products and Collections............................. 81

Nuts and Bolts: Adding Products to Develop Your Collections.......82
    Creating a collection 82
    Using product tags to refine your collections 86
    Adding collections to your menu 89
    Adding a new product to your store..........................90

Merchandising Your Collections 106
Activating Products in Your Store 107

CHAPTER 6: **Setting Up Shipping and Receiving Payments**. 109

One Size Does Not Fit All: Exploring Shipping Options 110
Free shipping versus paid shipping 110
Express shipping versus standard shipping 115
Shopify and shipping 117
Getting Started with Shipping in Shopify. .120
Adjusting your default package type 121
Shipping rates and profiles 124
Tax Time: Setting Up Tax Rates. 129
Setting up tax collecting in your store 130
Including tax in your product price. 133
The Fun Part: Getting Paid 133
Setting up Shopify Payments. 134
Accepting other payment methods 136
Viewing your Shopify Payouts 137
Setting up multiple currencies in Shopify Payments 138
Setting up a third-party payment provider 139
Fraud prevention. 139
Investigating suspicious orders. 139
Processing chargebacks 141

**PART 3: CURATING THE CUSTOMER EXPERIENCE:
THE CUSTOMER IS ALWAYS RIGHT**. 143

CHAPTER 7: **What's the Difference? Customer Service
and Customer Experience**. 145

Customer Service 101: Communicating with Customers 146
Creating clear policies and product information 146
Customer service channels to consider .149
Using Customer Service Metrics 154
Maximizing Customer Experience 155
Providing an excellent customer experience 157
Measuring customer experience. 158
Checking Customer Satisfaction 160

CHAPTER 8: **Reviews, Customer Loyalty and
User-Generated Content** 161

Why Reviews Matter 162
Onsite product reviews. 163
Offsite customer reviews 164
Selecting a review platform to use with Shopify. 166
Free offsite review platforms to use. 168
Why Loyalty Matters 169
Understanding the lifetime value of a customer 169
Loyalty, referral programs and Shopify .172

Utilizing User-Generated Content. 174
Customer Reports: Loyal and At-risk Customers 177
    Using customer reports in Shopify 177
    Customizing your customer reports. 184

CHAPTER 9: **Understanding the User Experience** 189
Understanding the Basics of a Good User Experience 190
    Getting to know how users behave 190
    Considering the theory. 191
Improving Your User Experience 193
    Conducting user research 194
    Monitoring and maintaining your page speed 198
    Fixing broken links. 199
    Running your own device analysis 199
    Optimizing your website's internal search. 200
Implementing AB Testing. 200
    When can I start running AB tests?. 201
    I've got the traffic, so how can I AB test in Shopify? 202

CHAPTER 10: **Getting Personal: Personalizing Your Website** 203
Creating a Personalized Shopping Experience 204
Tailoring Your Store to Suit Your Customers. 206
    Personalized banners 208
    Product recommendations 209
    People also bought 210
    Product quizzes and guided selling 210
    Recently viewed items 211
    Bestsellers 211
    Personalize by location. 212
    Location-based sizing 213
The Gift of Giving: Creating and Fulfilling Gift Cards 213
    Issuing a gift card. 214
    Making gift cards available for purchase 215
Giving Little Unexpected Extras. 218
    Handwritten notes 218
    Gift with purchase 219
    Personalized video 219
    Show off your personal side 219

**PART 4: TAKING STOCK OF THE SITUATION:
INVENTORY, LOGISTICS AND ORDERS** 221

CHAPTER 11: **Stocked Up: Buying, Receiving and
Managing Inventory**. 223
Defining Inventory Management 224
Starting from Scratch: Your First Purchase Order 227

Creating a purchase order 228
Receiving a purchase order 229
Storing Your Inventory 234
Shelving equipment 236
Locations. 236
Layout and design 237
Putting Your Stock to Work: Listing Inventory Across Sales
Channels. 238
Changing a product's availability status. 239
Making products available to your sales channels. 239
Catch Me If You Can! Tracking Stock Movement 242
Using Inventory Reports. 243
Month-end Inventory Snapshot 244
Average Inventory Sold Per Day 244
Percent of Inventory Sold. 245
ABC Analysis by Product. 245

CHAPTER 12: **So, You've Received an Order — Now What?** 247
Receiving and Confirming Orders. 248
The Three Stages of an Online Order. 249
Order placed: Capture payment 249
Order paid for: Fulfill the order. 251
Order has been paid for and fulfilled: Archive the order 251
Creating Draft Orders for Customers. 253
Managing Orders. 255
Viewing an order 255
Viewing an order's Timeline. 256
Editing an order. 257
Contacting a customer about their order 258
Checking an order's status. 258
Refunding a customer. 259
Creating returns. 260
Checking an Order for Fraud. 262
Fraud analysis indicators 262
How to handle potential fraud in your store. 264

CHAPTER 13: **From Here to There: Fulfilling Your Orders** 267
Fulfill Your Own Orders 268
Fulfilling your orders manually 268
Fulfilling your orders automatically 275
Using a Fulfillment Service. 276
Activating a custom fulfillment service. .277
Deleting a custom fulfillment service. 278
Using a fulfillment service with an app .279

Printing Shipping Labels and Customs Forms 280
    Creating and printing shipping labels. 281
    Printing a customs declaration form 284
    Printing packing slips 286
Using Local Pickup. 287
    Setting up local pickup 287
    Managing local pickup locations 288
    Customizing pickup notifications 289

**PART 5: ATTRACTING ATTENTION: SALES AND
MARKETING** 291

CHAPTER 14: **Pricing, Discounts and Promotions:
Creating Eye-Catching Offers**. 293
Pricing Your Products 294
Preparing to Run Sales and Promotions 296
Setting Sale Prices for Products: The 'Compare At' Price. 298
Delivering Discounts 301
    Creating discount codes. 302
    Create a free shipping discount 311
Discounting Shortcuts. 312
    Promote a discount using a shareable link 312
    Filter discounts. 313
    Edit a discount 314
    Disable a discount 314
    Re-enable a discount. 315

CHAPTER 15: **Getting Discovered: Finding New Customers**. 317
Introducing Digital Marketing 318
Building a Marketing Plan 318
    Step 1: Define your unique value proposition 319
    Step 2: Know your customer 320
    Step 3: Choose a marketing strategy 320
    Step 4: Consider how to measure the success of your
    marketing 321
    Step 5: Create a marketing channel plan. 323
    Step 6: Review performance 323
Implementing Marketing Campaigns and Automations 324
    Automating your marketing with Shopify 325
    Creating your first automation: Abandoned Checkout Emails. . .325
    Exploring other automations. 328

CHAPTER 16: Advertising and Promoting Your Online Store 333

Getting Started with Facebook Marketing 334
Audience building ads in Shopify 337
Creating your first audience building ad .338
Creating dynamic retargeting ads. 342
Trying Search Engine Marketing with Google Ads 343
The Google sales channel in Shopify 344
Create a Google Smart Shopping campaign 348
Track the performance of your Google Smart Shopping
campaign 349
Making the Most of Search Engine Optimization 350
Using SEO keywords in your Shopify store 351
Keeping your online store SEO-friendly. 356
Experimenting with Email Marketing 357
Email marketing using Shopify 358
Installing the Shopify Email app 359
Creating an email marketing campaign using Shopify Email 360

**CHAPTER 17: Getting Social: Using Social Media to Grow
Your Business** 363

All About Socials: The Rise and Rise of Social Media
in Ecommerce 364
Meeting the Social Media Marketing Channels. 365
Facebook. 366
Instagram 368
TikTok 373
Pinterest 374
Snapchat. 375
Linking Your Social Media Profiles 375
Tapping In to Influencer Marketing 376

PART 6: THE PART OF TENS 379

CHAPTER 18: Ten Helpful Apps for Your Shopify Store 381

Gorgias: Customer Service. 382
Okendo: Product Reviews 382
Klaviyo: Email Marketing 383
Glew: Data and Business Intelligence. 384
Oberlo: Dropshipping. 384
PushOwl: Web Push Notifications. 385
Back in Stock: Customer Alerts 386
Foursixty: Shoppable Instagram and User-Generated Content 386
ReferralCandy: Referrals 387
Plug in SEO: Search Engine Optimization. 388

CHAPTER 19: **Ten Ways to Improve the Customer and User Experience** 389

Check Your Page Load Speed 390
Optimize Your Site for Mobile 391
Fix Broken Links. 391
Include a Search Function 392
Use AB Testing as Your Business Grows 393
Give Little Unexpected Extras 393
Offer a Personalized Experience. 394
Create Surveys to Help You Understand Your Customers 395
Get to Know How Your Customers Behave. .396
Use Logistics as a Point of Difference. 396

CHAPTER 20: **Ten Ways to Prepare to Go Live** 399

Pop Quiz: Are You Sure You're Ready? 399
The Price Must Be Right!. 401
Manage Your Expectations 402
You Can't Be All Things to All People 403
There's an App for That! 404
Believe the Hype (Phase) 404
Not Too Heavy, Not Too Light: Getting Ordering Just Right 405
Shopify Reports to Watch. 405
Last-Minute Checks Before You Go Live 406
Ready, Set, Go: Time to Go Live! 408

INDEX 409

Introduction

There's never been a better time to sell online. I've lost count of the number of people I've met in ecommerce who have become self-made millionaires, let alone the millions of people around the world who've decided to make their living trading over the world wide web.

You may have something in common with just about all of them — they come from diverse professional backgrounds, and hardly any of them have studied how to sell online, and there's two good reasons for that:

>> Ecommerce is such a young concept; Shopify itself was only founded in 2006, so the chances are you've had a prior career and are looking for something new.

>> Hardly any courses teach end-to-end ecommerce, so there are very few ecommerce graduates.

Before you picked up this book, there's a pretty good chance you had already heard about Shopify. Shopify is certainly a buzzword around ecommerce, and it has been generating huge amounts of global interest in recent years — a simple search on Google Trends will show as much! Now, just because people are searching in droves for Shopify online, it doesn't mean you have to try it for your online store — but I definitely recommend you do.

I've used Shopify to sell clothes, shoes, pet accessories, furniture, beverages, beds, beauty products — you name it, I've probably helped sell it. I decided to write *Shopify For Dummies* because I'm passionate about online retail and I want to be a part of growing the ecommerce ecosystem. In my career, I've founded online businesses, advised online businesses and co-founded a digital marketing agency that focuses on online retail. I've decided to share my experience and knowledge, plus the odd trick or two, with a wider audience that's ready to pick up this book, grab their laptop and a cup of coffee, and start their own Shopify store.

About This Book

I've written this book as a practical guide to starting a Shopify store. With each chapter that goes by, you'll be developing a different aspect of your online store, with the end game being that by the time you finish reading the book, your online store will be ready to go live.

This book is a little different to what you might find on YouTube, or in other books, in that I use my experience to also teach you about the business fundamentals of ecommerce, like how to choose trending products, where to source them and how to price them. You won't just be learning about the ecommerce platform that is Shopify; you'll be learning how to grow a business, as well as create a digital shop front.

Throughout this book, I explain why I rate Shopify so highly and share how you can use Shopify to run a successful ecommerce business. I look at all the steps sequentially, in an easy-to-follow manner, so that anyone can pick up the book and develop their store as they go. I also include sidebars (boxes containing examples or some extra background information) and some technical information that you may or may not feel you need to know (look out for the Technical Stuff icons that occasionally appear), but don't worry — if they're giving too much information and you want to stay focused on your end goal, you can skip those and keep on reading (you can always come back to them later). And because the book is organized in a logical way, you can always jump back to key topics if you need to refresh your memory.

Foolish Assumptions

This book doesn't require you to have any prior knowledge of how to use Shopify — that's my job. However, I do make a few assumptions about you — I assume you've got some sort of interest in selling online, and you have an inkling that Shopify may be the platform that can enable you to create a successful online store. Perhaps you've read a few blogs or watched a few YouTube videos, or even read other books that piece together various aspects of ecommerce, and you're looking for something to help you get started.

I also assume you don't have a product lined up ready to sell (although you might have — if so, good for you!). Whether you have a product stockpiled in the garage or you're tinkering with your first few product ideas, I show you how to look for products that have the potential to be bestsellers.

Perhaps you've started an online store in the past and it hasn't worked, or perhaps this is your first attempt — or maybe you're simply looking to assess whether or not this Shopify thing is for you. Wherever you're starting from, I've got you covered in this book.

I do assume you've got a computer and the appetite to discover how to build an online store, big or small. If that sounds like you, read on...

Icons Used in This Book

To keep you on your toes, I throw in useful icons throughout the book. I use these icons to draw your attention to key points, little tricks or quick wins, and short-cuts and warnings. The icons are pretty self-explanatory, but here's a summary of what they mean.

REMEMBER

If this were a textbook and you were studying for an exam, you would highlight these parts. These are the key messages that will serve you well as you undertake each stage of building your Shopify store.

TECHNICAL STUFF

I try not to get too technical, but when I do, it comes with a warning. When you see this sign, I may well be talking about stuff that you can brush over, as it's usually extra information that explains technical features. Mostly, I keep the book practical, and avoid over-techy stuff — but some of these extra details may speak to you, depending on your store.

TIP

This is what I call the gold. Hold on to these tips; they're often time-savers or money-makers!

WARNING

I use the warning icon when I am highlighting a common mistake or something you need to look out for, so try and keep an eye out for this one — the chances are you'll be learning from one of my mistakes!

EXAMPLE

To help you understand how Shopify — and ecommerce — works in real life, I add a few examples so you can start to imagine how the decisions you make may play out for your business.

Where to Go from Here

I've written this book so that you can easily navigate to the correct chapter to find out about a particular topic, or how to perform a particular task using Shopify — simply turn to the relevant part or chapter of the book and dive in. Of course, you can read it from start to finish, which is what I recommend — it is written in a logical order that you can follow to gradually build up your online store and understand the intersecting pieces that complement your Shopify store (finding products, storing products, shipping to your customers and marketing to your customers, for example). However, after you've finished reading the book, you may want to flick back to certain chapters to revisit key topics.

Don't be afraid to jump around when you feel ready — you might turn to Part 2 to find out how to build your store, then jump ahead to read more about marketing in Part 5, before going back to Part 3 to develop a deeper understanding of your customer, or Part 4 to set up shipping in Shopify. Part 1 also contains plenty of useful information on sourcing products and identifying sales channels, as well as outlining the different parts of your Shopify admin (where the magic begins in Shopify — get to know your Shopify admin in Chapter 2).

I've tried to use my experiences, both good and bad, to take you on a straightforward journey towards building a user-friendly, visually appealing and financially rewarding online store. I hope that as you work your way through the book, you'll see ways to improve your evolving store and develop the confidence to get started in your new ecommerce career. I'd love to hear how the book has helped you sell your first product on Shopify too — after all, that's why I've written the book, to help more people use Shopify to improve their lives.

I've had a great career in ecommerce, and I absolutely love using Shopify. I hope you feel excited about starting your ecommerce journey. Thanks for allowing me to play a small part in your journey — I'm excited for you too, as I know what an adventure it can be.

1

Getting Started with Shopify

Understand the essentials of ecommerce, from product idea to shipping your goods.

Get to know the Shopify admin as you take the first steps to set up your store.

Discover ways to identify new products and explore the different sales channels you can use.

» Seeing how Shopify can help you plan for success

» Getting ready to build a user-friendly online store

» Managing inventory and fulfilling orders

» Marketing your online business

Chapter **1**

Introducing the Ecommerce Essentials

E commerce is a wonderful vehicle for positive change in so many ways. I've been lucky enough to witness many people make successful careers out of both starting an online store, or working in ecommerce. I've also seen the undeniable positive impact that trading online can have on the environment, and society in general, by giving wider reach and accessibility to promote good causes or raise money. For me, ecommerce is not only a career but a passion, and I take great pride in the ecommerce community as it continues to evolve into what surely must be the future of commerce.

In this chapter I introduce you to some ecommerce essentials, including looking at the inception and history of trading goods and services online. I then go on to introduce you to Shopify, the ecommerce platform that is the subject of this book, as I explain all the areas that I drill deeper into throughout the book.

My goal in this book is to help you understand Shopify's place in the ecommerce ecosystem, and to hold your hand as you build your own Shopify store. I aim to help you build more than an online store that just goes live — my goal is to help you build a thriving, sustainable online business using the brilliant platform that is Shopify.

Shopify is for everyone, and with the right guidance and learning, you can make Shopify work for you in ways that may change your life forever. It takes patience and hard work, but it can be done — and in this book I aim to show you how.

Explaining Ecommerce

So, what is ecommerce, aside from a fancy name for selling stuff online?

Well, *ecommerce* is exactly that — the electronic sale of goods, both physical and digital, hence the name ecommerce, which simply means electronic commerce.

Drilling down further, ecommerce involves selling goods and services via an online store or any other online sales channel, such as a marketplace (think eBay and Amazon).

Although it could be claimed that ecommerce in its earliest forms (such as the introduction of electronic funds transfers) dates back to the late 1960s and 1970s, in this book I focus more on products being sold online (rather than the transmission of data, such as electronic lodgements of tax and other information).

In the 1980s and early 1990s, companies such as the Boston Computer Exchange created online marketplaces for people to sell their old computers. Fast forward a few years to 1995, and you saw the launch of the online marketplace Amazon (which you've probably heard of — and if you haven't, I suggest you put this book down and google it!). In 1999, another giant was founded: the enormous Chinese online marketplace, Alibaba. The two founders of these companies, Jeff Bezos and Jack Ma, sit high in the rankings of the wealthiest people in the world. So, you're in good company.

Whether you're a multinational or global business, an experienced retailer with multiple stores, a 'Ma and Pa' style business with a local store, or a first-timer; whether you're selling bohemian crystals, heated dog mats, shoes or all of the above, there has never been a better time to try your hand at ecommerce, and in this book I'm going to show you how Shopify can help you succeed.

Introducing Shopify

'How do I Shopify?' 'I'll take three Shopifies please.' 'John, please can you pass me the Shopify?'

These are all things that don't make sense. I am going to assume, though, that you have zero knowledge of what Shopify is, so I start from the ground up. Even if you're already selling online with Shopify, you may discover something you didn't know.

Shopify is an ecommerce platform, and an *ecommerce platform* is the software that an online store uses to sell goods and services online. An online store needs a back end to hold stock, images, product info and data, and it needs a *front end* — a virtual shopfront where people can browse and transact. Shopify provides that platform — think of it as the engine that powers your online store.

Shopify is a Canadian company, founded by Tobias Lütke and Scott Lake, two snowboarding enthusiasts who had been trying to build their own website, Snowdevil. When Snowdevil morphed into an ecommerce platform, it was called Jaded Pixel (before it became known as Shopify). From their experiences selling snowboarding gear, the guys realized that the platform had the ability to be something that other ecommerce merchants could use and benefit from, and so Daniel Weinand was brought in to help build up what is now known as Shopify, which was officially launched in 2006.

By 2008, Shopify had taken its first investment round from John Phillips, who injected $250,000 (Canadian dollars) into the business, at a valuation of $3 million dollars. At this point, the platform was heavily focused on helping first-time online sellers navigate the complexities of selling online; however, its cost-effective solution attracted heavyweights like Tesla, which proved that Shopify could be just as attractive at both ends of the market, from start-ups to global enterprises.

Fast forward seven years and Shopify had continued its exponential growth, going public in 2014 with a valuation of $1.3 billion (CAD). By 2020, Shopify was powering over a million merchants and had global sales of more than $1.35 billion (CAD) going through the platform. These days, it's fair to say Shopify is more than just an ecommerce platform — it has thriving POS (point of sale) software and is growing in popularity among wholesalers for its easy-to-use wholesale application, which allows wholesale customers to place online orders from suppliers.

I love using Shopify because the barriers to entry are lower than you may think. You don't need a fancy degree or a million dollars in your bank account to get started. The average cost of fitting out a nice retail store in a good location can cost in excess of $100,000 — before you have even bought your stock or hired your staff. A savvy operator can open their online store with Shopify or a similar platform for free, only paying a monthly fee if they decide to continue past the free trial.

EXAMPLE

In my ecosystem, as an adviser and owner of online businesses, Shopify is by far the preferred platform for online retailers of all sizes. I've seen incredible success stories through Shopify, including a story I heard recently when I had lunch with a guy I have known for about five years. He had been struggling with his online business for years, after pouring all his money into building a brand. He was always on the cusp of success, but he couldn't quite make it work. However, when we met for lunch he told me the good news that he was on track to turn over $7.8 million dollars (AUD), with a 19 per cent profit margin! I was buzzing for him, and we spoke about the role Shopify had played in reducing his barriers to success.

If he had required a developer during those tough years, he may well have given up, but Shopify's usability meant that he could power through, making small changes at a minimal cost until his online store was thriving. To me, that epitomizes the nature of Shopify's platform, and I have plenty of stories like that — Shopify has helped make more millionaires than any other product I know.

Shopify is unique — I've never seen a platform or tool that can literally change someone's life so quickly, without them needing to spend millions or have in-depth web development skills. If that hasn't whetted your appetite, you may want to check your pulse, because I'm excited for your journey ahead with Shopify. It won't always be easy, but if you add the right elements, like great products and great people, there's no reason you can't be another Shopify success story.

Planning for Ecommerce Success

Throughout this book, I write a lot about good planning being one of the cornerstones of a successful business, and in Part 1 I take you right to the start of what you need to do to get started with Shopify.

As well as finding your way around how to use Shopify (getting to know its features, including your Shopify admin — which you can think of as the engine that powers your Shopify store), I also consider how you get started with ecommerce in chapters 2 and 3 — how you source your products and what prices you sell them at, as well as where you sell them and how you can make a profit along the way.

If you're not sure which sales channels you can use to sell your wisely sourced products, I introduce you to some options, including familiar marketplaces such as eBay and Amazon — or you can simply fly solo and only sell through your online store. The choice is yours, and the options are many and varied!

Getting Creative: Setting Up Your Shopify Store

When you come to build your online store, you have plenty of opportunity to start getting creative. Sounds like fun, right?

This stage of building a business through Shopify is crucial to get right, even if it can be a lot of fun. You need to consider the user experience as your site develops — for example, how easy is it to navigate, and can your customers find what they are looking for? Are you showcasing your products in all their glory or forgetting to add key information (such as colors, sizes, dimensions)? Does your site look the part as well as deliver on the details?

TIP

You can preview your store as you build it and add new features, and it is incredibly motivating to see the progress as you go. It also gives you the chance to check that the way you present your products works well in reality on your site.

Don't worry if you don't have a creative bone in your body — with Shopify, you get plenty of help with what to include on your site and where. In Chapter 4, I show you how you can use Shopify to create images, banners and videos that make your store look amazing.

Chapter 5 gets straight into creating products inside your store, including naming, pricing and describing your products, as well as publishing them across one or more sales channels. I also show you how to add products to your store that have variants, such as different colors and sizes.

The fun doesn't stop there though! In your online store, you can group your products together in collections, which are like categories. In Chapter 5, I also show you how to create collections of your products so you can showcase them in different ways.

Sadly, the fun takes a brief pause in Chapter 6, where I look at some of the inevitable admin that comes with running an online store using Shopify — this includes tax and shipping, though it also rather excitingly includes receiving payments.

Shopify is a global platform, and I'd love to see your store go global as well, so in Chapter 6 I also show you how to accept foreign currencies and how to set your store up to ship orders both domestically and internationally, with some advice around how to price your shipping (such as when to offer it for free).

Making Friends with Your Customers

This section is all about two key groups: the customer and the user. A *user* is someone who visits and uses your website, and ideally, you want to convert them into a paying *customer*.

Part 3 is all about providing the user and the customer with the best possible experience — which, fittingly, is called the customer experience and the user experience. I look at good old-fashioned customer service in Chapter 7, and explore how Shopify can help you provide top-level service across a variety of customer service channels, including email, live chat, Facebook Messenger and the faithful telephone.

In Chapter 8, I deep dive into how the overall experience can be improved, from the way you serve your customers to trying to convert them into loyal customers through loyalty programs. I also tackle customer reviews and user-generated content, and how you can turn customers into brand ambassadors through encouraging positive reviews. In Chapter 9 I offer some tips for making your online store and user experience as user-friendly as possible, while in Chapter 10 I attempt to demystify machine learning and personalization when it comes to ecommerce.

TIP

Artificial intelligence (AI) isn't only for the big end of town, as you'll discover. You'll be able to curate a unique experience for each user, both on your website and in your marketing communications, using personalization techniques.

Taking Care of Business: Managing Stock Levels and Delivering Orders

In this book I get right into the nuts of bolts of what's involved in building a beautiful and user-friendly Shopify store but also making it a successful online business, and that includes inventory management and logistics.

Inventory management is one of the most complex aspects of ecommerce, and in Chapter 11 I look at inventory by starting with the basics, from how to place purchase orders (POs) to how to receive products into your inventory in Shopify, make them available to sell, and accurately manage your inventory moving forward.

Order fulfillment (getting the order to the customer) and logistics can be the difference between getting a customer and keeping a customer. If you scroll through the reviews of some of your favorite online stores, you're likely to see comments around the delivery experience and the returns experience. In chapters 12 and 13 I show you how to use Shopify to manage and fulfill your orders.

Shopify doesn't just help you build good-looking websites — it's got tools to help with the end-to-end selling experience, including fulfilling your orders and, when need be, refunding them quickly when things go wrong. It also offers Shopify Shipping, which is a great solution if you live in Australia, Canada or the Unites States, where it is available (I provide you with different shipping solutions that cover other parts of the world too in Chapter 13).

Growing Your Business through Marketing

Digital marketing is an essential part of growing your business and reaching your customers, and from the dark arts of SEO (search engine optimization) to using Google Ads and Facebook Ads, Part 5 of the book has your marketing needs covered. I show you how and where to spend your money, to gain sales — profitably!

In chapters 14–17, I look at how to optimize your online store so you rank highly in search engine results, and how to pay your way to the top, if that's your modus operandi. I also show you how to use social media platforms such as Facebook and Instagram to gain new customers, considering whether or not you can still make money when using social media without paying for the privilege (spoiler alert, it's getting harder).

Taking your ecommerce journey full circle and back to planning for success, I look at building a marketing plan and how to gauge your success after you launch. I unpack some of the key marketing metrics, like ROAS (return on ad spend), to help you determine what a successful marketing campaign looks like.

My aim in this part of the book is to help you acquire and retain customers profitably — without burning through too much cash, and as such I show you how to set up some clever marketing automations using Shopify's inbuilt marketing tools, such as abandoned cart automations.

REMEMBER

With an understanding of digital marketing taken care of, you'll be getting very close to launching your online store but, importantly, you'll have a realistic idea of what's involved, including how much time and money you need to invest in your new business, and what sort of results you can expect.

Going Live!

By the time you're approaching the end of this book, you'll be itching to publish your store, or make it 'go live'. However, before I set you off into the Shopify wilderness, I share some helpful tips and tricks to help you get off to the best possible start with your Shopify store.

In Chapter 18, I tell you all about my favorite Shopify apps and how they can help with the smooth running of your online store. In Chapter 19, I remind you how important it is to put the customer first, as well as sharing some tips on improving the customer and user experience.

Finally, in Chapter 20, I run through some final checks before you go live. Your last piece of technical homework will be to remove the password that stops the general public from seeing your store — therefore keeping it private (you'll be asked to set up a password when you sign up to Shopify — for more on this, see Chapter 2). After you've set your store free, it's time to knuckle down and put all the things you've learned to good use, setting you on the path to a promising new online business with Shopify.

Chapter **2**

Finding Your Way Around Shopify

Ecommerce is an exciting place to be, and you may already have visions of the kind of Shopify store you want to operate — the products you want to sell, the way you want your store to look, the sales and marketing strategy that will see your business thrive...

For now, however, it's best you put that Ferrari down-payment on hold. You need to start with the basics: choosing a Shopify plan, getting to know the Shopify support services available and understanding how Shopify works.

Choosing a Shopify Plan

Shopify offers a range of plans to suit any business size, and you can even start a free trial before you decide on the best plan to suit your business. The free trial lasts for 14 days and it costs nothing to set up. You don't even need to worry about entering your card details, so you have no worries about paying for the service before you decide to go ahead: Shopify seems to understand how annoying it is to sign up to a free trial, only to find that your card has been charged when the trial ends! You also only pay for your Shopify service month to month and there are no contracts, so you can give it a go without worrying about any long-term commitments.

TIP

I encourage you to go ahead and register for the 14-day free trial as you start working through this book — by the end of the book, you may have built your store, all within 14 days!

Don't worry about creating a domain name right now — I cover this in the upcoming section 'Deciding on Your Domain Name'.

TIP

The good news is it's easy to change your plan at any time, whenever you need to, as your business grows. As an example, if you are looking at integrating a third-party shipping provider (which I cover in Chapter 6), it may be a good time to review whether your business is ready to upgrade to Advanced Shopify.

I think that it's fine to go ahead and start on the basic plan; however, I do like the reporting and building capabilities that Advanced Shopify offers. Here are your Shopify options — see what sounds good to you!

Basic Shopify

Starting at $29 (USD) per month, Basic Shopify is an entry-level plan that provides enough services to get you started with an online store. You can sell an unlimited range of products, and you can register two staff member accounts with Basic Shopify. You can sell your products in 133 currencies and up to five languages.

REMEMBER

You pay slightly more for credit card processing when using Basic Shopify with Shopify Payments (Shopify's own payment gateway; in other words, the software used to take payment from customers). Basic Shopify has a rate of 2.9 per cent per transaction (plus 30 cents, which is applied to each transaction across all plans), while Shopify's rate is 2.6 per cent and Advanced Shopify's rate is 2.4 per cent (plus the 30 cents per transaction).

I recommend starting on this plan if you're new to Shopify — you can then upgrade as and when you need to.

Shopify

The regular Shopify account is the next level up from Basic Shopify, and it's suitable for online stores starting to experience some growth. You can register up to five staff accounts, with your monthly bill increasing to $79 (USD) per month.

TIP

With regular Shopify you can set country-specific domain names, which is helpful if you're seriously contemplating selling your products internationally. If you have a specific website for each country you sell within, you can localize your content to your audience by offering local shipping rates or times, or including any other content specific to that country (perhaps for marketing purposes). For example, the United States has popular sales events every 4th of July for Independence Day, whereas other parts of the world don't — so you may wish to display a sale on your United States website's homepage only.

Advanced Shopify

Advanced Shopify is for serious online sellers who are starting to turn over yearly revenue in the millions of dollars. The monthly fee goes up to $299 (USD) per month, and Advanced Shopify allows you to utilize up to 15 staff accounts.

REMEMBER

The key differences — as well as extending your number of Shopify staff accounts — include reduced transaction fees when using Shopify Payments and the ability to set individual product prices for different countries/regions.

Shopify Plus

Shopify Plus is built for larger enterprises than *regular* Shopify (the Basic through to Advanced options listed previously). Don't worry if you start out with Shopify and upgrade to Shopify Plus — they have the same core features, and the same look and feel. Shopify Plus has extended features that go beyond Shopify.

REMEMBER

Shopify allows you to set up a store and start selling. As your business gets bigger, Shopify Plus can kick in and take you a little further through its increased capabilities.

SHOPIFY VERSUS SHOPIFY PLUS: WHAT'S THE DIFFERENCE?

Rather than put Shopify and Shopify Plus in a side-by-side comparison, I thought I'd cover some of the extra things that Shopify Plus can add to your business that the regular Shopify plans (Basic Shopify, Shopify and Advanced Shopify) do not:

- Shopify Plus allows you access to your own account manager, or *Launch Engineer*, whereas on Shopify you are limited to the Shopify phone, email or live chat — which is still very good support.

- Shopify gives you access to a large range of themes to help you design your store, whereas Shopify Plus does that and more — it allows you access to Shopify Liquid, which is Shopify's theme language. You'll be able to customize your themes with greater freedom using Shopify Plus.

  One of the best parts of Shopify is the fact that you can choose from hundreds of themes, many of them free, that you can simply install and start using. You can edit the themes yourself, with little to no experience in web development, using their drag-and-drop features. Many other platforms require the use of web developers, which can be costly and often presents a barrier for smaller start-ups to succeed. If you're at an early stage with your business, it's unlikely you need to consider Shopify Plus for its wider range of themes, as Shopify already offers the flexibility you need to build a great website from scratch.

- You get unlimited staff accounts with Shopify Plus, whereas other Shopify plans allow you only a set number of accounts (depending on your plan).

- Shopify Plus gives you greater control over your checkout design and function, allowing you to modify Shopify scripts, whereas with Shopify you have to change the checkout using apps, and you are limited with what you can change and what exists in your theme.

- Shopify Plus gives you greater access to different application programming interfaces (APIs). (In my companion book, *Selling Online For Dummies*, I talk about APIs in more detail, as well as the other ecommerce basics that provide a good foundation before you create an online store.) An API allows two applications to talk to each other.

  APIs are everywhere in ecommerce, and Shopify Plus gives you the flexibility to integrate custom apps — or even build your own. With Shopify, you're limited to using the existing API integrations, of which there are many.

  Regardless of which Shopify plan you're on, your store will be using APIs to handle all sorts of tasks, from processing payments and running email marketing campaigns through to sending shipments.

- Shopify Plus gives you access to a larger range of apps in the Shopify App Store, including Shopify Flow, one of my favorite intuitive apps that automates certain processes in your business, such as notifying you when your stock drops below a certain level.

- Shopify Plus has a cool wholesale channel where retail customers can shop online and place wholesale orders with their suppliers, which Shopify doesn't provide access to.

- The pricing between Shopify and Shopify Plus is very different. You may be looking at $2,000 per month plus a percentage of sales each month (capped at a certain point).

To get your online store started, one of the three regular Shopify plans (Basic Shopify, Shopify and Advanced Shopify) will be absolutely fine. And rest assured, if you do get to a point where you need to upgrade to Shopify Plus, it's a seamless transition rather than a new website build. So, if or when the time is right and you're turning over millions of dollars, you can make the jump to Shopify Plus without any headaches.

To find out more about the differences between Shopify and Shopify Plus, check out the nearby sidebar 'Shopify versus Shopify Plus: What's the difference?'

Shopify's Support Services

Shopify's support is first class. It really is geared towards helping you become successful. I've been using Shopify for years, and I have clients putting over $500 million a year collectively through Shopify, but I still use Shopify's support services on a regular basis.

TIP

Once you have signed up to Shopify and logged in to your account, you'll be able to access various Shopify support solutions by clicking on your name, in the top-right corner, where you'll be presented with the following options:

>> **Shopify Help Centre (help.shopify.com):** Here, you can find help for just about anything, and it's updated often, which is why I like to check in occasionally and see what's new. It's available in plenty of languages and can be filtered by topic.

>> **Community Forums (community.shopify.com):** Currently, Shopify's community forums host around a million posts by over 800,000 members, so it is a vast resource worth checking. If you're ever looking for feedback on apps or ideas to grow your store, this is a great place to learn from other Shopify users and see what has worked for them.

>> **Hire a Shopify Expert (experts.shopify.com):** This is a useful resource for finding specialist Shopify contractors, posting a job (for example, if you're looking for someone to customize certain parts of Shopify) or searching for marketing help. Trusted experts can then apply to win your work, and you can hire and engage them through the platform.

I'm a big advocate of continuing to learn as much as I can from as many people as I can. By far the most common mistake I see people make when they get started in ecommerce is not taking the craft of ecommerce seriously enough. It doesn't matter if you're selling dog beds, women's clothes, alcoholic beverages or fine art — if you're planning to sell them online you're in ecommerce, whether you like it or not, and you need to become an expert in ecommerce if you want to make a living from it (no matter how much you know about your products — the dog beds, the dresses, the art or the cocktails).

TIP

Where am I going with all this, you may ask? The truth is that I love learning, and Shopify has a great educational platform (Shopify Compass) that can provide you with additional resources to build your understanding of ecommerce. You'll be able to watch videos and take courses run by experts who know their craft and can show you how to succeed. I'd encourage you to check out the courses at shopify-compass.com to discover more about what makes Shopify tick.

REMEMBER

My advice to newcomers to online retail is always the same. If you wake up one day and decide you want to be a landscaper, you don't just go to the hardware store, buy a shovel and a pair of gloves, and start hacking up the garden in the hope that it's going to win awards. That would be silly, and disrespectful to actual landscapers who have honed their craft over time: people who have studied it, lived it and made a career from it. Ecommerce is no different. You don't just wake up one day, decide to open a store and automatically become good at ecommerce. You need to work at it.

I also recommend that you gain a broader understanding of how ecommerce works before you start selling online. While this book touches on the key aspects of ecommerce, it's focused more on using Shopify in particular, so you may like to check out my companion book, *Selling Online For Dummies*, which deals with some of the broader principles of selling online.

REMEMBER

Don't put the cart before the horse: You need a methodical approach to starting your online business, and this involves understanding ecommerce in detail. With the help of this book and the excellent Shopify support services available, you'll be well on your way to mastering ecommerce and building a successful online business.

Opening an online store and not knowing enough about ecommerce is a recipe for failure. If you asked me why your online store wasn't making any sales and you couldn't tell me your paid media strategy, your conversion rate, how your keywords are ranking or what your conversion rate optimization strategy is, I'd send you back to the books to brush up on these essentials.

REMEMBER

Understanding the terminology is a key part of creating an online store. It is essential for you to get a solid grasp on the lingo before you get started if you intend to be successful.

Deciding on Your Domain Name

Before you create your website, you need both a domain name and web hosting. A *domain name* is the address of your store: your www.something. It is what people type into the URL (uniform resource locator) bar of a web browser to help them find your business when they are 'surfing the net' (do people still say that?).

TIP

A domain name is as important as your brand — it's how many people will refer to your business, so it's a good idea to match your domain name to your business name/brand. Keep it simple — a hard to spell or pronounce website or brand name may cost you in *organic sales* (sales generated without you needing to spend money on marketing) later.

Fortunately, Shopify offers you a turnkey solution. You can register a domain name through Shopify, and if you've registered a domain elsewhere you can easily connect it to Shopify. Although there are many variations of domain names available, like .com, or .biz, I suggest keeping to .com, which is universally recognized.

TIP

You may choose to register the .com domain and your country's domain, such as .com.au in Australia or .co.uk in the UK — this may come in handy later if you start selling internationally.

Web hosting is simply your website's home. Many hosting companies exist that can take care of this, but as a Shopify user you don't need to worry about this at all — thankfully, Shopify does it all for you.

WEB HOSTING: GETTING YOURSELF CONNECTED

You don't really need to understand the ins and outs of how the internet works to start selling online — and Shopify can take a lot of the technical headaches out of your hands by making it easy to secure your domain name and host your store's online activity — but it is rather fascinating stuff. When someone types your business's URL into their browser, it sends a request to the DNS (*domain name system* — essentially, a global network of websites, like a phonebook), which looks up the name servers associated with your domain and forwards the request to those servers. Your website will have a web host, and that web host will manage those name servers (which are essentially a large group of computers). The request to access your site is then sent to the appropriate web server that stores your website. The data is then sent back to the original browser, which enables your future customer to access your website.

If you don't yet have a domain name, you can check the availability of some of your ideas at shopify.com/domains — pricing starts at $11 (USD) per year.

TIP

Email hosting isn't provided by Shopify; however, you can connect your email hosting to your Shopify domain. If you already have a domain that you've registered through a third party, you can transfer or connect it to Shopify. Simply visit the Shopify Help Centre to find the latest advice on connecting a third-party domain to your Shopify plan.

Where Am I? Signing Up with Shopify

It's getting real now. It's time to log in to your free Shopify trial.

REMEMBER

You've got 14 days absolutely free from the moment you sign up — so it's time to get cracking!

If you already have your Shopify store set up, please feel free to put the kettle on, take a bathroom break, or spend a moment visualising your future success before you start exploring Shopify in more detail. However, if you're still staring at a blank screen, go ahead and complete the initial set-up of your store:

1. **Visit the Shopify website at shopify.com and click on Get Started for the 14-day free trial.**

    A pop-up dialogue box appears titled Start Your Free 14-Day Trial of Shopify.

2. **Enter your email address, create a password and give your store a name, such as 'Shoes by Paul', which you enter with no spaces in the Your Store Name field (so 'shoesbypaul', for example).**

TIP

If you're still stuck on this an hour later (I'm terrible at choosing store names), don't worry — you can change it later!

REMEMBER

Your store name will be used in your domain name, so the domain name for my example store here becomes 'www.shoesbypaul.myshopify.com'. You can always create a new custom domain to replace this automatic one (turn to the earlier section 'Deciding on Your Domain Name' for more on this), such as 'www.shoesbypaul.com', or 'www.paulsshoes.com'.

3. **When you're satisfied with your new store name, click on Create Your Store in the same dialogue box.**

A new page appears, titled Tell Us a Little about Yourself.

4. **You are asked to answer a few self-explanatory questions (such as your business address) over two pages as part of your Shopify sign-up process, so go ahead and complete these questions, clicking on Next at the bottom of the first page so that you can complete page two.**

TIP

You aren't a web developer or designer, so don't worry about ticking the developer/designer box near the bottom of the page (and if you are, I don't judge). You only need to tick this box if you are a developer who is building a Shopify site for a client, not for yourself.

5. **Click on Enter My Store.**

REMEMBER

After you've signed up for your free trial, what you'll see in front of you is what's commonly known as the *Shopify admin* or *Shopify admin panel* — it's the engine room of your website, where you'll manage your store's content, from designing your store and editing your theme to uploading your products and checking your sales (see Figure 2-1, which shows a typical Shopify admin panel). You may hear people call the Shopify admin the *back end* of your Shopify store (as opposed to the *front end*, which is the customer-facing part of the website).

Woohoo! You've started your free Shopify trial, and you haven't even had to hand over any credit card details — how good! The sign-up process is pretty easy, which sums up Shopify perfectly — Shopify aims to break down the barriers involved with starting an online store, not set up hoops for you to jump through. You'll appreciate this accessible and manageable approach time and time again throughout your journey as a Shopify online retailer.

REMEMBER

When you start an online business, you need to understand what's involved in making sales in your country, including taxes and general legal matters (such as business name registration, trademarks and patents), so be sure to do your own due diligence and get the correct legal, taxation and business set-up advice for your region. If you want to find out more about the legalities and requirements relating to starting an online business, my book *Selling Online For Dummies* covers the process.

FIGURE 2-1:
The Shopify admin panel, with the Home page selected.

Source: Shopify

TIP

Before you explore the Shopify admin further, one of the first things I'd recommend you configure in your Shopify admin is a password, which will hide your store from anyone who doesn't have it until you are ready to go live to the world. Because your store will be password protected until then, if you want someone to check out your online store while you're building it, you'll need to give them your password (in Chapter 20, I show you how to remove your password — the last step before going live with your online store).

REMEMBER

This password is different to your account password, which you created when you completed the initial set-up in the earlier steps in this section. This password hides your store from anyone who doesn't have the password. Anyone who visits the customer-facing part of your store (your online store's front end) will not be shown any of its contents unless they can enter this password. (The password you create when you initially set up your Shopify account is the password you use to log in to your Shopify admin section — in other words, the back end of your online store.)

To set up a password for your online store that hides your store's front end, follow these steps:

1. **From your Shopify admin (see Figure 2-1), click on Online Store in the menu on the left-hand side of the page, and then click on Preferences.**

The Preferences page appears.

2. **Scroll to the Password Protection section, and check the box named Enable Password.**

3. **In the same section, you see the word Password next to a text field. Here, enter the password that you want to give people so they can access your online store (such as friends who you may ask for feedback while you're designing your store).**

Don't use the same password that you use to log in to your admin. It's a good idea to have strong passwords that you aren't using across multiple devices or sites, just in case your password ends up in the wrong hands. Remember, your online store contains private information, such as customer addresses, so you need to keep it under lock and key.

4. **In the text field named Message for Your Visitors, enter the message that you want to show anyone visiting your store before you go live. (If you don't want to show a message, you can leave this field blank.)**

For example, you could create a message called 'Under construction' while you're building your online store.

5. **Click on the Enable Password box at the top of the Password Protection section, and then click on Save in the bottom-right corner of the Preferences page.**

Your site will now only be visible to people who use the password when visiting your website.

Navigating the Shopify Admin Panel

Now that your Shopify trial is up and running, it's time to take a look under the hood of your new ecommerce machine and get to know your Shopify admin.

TIP

The Shopify app (which you can download to your smartphone or tablet) provides you with certain controls over your store, but I mostly use the app to check sales and monitor reporting (and to enjoy the catchy 'cha-ching' sound every time a sale is made!). Your computer's desktop is a better place for doing most of your store updates in the Shopify admin section.

Note the sidebar on the left — the headings that start with 'Home' and end with 'Settings', right at the bottom — this sidebar is the home of all the features you need to access to manage your online store. The sidebar is shown in more detail in Figure 2-2.

Over the course of this book, I show you how each aspect of the Shopify admin ties into the success of your new online store. However, here I introduce you to the different sections of the Shopify admin that you'll soon get to know in more detail.

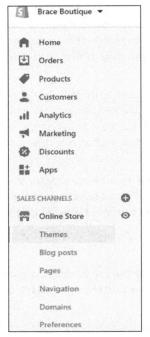

FIGURE 2-2:
The sidebar of
the Shopify
admin panel.

Source: Shopify

Home

Shopify Home is a page you'll spend a lot of time on. When you start your free trial, it's likely to show you suggestions for your next steps (such as finding products and adding a domain), but when you start trading, it's going to show you a great snapshot of your store's activity, including sales, orders needing to be fulfilled, useful marketing tips, any errors that need fixing, the top searched terms on your website, your most viewed products and tips for recovering abandoned checkouts. Shopify Home also shows you today's orders, today's visits and the number of visitors that are on your website right now!

TIP

An activity feed runs down the middle of your Home page, and this reveals some additional features that are worth noting in Shopify. Before you launch your online store, this activity feed may show you how to perform certain functions, such as getting your store ready for marketing or adding a shipping policy. This section is well worth keeping an eye on, as it provides you with meaningful insights and prompts you to finish setting up your store correctly.

You may not see many tips and insights into your store's performance until you launch it — which is when Shopify can give you the insights and metrics you can use to optimize your business, such as your daily sales across all your sales channels and your bestselling products.

Your store's activity feed may reveal other useful insights, including what actions you need to take, how many orders you need to fulfill and which customers haven't been back to your store in a while.

Orders

This is where you go to check orders that have been placed on your online store. You can manage all aspects of your orders here, including raising manual orders, handling refunds, editing order details and, of course, sending orders out — also called *order fulfillment*.

Products

This is where you'll manage the products that you're selling through your online store. This includes creating products, pricing them, writing product descriptions, uploading product images and making products available on your store (and other sales channels) for customers to view and purchase.

Customers

Making the most of your customer list is an important part of any ecommerce business, and retaining customers is every bit as important as acquiring them. In Part 5 I talk more about driving new customers to your site — and when you get them, this is where their details will be stored.

Analytics

Analytics is the next section of the Shopify admin, and this section is broken into three parts: Dashboards, Reports and Live View.

» **Dashboards:** Here, you can select a date range at the top (for example, 'today'), then you'll see a dashboard showing your total sales for the day along with your store sessions or visits, your returning customer rate (which is the number of customers who have come back for a second or third time), your conversion rate, average order value, total number of orders and, depending on the plan you're on, a whole lot of other metrics, including sessions by traffic source, top product sold, sessions by location and top landing pages.

TIP

I recommend you gain an understanding of all the metrics in this dashboard if you're seriously considering a career in ecommerce. I consider the two most important metrics on this page to be conversion rate (CVR) and average order value (AOV).

>> **Reports:** Here you'll see all sorts of sales reports, marketing reports, profit margin reports and reports on your customer — for instance, first time versus repeat customers. You can also access inventory reporting here, such as average inventory sold per day and month end inventory value (which is important for your bookkeeping). As you find out more about marketing, you'll circle back to these reports and be able to do all sorts of cool things with them, such as segmenting your customers by location, frequency of shopping, and how much they spend. You'll then be able to use these segments to send out more targeted marketing campaigns.

>> **Live View:** I use this page many times throughout the day as it tells you how many customers are on your website at any given time, how many are at the checkout placing an order, and how many have purchased from you in the last ten minutes. It's always fun to check your live view after you've sent a newsletter or EDM (electronic direct mail) to see what sort of reaction it's had.

The level of reporting you get in this section depends on the plan that you use. Shopify, Basic Shopify and Advanced Shopify all have very good reporting, and Shopify Plus has the full suite of reporting.

Here's a summary of some of the key metrics used in Shopify's analytics dashboard:

>> **Average order value (AOV):** This is the average value of your orders for a given time period, it is calculated by dividing the total value of all orders by the number of orders. AOV is one of the most important metrics in ecommerce, and you should never stop trying to increase it (remember, a 10 per cent increase in AOV means a 10 per cent increase in your online revenue!).

>> **Online store conversion rate (CVR):** Conversion rate is one of the top metrics in ecommerce. It shows the number and percentage of customer visits that result in an order being placed.

>> **Added to cart:** This metric shows the number and percentage of customer visits that result in an item being added to a shopping cart.

>> **Reached checkout:** The number or percentage of visits to your website that result in a visitor reaching the checkout page and performing an action, such as a mouse click.

Reaching the checkout does not always mean a sale has been made as users will often drop off or abandon the checkout.

>> **Online store sessions:** The number of sessions (or customer visits) to your website. This metric also shows the kind of device used, for example a smartphone or desktop computer.

>> **Online store sessions by location:** This shows sessions by country.

>> **Online store sessions by traffic source:** This shows the number of sessions sorted by the *traffic source*; in other words, the channel that brought them to your store, such as through a search or clicking through from your newsletter.

>> **Online store sessions from social source:** Shows the number of sessions coming from social media channels such as Facebook and Instagram.

>> **Repeat customer rate:** Shows the percentage of repeat customers — customers who have placed more than one order on your store.

>> **Sales by POS location:** For those that have Shopify POS, this shows the sales per POS location. (I explain what Shopify POS is in the later section 'Using Shopify to Sell In-store and Digital Products'.)

>> **Sales by staff:** Another metric for Shopify POS, this shows who handled your sales — in other words, which specific staff member(s) made each sale.

>> **Sales by traffic source:** This shows the sales that come from specific traffic sources, which is a useful guide for where to spend your marketing time and money.

>> **Top landing pages:** Shows the pages of your website where customers land on your site and start their browsing journey, such as the home page, or a certain product page.

Monitor your top landing pages closely to optimize your site's sales potential and maximize your conversion rate.

>> **Top products by units sold:** Lists your products in order of the number of orders in a given time period. Always lead your marketing efforts with your top products.

>> **Top referrers by session:** The number of sessions on your website that came from referring websites. For example, you may have published an article online that links back to your website, and you'll see the traffic that your article has driven to your site.

>> **Total online store sessions:** The total number of sessions on your store. One user could have two or more sessions if they viewed the site on two or more separate occasions.

A user is a person (your potential or future customer); a session is a visit (by this customer).

>> **Total orders:** This is, you guessed it, the total number of orders in a given period.

>> **Total sales:** Another self-explanatory one, this shows the total sales in a given period.

>> **Sales attributed to marketing:** This shows sales attributed to certain marketing campaigns you may have run, such as an email marketing campaign. This is tracked using Urchin Tracking Modules (UTMs), which I cover in Chapter 15.

I consider understanding these metrics to be essential for someone who wants a career in ecommerce, so why not try and quiz yourself. If you get them all right then you're on your way, and if you don't — try again!

Marketing

This is the next heading in the sidebar menu, and it splits out into three sections: Overview, Campaigns and Automations. As well as providing useful recommendations for growing your customer base or driving traffic, the Marketing section of the admin allows you to launch and manage marketing campaigns.

You'll notice suggested apps that your store can use to find and retain customers, as well as a summary of any marketing activities you're running through the platform. I'll save the in-depth marketing chat for Chapter 15, where I'll explore this section of Shopify in detail.

Discounts

The next cab off the rank is discounts. From here, you can create and manage your discount codes. Discounts are useful for a variety of ecommerce strategies, and at some point you're bound to use them — unless you're one of the few businesses that never needs to discount. More on that in Chapter 14!

Apps

This page lists all the apps that you have integrated into your Shopify store. The Shopify App Store is one of the best parts of Shopify. You can find an app for just about anything, and best of all, you'll be able to integrate most of them into your store without paying a cent to a developer!

You can access your apps from this page too, which is useful for when you forget your passwords! You also get handy recommendations for apps that may be suitable for your store.

Sales channels

Here, you see all the sales channels you have connected to your store. While you're getting started, you may only see 'Online Store' (which is the store you're creating now), but later you may like to add other channels, such as Amazon, eBay or other forms of marketplaces (even your physical store, if you have one).

If you click on the eye symbol next to Online Store, you can preview your store as you build it. In the rest of the Online Store section of the Shopify admin, you can design your store and its pages. Shopify covers all elements of designing your website (your Online Store sales channel) in six sections: Themes, Blog posts, Pages, Navigation, Domains and Preferences.

Themes

You can have a lot of fun on this page — it's where you go to find themes that you can adapt to suit your store. A *theme* is a template that someone has created and listed for people like you to use, without needing to hire a developer or work out how to code.

Themes can be free or you can purchase one to suit your store. You can find a theme to suit all different types of products and services. I cover theme selection in Chapter 4.

Blog posts

If you intend to create blog posts, this is where you need to go.

Pages

Here, you create pages for your website, such as About Us, Shipping Information or any other pages that you want to include on your website. You can style them, add content and optimize them for SEO (search engine optimization). I talk through the process of creating pages in Chapter 4.

Navigation

The 'nav', as it's commonly called, is one of the most important parts of your website's CX (customer experience) as it helps your customers discover your products. A good nav can make or break a store. You visit this section to create your nav, which I cover in more detail in Chapter 4, when I take a look at adding menus, and in Chapter 5, when I show you how to create products and collections.

Domains

I cover domains in more detail in the earlier section 'Deciding on Your Domain Name'. This is where you register your domain through Shopify (or add an existing domain to Shopify).

Preferences

Preferences is where you'll set up Google Analytics and your Facebook pixel. You can also add a website title and meta description in your Preferences, which will help your search engine rankings.

Settings

The sidebar ends with settings, which is where you go to update your store information and to view and edit your Shopify plan (for example, if you want to upgrade to Advanced Shopify or Shopify Plus). In Settings you can do all sorts of things, such as set up shipping rules, adjust the ways you accept payments from customers and create your refund policies.

TIP

At various stages of the book, I'll be referring to this Settings section so you can action these things as you come to them, but at this stage of getting to know the Shopify admin panel you may like to check that your contact information is up to date (look under 'General').

Using Shopify to Sell In-store and Digital Products

Although this book is geared towards retailers selling physical products online, Shopify's suite of products does extend further. Here are a few other ways you can use Shopify to make sales online.

Shopify POS

Shopify POS is a point of sale software for retailers with physical storefronts. It's great for *omnichannel retailers*, which are retailers with more than one sales channel, such as online plus physical storefronts. The main selling point of using Shopify POS in conjunction with Shopify (as your ecommerce platform) is to unify your back end, which brings all your data and reporting together.

By combining the ecommerce platform (Shopify) with Shopify POS, you can do cool things to connect different channels, such as allowing customers to redeem online vouchers in store or allowing your customers to return online orders to a physical store. I've also seen Shopify POS work well for online stores that run warehouse sales throughout the year — for example, you can use the Shopify POS app to walk up and down long queues of customers, processing payments as you go to keep your customers happy.

The way I have seen this combination work best is when a physical store runs out of inventory of a certain product, and the salesperson is able to check the back end of Shopify to see if the online store has any stock left. The salesperson can make the sale by logging in and placing a manual order for the customer, which means you still get the sale.

If you're an online retailer with physical stores, Shopify is a great option for bringing together all your data to improve the customer experience — and it's cost-effective too, at $89 (USD) per month, per store location.

Using Shopify to sell digital products

A *digital product* is an intangible product, in that it has no physical component to it. A physical product is typically a form of media that can be streamed or downloaded, such as music, movies and courses.

Digital products can be a lucrative business, due to the repeat (or *passive*) income you can generate once you've launched the product. My digital courses at learnecommerce.com.au were time-consuming to create at first, as I needed to make sure the format was user-friendly and the content was useful and up to date, but once they launched, they became easier to maintain, and I began to get a following of people that I could introduce to my new material as well.

Shopify actually suggests a few categories within this field. Here are a few to give you an idea of the potential of selling digital products:

>> **Digital templates and tools:** A great example in this space is canva.com, a website where users can go and pay for templates to help them create logos, flyers, or other types of graphics and marketing material.

>> **Educational products:** Think online educational courses here, such as my Learn Ecommerce courses. There's a lot of up-front work to produce resources like these, but you have little maintenance once they're out there in cyberspace.

>> **Licenses to use your digital assets:** Think stock photos and videos, or music and sound effects here. A *license* provides the retailer with a fee (or *royalty*) in exchange for an individual or organization using your digital assets.

>> **Membership sites:** You may decide to sell a recurring membership to your content. For example, you may consider streaming or hosting a webinar where you reveal your content to your audience, rather than selling your expertise through a downloadable digital course.

>> **Music or art:** Musicians and artists can monetize their work by selling things like ringtones, wallpapers or even artwork (to be used on a t-shirt or novelty

items such as mugs). Digital versions of books (like this one) may also fall into this category, where inventory isn't required and customers can download the book to their device.

>> **Services:** Digital service offerings are a great way for people in a professional field to add value to potential customers through the things that they do every day. One example is personal trainers who offer fitness plans (they may also offer membership-based services). Another example could be a business consultant who offers a 12-month budget plan in Excel, along with a training guide on how to use it.

Shopify has many apps that can help digital product retailers thrive. Here are eight apps that Shopify recommends for selling digital products:

>> **BookThatApp, Tipo, or Sesemi:** All three of these apps allow your customers to book a time in your calendar via your Shopify store, which is perfect for booking online lessons — for example, the guitar lessons that I've been taking online.

>> **Courses:** Courses allows you to create courses, tutorials and manuals and sell them in your Shopify store.

>> **Digital Downloads:** This app allows you to add digital products to your Shopify store.

>> **FetchApp:** This app allows your Shopify store to automate the delivery of digital downloads like music, books and anything else that's able to be downloaded.

>> **SendOwl:** This app delivers digital products to your customers (with an expiring download link to restrict unlicensed shares).

>> **Single Music:** This app does what you'd expect it to do — it allows musicians to distribute their music via downloads, including private livestreamed concerts and events.

>> **Sky Pilot or Bold Memberships:** Sky Pilot is an app that allows Shopify stores to deliver files and streaming videos to your customers. Bold Memberships is a favorite of mine: It allows your store to facilitate recurring billing or subscriptions for your customers. If you have any form of membership or subscription-based business, Bold Memberships is a great app to consider.

>> **Thinkific:** This is another good app for creating online courses in Shopify.

TIP

Search for these apps in the Shopify App Store at apps.shopify.com.

Chapter **3**

Sourcing Products and Identifying Sales Channels

Make no mistake, it's rare to succeed in ecommerce without a great prod-uct, and a great product is one that fills a gap in the market or solves a problem for your customer.

Many online retailers sell a generic line of products, such as clothing, without really identifying their niche in the market, which is why I'm going to help you find the products that you can take to the bank!

In this chapter, I give you some tools to check if your product ideas are trending up — meaning you are supplying a product that is in demand. Luckily, Shopify provides some great resources for new online business owners to help get your creative juices flowing so you can find products that sell, so I share some advice on using these resources.

To ensure you have a good handle on all the channels through which you can sell your awesome products, I also review the different styles of selling (business to business, business to consumer or direct to consumer) so you can decide which route is best for you.

You may have seen a bunch of YouTube videos about how to get rich using drop-shipping, so I take some time to unpack the pros and cons of this ecommerce model too. Finally, I cover selling through marketplace channels, such as eBay and Amazon, and choosing the marketplace that's right for you and your business.

Sourcing the Right Products to Sell

There's a good chance that many of you have a product in mind already that you're working out how to sell and make a living from it — or at least an income — and that sure is exciting! However, it's important to make sure that your product is in demand, or *trending*, as the best online businesses I have seen are always driven by good products — followed by well thought out operations, great people and effective marketing.

TIP

If you decide that you want to start your own brand, the chances are you'll have to work harder to find products by going directly to manufacturers, often offshore. If you choose to stock brands, you're usually dealing with local wholesalers who sell you the product, which you then on-sell on your online store. In my companion book *Selling Online For Dummies*, I talk more about the pros and cons of starting a brand of your own versus stocking existing brands.

WARNING

I strongly advise against diving head first into a product that you *think* is going to work; instead, focus on product you *know* is going to work.

A favorite saying of mine is to fish where the fish are. In other words, dangle your products in front of the people you know want them, rather than trying to convert cold leads that aren't really that interested in what you're selling.

In the following sections, I share some tips on where to start your product search and how to assess the demand for your products, plus I look at the ways Shopify can help you identify trending products.

Locating products to sell

There are plenty of websites where you can browse products to start your online store. You can also visit *trade shows* (which are expos or conventions where suppliers of products will exhibit in booths, and potential customers can visit and browse their products and place orders). However, with travel restrictions resulting from the COVID-19 pandemic, you can expect to see an even bigger swing towards using websites to source products, so I'm going to focus on digital platforms for sourcing products.

Here are three of my favorite digital platforms for sourcing new products, in my order of preference:

1. Alibaba.com

2. Made-in-China.com

3. Etsy.com/market/wholesale

Using any of these three websites, the principles of sourcing products are the same. You simply search for the product you are interested in and apply any filters that are relevant.

EXAMPLE

Imagine you want to sell beach towels from Turkey. If you're using Alibaba, you navigate to the top of the homepage — where you will see a search bar. Simply type in 'Turkish beach towels', click on the search button and hey presto — you're looking at your first potential products! You can then apply filters from the left-hand side of the screen, such as the preferred country of your manufacturer, your minimum order range or your target price (most suppliers operate in a similar way, but each website differs slightly). Start browsing the available products, and when you find a few you like you can call, email or live chat with your potential new supplier.

TIP

Try and work with trusted suppliers who have been on the platform for three or more years, and always review their feedback or customer ratings.

Supply and demand: Tools to check for trending products

The concept of supply and demand is a simple one, however you may be surprised at how often it's not considered during new product launches. Put simply, *supply* is the products you provide, in a certain quantity, to match the *demand* — the interest in your products from consumers. Ideally, you want to match supply to demand so you can maximize profits and minimize spend. When I say minimize spend, I mean that you don't want to be outlaying capital (your *initial cash outlay*) on stock that isn't going to move or that will sell slowly. You need to find the balance of the right product, at the right time, in the right quantity.

REMEMBER

There's an age-old debate and tension between creative types and numbers types, with the creatives wanting products that are aspirational and match the vision and the aesthetic of the business, while the number-bods want products that are trending, are commercial and have a high sell-through. There is of course, a happy marriage to be found between the two, and your job is to find it.

When you think of how people search for products online, you probably think primarily of Google or Amazon. Imagine if you could collate the search data of millions of people all over the world to get an insight into what they are actually looking for! Well, the good news is you can.

Data-led buying is a strategy you can use to find out what people are actually looking for by scraping various pieces of data from a variety of sources. Don't worry, I'm not about to get the tarot cards out or show you how to read minds — thankfully, tools are available to help you figure out what people want to buy.

One such tool is Google Trends. Go ahead and type trends.google.com into your browser — this will show you the current trending topics, in terms of what people are using Google to search for (Googling) in different countries. If I do this today, the example Google Trends shows me is Kim Kardashian and Taylor Swift.

While celebrity stories may be interesting, you will not find them particularly useful for your product research. You primarily want to see if your product idea rises or declines in popularity, in terms of trending searches, so you can check the validity of your product idea. You can also use these tools before you have a product in mind to give you ideas around what you can sell on your online Shopify store.

REMEMBER

You want to be an early mover and catch the product wave when its growth trajectory is just starting, not when it's near the top or coming down. Early mover advantage is a core business principle and puts you at a competitive advantage over new entrants to the market.

EXAMPLE

If I search for 'smart watches', the search volume shows an upward trend (see Figure 3-1), so I know this is a product that people are actively searching for on Google. A graph trending up equals increasing demand that you can expect to organically boost your sales.

Conversely, if I type the word 'DVD' (see Figure 3-2), the search volume appears to be in steady decline (although there is an interesting bump at around Christmas, which probably indicates that DVDs are still a Christmas present for some). It's safe to say that DVDs show decreasing demand. If I were weighing up selling one of these two products, smart watches are by the far the more lucrative in terms of matching a product to demand.

You can also use Google Trends to compare products over time, if you want to see one product pitched against another. Similarly, you can search for topics; for instance, you may want to create something in the field of environmentally sustainable products. If you find a trending topic, you can then play around with products in that field to see if any are trending. It's a little like going down a rabbit hole, but it's a lot of fun and can be incredibly useful.

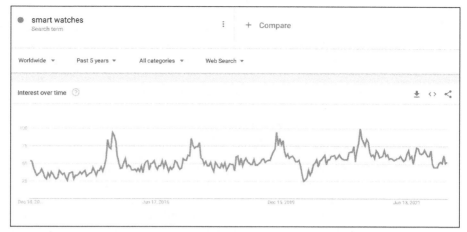

FIGURE 3-1:
Google Trends search results for 'smart watches'.

Source: Google Trends

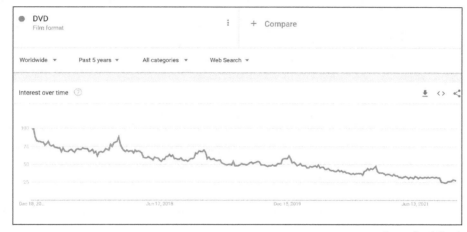

FIGURE 3-2:
Google Trends search results for 'DVD'.

Source: Google Trends

The homepage of Amazon is also really useful, as it will generally fill the homepage with 'Trending Products' and 'Top Sellers'. If you stick to these two websites, you're likely to get some good ideas flowing! Checking Amazon at the time of writing, the trending products include Apple AirPods, a Wi-Fi Extender, a Nintendo Switch and a Lamaze Peek-A-Boo book for children. If that's too generic and you want to check what's trending across a particular category — for instance, if you have decided that your online store is going to be based around pet supplies — then you can click on any of the trending products on the Amazon home page and then scroll through the filter on the left-hand menu, until you find 'pet supplies', which you can click through to. By following that path, I find cat litter, poop bags, scent-removing spray and a roller hair remover listed.

Alibaba provides much of the same, although more from a bulk ordering, or business to business (B2B), perspective, which of course is still useful (I talk about B2B and other sales channels in the section 'Introducing Online Sales Channels'). For example, if I navigate to the 'Top Ranking Products' section and narrow this down to 'Sports and Entertainment', the top products are bicycles, fishing lines, baseball bats and plastic jump ropes. The great part about researching trending products on Alibaba is that you can then connect with the leading manufacturers of those products and commence the product sourcing process.

If you want to have any sort of commercial scale to your online business, you need to dive deeply into your product research, unless you are one of the very, very, very few who manage to master a niche that few others can — for example, perhaps you have a unique set of skills that means you can craft a certain kind of in-demand product yourself, such as custom-made surf boards. That's great, but if you're a generic brand aiming to sell printed t-shirts then you're joining a long queue, because it's busy inside that category unless you can stand out.

REMEMBER

Avoid the temptation to believe that charm alone will drive your success — it plays a part in the story and the content, but your online business will be driven by great products. Uncover a great product, and you've made an amazing start to your journey towards ecommerce success.

Checking trending products in Shopify

Shopify provides great data on what products are trending on Shopify — and given the number of products it has listed, it's no surprise that you can do much of your trending product research on Shopify directly!

Here's a list of Shopify's 'Trending Products To Sell' from early in 2021:

1. Peel-off face masks
2. Nail polish
3. Exercise bands
4. Water bottles
5. Blankets
6. Yoga and Pilates mats
7. Kayak accessories
8. Jigsaw puzzles
9. Kitchen and dining room furniture

10. Rugs

11. Board games

12. Laptop skins

TIP

Visit shopify.com/blog/trending-products to check what is trending on the platform and to help generate new product ideas.

Introducing Online Sales Channels

There are different kinds of sales channels to suit just about any business or individual. Whether you're selling your boyfriend's old size 32 Levi's that he just won't fit into anymore (despite what he thinks), or you're wholesaling product all over the world and you want to make it easier for your clients to log in and place orders, the chances are that there's an online sales channel for you, and it's probably available in Shopify.

Wholesale trade is the practice of a supply or manufacturing business selling products to a retail business, which then sells them to the end customer. People often refer to wholesalers as an intermediary or 'middleman'.

If you think about all the times you've used the internet to purchase something, it can seem pretty ridiculous how many options you have. I've bought and sold cars online, found a breeder for my Rottweiler, studied from afar, paid my council rates, sourced cheaper gas and electricity . . . and I can't remember the last time I bought clothes in a physical store. The breadth of industries that can prosper via some form of online sales channel is enormous!

In the following sections, I introduce you to a few of the most common online sales channels.

D2C: Direct to consumer sales

This is probably what springs to mind when you think of a typical ecommerce business — and it's probably what you've signed up to do using Shopify. *Direct to consumer (D2C) sales* are when a brand or manufacturer sells items directly to consumers without the need for an intermediary (like a wholesale or retail store). D2C sales can be applicable across a whole range of industries, whether it be a winery selling wines online without going through the local liquor store, or your favorite fashion brand starting a website and taking customer orders, rather than, or in addition to, stocking retail stores.

Many early online shoppers favored online shopping for the perception that there were discounts to be had thanks to businesses cutting out the person in the middle, who needed to make a share of the profits. Going direct to customers allowed manufacturers to reduce their retail prices, rather than having to cut in the wholesalers.

Platforms like Amazon and Alibaba are examples of online marketplaces where manufacturers can engage in D2C sales by creating their own stores on the marketplace and listing their products so that customers can place orders directly with them. In many cases, selling online via D2C channels has opened up a huge new revenue stream for manufacturers who were previously focused on B2B (business to business) revenue.

D2C channels have put a lot of strain on the traditional wholesale customers of manufacturers, as often they can end up competing against one another. I've seen this happen to a business I was involved with. We had placed a large order of men's footwear, only to see that our manufacturer had also listed the same styles on Alibaba at half the price we were selling them for. Pricing rules and other agreements and restrictions are sometimes agreed upon to ensure that manufacturers don't undercut their wholesale customers. On the flip side, a lot of wholesalers have gone further upstream or become more vertical and explored creating their own brands or manufacturing plants as a way to enjoy D2C benefits. Going *vertical* (or upstream) is essentially going back up the supply chain to source your product. If you're a retailer buying from a wholesaler, you may decide to skip the wholesaler and try and go directly to the manufacturer.

B2C: Business to Consumer sales

Business to consumer (B2C) sales are when businesses that are not manufacturers, like Walmart, stock multiple brands to sell on to consumers. The business is not manufacturing the goods themselves but buying them from manufacturers, before on-selling them to consumers.

Shopify powers many of these sites around the world. Shopify is not concerned with how the product is sourced, or whether or not an online retailer manufactures their own products or buys them, as its purpose is to display content and help you sell it.

In an online context, think of websites like Revolve, Zalora, The Iconic, or the digital versions of retailers like the afore-mentioned Walmart. Most of these kinds of businesses are likely to have their own *private labels* as well; in other words, labels or brands that they have created, where they source its products from a manufacturer to increase the profit margin.

One of the criticisms of larger B2C businesses is that they use the sales data from the brands they stock to then go and copy their products to sell themselves. They may then use their significant buying power to get discounts from the manufacturers of the copied products, which allows them to undercut the original brand they stocked. If this happens to your own manufactured products, you need to regain control, put an end to the business relationship and rethink your strategy, or shift more towards selling online only rather than stocking other businesses.

Typically, a B2C online store carries desirable brands, which is often a method to attract customers to their online store, at potentially a lower cost, as customers are actively seeking the brands. If you are contemplating starting your own brand, you may have to work a little harder or spend a little more money to bring traffic to your store and alert people to who you are. (My book *Selling Online For Dummies* talks more about the pros and cons of creating your own brand versus stocking existing brands.)

A common mistake that many new online retailers make is to think that once your online store is open, there will be a natural procession of customers waiting for your virtual doors to open — but there isn't, and it can be a lonely place unless you actively start acquiring visitors. Part 5 explores sales and marketing in more detail to ensure you get people clicking on your online store.

B2C retailers may make a little less profit per product than a D2C business (as they are effectively the intermediary), but this is not always the case, and it varies from industry to industry. Some of the largest online retailers in the world are B2C businesses — think Walmart, Target or the Zalora websites across Asia.

B2B: Business to Business sales

Although not the focus of this book, the flexibility of many ecommerce platforms allows for businesses to sell to other businesses — *business to business (B2B) sales*; in other words, a wholesale distributor can offer products online to retailers to buy, and then on-sell them to individual customers. An example of this may be a manufacturer receiving wholesale orders through a website, or from its stockists or distributors. This method has allowed for sales to be made from the office, with less dependency on travelling salespeople or print catalogues.

Online wholesale sales portals are commonplace these days. Shopify has created an app called Handshake (which can be found in its app store) where retailers can log in and order stock from their wholesale supplier without needing to visit their showroom or meet with a salesperson.

Wholesale trade conducted through online channels allows for a reduction in friction. The buyer can log on at any time and place an order whenever they want, from the comfort of wherever they are. I was recently part of an ecommerce build for a B2C business with 150 stores across Australia, and as part of the scope of its website build, the business constantly repeated the need for its stores to be able to log in to the website and place stock replenishment orders; in fact, the business was more excited about the potential of this service than the opportunity the new website provided for finding new customers across the country who had never seen their stores!

All about Dropshipping

Dropshipping is when an online store lists products on its website that it does not actually have on hand. It is essentially all about how you fulfil an order. As a dropshipper, you don't hold any inventory and your supplier sends the orders to your customers directly. Your role in this relationship is to build an online store, list a supplier's products on your site, market the products, gain sales and forward the order details to your supplier to ship. You only pay the supplier after the customer pays you.

For example, if I started an online store and researched manufacturers in China who make single unit orders, I might ask them if I can list their products on my site and send them notifications when I get an order, so that the manufacturer may then send the order to my customer. Thankfully, Shopify automates this process for you, using cool apps like Oberlo, which I talk about in the later section 'Dropshipping on Shopify'. It can be perceived as a little sneaky but, if fully disclosed, there's nothing ethically wrong with engaging in good dropshipping.

MAIL ORDER OR DROPSHIPPING?

The history of dropshipping is an interesting one. While some may think it's a recent phenomenon, the concept appears to have existed in various formats for many years. Mail order shopping was enormously popular in the 1960s and 1970s, and many of the suppliers did not need to stock the product on their shelves; instead, they sent it direct to the customer. However, for this method to be strictly considered dropshipping, the seller wouldn't keep the stock at all, either in store or in a warehouse, until the order from the customer had been placed.

There's more than one way to run an online store that relies on dropshipping, and in the following sections I look at the different kinds of dropshipping, the pros and cons of dropshipping, and how dropshipping works on Shopify.

Comparing the different kinds of dropshipping

Dropshipping is perfectly legal, and some retail dropshippers will even inform their customers that the order is being shipped from a third party (it will also be made clear that the paperwork will be from the dropshipper rather than the third party). This more transparent process is known as *white hat dropshipping. Black hat dropshipping* is when a retailer simply lists products from other suppliers but doesn't disclose anything about the supply chain to the customer; in fact, the retailer will even leave all the paperwork from the original supplier, which can leave a very bad taste in the customer's mouth because the customer may feel deceived by the fact that they have purchased from an intermediary when they could have gone directly to the supplier, often at a cheaper price.

I've seen black hat dropshipping in action, and it wasn't pretty. In an omnichannel business I was working with (*omnichannel* meaning multiple sales channels, in this case online and wholesale — as opposed to *pureplay online*, meaning online sales only), a wholesale customer was bidding aggressively on our keywords on Google, meaning they were paying to rank higher than us in search results when shoppers were searching for our brand. However, the wholesale customer wasn't carrying any of our stock — not since its first orders when it became a wholesale customer! We found out that this customer was listing our products online at 30 per cent cheaper than our retail price to gain traffic, advertising this discount in its ads (to entice shoppers to its own website, instead of ours) and then placing wholesale orders with our wholesale department (at a 50 per cent discount!) so that it can pocket the 20 per cent difference. The wholesale customer established a wholesale relationship with us, but then stopped ordering stock at a wholesale level and started dropshipping products without our knowledge!

This is typical black hat dropshipping — and although the customer in this instance got a good deal, they may not be so happy if the next order they purchase in the same way is available cheaper than the price listed on the online store they shopped from. Needless to say, the practice outlined in this example was not sustainable as the retailer was no longer allowed to stock the brand.

If a wholesale account is undercutting the prices of the brand they are selling, the business relationship goes south pretty quickly. Bidding on your suppliers' keywords and using clickbait (like discounted pricing for a specific brand) in your ads is considered unethical, although not illegal.

An acceptable dropshipment model here would have been for the seller to ask permission to become a dropshipper, as opposed to taking the customer's money and then placing orders without making it clear to the brand that this is what they were doing.

Here are some of the fair, white hat dropshipping models you may consider trying when you set up your Shopify store:

>> **Product reselling:** The dropshipper sources products from a variety of suppliers and lists them on his or her site for resale. Typically, the website has a theme, such as pet supplies, and the online store focuses on that niche product range while providing value to the customer through offering benefits such as good customer service, excellent product knowledge and fair pricing.

REMEMBER

This model relies on your business being an effective marketing machine — the product is sourced from a third party, so there is little to no product development, and the dropshipper's goal is to bring in traffic to move the product.

>> **Business extensions:** This occurs when a retail store that doesn't have an online presence gets a dropshipper to list its products, essentially becoming their digital footprint. When an order is placed, the dropshipper asks the retail store to fulfil the order. This is a useful model for physical retailers who are looking for an online partner because they don't have the technical ability, or the capital, to start an online branch of their business.

>> **Product creation:** This occurs when a dropshipper bundles items together and the customer orders them as a group, such as supplying the products for a DIY craft project. The dropshipper aims to work with a supplier that has a large range of items that can be bundled together and sold as a group.

>> **Print on demand:** Print on demand is a popular dropshipping business strategy. An example is where a dropshipper sells a product that can have an image or print on it, such as a mug, apron or t-shirt. Every time a sale is made, the dropshipper raises an order with the print on demand supplier, which sends the order out. For this style of dropshipping, you need an arrangement with a print on demand supplier that considers all the product requirements — for this example, you'd need to agree on the image format the supplier can accept to produce the products to an acceptable quality standard, and also agree on the range of products the supplier will print on.

TIP

If you find a niche market, such as 'we print your pet's face on a t-shirt', this dropshipping model can lead to a fun novelty gifting business.

Considering the pros and cons of dropshipping

Dropshipping can be a good way to get started in ecommerce, but remember to weigh up the pros and cons before you rush on in.

Pros of dropshipping

The benefits of dropshipping are impossible to ignore: zero capital outlay on stock; the ability to hold an enormous range of SKUs (stock-keeping units); and fairly low barriers to entry (which is why you see so many young people, sometimes still in school, telling their story of how they got rich quick via dropshipping). You only pay for stock when the orders come in, so it's a *cash-positive business*, meaning you have the cash from the sale to pay for the order from the manufacturer and pay for other costs, such as marketing and wages.

Cons of dropshipping

Profits from dropshipping are generally slim, so you will need to move some serious volume in order to scale the business to a substantial size. It isn't uncommon to see profit margins of 10–20 per cent on products, which doesn't leave a heck of a lot for wages, marketing and other expenses — there isn't much fat, in other words.

The other thing you lose is control — control over your shipping times, control over the accuracy of the picking of orders, and quality control of your products and packaging. You need to trust your suppliers if you're planning to set up a sustainable dropshipping business model.

REMEMBER

It's good to try at least one dropshipping store to cut your teeth on, but it's not as easy as some of those 'get rich quick' videos on YouTube make out. As the margins are slim, you need to drive a lot of traffic to your site to be successful — and web traffic costs money.

Dropshipping on Shopify

I've built two dropshipping stores on Shopify, mainly in my early days of using the platform, as a cheap way to get started and work out how to use Shopify. I found the process to be straightforward, and Shopify has some great resources for sourcing products you can dropship and automating the order process.

Oberlo.com is Shopify's secret weapon when it comes to dropshipping. *Oberlo* is software that bolts on to your browser. It allows you to access over 30,000 drop-shipping products through AliExpress. Rather than having to go one by one through each supplier, asking if they'll dropship, Oberlo identifies the suppliers who will dropship and allows you to list their products directly on your store, with a click or two of your mouse.

You can find just about anything through Oberlo. As well as listing the identified products on your site, Oberlo automates the ordering and fulfilment process for you. When your online store gets an order, Oberlo raises an order to the supplier of the SKU in your store and places the order automatically, including the delivery address of the customer — asking you only to enter the payment details and select your shipping service.

If you want to go ahead and try Oberlo, you can add it for free to your Shopify website. Just visit apps.shopify.com/oberlo and follow the instructions to add the app to your store — no web developer needed.

As well as providing Oberlo, Shopify also recommends another group of dropshipping sites:

>> CJdropshipping.com

>> Supplymedirect.com

>> Crov.com

>> Modalyst.co

>> Dropnshop.com

Be sure to check your potential dropshipping partner's feedback, particularly with regard to shipping times and product quality. You're placing a lot of trust in your supplier, so choose carefully!

Selling on Online Marketplaces

When you hear the word marketplace, the obvious ones that come to mind are eBay, Amazon and, more recently, Facebook Marketplace. An *online marketplace* is exactly as the name suggests — a platform to bring together sellers and buyers in a common environment. Sellers can be retail merchants or individuals, and they are open to selling virtually anything lawful.

Some marketplaces are free, like Facebook Marketplace, while others charge a commission for each item sold, or a monthly subscription fee. Some online businesses offer a hybrid model that includes a D2C or B2B website, as well as offering a marketplace where brands can list additional products. An example of using a hybrid model is Zalora, which buys stock up front from brands under a traditional wholesale model but also provides a marketplace offering.

If a brand is unhappy with its initial order from Zalora (perhaps because Zalora has ordered ten product styles, but the brand was hoping Zalora would stock 20 of its product styles), it may be able to extend its product offering by adding further products to the Zalora online store through the Zalora marketplace, on a consignment model — in other words, the supplying brand only gets paid when a sale occurs (as opposed to wholesale, where full payment on the order is guaranteed). The risk of slow sales or high expenditure is reduced for Zalora, which only pays for the goods if and when they sell.

The benefits of a marketplace model for businesses is that they do not have to outlay capital for the stock; instead, they make their money when an item is sold, when they can charge a commission. Stock can be either held at the marketplace's warehouse or at the brand's location, depending on the agreement.

Typically, a marketplace integrates with your ecommerce platform or your inventory management system via an API (application programming interface) or PIM (product information management) system. API is an abbreviation you're going to be hearing a lot. Basically, an *API* is software that connects two applications to each other. An API is like a messenger delivering a request from one application to another, and then brings back the response. So, you have an API connection to a marketplace, from wherever your inventory is housed, and the inventory details, including quantity, cost and often product descriptions, are pushed into the marketplace, which saves you the time of listing each product individually.

In the absence of an API (such as when smaller businesses are just getting started), some marketplaces will offer the option of a spreadsheet to upload your products to their platform; however, this method doesn't operate in real time, so it doesn't update your master inventory records — relying on you to do it manually. An API deducts the inventory as the sale occurs, which provides more accurate and current data on available stock.

Without getting too much into the technicalities of it (that will come in Chapter 11, where I look at managing your inventory), a marketplace is a great way to get new eyeballs on your brand, particularly in a new market. The downside is that the marketplace owns the customer, so in reality you are bringing them customers, and they are bringing you orders, but you don't really get the chance to nurture that customer for life, whereas there are various methods to communicate to the customer, post purchase, when you sell through your own website. Marketplaces are very protective of their customers, and usually won't even let you use your own branded mailers.

REMEMBER

Shopify is incredibly friendly to marketplace sellers, and it provides apps for integrating with most of the major marketplaces. You can download these solutions from the app store and usually set them up yourself.

Usually, these apps are third-party apps. For example, eBay has an app in the Shopify app store, so Shopify isn't responsible for integration with eBay, or providing support — eBay are. Shopify simply allows you to add the app to your store and list your products on eBay using the app.

If you browse apps in the Shopify App Store (apps.shopify.com) and search for 'eBay', you'll see plenty of options to add eBay to your Shopify store — meaning you can list your products on eBay via your Shopify store rather than having to list products one by one on eBay. The trick to choosing any app you install in your store is to go and read all the reviews and look at the demonstrations inside the apps before you choose one. For instance, the app 'eBay App Integration' has a higher star rating than the actual eBay-owned app, so just because eBay created that app, it doesn't mean it's the best one out there.

TIP

Shopify shows you where an order is from, so you will be able to see when orders are placed through a different channel (such as a marketplace) rather than your normal sales channels in case you want to use specific packaging or marketing materials for that order.

I'm a fan of using marketplaces to grow your business, particularly in the early days when you may find it hard to grow sales and get traction. Marketplace sales help to boost your cashflow and can be quite lucrative, despite the commission you pay on each sale.

WARNING

Some marketplaces let you list at your discretion; others require permission, particularly if you're selling designer clothing. For example, you don't need permission from eBay to sell most products — eBay sells just about everything! However, marketplaces such as farfetch.com are more selective about the brands that they list on their platforms, so you need direct approval from the marketplace — or to be invited onto the platform to sell your products.

Here's a list of some of the marketplaces that you will have access to when you build your store on Shopify:

>> eBay.com

>> Amazon.com

- Walmart.com
- Etsy.com
- Wish.com
- Ecart.com
- Catch.com.au
- Sears.com
- Mydeal.com.au
- Onbuy.com
- Rakuten.co.jp
- FR.shopping.rakuten.com

All told, I recommend marketplaces to new or existing brands looking for expansion, as long as the commission suits your gross profit margins — a commission over 22 per cent rings alarm bells for me. So, remember to check the marketplace's commission and try and keep your gross profit over 50 per cent — there's no point gaining sales if they aren't profitable.

TIP

Most successful marketplace sellers allow a budget for marketing, and there is a tendency for marketplaces to move more and more towards prioritizing brands that are paying to advertise on their platforms.

2

Preparing Your Store for Launch

Create the foundations of your online store.

Add products and develop collections to showcase your wares.

Tackle the admin and set your store up for sales success.

IN THIS CHAPTER

» **Going behind the scenes of web development**

» **Navigating your site**

» **Choosing a theme**

» **Designing your homepage**

» **Creating menus and pages**

Chapter **4**

Designing Your Shopify Store

t's time to start the process of designing your store, which, in Shopify, starts with choosing the right theme.

Before I get to themes, however, I discuss the role that web developers play in ecommerce — as well as highlight the importance of user-friendly site navigation (in other words, how you get your customers to the products they want to see in as few clicks as possible).

I also take you through one of your website's most important pages, the homepage, where you can find out how to set up your menus and pages to ensure visitors can get around your site with minimal friction.

So put the kettle on, clear your desk, clear your mind and charge your laptop — there's a lot of ground to cover in this chapter!

Coding, Web Developers and Shopify

Before you dive into designing your store, it's a good idea to touch on some of the fundamentals of web development and *coding* — the language used to create websites — and to figure out where Shopify sits within this world of website development.

As a Shopify merchant, you won't be asked to write or understand *HTML* (hypertext markup language), which is a code used by web developers to build websites and other cool things. So you can keep your coding course under wraps for now . . . however, it will help if you know some of the basic web development lingo so you can understand how your business's ecommerce platform — Shopify — operates.

Web development is the practice of building a website or application. A common mistake is to think of web developers as web designers, but *web developers* (or devs) are not concerned with the design or layout of a website; instead, they focus on the function and performance of the site.

Web developers (sometimes known as *programmers*) are focused on coding a website to build or maintain it, not designing websites. One of the beautiful things about Shopify is that you won't need a web developer to get started — and smart Shopify sellers who are willing to invest time in getting to know all that the Shopify platform has to offer can scale a very long way before they need to look at bringing a web developer on board.

Most of the systems, platforms and applications that integrate with Shopify are built by web developers.

TECHNICAL STUFF

Typically, web developers fall into three categories:

>> **Front end developers:** Front end developers are responsible for the look and feel of the website. When you see a design change on the homepage of your favorite site, or a new layout for the product pages, they have been updated by a front end developer. This is not to say the developer has designed those features; usually, this is done by a UX (user experience) designer, or a web designer. Shopify gives you all the tools you need to adjust your design by yourself, so you won't need a developer at this point — which is one of the reasons that Shopify is such a great platform for those new to ecommerce.

>> **Back end developers:** A front end developer needs to be supported by a back end developer. Back end developers keep the website's engine running smoothly. While not dealing with the fun stuff that the front end developers do, the back end developer plays a very important role. A back end developer

spends their time writing code and dealing with the server side of the website, including updating a store's prices, inventory and products. Fortunately, with Shopify, you have pre-built themes that include just about any feature you can think of, from wishlists to inventory management and general content management, so you can build your site without needing a back end developer.

» **Full stack developers:** These are the big cheese in the hamburger! The full stack developer is comfortable managing both the front end and back end parts of a website. A full stack developer isn't technically better or more skilful than either a front end or back end developer — they are simply proficient in both areas.

TECHNICAL STUFF

Liquid is Shopify's *template language* — in other words, the code used to build your website. It was developed by Tobias Lütke, Shopify's co-founder, and Liquid is used across many different software projects (in addition to Shopify). At a technical level, Liquid creates a bridge between an HTML file and a data source. The data source is Shopify, and an HTML file is a text file designed for digital viewing (meaning it's perfect for displaying on a screen, rather than in print); in other words, it's designed to display content on your website.

Essentially, the Shopify platform retrieves data from the themes that you use to build your online Shopify store, as a result of the Liquid code used in the theme. The retrieved data may be anything from the title of a product to a gallery of images. The data is then displayed on your front end, which is the customer-facing side of your website. Shopify Liquid is the developer's language that allows data, design and content to come together to form your website.

Thankfully, you don't need to understand how to use Shopify Liquid, as part of the beauty of Shopify is that the heavy lifting has been done for you, which means when you choose your theme it will be ready for you to customize.

Finding Your Way: Website Architecture

Website architecture (or *site architecture*) refers to the way a website is structured and organized. Website architecture aims to keep people on your site, helping you avoid the dreaded *bounce* — which is when visitors to your site leave after only viewing one page. A high bounce rate is a sign of a poor user experience and can be due to a variety of reasons, which I consider further in Chapter 9. Website architecture also plays a part in SEO (search engine optimization), which I cover in Chapter 16.

Why is website architecture important when building your online Shopify store? It helps your customers find what they're looking for. The overall goal of your site's UX is to nurture the customer through the purchase journey smoothly, in such a way that makes them want to come back and buy from you again. The UX is what separates selling through your own website from selling through other channels, such as a marketplace — you need to give your customers a brilliant experience, rather than simply provide them with another way in which to shop.

Before you start building your website, it's helpful to consider the UX that will encourage your customers to become returning customers. Here are some ideas for maximizing your Shopify store's website architecture:

>> **Keep it simple:** The more difficult it is to navigate your website, the more likely your visitors are to bounce. If you send a customer around the world to find the perfect pair of black jeans, the chances are they won't buy them and they'll continue their search elsewhere — which is a real shame for you, and also for your customer if your products are the real deal.

WARNING

'Keep it simple' applies to your whole website, not just your product pages. If a user clicks on your 'About Us' page and a video appears that takes five seconds to load, many of your website's visitors may bounce without waiting to find out more about who you are — your potential customers can be an impatient lot sometimes!

>> **When in doubt, learn from the best:** You can be sure the likes of Amazon, eBay, Revolve, ASOS, and so on *AB test* (in other words, trial variations on a specific site feature to determine which option provides a better result, such as a higher conversion rate) their website architecture constantly, so why not follow their lead? This is particularly important in the early days — when you probably won't have set up any kind of website testing.

WARNING

If your website's structure differs greatly from the norms put in place by the big ecommerce players, it's more likely that you have got it wrong — as opposed to the unlikely possibility that you have discovered a revolutionary way to structure your site.

>> **Check your links:** Broken links stink. If you've got links on your website that direct visitors to other pages, make sure they work. When I see a link on a website that takes me nowhere it feels like amateur hour, and I won't trust a website with broken links to process my credit card.

>> **Travel in no more than three or four clicks:** A visitor to your website should be able to get to any of your website's pages within three or four clicks. Don't take them on a journey through your ecommerce platform — get to the point.

>> **Choose your theme wisely:** The next section talks all about themes, but here's the clincher — if you're using a theme, choose one that has good UX reviews. Just because it looks good, it doesn't mean it is. Your theme has to work well *and* look good.

There's no need to reinvent the wheel. Resist the urge to build your website based on what you think your customers will like. With AB testing, there's no excuse not to develop a site you know they'll love!

Team with the Theme: Exploring Shopify Themes

A *theme* is a pre-built website template that you can choose to adopt for your own website, saving you the hassle of having to build your website (or hire someone to build a website for you). Themes can be either paid or free and may be created by Shopify or by third parties. Browsing Shopify's themes is one of my favorite things to do when starting a new Shopify store, because there are so many great-looking themes that you can apply within minutes to your own website. Themes drastically speed up the time it takes to create a website.

To get you started with searching for and choosing a theme, go ahead and visit themes.shopify.com — or log in to your Shopify admin, scroll down the sidebar till you reach 'Online Store', and when that expands, click on 'Themes' and then 'Visit Theme Store'.

Most themes are made by third parties, and Shopify isn't responsible for providing technical support for third-party themes. Be sure to check out the support available for a theme you're interested in using for your store.

If you want to look at the themes Shopify has built, you can access these themes through your Shopify admin panel by clicking on 'Explore Free Themes'. Shopify provides support when needed for these themes.

Now you're immersed in the world of Shopify themes, it's time to investigate your next steps — from choosing a theme to publishing and customizing your theme. And don't forget to preview how your chosen theme looks and works — all while keeping the user experience (UX) of your future customers in mind.

Choosing a theme

The theme store has pages and pages of themes — some free and some paid. Menus at the top of the theme store allow you to browse themes in a variety of ways, including searching by what's trending, what themes are suited to large or small inventories, or even what themes work well with video and 3D. You can also browse by industry — for example, Toys & Games. As you browse through the available options, you can start to envisage what your store may look like.

On the left-hand side of the theme store, there's also a sidebar that allows you to filter your search based on a variety of options, including paid and free themes, product page style, and homepage style. You can also use the search bar in the top-right corner to search for things that you consider to be must-haves for your store — for example, 'product zoom', so customers can zoom in on the details of your products — and the results will show you themes that include your requirements (in this case, all the themes with product zoom features will show up).

When you click into a theme, as well as being able to read about all the features and technical specs of the theme, you can check the look and feel of the site by using the demo feature — just click on 'View Demo' and you'll be taken to a demo site that uses the selected theme. Have a good look around all the pages and try the various features before you select that theme for your store.

REMEMBER

Don't skip the reviews when you're selecting a theme — it may save you time and help you pick the most suitable theme for you. If you're just starting out, you probably want something that has an easy set-up and simple integration, so check for feedback around ease of use.

Eureka! You've found your theme

Many of the themes look great, but I'm sure it will feel extra special when you find 'the one'. When you've found your theme, you can add it very simply to your store by clicking on 'Add Theme', which adds your theme to the Themes page of your Shopify admin panel.

TIP

If you're not quite sold on a certain paid theme, you can click 'Try Theme' and you'll be able to preview the theme in your store. You can make modifications if needed and then decide to buy it if you like it. You can preview up to 19 paid themes, so you have several opportunities to make the right choice.

You can store themes in your theme library (which is located in your Shopify admin) and switch between them as you please. If you manually customize a theme, it will appear as a new theme, with the original version of the theme also showing in your theme library.

REMEMBER

Changing themes doesn't impact your inventory or content, as that's stored in your admin — however, you will lose the styling that the theme provides, including the colors and fonts, if you decide to change themes.

TIP

If you want to show a few people your theme to get feedback (and it is a great idea to get feedback when you can), follow these steps:

1. **From your Shopify admin panel, go to Online Store (located below Sales Channels in your left-side menu) and click on Themes.**

   The theme library appears. The theme that you want to share to gather feedback is the one you have currently installed on your site, so you see this theme listed at the top of the Themes page, under Current Theme.

2. **For the theme that you want to share, click on Actions and then select View.**

   When you select View, you'll be taken to a preview of your website.

3. **Copy and paste the URL link to the website preview page from your browser. Send the link to friends and family to gauge their opinion.**

Publishing your theme

While you can have up to 20 themes in your admin, only one can be published at any given time. Your published theme is what your customers see (and it's also labelled as your 'Live Theme' in your Shopify admin panel), while your unpublished themes remain in your theme library.

To publish one of your chosen themes, therefore making it your Live Theme:

1. **From your Shopify admin panel, go to Online Store (located below Sales Channels in your left-side menu) and click on Themes.**

   The theme library for your site appears, which is a selection of themes that you have added to your store while exploring your theme options.

   The Live Theme is the one you're currently working on and will always be the theme at the top of your Themes page.

REMEMBER

2. **Click on Actions next to the theme that you want to become your Live Theme, and then click on Publish.**

   The Publish window opens.

3. **In the Publish window, click on Publish.**

WARNING

Don't forget to make a back-up copy of your theme. It's good to have in case something goes wrong as you start getting further into customizing your theme — this way, you'll always have a theme to fall back on. You can back up your theme by clicking on 'Themes' then 'Actions', and then clicking on 'Duplicate'.

TIP

Your theme is only licensed to the store you bought it for — if you need to transfer a theme to a new store, you need to contact Shopify's support.

Customizing your theme

The theme you choose gives you the skeleton of the look and feel of your online store, but it's up to you to bring it to life in a way that suits your brand's identity.

Shopify offers a lot of flexibility when it comes to customizing your theme. To illustrate, it's possible for two businesses to use the same theme but have websites that look completely different — so much so that a customer wouldn't be able to identify that they shared the same theme.

REMEMBER

To customize your theme, click the 'Customize' button in the Themes section of your Shopify admin panel (the 'Customize' button is next to the 'Actions' button). The structure of a homepage is then in front of you, with spaces to drop images and text. A new sidebar appears to the left, and a drop-down menu appears at the top of the page, which indicates which page of your website you're currently editing.

I take you through customizing your website as I introduce each part of your website's functionality throughout this book.

Designing Your Shop Window: The Homepage

The homepage is a constant source of debate among ecommerce professionals, who all have their own views on what should be there. Commonly known by its cute nickname, HP, your *homepage* is often the first port of call for your customer — it's your shop window, so it needs to look good and load fast.

TIP

I am a big believer in designing, building and buying for what you know your customer wants, not what you *hope* they want, so thank goodness for AB testing, which allows you to better understand your customer. I talk about AB testing in more detail in Chapter 9.

In the following sections, I walk you through the shape and structure of your homepage, including how to customize the key features of your homepage and make the most of your theme. But first, I talk about some of the menu options that may help to shape and style your store, making it easy to navigate for your customers.

What's on the menu?

The *menu* of an online store is part of its *navigation* (or *nav*). It's the section of a website that displays the categories and sub-categories of items that the online store is selling. The menu is usually located in the top-left corner of an online store's homepage.

REMEMBER

An online store's homepage looks different depending on what device you're viewing it on; however, if it has been mobile optimized, it almost always shows the menu at the top.

Menus in desktop view tend to run from left to right across the top of the site, calling out the main categories (or pages) of the site — for example, Men, Women, Kids and Sale for a clothing website. Often, more options appear when you click on these sections — for example, clicking on Men may lead you to different types of men's clothing, such as jeans and t-shirts (this is known as a *drop-down menu* — where additional sub-categories of the main category, in this case men's clothing, appear to further direct the customer to the area they are interested in). When your *cursor* (the little arrow that moves around the screen on your desktop, directed by your mouse) leaves that part of the menu, the men's jeans and t-shirts (and so on) disappear — so the drop-down menu appears when you click on the main menu item and then disappears when you leave it.

An expansion on the drop-down menu is a *flyout menu* — a list of additional options that appears to the side of each option (or some options) on the drop-down menu. Going back to men's jeans, if you click on 'Men' and then 'Jeans', a sub-menu may appear to the side to show the different types of jeans you have for sale, such as casual jeans and dressy jeans. If you click on 'Casual Jeans', you may even see an additional flyout menu at the side that provides different size options. It may seem like overkill, but the idea is to guide your customer closer to the product that they want to buy.

You have more options than drop-down menus and flyout menus, however, when you are building your online store. Here are a few of the other menu styles that you may like to try:

>> **Accordion menus** are similar to drop-down menus in that the menu links drop down vertically, but when you click on the menu item, another set of

menu items appear below it. To close the second set of menu items, simply click on the first menu item again.

» **Dropline menus** appear when you hover your cursor over a main menu category (such as Men on a clothing website). Instead of a drop-down menu of options, the sub-categories appear below, running from left to right across the screen and forming a horizontal sub-menu under the main menu.

» **Mega menus** are drop-down menus that use text plus visual content, such as imagery of the items in the menu — for example, if you're browsing the menu of an electronics store online and you click on laptops, a mega menu shows you the names of the laptops, plus accompanying images of the laptops. Mega menus work well when you have a large range of categories; for example, large electronics retailers who need big, bulky menus to help customers navigate multiple departments, categories and sub-categories within their online store.

» **Split menus** are when a menu and a sub-menu appear on different locations on the homepage; for example, if you click on 'Men' on the top menu (the main menu), different men's clothing categories may appear on the left-hand side of the website, such as jeans, shirts, shorts, and so on.

A fun fact — when you are viewing websites on a smartphone or tablet, they often have three horizontal lines to represent the menu, which is called a *hamburger menu* (see Figure 4-1) because apparently the icon looks like a hamburger!

FIGURE 4-1:
The hamburger menu icon.

Source: Shopify

Later in this chapter, in the section 'Adding Menus and Pages', I show you how to create pages (such as About Us and Shipping) and menus within Shopify, and in Chapter 5, I show you how to create *collections* (another name for categories) and place them inside your menu.

Styling your homepage

Your homepage can vary in length and content. Some online stores like you to scroll and scroll and scroll, jamming as much content as they can onto that one page, whereas others simply have a homepage banner with a call to action (like 'Shop Now') and a menu, from which customers can navigate to other pages.

The homepage banner is really important, as is any content that is above the fold of a homepage. *Above the fold* is a term taken from print media. If you picture a folded newspaper, the content above the fold in the paper is on the upper half of the front page, where a key headline or image is placed. In ecommerce, above the fold is the content you see before you need to scroll. When you begin to scroll, the content below the fold appears. Online shoppers can be a fickle bunch, and even the act of scrolling can be too much effort, so typically you want to grab a visitor's attention as quickly as you can by including priority content above the fold, without giving your site visitors any cause to abandon the page (or bounce)!

TIP

Content *below the fold* is typically reserved for more banners, smaller in size than the main homepage banner, that advertise secondary offers or products. I like to use this web page real estate for talking about the history of the brand or showing photos of the team, in a sort of 'get to know us' kind of way — remember, building trust is important, and authenticity is difficult to replace.

Another useful piece of below the fold content is what is known as *social proof*. Without going into the science of social proof in marketing, it's essentially convincing people that buying your product is the right thing to do — perhaps because other people the customer looks up to are doing it. Social proof is not a means of underestimating a customer's intelligence, it's simply helping to convince them that they can trust your store, and should buy from you, if they are so inclined — more of a gentle push, if you will.

You can make changes to style and personalize your homepage to fit with your brand through the theme customization areas of your Shopify admin.

To access the theme customization area, follow these steps:

1. **From your Shopify admin panel, go to Online Store (located below Sales Channels in your left-side menu) and click on Themes.**

   The Themes page appears (see Figure 4-2).

2. **Click on the green Customize button, which appears on the Themes page — you can find it over on the right-hand side of your screen, next to Actions.**

   You'll then be taken to what is beginning to look like a website — at least in its basic form. It's here you'll be able to make changes to the design of your website using the theme customization menu on the left-hand side (see Figure 4-3) and preview your changes as you go.

TIP

   Stay in the Customize section as you work through customizing your homepage in the following sections, as I show you how to make changes to your online store's look and feel here.

FIGURE 4-2:
The Themes
page.

Source: Shopify

FIGURE 4-3:
The theme
customization
menu options on
the Customize
page.

Source: Shopify

TIP

From time to time you may see options to Explore Free Images appear. If you click on this, it brings up a free library of images provided by Shopify that you can add to your store, which saves you time and money on paying for your own photo shoots.

After you start customizing your theme, you can view the skeleton of your first Shopify homepage by selecting View Your Store, in the top-right corner of the Themes section in your Shopify admin — see Figure 4-4.

Source: Shopify

REMEMBER

Don't forget to save your changes!

As you work your way through the theme customization menu options (see Figure 4-3), you'll see your homepage broken into sections, starting with Header.

TIP

The following sections take you through customizing your homepage using Shopify's default Debut theme. If you have chosen a different theme, there may be some differences in the layout or sequence of options below; however, the principles remain the same. To deepen your understanding of how Shopify works, you may find it helpful to use the Debut theme while you get to know your customization options — you can always change your theme later.

Customizing the header

The *header* is the bar at the top of your website that runs horizontally across each page. It usually contains your menu, the name of your business (often as a logo) and a search bar. Your logo should be large and clear, and it is typically positioned in the top-left corner of the homepage.

The main function of a website's header is to house your menu. Your menu is how a customer finds their way to your products and the other pages of your site, such as your shipping information. I'm going to talk about configuring your menus to house pages like About Us and Shipping later in this chapter (in the section 'Adding Menus and Pages'). I also return to building your menu in Chapter 5, when I show you how to create collections and position them in your menus.

FIGURE 4-4:
View how your Shopify store is shaping up by clicking on View Your Store in the Themes section of your Shopify admin.

To edit your header, click on — you guessed it — Header in the theme customization menu (see Figure 4-3).

You can upload your logo right away by clicking on Select Image (under Logo Image) in the Header section of the theme customization menu (see Figure 4-5). If you don't already have a logo, you have the option to choose one from Shopify's library of free images — although you probably want to design your own logo. You can also change the dimensions of your logo by dragging the Custom Logo Width bar (see Figure 4-5) from left to right, and change the alignment of your logo by selecting either Left or Centered for your Logo Alignment (as you tailor your logo image, the changes take effect in an updating preview that is constantly visible).

FIGURE 4-5:
Logo Image selection within the Header section of the theme customization menu.

Source: Shopify

TIP

Canva.com is a great resource for creating a new logo, plus other useful pieces of creative elements you can use on your website, such as social media material, infographics and GIFs.

The other part of the header you can change in this section is what's known as the *announcement bar*, which is the strip of text at the top of the homepage. You can edit the text and link it to anywhere you like; you can also change the background color or leave it as text only. The announcement bar settings are found halfway down the Header section of your menu — simply type over the text that says Announce Something Here (see Figure 4-5).

TIP

I tend to use the announcement bar to highlight free shipping messaging or to promote a sale. I generally also leave such announcements on all pages of the website (as opposed to selecting Home Page Only, in the announcement bar settings — see Figure 4-5) as this ensures your key promotions or free shipping offers are visible on every page of your website.

Building the homepage banner

As you move through the theme customization menu, the next item down is called Image with Text Overlay. This option allows you to create and edit your website's *homepage banner*, which is usually the first banner a visitor to your website sees when they arrive at your online store.

When you click on Image with Text Overlay, you see a placeholder image that Shopify uses for all new stores — a grey box with shapes on it. You can replace this grey box with your own homepage banner image. A new set of menu options also appears on the left-hand side of the page (see Figure 4-6).

FIGURE 4-6:
The homepage banner customization menu options.

Source: Shopify

Here's a rundown of the changes you can make to your homepage banner with each of these menu options:

>> **Image — Select Image:** Clicking on this option allows you to upload your own homepage banner, or you can choose one of the images in Shopify's free image library.

>> **Image Alignment:** Choose from Top, Middle or Bottom, and watch your image move in the preview on the right-hand side of the page to help you decide the position that works best. The Image Alignment feature changes which part of the image you want to display — for example, selecting Middle shows the majority of the homepage banner, while selecting Top only shows the top of the image you have uploaded.

Play around with all three and see which looks best — it's likely Middle is where you'll land.

>> **Layout:** Here you can choose between Full Width and Fixed Width. Full Width occupies a larger horizontal space on your homepage, while Fixed Width shows space on either side of the banner. Again, the banner preview moves as you try out both options, so you can make an informed choice between the two.

>> **Section Height:** As with the Layout options, you can change the vertical size of the banner, with six different height options available: Adapt to Image (which adjusts according to your image size), Extra Small, Small, Medium, Large and Extra Large.

>> **Text Size:** Use this option to change the size of your overlying Heading text from Large to Medium (see the next item in this list).

>> **Heading:** Choose this option to add a Heading to your homepage banner — the text appears over the top of the homepage banner image. An example of a heading might be your store's name or the name of a product range, such as Summer Collection.

>> **Text:** The next section down allows you to add another text section, which is smaller-sized text that appears under your Heading. You can use this for a call to action, such as Sale Now On or Limited Edition. You can add a link from this text section to any page on your website (or an external website) and you can change the font to bold or italic (the text default is regular, not bold or italic).

>> **Button Label:** This option allows you to create a button on your homepage banner, such as a Shop Now button. Simply type in the text you'd like to see on your button.

>> **Button Link:** A button isn't much use unless it takes the customer to another point on your website; fortunately, this option allows you to add a link to the page you want to send the customer to when they click on the button. You can put a link in here (such as www.something.com), so that when a shopper clicks the button you just created, it will take them to a particular page. For example, if your banner is advertising a new range of scooters (with the heading New Scooters), you can add a button that says Shop Scooters, which you can link to your scooter collection.

TIP

When you click on the Button Link field, a list of all your website's available pages and collections appears, so you can choose which page you want to link your button to.

REMEMBER

Don't forget to click the green Save button in the top-right corner, and then click the left-facing arrow button in the top-left corner to go back to the main theme menu, if you want to continue designing the rest of your homepage.

When you return to the theme customization menu, you may notice that the Image with Text Overlay menu option has changed to the name of the Heading for your homepage banner, such as New Scooters.

TECHNICAL
STUFF

If you're designing your own homepage banner or using a graphic designer, the dimensions of a typical homepage banner in Shopify are 1200 x 400–600 pixels.

Boosting your homepage with extra images with text

The next section under your homepage is Image with Text. Here you have space to add another smaller image under the homepage banner. For example, if your homepage banner features new scooters, your secondary banner may feature helmets and kneepads, or a similar secondary collection. The options are basically the same as your homepage banner (refer to the preceding section, 'Building the homepage banner') — you can upload an image or choose from Shopify's free image options, and you can add buttons and text, all the while viewing the live preview to see how it looks.

Adding text columns with images

This is a basic section that allows you to upload images with text underneath. When you click on this menu option, you're taken to a page where you can first create a Title, or Tag Line. When you click on that option, you are presented with the option to add an image, once again with headings, text and a button that can link to wherever you want it to.

You can use this section to create an About Us section (though this section can also commonly be found in your homepage footer), where you display an image of yourself or your team on your homepage, with text that tells the story of your store's history. Alternatively, you may like to feature a special product or collection of products, or even to promote a blog post that you've written. You can use this section to include virtually any content you'd like.

Making a feature of your key collections

Collections (or categories) group together products with similar properties, such as men's clothes, children's toys, dog treats, women's shoes — you get the picture! By grouping similar items together, your customers can browse through the categories of interest to them, without wading through pages of items they don't want.

The theme customization menu gives you the option to feature a collection on your homepage. To use this feature, you need to have created at least one collection in your store, and then added some products to that collection in order to preview them on your homepage. (In Chapter 5, I show you how to create a collection and add products to your store.)

When you click on the Featured Collections option, you can edit the name of the collection to whatever you want, for example Men's Jeans or What's New.

In the space beneath the collection name heading, you have the option to Select Collection — when you click on this, a list of all the collections you have created in your store appears, and you can click on one to display its products on your homepage.

TIP

You can change the number of products per rows, and the number of rows overall that you want to show on your homepage — see Figure 4-7.

FIGURE 4-7:
Adding a
Featured
Collection to
your homepage.

Source: Shopify

Adding an extra banner

The next heading on the theme customization menu is Image with Text Overlay — which may ring a few bells. This extra banner follows the process of setting up your homepage banner exactly. With this option, you can create a similar banner further down the homepage, which you may decide to use to advertise another offer or collection. This is another section where you can show off your products or more about your store.

TIP

If you don't want to add an extra banner, or you want to remove any other section, click on the section you want to remove, such as Image with Text Overlay. An option at the bottom of the menu appears, called Remove Section, with a rubbish bin icon — click on it, and your section (in this case, Image with Text Overlay) will disappear from your menu, and therefore from your homepage.

If you want to add a section to your homepage — for example, you may decide to add another Image with Text Overlay section, or a new image gallery — there's a blue button with a + symbol at the bottom of the theme customization menu with Add Section next to it. Click on this, and select any of the sections that appear from the list of options that appear. The sections that can be added are the same as the sections you've been editing in this chapter, along with some others, such as a map to your physical store (if you have one), videos or more image galleries.

To add an extra homepage banner, follow the process outlined in the earlier section, 'Building the homepage banner' and apply it to this section of the theme customization menu.

Selling yourself: Testimonials

The Debut theme comes with a Testimonials section, where you can add positive reviews and feedback to your online store to highlight the reliability of your service. Simply click on Testimonials and type in the testimonial text you want to appear, along with the author's name, in the two fields that appear. Remember to click on the green Save button in the top-right corner when you're done.

TIP

Ask enthusiastic friends or willing early customers if they are happy to provide you with a testimonial. Chapter 8 talks about how to gather product and customer reviews, as well as utilizing the Shopify App Store to make the most of your positive feedback.

Adding an image gallery

The Gallery section allows you to upload a group of images. Typically, here you may choose to feature some products or marketing materials you have created for a collection. When you click on Gallery in the theme customization menu, you see three options drop down, as an extension of the Gallery menu, each labelled Image, with a grey square icon next to each Image label (so, the word Image is repeated three times, with grey squares next to each word). When you click on any of the three Image words or grey square icons, a new section appears within the menu that prompts you to upload the image you want to add to your homepage. Click on the Select Image button and upload the image from your computer. You can then add a caption, such as 'The Paul Shoes in Black' and link the image to any page on your site by clicking on the Link field and browsing the pages that appear in the list.

Another idea for this section is to create a gallery for user-generated content — which is content your customers have sent to you, such as an image of a happy customer using your product. You can then link that image to the product page on your site so that shoppers can view it and purchase it. You may also decide to use this section for adding influencer content — Part 5 covers marketing and influencer content.

Customizing the footer

Your *footer*, the helpful and informative resources section of your website located at the bottom of your homepage, can be edited from the bottom of your theme customization menu. Your footer usually contains links to other informative pages within your website, such as Shipping, Returns, About Us, Privacy and anything else that is valuable for the customer to know. (I show you how to create these pages and insert them into your footer menu in the later section 'Adding Menus and Pages'.) You may also choose to display links to your social media pages, although increasingly you see Instagram and other social media marketing channels incorporated in higher positions on the homepage — for example, when using apps that feed Instagram images into a gallery for users to browse (more on Instagram in Chapter 17!).

TIP

Check out the policies of other online stores to better understand the policies they hold for topics such as returns — and what your online store may need to include in its own policies. By understanding what your competitors (or some of the bigger ecommerce businesses) are offering, you can get an idea of what your customers may expect from your policies. I cover more general ecommerce practices — including store policies for shipping, returns and privacy — in my book *Selling Online For Dummies*.

Adjusting your theme's settings

While in the theme customization menu, you'll see down the bottom of the menu, another section titled Theme Settings. Go ahead and click on that, and you'll be able to continue editing and styling some of the other features and functions of your homepage that may also impact other parts of your online store, such as your font styles and colors (see Figure 4-8).

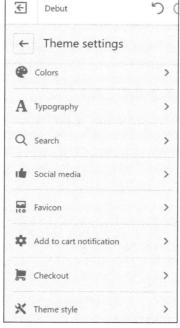

FIGURE 4-8:
The Theme
Settings section.

You can use the following items in the Theme Settings menu to adjust your theme further:

TIP

>> **Colors:** This section allows you to change the colors across your website, from the color of the text your site uses to the color of the buttons on your site — and everything in between. You can also change background and border colors.

As with many of the customization options in Shopify, you can visualize your changes using the live preview feature to the right of the page as you experiment with different colors.

>> **Typography:** Clicking into this section allows you to change the font your store uses and the size of the text across your headings, on your buttons, and across your website.

>> **Search:** This section refers to the search bar, which customers use to search for certain products or pages in your website.

You'll be presented with the option to Enable Product Suggestions, which is ticked by default. Leaving this ticked is useful, as it predicts the products customers may be searching for as they begin their search. For example, if your visitor starts typing Jeans in the search bar, any Jeans in your store may begin to appear below the search bar, to help the customer find what they're looking for.

>> **Social Media:** You can add social media icons to the footer on your homepage. In this section you can set up links on your store that connect social media icons to your social media pages for Twitter, Facebook, Pinterest, Instagram, Tumblr, Snapchat, YouTube and Vimeo.

>> **Favicon:** Although it sounds like a creature out of *Star Wars*, a *favicon* is a nice little badge for your store to have. It's that tiny icon or logo that appears as you search for a website. For example, if you type www.shopify.com into your browser, the green 'S' logo — Shopify's favicon — appears as you type. This lets you know you're on their official site, which helps build trust and brand identity.

In this section of the menu, you can upload your own favicon — the recommended dimensions are 32 x 32 pixels, so you may need to adjust your logo to something even smaller than it usually appears.

>> **Add to Cart Notification:** You only have one option when you click on this, and the default position on the Debut theme is to notify customers when an 'add to cart' has occurred. It's just a nice way to let a customer know that they have successfully added something to their cart, rather than having them check their cart to see if the item was added.

I recommend keeping with the default setting and leaving this ticked.

>> **Theme Style:** When you click on this option in the menu, you see that the Debut theme has two styles, Default and Light, which change the overall color scheme of your site, basically giving you two different looks within the one theme. Try both to see which you prefer.

You won't be able to click on this until your changes so far have been saved, which is a timely reminder to do so!

Adding Menus and Pages

Menus exist in two places in your online store — your header and your footer (for more on the different types of menu, check out the earlier section 'What's on the menu?'). In this chapter, I've introduced some of the menu items that may exist in your store, such as product collections, as that's how your visitors navigate their way around your store. I look at adding collections and linking them to your main header menu in Chapter 5.

Pages are where visitors to your store are taken when they click on certain menu items, such as a collection, About Us or Shipping. Your footer menu is a great place to keep some of the more informative pages that aren't product-focused, such as the About Us page — which is a page that talks to the customer about who you are, what your store sells and how you got started. Stores with an authentic About Us page tend to get more sales than stores with those with a vague or unhelpful story to tell about themselves.

TIP

I recommend adding the following pages to your footer:

>> About Us

>> Contact Us

>> Shipping

>> Returns Policy

In the following sections, I show you how to create pages and link these to your menu, using the footer as an example.

Creating a page

To create a page:

1. **Navigate to your main Shopify admin menu (not the themes customization menu, where you have spent much of your time in this chapter!).**

2. **Click on Sales Channels → Online Store. Select Pages from the list of headings that appears.**

    You'll be taken to a new page, that is aptly titled Pages. It's here that you'll create . . . you guessed it, pages!

3. **Click on Add Page.**

    A new page appears asking for some input into what sort of page you're creating (see Figure 4-9).

4. **Give the page a title — for example, About Us.**

Source: Shopify

FIGURE 4-9:
Populating the
About Us page.

REMEMBER

TIP

5. **Enter your About Us content into the text box below the title field.**

A good About Us page lets the shopper into your brand and is authentic and genuine. In your early days, it's important to remember that a potential customer has no idea who you are, so before they part with their money, they often want to know who the people behind the brand are. A lot of brands have fun team photos or videos here — and don't forget to show the office dog!

The About Us page is a great opportunity to showcase your brand's fabric, or innate qualities. Are you humorous, cheeky, serious, safe and trustworthy, or technically the best? Here's your chance to convey that!

You can easily add images and videos in the text box — just click on the icons that represent the feature you want to add and upload your images and video.

You may also see a space for SEO (search engine optimization), but perhaps leave that for now — I look at SEO in Chapter 16.

6. **In the top-right corner, you have the option to hide the page or make it visible, or even set a date you want it to become visible (click on the link that says Set Visibility Date — see Figure 4-9). When you are happy with the content, hit Save in the bottom-right corner.**

Creating a menu item

To create a menu item:

1. **Navigate to your main Shopify admin menu. Click on Sales Channels →
   Online Store. Select Navigation from the list of headings that appears.**

   The Navigation page appears, showing you two default menus — Main Menu
   and Footer Menu. The About Us page you created in the preceding section
   belongs on the Footer Menu, which is where the About Us page you just
   created will live.

2. **Click on Footer Menu.**

   A new page called Footer Menu comes up (which you can rename, but there's
   no real need to do that).

3. **On the Footer Menu page, under Menu Items, click on Add Menu Item.**

   A dialogue box called Add Menu Item appears.

4. **Name the menu item by typing the name of the item in this box —
   for this example, you would type About Us.**

5. **In the Link field that follows the Name box, click on Pages from the
   drop-down menu that appears.**

   A list of pages that you have created appears — if you have only created the
   About Us page so far, this will be the only one that appears.

6. **Click on the page that you want to add to your menu — in this case,
   the About Us page.**

   The About Us page title appears in the link field.

7. **Click on the green Add button at the bottom of the Add Menu Item
   dialogue box.**

8. **Click Save Menu in the bottom-right corner.**

   You've just created your first menu item — an About Us page in your
   Footer menu!

TIP

If you want to preview what it looks like live, then click on the eyeball icon next to
Sales Channels in the main menu, which directs you to a fully functioning preview
of how your site looks and works.

Repeat the page and menu item creation process for each page you'd like to add to
your store (such as About Us, Shipping, Returns Policy and any other pages you
want to add to your store). Chapter 5 goes into the detail of adding product pages
and linking your products to collections.

Chapter **5**

Filling Your Virtual Shelves: Creating Products and Collections

You are making your way towards publishing your first products and collections on your online store, ready for sale. However, you still have some crucial steps ahead before you can activate your store.

In this chapter, I explore developing and curating your collections — adding products to them, describing them in an appealing way, and visually merchandising them so they look great and are easily discoverable on your website.

I also look at using Shopify's tag feature, which helps your products find their home within a collection — as well as helping your customers to search for them in your store.

Nuts and Bolts: Adding Products to Develop Your Collections

Collections (also known as categories) consist of groups of products that contain similar properties, making it easier for a potential customer to find what they are looking for. Collections can be grouped by a variety of criteria, including season or range, gender, types of products, bestsellers and sale.

After your collection has been published with products inside, it then appears on your website. Upon clicking on a product within a collection, a visitor will be able to look at a product individually in a product page, where they'll be able to make a purchase if they so choose.

REMEMBER

You need to be in the Collections section, located within the Products menu of your Shopify admin, in order to create, develop or maintain a collection.

In Chapter 4, I encourage you to start thinking about the layout of your online store. In the following sections, I guide you through adding products to your online store and creating collections, as well as adding tags and products to your collections.

Creating a collection

In Shopify, you have the option to create one of two types of collection — automated collections and manual collections.

An *automated collection* uses certain conditions to automatically include certain products into collections. You can add up to 60 selection conditions to your Shopify store. You can also specify whether products need to meet *all* of the conditions or *any* of the conditions to be included in the collection. When you add a new product to Shopify that matches your selection conditions for a collection, Shopify automatically adds the product to the collection.

REMEMBER

You can save a lot of time by using automated collections if you have a large selection of products or if you have seasonal or rotating inventories. For example, if I create an automated collection and add the selection condition 'mens-clothes', every product that I add and tag with 'mens-clothes' will automatically go into the 'Men's Clothes' collection (the next section talks more about product tags).

A *manual collection* includes only the products that you choose to add to a collection. Therefore, the collection always contains the same products unless you specifically add new products or remove old ones.

TIP

Manual collections take more work to maintain, but they can be a good choice for small or specialized collections that you intend to curate personally. For example, if you plan to hold a one-time flash sale of just a few products, you can create a manual collection for them and set up a discount for just the products in that collection.

To create a collection:

1. **In the Shopify admin sidebar, navigate to Products → Collections. In the top-right corner, click on Create Collection.**

   A new page appears (see Figure 5-1), which has a variety of empty text boxes for you to input the information about the collection you want to add to your store.

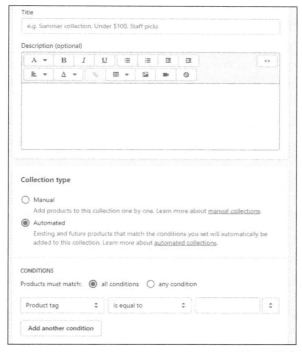

FIGURE 5-1:
The Create Collection page.

Source: Shopify

2. **In the Title box, enter the name of your collection — for example, 'Men's Clothes'.**

   You can leave the description empty for now, as I talk about the SEO (search engine optimization) benefits of writing an effective collection description in Chapter 16.

The title you choose will be visible on your store as it is the name of your collection.

3. **Select Manual or Automated collection from the checkbox options below the Description field.**

Doing this means that your collection either automatically populates with items as you add certain tags/conditions to new products (for automated collections), or it means that you will manually add products to your collection.

4. **In the Conditions section, select either the All Conditions or Any Condition checkbox.**

Here, it's usual to leave the existing selection, which is All Conditions (though later in this section I explain when it's helpful to use the Any Condition option).

5. **Type a product tag in the blank field after Product Tag and Is Equal To.**

This is the default selection, though you can choose other condition criteria. Here, for example, you can enter the tag 'mens-jeans'.

As well as Product Tag, you can choose from other conditions for your collections, such as Product Title, Weight, Product Type and Variant's Title. These are all aspects of the products that you add to your store. These conditions serve as different ways to automatically add products to your collections. So, if you have a collection called 'Everything Under $50', you can change the condition to Product Price, select Is Less Than and type '$50' in the blank field that follows. Then, when you add a product to your store with a price that's less than $50, it's automatically added to your Everything Under $50 collection.

Experiment with the different conditions you can apply to your collections to work out which options are most useful for your store.

6. **Press enter on your keyboard.**

Voilà, your product tag will save automatically.

You have the option to add more conditions here (click on Add Another Condition) or you can add further conditions at a later time. I talk more about adding additional product tags in the next section, 'Using product tags to refine your collections'.

7. **Click on Save in the top-right corner to create your collection.**

You can come back later and add more text and images to your collection before you publish your website. Whenever you want to come back and make any edits, just go back to your Shopify admin, click on Products → Collections, select your collection, and then make your edits.

When you are editing your collection, you see a section in the top-right corner called Collection Availability. When you tick the checkbox labelled Online Store, your collection publishes in your store (your collection only shows in your store when you check this checkbox — until then, it is a work in progress). You can also add a collection image when you are ready to publish. Click on Add Image, just below Collection Availability, and upload the image that you want your shoppers to see as they enter your collection.

If you add more than one condition to a collection, then the option that products must match All Conditions or Any Condition becomes important.

Imagine that you're creating the collection described in the preceding steps and you decide to add a second condition. You click on Add Another Condition, and as you scroll through the condition options (which defaults to Product Tag), you instead select Product Vendor (*vendor* is another name for supplier; the later section 'Organization' talks about adding vendors to your products). If your product's supplier is called ABC Jeans, you will also enter that information into the Product Vendor section of your product page; to bring all the ABC Jeans products into this collection, you select Is Equal To after Product Vendor, and in the blank field you enter ABC Jeans.

Now, in this collection, you have two conditions:

>> A Product Tag that Is Equal To mens-jeans

>> A Product Vendor that Is Equal To ABC Jeans.

This is where All Conditions versus Any Condition becomes important. If you selected that products must match all conditions in order to automatically become part of the collection, then a product will only appear in the collection if it meets both of these conditions.

Products that you want to become automatically added to the collection therefore need:

>> A product tag called mens-jeans

>> For ABC Jeans to be named as the product vendor.

In the same way, if you selected Any Condition rather than All Conditions, then any product you add to your store that matches one of these two conditions will automatically appear in your collection.

Find out how to add these details and many other pieces of helpful product information in the later section 'Adding a new product to your store'.

Using product tags to refine your collections

Tags are labels you can add to a product to help customers search and find specific products within your online store. Tags are also used to add products to their correct collections (for example, making sure that your blue jeans are displayed in the Jeans collection). I'll be explaining how to upload products into collections throughout this chapter — first by creating product tags, and then by adding products (see the later section 'Adding a new product to your store'). Shopify allows you to add up to 250 tags to each product, separated by a comma — although I haven't seen more than 50 attached to a product.

TIP

Keep in mind the following guidelines when setting up tags in your online store:

>> **Use simple characters:** Use only ordinary letters, numbers and the hyphen (-) symbol in your tags (although you aren't required to use a hyphen). Avoid accented characters and other symbols.

Although you can create tags that use some special characters, they may not work as you expect in searches or as conditions in automated collections. Special characters in tags may either be ignored or treated the same as other special characters, making them unhelpful for your store's search function.

>> **Keep tag lengths short:** For ease of use, keep your tags short. Misspelling a tag may land your product in the wrong collection, or mean it doesn't show up on your site at all!

>> **Ensure your tags are simple and understandable:** Name your tags in a way that makes sense to you and your staff so that each tag has a clear purpose and is easy to remember.

>> **Check your tags are clear to customers:** In some online store themes, your product tags are shown to your customers (such as in drop-down filter menus). Because the tags are visible, you need to make sure that they make sense to customers.

For example, imagine you want to create a tag for the products in a collection for the Autumn 2019 season. You could create the tag myautumn19, but if that tag is shown in a filter menu in your online store, your customers may not understand what it means. A better choice is Autumn-2019.

EXAMPLE

Jack is selling women's shoes online. He's using tags to indicate the heel size of the shoe, such as flat, wedge and high heel. He's also using tags to indicate the shoe color, such as black, navy and red (when a product has more than one color or size option, that's referred to in Shopify as a product *variant*, which I'll be running through in the later section, 'Step seven: Adding variants'). The theme Jack uses in Shopify has a filter in the collection page, which allows customers to filter products by tag, so if a customer filters products by 'flat' shoes, all of Jack's flat shoe products that are in that collection appear. If the customer then adds a filter that says 'red', all of Jack's flat red shoes that are in that collection appear.

TIP

If you like the idea of including a filter option to your online store, make sure your theme has one by checking the theme's demo website in the theme store (`themes.shopify.com/themes`) or by using a third-party app from the Shopify app store — for example:

>> Collection Filter by Supple

>> Smart Product Filter & Search by Globo

>> Product Filter & Search by Boost Commerce

>> Collection Filter & Search Bar by SoBooster

To use tags to automate the grouping of products within collections (known in Shopify as setting up an *automated collection* — refer to the preceding section 'Creating a collection' for more on this), you first need to create the tag name when you create the collection — for example, you need to create the tag mens-jeans when you create a collection called Men's Jeans. You can then use that collection when you set up each product that goes into the Men's Jeans collection.

You marry your products to your collections automatically with every product you add to your store if you have your collection tags set up, ready to accumulate new products. When you add products to your store and include a correlating product tag, they automatically join any collection containing the same collection tag. For example, if you have a collection called Men's Jeans (with the collection tag mens-jeans) and you add a new pair of jeans as a new product (with the product tag mens-jeans), the jeans will be added to the Men's Jeans collection.

REMEMBER

Only automated collections can use tags to automate the grouping of products to a collection. A manual collection requires you to add products to a collection one by one.

To add a tag to a collection (to illustrate here, I continue with the Men's Jeans example):

1. **In the Shopify admin sidebar, navigate to Products → Collections.**

   A list of the collections you have created appears.

2. **Click into the collection you want to prepare to add products to, and scroll down to Conditions (see Figure 5-2).**

   For example, click into the Men's Jeans collection.

   The Conditions section only appears if you selected automated collections when you created the collection.

Source: Shopify

FIGURE 5-2: Adding collection tags to an automatic collection in Shopify.

3. **In the drop-down menu under Conditions (in the Conditions section of the Men's Jeans collection page), select Product Tag, Is Equal To and type in your product tag (for example, mens-jeans).**

   Product Tag should already be selected as a default in the Conditions section, and using product tags is the most common way to use automatic collections.

By selecting Is Equal To, you are confirming that only products that match the product tag can be added to the collection. Finally, by entering the product tag mens-jeans, you are indicating that any products tagged with mens-jeans will be added to the collection.

4. **Click on Save in the top-right corner.**

Now that the product tag mens-jeans has been added to this collection, any time you create a product and enter the tag mens-jeans in the Tags section of the Add Product page, that product will automatically be added to your Men's Jeans collection, meaning all products tagged with mens-jeans will appear in the collection. See the later section 'Tags' for more on adding product tags to your products.

If you prefer not to use collection tags and would rather add products one at a time to their respective collections, ensure that you select Manual Collection when you set up your collections (refer to the earlier section 'Creating a collection'). Look out for the steps in the later 'Collections' section for more on populating products into collections manually.

Adding collections to your menu

In Chapter 4, I showed you how to create menus and add pages to your menu (such as your About Us and Shipping pages). Here, I'm going to show you how to add your newly created collections to your header menu.

REMEMBER

Your *header menu* is where shoppers go to browse your collections. Think of your menu as a gateway to your collections — every collection you create should have a place in your store's menu.

Imagine you have a collection called Men's Jeans. To add this collection to your menu, follow these steps:

1. **Navigate to your main Shopify admin menu. Click on Sales Channels → Online Store. Select Navigation from the list of headings that appears.**

   The Navigation page appears, with two menus listed: Footer Menu and Main Menu.

2. **Click on Main Menu.**

   The Main Menu page appears.

3. **On the Main Menu page, under Menu Items, click on Add Menu Item.**

   A dialogue box appears on the right-hand side of the page, which prompts you to fill out two fields: Name and Link (see Figure 5-3).

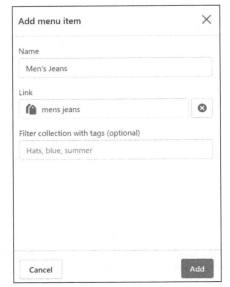

FIGURE 5-3:
Adding
collections to
your header
menu in Shopify.

Source: Shopify

4. **In the Name field, type your collection name; for example, Men's Jeans.**

5. **In the Link field (which prompts you to search for or paste a link), start typing your collection name (in this case, Men's Jeans). Because your collection already exists in Shopify, as you start to type it will recognize your Men's Jeans collection and it will appear on a drop-down list of options. Click on Men's Jeans.**

   Men's Jeans appears in the Link field (see Figure 5-3).

6. **Click the green Add button in the bottom-right corner of the dia-logue box.**

   You'll be taken back to the Main Menu section, where you can now see your new menu item, the Men's Jeans collection, listed under your menu items.

7. **Click on the green Save Menu button in the bottom-right corner.**

   Visitors to your store will now be able to see your Men's Jeans collection in your main menu, and when they click on it they will be taken to your Men's Jeans collection, where they can browse all the men's jeans in your store!

Adding a new product to your store

By now you've probably spent countless time (and possibly a fair bit of money in the process) sourcing what you hope to be your breakthrough ecommerce prod-ucts, so now it's time to add these products to your store, bringing you one step closer to opening your doors and going live.

Adding products in Shopify means creating product listings for the products you have sourced and intend to sell through your online store. You create product listings in the Shopify admin panel (the back end of your site), and they are displayed to your store's visitors on your website (the front end).

REMEMBER

Adding a product to your store is a major deal. You can't just throw your products online in the hope they'll sell themselves; like all the pages of your online store, each product page needs to be compiled strategically — with appropriate and engaging images and product descriptions — to lure the customer further down the path towards purchasing.

The main components of a product listing are the images of the product and the product description. In the following sections, I talk you step by step through how to create a product, including setting an initial price and inventory level, so that you are ready to start selling online.

TIP

Because this is a process following many steps, I break the steps into subsections, with their own headings — but each section follows part of an overall process. Read through the following sections before you get started so you can gather all the information you need before you begin — including your product description and the product images you want to add to your image gallery.

If you only partially create a product — for example, you enter a title but nothing else — as long as you hit Save, then your product will be ready for you to return to editing when you can. Find any products you want to edit in the All Products section of the Products section of your Shopify admin.

If you forget to save your progress, you'll be prompted to either save or discard your work. Hit your favorite green Save button in the top-right corner to save your new product.

TIP

When you've worked through all the steps and saved your product, remember to check out your product through the eyes of your customers by clicking on Preview in the top-right corner of the Add Product page!

Step one: Getting started with adding a new product

To create a new product in Shopify:

1. **From your Shopify admin, click on Products → All Products.**

    This takes you to a new page that displays all of your store's products, with a green button in the top-right corner labelled Add Product.

2.   Click on Add Product.

The Add Product page appears (see Figure 5-4). This is the money page — the all-important page where you will add each of your new products.

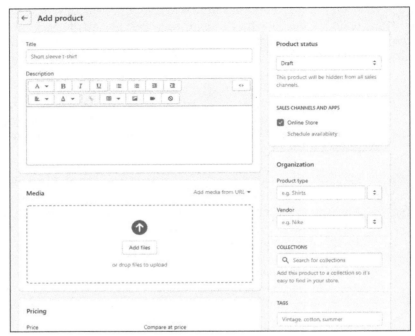

Source: Shopify

FIGURE 5-4:
The Add
Product page.

3.   Add a product name in the Title field of the Add Product page.

Check out what some of your competitors are doing with their product names, and when you have one, go ahead and place your product name in the title field.

For example, if you are adding a pair of men's jeans to your store, you want to choose a name that makes it clear you are selling a pair of jeans — so include 'Jeans' in the product name.

Naming your products is much like naming your children — throw a few names in a hat, swirl them around and pluck out the lucky winner! Okay, so I may have simplified that, but the chances are your supplier or manufacturer has a very boring serial number, or product code, so your job is to rename that product into something that resonates with your customers and suits your brand.

You can change your product name (and any other product details) at any time, but changes may impact your reporting — for example, changing 'Charlie Jeans in Blue' to 'Charlie Blue Jeans' means the same item appears as two different products in your reporting. I'd suggest trying your best to set it up cleanly from the start — your future self will thank you.

Step two: Adding a product description to your product

It's a challenge to constantly write and produce content that pays homage to one product, particularly if you have a large range of SKUs (stock-keeping units). You want the meaty stuff to appear in the product description, as it should appear *above the fold* of the product page (the content that sits in plain sight before a shopper needs to scroll down; therefore, it's the MVP real estate on any web page) — in other words, this will stand out and be seen by potential customers, so think key features, measurements and technical specs.

Different themes display part or all of the product description above the fold, and some prefer to have it lower down, with the Add to Cart button or other information sitting higher above the fold. Browse your theme's product pages to find one that suits. I don't think there's a hard and fast rule to follow — though I recommend you always AB test different layouts (I explain AB testing in Chapter 9) — but as a general rule I suggest trying to keep the meaty stuff on your product page above the fold.

Here's a few ideas for what to include in your product description:

>> Weight and dimensions of the product

>> A description of the material used

>> Any technical specifications that come with your product

>> A clear summary of your product's unique selling points (USPs)

Keep your product descriptions practical — *why* is your customer shopping for a product like yours? One likely reason is as a solution to a problem — a dress to wear at a party, a pair of boots to wear hiking or a trampoline for the kids. Tell the customer why your product is the one for them — for example, the dress can be worn two ways; the boots are waterproof; the trampoline is rated AAA for safety.

Within a product description, more is more — *if* it's useful. If the product description content isn't adding value to the decision-making process, you may need to rework it. There's no real guide to how much you need to say in a product description, so stop when you think you've covered everything.

To add a product description to your product:

1. **Return to the Add Product page from the preceding section 'Step one: Getting started with adding a new product'.**

   Directly below the Title field you'll see the Description box (what Shopify calls the *rich text editor*).

2. **Enter your product description in the Description box.**

   Your product description is the information your customers read when they're weighing up whether to buy your product. This is where you can solve your customers' problems using the written word!

REMEMBER

Your job is to inform and persuade, not to write the next great play. You want to talk about everything glorious about your product, and above all, explain how your product solves the customer's problem. If you can't answer that question yourself, there's a fair chance you need to rethink your product selection.

Step three: Adding media to your products

The product description (refer to the preceding section) may help to sell your customers on the technical aspects of your products, but visual media is the eye-catching way you attract customers to your products at a glance — and you can add visual media in the Media section of the Add Product page (the Media section appears after the Description section on the page).

Media is another name for photos, images, GIFs (graphics interchange format), videos, augmented reality (think of an online rug store that allows you to upload a photo of your living room to its site, then shows you how your rug looks in your living room) or any other form of graphic that you can use to display your products.

REMEMBER

When it comes to product page images, I think both quality and quantity are important, alongside a good product description. If you're selling dog food online, you may not need as many images, but the product description and ingredients are likely to be more important to customers; however, if you're selling clothes, you're best advised to provide a lot of photos, along with a clear product description.

If your online store sells something visual — something that people display, either on themselves or in their households — it's a good idea to show off that product in various scenarios, including real life, so aim to include product photos and lifestyle photos. For example, if you're selling a rug, you can show images of the front and back of the rug, as well as picture the rug positioned in a living room (or in various living rooms), so that the potential customer can envisage that rug in their own home (you can also offer an augmented reality option to see how it may look against a photo of their own living room).

TECHNICAL STUFF

If you want your customers to be able to view your products in augmented reality (AR), you need 3D models of your products. Try the Shopify Experts marketplace (`experts.shopify.com`) to find an expert to help with creating 3D models. You need to use a theme that supports 3D or augmented reality — the default Shopify Debut theme does not do this 'out of the box'.

The same applies for clothing — while some stores show an outfit against a white background, most successful online clothing stores show the clothes on a model, in various poses.

TIP

Show clothing items on a diverse range of models, as obviously not all people look the same. People want to get an idea of how a product will look on them in real life.

Product photos aren't all about showing off how a product looks; they can also be used to demonstrate functionality. If you're selling a bag that looks great but the unique selling point (USP) is its ability to hold a large variety of items, then you need to show that functionality through your images. For more functional items, instead of the showy model poses you may instead opt for detailed photos of the inside of the bag, or images that show how a laptop and diary fit in the bag.

Of course, an evening bag is a different proposition — and modelling the bag with different outfits may help to sell the bag more than a photo of the inside of the bag. But functionality may still be a feature to consider — does it fit a phone, purse and keys, for example? Do you need to show this too?

REMEMBER

Sellers need to understand their value proposition for each product: Are you going for fashion, function or (sometimes) both? If it's function, make sure you talk to that function through your product description and your range of product images.

When it comes to the number of product images to show, I tend to suggest more rather than less. It isn't uncommon for fashion brands to use more than 10 images on the product page, including a mixture of product and lifestyle shots.

You can also include video and movement in the product images section, and I'm seeing this a lot more these days. It doesn't need to be a long video, and it may only be a GIF that has an element of movement, without requiring full video production resources. For example, if you sell a product that is made from recycled plastic, you may have a GIF or some form of motion graphics that illustrates the plastic being turned into your product. The plus side of motion like this is that it's often well-received across social media.

TIP

You can hire talented motion graphics specialists on platforms like Upwork to create content for you, often relatively cheaply.

The downside of video can be the impact it has on your website's speed, although Shopify is great at handling this so you can expect to be able to load video on a decent theme. If in doubt, test how well — and quickly — the added video works on your site across a range of devices.

A product zoom feature (which allows the user to zoom in on the details of your products) is always helpful, and most Shopify themes provide this option. Zooming in is particularly useful if you're selling products with a lot of detail. If you add a zoom feature to your items, remember to test how it works on both a desktop and a smartphone.

To add product media, follow these steps:

1. **Return to the Add Product page from the earlier section 'Step one: Getting started with adding a new product'.**

If you've saved a product you were adding to your store, but hadn't quite finished, you can always go back to it and keep going with any of these steps — just click on Products → All Products from your Shopify admin. All your products, including draft products, will be listed here — just click on the one you want to keep editing.

Directly below the Title field and the Description box, you see the Media section.

2. **Click on the Add Files button located in the Media section.**

A box showing your computer's file contents appears.

3. **Select a media file from your computer, and click on Open.**

The image or media file that you clicked on appears in the Media section of the product creation page.

Repeat the process until you have as many photos or media items as you want to include for your selected product — for example, I may decide to include five images of my Charlie Jeans in Blue.

4. **Drag the images into the order that you want them to be displayed on your website.**

The first image (the image in the first position) will be the image shown in any collections in which the product appears (for example, Men's Jeans); therefore, this image will be the first image a shopper will see. Make it a good one!

If you also want to add a video, follow the same steps but select the video you want to upload, rather than images.

REMEMBER

You can have up to 250 media items across all products on Basic Shopify, 1,000 on Shopify, and 5,000 on Advanced Shopify.

Step four: Pricing your product

The next cab off the rank is pricing (the Pricing section appears after the Media section on the Add Product page).

The Pricing section has three fields in which you can enter information: Price, Compare at Price and Cost Per Item (see Figure 5-5).

Source: Shopify

FIGURE 5-5:
The Pricing section on the Add Product page.

To update your Pricing section, complete the three Pricing fields as follows:

>> **Price:** Enter your original recommended retail price (RRP) into the Price field.

   Imagine you are selling my Charlie Jeans in Blue at $99. Enter 99 or 99.00 (the decimal only matters if I'm selling them at a price that is not rounded to the nearest whole number, such as 99.95).

>> **Compare at Price:** Use this field to provide a price comparison when you want to discount your product.

Imagine you now want to discount the Charlie Jeans in Blue. To do this, you move the original price ($99) into the Compare at Price field, and put the new price (say, $50) into the Price field. This allows your customers to see the original price with a line through it, and the new bargain sale price.

» **Cost Per Item:** Here, you enter your *landed cost price* (the cost of your products, including the cost of shipping them to you).

TIP

Adding your landed cost price to your products helps you generate accurate profit margin reports.

Tick the box that says Charge Tax on This Product if you're registered to collect and pay tax. Chapter 6 shares more information on tax.

TIP

If you ever need to adjust your pricing, or put a product on sale, you can find your product under Products → All Products in your Shopify admin. Simply search for your product and make the edits you require.

Step five: Adding your initial inventory quantity

The Inventory section appears below the Pricing section. It includes three sections: SKU, Barcode and Quantity (see Figure 5-6).

FIGURE 5-6:
The Inventory section on the Add Product page.

Source: Shopify

I dedicate Chapter 11 to managing inventory, so all you need to do for now is set up your initial inventory quantity, also known as your *stock on hand* (SOH).

To enter your opening inventory, simply enter the quantity of the product that you're making available to sell in the Quantity field of the Inventory section on your Add Product page. For example, if I have 100 pairs of the Charlie Jeans in Blue to sell, I enter 100 in the Available box located under Quantity.

The other two fields within the Inventory section ask you to enter a SKU and a barcode (although it's not mandatory). If you have a SKU (stock-keeping unit) code or barcode, enter them here. A *SKU* is a code you or your supplier creates, which usually goes onto a barcode or product label; a *barcode* is a little sticker that sits on your product label, containing information such as size, color and price. Both are ways of identifying each product and are particularly useful for barcode scanners and inventory management systems (IMSs). Although you're not likely to be using scanners at this point, I recommend entering your SKU as it's going to be used to generate reports, and if you decide to sell on marketplaces like eBay or Amazon, or use a warehouse management system (WMS) or external warehouse to store your goods, or even list your products in Google Shopping or Facebook, the SKU is a universal way of deciphering one product from another.

I explain more about SKUs and barcodes in relation to logistics in Chapter 11.

TIP

Do you want to pre-sell stock before it lands in your warehouse? If so, check the Continue Selling When Out of Stock box in the Inventory section of your Add Product page (the checkbox is just below the SKU field). For each additional order after you reach zero stock, your inventory drops below 0 and into negative quantities. If you adopt this strategy, make sure you communicate delivery times with your customer, and keep them updated.

Another option in the Inventory section of your Add Product page is to tick Track Quantity (also under the SKU field) if you want to keep track (through your reporting) of how many units you've sold. Leave it unticked if you have an unlimited supply of products (which may be useful when you're not actually holding the inventory, such as when you're using a dropshipping model).

Step six: Selecting shipping options

The next section of the Add Product page is Shipping (see Figure 5-7).

The first item you see in the Shipping section is a checkbox (This Is a Physical Product). You check this for any product that needs shipping — so any physical product. You may think that this always applies, but if you are selling digital products, such as a digital course, you don't check this checkbox as there's nothing to physically ship.

The next part of the Shipping section asks you to add your product's Weight. Adding the weight tells your carrier how much your parcels weigh, or it can help Shopify calculate your shipping rates if you have weight-based shipping rules. Enter your product's weight in the Weight field.

Source: Shopify

FIGURE 5-7:
The Shipping section of the Add Product page (located under the Inventory section).

TIP

If you're charging a flat shipping rate, you can leave the weight at 0.00; otherwise, you need to weigh each product and enter the weight here.

WARNING

You don't need to add a weight, but if you do, resist the urge to under-declare the weight of your products, as shipping companies often hit you with increased rates based on the true, adjusted weight. Always be extra careful when providing weights (especially volumetric weights) to shipping companies.

The final part of the Shipping section covers Customs Information and only applies to international shipping. If you're planning to ship internationally, you can enter your country of origin (in other words, where your product was manufactured) in the Country/Region of Origin field. You can also enter your HS (Harmonized System) code, if you know it.

If in doubt over any element of product shipping, turn to chapters 6, 12 and 13, where I cover your shipping options in more detail.

Step seven: Adding variants

The next section of the Add Product page covers Variants (you find this section under the Shipping section). Figure 5-8 shows the Variants section of the Add Product page.

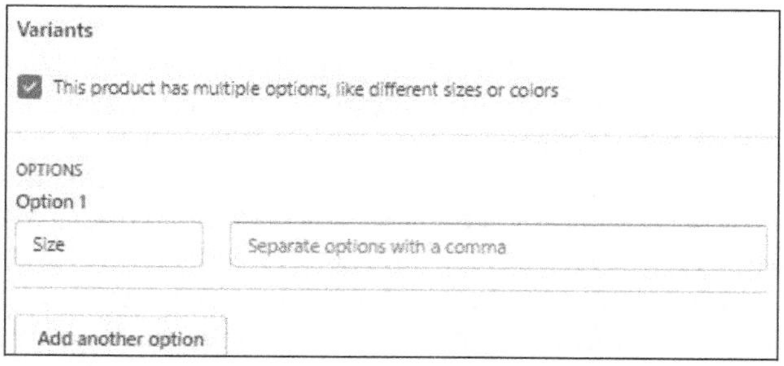

FIGURE 5-8:
The Variants
section of the
Add Product
page.

Source: Shopify

Variants are extensions of products or extra options within products, such as colors or sizes. For example, my Charlie Jeans in Blue may come in three sizes (small, medium and large), where each size is a variant.

Each product can be described in up to three different ways, such as by size, color and style.

To add a variant to your product:

1. **Return to the Add Product page.**

   If you are editing your product at a later time, click on Products → All Products from your Shopify admin. All your products, including draft products, will be listed here — just click on the one you want to keep editing.

2. **Scroll down to the Variants section of the Add Product page.**

   This is the section after the Shipping section in the Add Product page.

3. **Check the box marked This Product Has Multiple Options, Like Different Sizes or Colors.**

   The Options area appears.

   By default, the Options area shows you Option 1, which Shopify has named Size (because size is the most commonly added variant for online sellers, although you can edit it to Color, Material or anything you want). There's a space then left next to Size, with grey text that says Separate Options with a Comma.

4. **Enter your sizes, for example Small,Medium,Large (each size/variant is typed with no spaces, just separated by a comma).**

   Once you've entered in your Size options, you can move on or create a new option (by clicking on Add Another Option), such as color.

   Option values may be sizes, styles or colors. Customers see these option values when they are choosing a variant.

REMEMBER

EXAMPLE

In Figure 5-9, you see two options that have variants: Size and Color. I have entered three size variants (they appear here as S, M and L). I have also added another option called Color with two variants (they appear here as Blue and Black). From here, a box appears, asking you for the price, quantity and SKU of each variant. The price will be pre-populated, as most colors or sizes are the same price (most customers would be baffled if my M Blue Jeans cost more than my L Blue Jeans), but your quantity in stock of each color and size may be different, so you can enter those quantities here. Each variant requires its own SKU too — this is important in areas like warehousing, where a picker won't necessarily look at the item they are picking to send to your customer; instead, they scan the barcode or look at the SKU. (Some warehouses have thousands of products, so it's impossible for one person to visually recognize what each product looks like, which is why warehouses use barcodes and SKUs — and scanners to recognize them!)

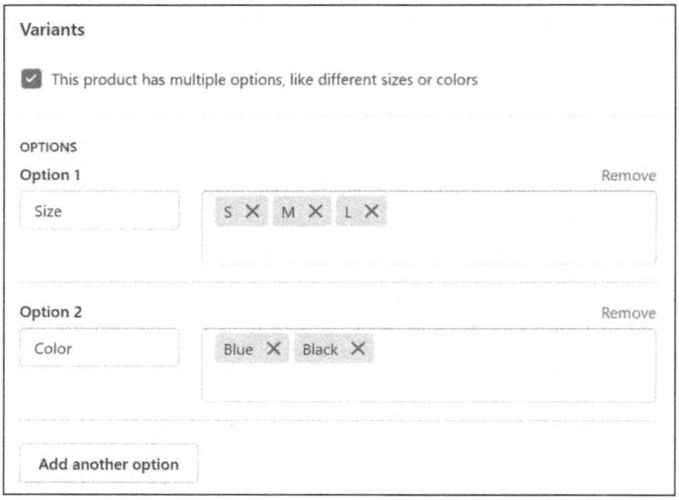

FIGURE 5-9:
The Variants section of the Add Product page with initial variant details added.

Variants

☑ This product has multiple options, like different sizes or colors

OPTIONS

Option 1   Remove

Size | S ✕ M ✕ L ✕

Option 2   Remove

Color | Blue ✕   Black ✕

Add another option

Source: Shopify

Each product can have up to 100 variants, although I've never seen any store come close to that number of variants of one product! (If you need more variants, you can find third-party applications to help with this — but I've never seen a store require this.)

TECHNICAL STUFF

Sometimes a variant is known as a *child* or *simple product*, with the style itself called the *parent* or *configurable product*.

Step eight: Making some final adjustments

The final section of the Add Product page is the SEO Preview section, which is not something you need to set up now. I give more context on how you can use this section to optimize your products and how they appear in search engine results in Chapter 15 on marketing.

However, just because you've reached the end of the Add Product page, it doesn't mean you can't make some final changes before your product is ready to launch. In the following sections I talk through some additional options you can access on the right-hand side of the Add Product page to make some extra adjustments to your added products (see Figure 5-10).

FIGURE 5-10:
Additional
options on the
Add Product
page.

Source: Shopify

PRODUCT STATUS

The first section is Product Status, which is set to Draft mode until you are ready to launch your product. Change this to Active mode when you're ready for the world to see your product — it will go live on your front end (the customer-facing part of your website), ready to be purchased by your customers.

SALES CHANNELS AND APPS

Next in the right-hand menu at the top of the Add Product page is the Sales Channels and Apps section. This shows you a list of all your sales channels, for example Online Store, which is, you guessed it, your online store sales channel. Check the boxes for all sales channels you want to sell your product on — for now, you should only see Online Store, so make sure you check that box.

This section also shows any other sales channels you add to your store, such as eBay or Amazon. Turn to Chapter 3 to look at some options for other marketplace sales channels.

ORGANIZATION

Next up is Organization, and in this section you can update your Product Type and Vendor.

Your *product type* is often a repeat of your collection name, like jeans, or shoes, and is used in product reporting, which I cover fully in Chapter 14. So, for my Charlie Jeans in Blue, I enter Jeans in the Product Type field.

Your *vendor* is your supplier — the company you bought your products from. So, for my Charlie Jeans in Blue, I enter the name of the company that I bought the Blue Jeans from in the Vendor field. You can use vendor information to generate reports (see Chapter 14) or create purchase orders through third-party apps like Stocky.

COLLECTIONS

The next section on the right-hand side of the Add Product page is Collections, which has an empty box prompting you to Search for Collections. You can use this search function to manually add products to collections.

EXAMPLE

Imagine you are selling jeans and you have set up your Jeans collection to be a manual collection. To add your new product — for example, I may add my Charlie Jeans in Blue here — to a collection of jeans, you can search for Jeans in the Collections search field. What you will see by default when you click on the Search for Collections box is a list of all the manual collections you have set up in your store. You can scroll through the list, ticking the checkbox next to the collection name that you want the Charlie Jeans in Blue to appear in, or you can start typing the name of the collection (Jeans) in the search box, and the Jeans collection should appear as you type. Select the Jeans collection by ticking the checkbox, which ensures that the Charlie Jeans in Blue are added to the Jeans collection.

You can have products in more than one collection — for example, you may want to create a New Arrivals collection that you'd also like to add the Charlie Jeans in Blue to.

TAGS

Tags are used in Shopify to help customers find your products when they use the search function on your site, and they're also used to slot products into their respective collections! In the earlier section 'Using product tags to refine your collections', I talk you through what tags are and how they can help you refine your collections; here, I show you how to close the loop on connecting your product tags to your collection tags using automatic collections.

To illustrate, I return to my example of the Charlie Jeans in Blue.

EXAMPLE

Imagine I want to add the Charlie Jeans in Blue to a collection of Men's Clothes. First, I need to ensure that I have already set up the collection Men's Clothes. When I know my Men's Clothes collection is in place and set up as an automatic collection, I can add a product tag in the Tags field here to ensure that the Charlie Jeans in Blue go into this collection.

To do this, I enter mens-clothes into the product tags field and press the Enter key on my keyboard. The product tag mens-clothes appears in the Tags field. The Charlie Jeans in Blue now live in the Men's Clothes Collection, thanks to the tag I have added here in the product page, which marries up to the tag in the Men's Clothes collection page.

You can add more than one product tag to each product, such as mens-jeans or blue-jeans, as a product can and usually does sit in more than one collection in your store.

Remember to click on the Save button to ensure that these product tags are saved to your product.

TIP

To remove a product tag, simply click on the 'x' symbol next to the tag you want to remove.

ONLINE STORE

The final section of the right-hand sidebar of the Add Product page is called Online Store. You're not likely to ever use this. It has a subheading titled Default Product. *Default Product* is the standard product page theme that is available within the theme you select for your website, and you won't be required to deviate from this.

If you hire a web developer to add a selection of product pages on top of what your theme comes with, they appear here. For example, you may want a product page that looks one way for jeans, and completely different for hats (which is not common in the early days of an ecommerce career). If you do get to the stage where you want to hire a developer to extend your website's capabilities, they will know what to do — so you don't have to!

Merchandising Your Collections

The products that you show first in your collections are likely to get the most eyeballs on them. Online shoppers can be an impatient bunch and may bounce off your site at the slightest friction — for example, if they see too many products they don't want to buy.

By default, Shopify displays the products in each collection in alphabetical order. However, you can change that to sort your products in different ways:

>> Alphabetical (or reverse alphabetical) order

>> Bestselling products first

>> Highest (or lowest) price products first

>> Manually (so you order them however you choose)

>> Newest (or oldest) products first (based on the date created)

In my experience, if you have a reasonable range of SKUs (say, 50 or more) and you're dropping new products every three months or less, a New Arrivals collection tends to get a good share of traffic. In the case of New Arrivals, you can set the default sorting to newest to oldest, but in all other cases, I suggest having your bestselling products within the first few rows of a collection, and then manually scattering in other products (perhaps new items or even other collections that have been well received).

Group like products together, so if you have a bag in both black and tan variants, it's visually pleasing to see these displayed alongside each other in a collection. Turn to the earlier section 'Step seven: Adding variants' to find out more about adding variants in color, size and style to your products.

I've worked with businesses that are obsessed with listing old products first because they need to go — but if they've been hanging around for good reason (that is, no one wants them!), they may never sell well. If you have a physical retail store and someone walks by and glances at your shop window, you want them to see your best products so that they stop and come in for a closer look. Ecommerce is no different — you want your best products front and center as they will get the highest click-through rate (the percentage of clicks versus views).

TIP

Third-party apps are available to help you visually merchandise (VM) your store, but I recommend always putting your best foot forward and giving prime real estate to your bestselling products, especially at the start of your ecommerce journey.

When you're further along your ecommerce path, you may look to introduce some artificial intelligence (AI) into the mix. *AI* is a form of machine-learnt intelligence that provides insights or takes actions based on certain behaviors. Some great AI solutions are available that you can integrate with Shopify, including Klevu and Nosto — search for these in the Shopify App Store. I talk about these sorts of AI solutions in Chapter 10 when I look at personalization, as they cover a whole range of personalization techniques as well as merchandising your products within collections.

Activating Products in Your Store

After you've finished creating your first product, you've previewed it in both desktop and mobile, and you're happy with it, you can go ahead and save it, or change it from Draft to Active in the top-right corner of the Add Product page.

Select Active when you're happy with your product. As soon as your store is published (or goes live), your customers will be able to discover your active products.

REMEMBER

If your store is already up and running, any new products go live as soon as they are made active.

Chapter **6**

Setting Up Shipping and Receiving Payments

Admin . . . it's unavoidable, but get this part right and you're setting yourself up for Shopify success.

In this chapter, I show you how to set up shipping rates in your store and share some of the strategies online sellers use to optimize shipping to convert more sales.

I walk you through collecting tax and navigating your store's payment settings, where you discover how to set up Shopify to accept payments in multiple currencies. On the subject of money, I also provide some advice on protecting your store from fraudsters and minimizing chargebacks, which occur when customers ask their banks to reverse the charges for orders placed on your store without their knowledge.

TIP

You need to use your Shopify admin a lot in this chapter, which is where you find your store's settings. You use the Settings section to help you set up many of your store's fundamentals.

One Size Does Not Fit All: Exploring Shipping Options

Shipping is one of the determining factors in whether or not a visitor to your website turns into a customer, and whether or not they come back. In fact, according to a recent UPS survey, 43 per cent of customers research shipping costs before making a purchase.

An online business needs to have a strategy around two aspects of shipping:

>> How much it charges for shipping

>> What services it offers (that is, express or standard shipping)

In the following sections, I cover the ins and outs of shipping, from weighing up free versus paid shipping options to looking at using a courier service. I also start looking at how Shopify supports the all-important element of shipping out your products to your customers.

Free shipping versus paid shipping

You hear the term *free shipping* a lot in ecommerce, and for many of today's online shoppers the notion of free shipping has become an expectation rather than a pleasant surprise. In 2020, a survey by RetailMeNot showed that 82 per cent of Americans prefer free shipping over fast shipping!

In my opinion, it can't only be the customer that dictates whether or not you offer free shipping. You also need to consider whether your pricing — and your gross profit margin — can withstand the costs of covering the shipping.

In the following sections, I run some calculations to help you work through the financial implications of free shipping versus paid shipping. I also suggest some alternative shipping approaches that may work for your business.

Testing whether free shipping is cost-effective

Your *gross profit* is your sales minus your cost of sales (your *cost of sales* being the landed costs — or cost of goods sold — plus the cost of shipping your orders to the customer), which is usually known as your *gross profit margin* (expressed as a percentage).

In a healthy online business, your gross profit margin needs to hit a certain level if you are going to cover your fixed costs and have some profit left over.

Generally, if your gross profit margin is below 45 per cent, you run the risk of not generating enough gross profit to cover your other expenses, such as wages and marketing. If you are a business that has a gross profit margin of less than 45 per cent, you want to consider charging for freight in order to increase your gross profit margin, because freight revenue is added to overall company revenue.

To calculate your gross profit, you start with the sales price of your product (exclusive of tax) and take away your cost of sales, which consists of your *landed cost* (the cost of your product plus the freight and duties required to get the product to you) and the *outbound freight costs* (the cost of sending your product to the customer) combined. (Note, some businesses include other costs such as marketing and merchant fees as part of their cost of sales, however, for this example I'm just using landed costs and outbound freight.) Effectively, you are calculating sales minus expenses:

> Sales price (exclusive of tax) – Cost of sales (Landed cost + Cost of outbound freight) = Gross profit

Gross profit is frequently displayed as a percentage — your gross profit margin. To turn your gross profit figure into a percentage (the gross profit margin), divide your gross profit by your sales:

> Gross profit/Sales = Gross profit margin

EXAMPLE

Imagine you're selling an apron for $10 exclusive of tax, which has a landed cost of $2. Your courier company has quoted you a flat fee of $5 delivery, for a 500-gram mailing bag (meaning you will pay $5 for whatever you can fit into that 500-gram satchel, as long as it fits, and as long as it weighs less than 500 grams), going to anywhere in the same country. Here's how to look at the gross profit, and gross profit margin, on that order.

Sales

Online order: $10

Total sales: $10

Cost of sales

Landed cost (Cost of goods sold): $2

Cost of outbound freight: $5

Total cost of sales: $7

Sales minus cost of sales to calculate gross profit:

$10 – $7 = $3 gross profit

Gross profit margin (expressed as a percentage):

$3/$10 = 30%

Now, 30 per cent may not seem too bad for a profit margin — but it isn't great, and here's why. This is your *gross* profit, meaning your sales minus your cost of sales, so it doesn't factor in any of your regular operating expenses, such as wages and marketing. Considering that many online businesses operate with around 30 per cent operating costs, you can expect to see your 30 per cent gross profit vanish after paying your operating expenses!

REMEMBER

You want to be aiming for a gross profit margin of over 50 per cent, particularly if you're starting your own brand (which means you have to spend more on marketing to build the brand and generate traffic to your website).

If you run these numbers again, with the variable that you're charging the $5 for shipping to the customer (instead of paying for shipping yourself and making it free to the customer), this impacts the gross profit margin as follows.

Sales

Online order: $10

Shipping revenue: $5

Total sales: $15

Cost of sales

Landed cost (Cost of goods sold): $2

Cost of outbound freight: $5

Total cost of sales: $7

Sales minus cost of sales to calculate gross profit:

$15 – $7 = $8 gross profit

Gross profit margin (expressed as a percentage):

$8/$15 = 53%

Just like that, you've more than doubled your gross profit!

REMEMBER

If an extra $5 gross profit seems small, consider the impact on your bottom line when you're selling 100,000 aprons per year!

By now you may be thinking that charging for shipping is a no-brainer, even if your customers ideally prefer free shipping, but before you make your mind up, consider this scenario.

EXAMPLE

Imagine your customer buys two aprons and a chef's hat, and you are also offering free shipping. The chef's hat costs and sells for the same amount as the aprons, and the postage cost is $7, because all three items fit into a 1-kilogram mailing bag (as opposed to the 500-gram mailing bag that costs $5 to ship), so you now have to factor in a flat fee of $7 for shipping (because the weight and dimensions of the customer's order have increased).

Sales

Online order: $30

Shipping revenue: $0

Total sales: $30

Cost of sales

Landed cost: $6

Outbound freight: $7

Total cost of sales: $13

Sales minus cost of sales to calculate gross profit:

$30 – $13 = $17 gross profit

Gross profit margin (expressed as a percentage):

$17/$30 = 57%

Your gross profit margin has actually increased, even though you're offering free shipping! This is because your average order value (AOV) has increased by three times, whereas the postage costs have only increased by a small margin.

REMEMBER

This outcome illustrates the effect of *economies of scale* — the greater the volume of orders you can fit into a mailing bag (which often go up in 500-gram increments), the more cost-effective your shipping costs will become. In other words, if your AOV increases, your shipping costs become easier to absorb without denting your gross profit margin too heavily.

The one caveat here is that every business is different, and selling different products, so you have to evaluate whether this general rule works for your products. For example, if you are selling dumbbells that weigh 50 kilograms each, you may not enjoy the benefits of economies of scale by fitting more into your mail bags; however, you can always add small, lightweight items to increase your AOV that barely touch the shipping scales — such as gym gloves or a sweat band.

TIP

Offer free shipping if you can — but only if your gross profit margin allows for it. An online retailer that offers free shipping has to constantly crunch the numbers to select a cost-effective free shipping threshold that protects gross profit. Fortunately, one of the best levers an online retailer has to increase AOV and protect profit is to offer a free shipping threshold. In the example above, the online retailer may offer free shipping on orders over $30, as that's the sweet spot where the gross margin soars while the shipping increases slowly.

WARNING

Don't offer free shipping at the expense of your gross profit as this is a recipe for disaster. The single biggest reason that I have seen online retailers close their doors is due to not protecting their gross profit. High sales don't necessarily mean high gross profit, and freight can chomp into your gross profit quickly if you haven't modelled it out properly. Don't press 'go' on your online store until you can answer the question, 'What is your gross profit?'

Free shipping can be a great lever for increasing your conversion rate (CVR), and if your gross profit margin supports it then I recommend offering it. However, if your gross profit margins can't cope with offering free shipping on all your products, choose an order value threshold where the economics of scale add up across your store.

TIP

Consider offering free standard or economy shipping but asking the customer to pay for express delivery — either way, be sure to only offer free shipping when you're encouraging the customer to add more to their cart. If the average selling price of your products is $45, you can set your free shipping threshold at $50 in order to nudge the customer towards buying an extra item and therefore making free shipping a win-win for your customer and your gross profit.

Opting for flat rate shipping

One popular approach to paid shipping is to offer *flat rate shipping* (a shipping cost that doesn't change, regardless of what product the customer orders or where they're located within the same country), either as your sole shipping strategy or as a shipping option when customers order items that add up to a total under your free shipping threshold.

TIP

Make sure that you don't drastically undercharge or overcharge your customers. Flat rate shipping works best when you sell products of a standard size and weight. Flat rate shipping tends to become complicated and less effective if you sell a wide variety of products of different sizes and weights. A good example of a suitable product line for flat rate shipping is clothing, whereas a furniture store may find it hard to offer flat rate shipping due to the inconsistent weights and sizes of the orders.

Choosing real time (dynamic) shipping rates

Shopify integrates directly with carriers such as USPS, Canada Post, Australia Post and plenty more, as well as integrating with *shipping aggregators*, services that offer you access to hundreds of carriers across the globe. Using these carriers, you can use a shipping strategy where you offer *dynamic shipping rates* (also known as *real time shipping rates*) that adjust instantly according to the delivery address and the weight and dimensions of an order.

Typically, online retailers who sell bulky goods (such as furniture or gym equipment, or even department stores with a huge range of different products) use dynamic or real time shipping rates, as the rates can vary by small weight increments (perhaps with every 100 grams, 500 grams or kilogram added), depending on which carrier you use. This shipping strategy allows you to simply pass on the raw costs of the shipping to the customer.

Express shipping versus standard shipping

Another useful comparison to keep in mind is standard versus express shipping, which vary in cost as well as shipping time. *Standard* shipping, also known as *economy* shipping, is cheaper and generally slower when it comes to getting your parcel from A to B, while *express* shipping is faster and more expensive.

Do you absolutely need to offer both? Not really, but speed in delivery is important to some customers, who will pay extra to have their order with them sooner — so it doesn't hurt to offer it. A common shipping strategy is to offer a free standard shipping service and cover your costs (or close to your costs) by charging for express shipping if the customer elects to upgrade to the faster service.

TIP

If you're electing to charge for shipping, try to cap your domestic express shipping rate at a cost of no more than $10 to the customer (if you're selling products that weigh less than 2 kilograms). This prices your shipping competitively — anything more may stop customers from ordering.

REMEMBER

Customer enquiries asking about the whereabouts of an order are one of the most common enquiries you can expect to see, which suggests there's always a sense of urgency when customers place their orders. Speed of delivery is often of the utmost importance in a customer's decision-making process, and a positive shipping experience can be a key determining factor as to whether or not they will shop with you again.

Amazon is famous for continuing to raise the bar when it comes to the delivery of online orders. Amazon launched Prime in 2005, which promised two-day delivery on over one million items across the United States — and Prime has since upped the ante by offering same-day delivery in some places! The reality is, customer expectations around speed of delivery are increasing, so it's a good idea to review your delivery options and make sure that you're offering something at least as good as your competitors.

One of the reasons that express shipping is faster than standard shipping is that parcels are often delivered by air across the country, except when delivery destinations are close to the sender, in which case a driver can deliver within an express time frame. Deliveries are carried out by in-country mail systems, such as USPS, Australia Post, Royal Mail, and so on, or by carriers, also known as couriers. A *carrier* is any person or vehicle involved in carrying or delivering a parcel from a retailer to a customer.

In order to achieve fast delivery across the country (and not just in the city or area that your business is located), it's important to select a carrier company that is both reputable and has a good delivery network.

TIP

Try and cover your costs, but don't get greedy and try to profit from shipping. If you are having trouble working out what to charge your customers, check out some of the major carriers (such as Australia Post, Canada Post, FedEx, UK Royal Mail, UPS and USPS) to get an idea of what they charge for different shipping services.

TIP

As well as requesting prices (or rates) from your potential shipping partner, I suggest you also request a copy of their delivery times to each area (or zone) across the country you're located in. The same applies for international shipping.

When shipping internationally, you need to consider the profitability of offering free shipping, even more so than usual, due to the higher costs of international shipping. Use the same principles as outlined in the earlier section 'Testing whether free shipping is cost-effective' to see if it's cost-efficient for your store to ship internationally for free. Perhaps you could offer free shipping on an international economy service, while asking the customer to pay a fee for international express shipping. You may even have different prices for your shipping fees depending on the country — for example, shipping from the United States to Canada may be cheaper than shipping from the United States to Australia.

Logistics and fulfilment are a huge part of ecommerce, so they deserve their own chapters. In chapters 12 and 13 I talk more about the finer details of order fulfilment and logistics.

Shopify and shipping

When I first started out selling products online, at the end of each day I would review all my orders, pick the items from my inventory and then take the products to the local post office, filling out each postal slip, including the address details, by hand. Eventually, I opened a commercial account with the postal company, and they sent a driver to my address each day — but I still had to write out each address.

I then got slightly (very slightly) smarter and invested in a label printer, so instead of writing the labels I was typing them — not much of a time-saver, really! While this worked for a while, it wasn't scalable, and the best use of my time was certainly not writing out labels — I needed to free up my time to grow my business.

Fast forward a decade (okay, maybe two), and Shopify not only integrates with most major carriers but it can print your shipping labels and update your orders with the click of a mouse — no pen and paper required. This doesn't mean you are tied to any specific carrier or price structure, either — Shopify gives you the flexibility to find the best shipping strategy to suit your business.

You can handle shipping three ways in Shopify:

>> **Carrier accounts:** Bring your own shipping rates over to Shopify if you already have a great deal with your preferred carrier, including your own account number. If you use a shipping aggregator, such as ShipStation, Starshipit or Easyship, you can plug them right into your Shopify store, giving you the option to use their negotiated rates with a wide range of carriers or load your own rates into their system. I talk more about making the right choice for your business in Chapter 13.

>> **Shopify Shipping:** Shopify Shipping is already built into Shopify and has a set of negotiated rates for Shopify merchants. Shopify Shipping shows merchants real-time shipping rates in the United States, Canada and Australia, allowing merchants to print labels and track shipments.

TIP

Shopify Shipping partners with USPS, UPS, DHL Express, Sendle (in Australia) and Canada Post to offer discounted rates on many shipping services. These discounts are often around 20–50 per cent, but they range all the way up to 90 per cent. Accessing these shipping carriers' rates allows you to list real-time shipping calculations both on your order processing page and in your checkout! This allows you to charge precise amounts for shipping, reducing the risk of underestimating your shipping expenses.

>> **Manual shipping:** You won't see this terminology used in your Shopify store — it's just my way of explaining the process of using Shopify to facilitate online orders, and then arranging your own delivery. You can still print invoices or packing slips out of Shopify, but this way you have your own courier come and collect from you when you book in a delivery — or you take your items to the post office.

The downside of this process is that it's a manual process, so unlike the previous two automated options, you need to enter your tracking numbers manually into each order, as opposed to integrating with automated solutions that do cool things like entering your tracking numbers into your orders (which is super helpful for when a customer emails in, asking you to track their order). You can still send an email to a customer, with their order tracking number, it just doesn't happen automatically, like it does when you use Shopify Shipping.

Most of the online businesses I work with are exporters, meaning they ship internationally as well as domestically (in other words, they send orders overseas as well as within their domestic market). In Chapter 13 I look at the logistics of shipping internationally, and if you're using Shopify it's easy to access a wide range of carriers that can transport your products into new markets.

Using Shopify Shipping

Shopify Shipping is available for orders shipped from fulfilment locations based in the United States, Canada and Australia. It's super simple to use and offers you really competitive shipping rates that you're otherwise unlikely to get when starting out as a new business.

Shopify Shipping allows you to connect your Shopify account with Shopify Shipping carrier accounts, which has the following benefits:

>> Your store displays calculated shipping rates, instead of flat rates, to your customers at checkout.

>> You get reduced shipping rates.

>> You can print shipping labels directly from your Shopify admin.

Purchasing a shipping label essentially means booking a courier and then printing a label to apply to your order. Depending on your fulfilment locations, Shopify Shipping enables you to purchase labels from the following carriers:

>> **Australia:** Sendle

>> **Canada:** Canada Post

>> **United States:** USPS, UPS and DHL

TIP

If Shopify Shipping is available to you, I recommend that you use it — in my experience, the rates are good and the partnerships are with reputable carriers. The fact that shipping is already integrated into your store is a huge bonus as well.

If Shopify Shipping isn't available in your country, it won't stop you from using Shopify to its full potential. I look more at Shopify Shipping and other shipping alternatives in more detail in Chapter 13.

Setting up Shopify Shipping

In this section I show you how to set your store up to be compliant with Shopify Shipping — and in Chapter 13, I show you how to send shipments using Shopify Shipping. If you sign up for a Shopify account in the United States, Australia or Canada, then some courier shipping rates are added to your Shipping settings by default (this is the Shopify Shipping option covered in the preceding section). If you're outside of these countries, the process of setting up shipping is a little more involved, which I discuss further in Chapter 13.

Here are some of the couriers and postal services available in Shopify Shipping:

>> If you're in the United States, USPS rates are added by default.

>> If you're in Canada, Canada Post rates are added by default.

>> If you're in Australia, flat rates are added by default.

You can change what shipping rates are available to customers in your Shopify Shipping settings (go to Settings in your Shopify admin, and then click on Shipping and Delivery), but before you look at that, you need to set up different package types to send your products in, and shipping regions that will get their own shipping rates — for example, you will most likely charge your international customers more for shipping than your domestic customers.

Getting Started with Shipping in Shopify

Now that you've considered some of the different shipping strategies, it's time to start adding some competitive shipping options to your store. In chapters 12 and 13 I look at the process of fulfilling orders, including shipping them out; however, at this stage you need to look at shipping in Shopify in brief because setting up shipping rates is one of the basic elements of setting up your Shopify store.

TIP

Before you begin to set up your shipping options, double check that the address you entered when you set up your Shopify store is where your orders will be shipping from.

If you need to add a location, change a location or add extra locations (for example, if you have multiple locations, such as a warehouse and a physical store that you will be shipping from), Shopify caters for that — just follow these instructions:

1. **From your Shopify admin, go to Settings → Locations.**

   The Locations Settings page appears.

2. **Click on Add Location in the top-right corner.**

   The Add Location page appears. This page displays text fields that ask you to fill out two sections: Location Name and Address.

3. **Enter a unique name for the location in the Location Name field.**

4. **Enter the location's address in the Address field.**

5. **If you want the inventory at this location to be available for online purchases, then check the Fulfil Online Orders from This Location box.**

6. **If this is a physical bricks-and-mortar location that you regularly sell from, then check the This Location Is a Retail Store box.**

7. **Click on Save in the bottom-right corner to save your location.**

TIP

You can assign inventory to each of your locations, but I cover that in Chapter 11 when I talk through managing inventory.

In the following sections, I show you how to create shipping profiles for your store in Shopify, as well as how to set up package types. You need to do this if you're planning to use Shopify Shipping, which is available in Australia, Canada and the United States. However, the following sections are not specific to any one of the three shipping options — instead, they deal with setting up pricing for your shipments, based on the weight and dimensions of your products and the country you're shipping to.

TIP

If you're not planning to use Shopify Shipping, you can integrate your own carrier — such as USPS, Royal Mail or Australia Post — into your online store, or you can leave out shipping integrations completely, choosing instead to book your own couriers outside of Shopify (refer to the earlier section, 'Shopify and shipping', for more on your options). (In chapters 12 and 13, I take the next shipping step and show you how to fulfil and ship your orders to your customers.)

Adjusting your default package type

When you create new products in your online store, you have the option to add accurate weights to assist with calculating your shipping rate. The weight of the product, combined with the weight of the box or package you use to ship your product, is then used to calculate the cost to ship your order.

Shopify has a default package type already in place in your Shopify admin. You can set up the weight and dimensions of the default package type you intend to ship your orders in. If you intend to use multiple package types when shipping your products (for example, because you sell products of different sizes, such as shoes and earrings), then you can adjust the dimensions of the package when you purchase the shipping label, which occurs when you ship your order (I explain this in more detail in Chapter 13); however, the easiest approach is to adjust your default package types within Shopify, which saves you having to adjust them with each shipping label you purchase.

If you want a shipping carrier to calculate the cost of packages other than your default package, you can use a suitable shipping app, many of which are available to browse in the Shopify App Store (apps.shopify.com).

To change the weight and dimensions of your default package:

1. **In your Shopify admin, go to Settings → Shipping and Delivery.**

   The Shipping and Delivery page appears.

2. **Scroll down the page until you see the section Saved Packages.**

   You see a sample box listed in the Saved Packages section, with the word Default next to it. This is your store's default package option.

3. **Click on the Edit button next to the Saved Packages section heading, and enter the dimensions in the dialogue box if you want to change them (you see some default dimensions in place already — simply type over them).**

   For example, if you sell shoes, enter the dimensions of your shoe boxes (or the box that you send your shoe boxes in). If you sell shoes, plus earrings, then you may want to add a new, smaller package, so that your courier isn't charging you for a shoe-box sized package when you're sending your earrings in a small envelope. The weight and dimensions you add here need to reflect your package size as accurately as possible to ensure that you are not overpaying for shipping — or providing inaccurate information to your shipping provider.

4. **Click on the green Save button inside the dialogue box to save your new dimensions.**

You get to select the packaging type when you buy a shipping label through Shopify Shipping — more on that in Chapter 13.

Setting up packages and shipment weights in Shopify is important if you have different-sized packages, and you wish to be charged correctly by your courier and pass the charges on to your customer, because most couriers charge by weight and dimensions. If you're integrating a courier into your Shopify store, you'll be able to get accurate pricing for each of the parcels you intend to send. Online retailers often use this pricing to display the shipping price at checkout to customers. If you're intending to offer free shipping, or a set price, then package types aren't so important.

You can leave all your package types as they are, without ever touching this section in your Shopify admin; however, you run the risk of being incorrectly charged by your courier, whether you use Shopify Shipping or a third-party integrated carrier, as the weight and dimensions you provide the courier will revert to Shopify's default weight and dimensions.

To add another package type to your Shopify store (so you can send packages containing products of different weights/dimensions):

1. **In your Shopify admin, go to Settings → Shipping and Delivery.**

   The Shipping and Delivery page appears.

2. **Scroll down to Saved Packages.**

3. **Click on the Add Package button and enter the packaging dimensions and weights for your new package type.**

4. **Click on Add Package in the bottom-right corner, which saves your new package and takes you back to the Shipping and Delivery page within Settings.**

   Your new package appears next to your Default package on the Shipping and Delivery page.

If you ship products of all sizes, it's important to either set up a range of package types (in addition to your Default package, which ideally ships a large portion of your typical orders) or remember to manually change the dimensions of the product when you buy the shipping label. If you are sending earrings but you forget to change your package type from a box to an envelope, you'll likely be overcharged for your shipping.

TIP

Some Shopify Shipping options offer their own packaging types, so you may not need to add extra package types. For example, if you're in Australia, you can choose between carrier packaging or customer packaging when you add a new package type.

If you choose carrier packaging, you're presented with the option to use Sendle packaging (which is Shopify Shipping's Australian carrier). The main benefit of using carrier packaging via Sendle in Australia is that Sendle has what it calls an Unlimited Satchel, which measures 33.5cm x 24.5cm x 1cm — a typical size that's big enough for many popular ecommerce items, such as clothing. If you select this option for your package size, Sendle charges you a flat rate for whatever you can squeeze into that satchel, so it's simple to calculate your shipping costs. As a bonus, you can order the satchels from the carrier inside the Shipping and Delivery section of your Shopify admin — see Figure 6-1.

TIP

If the Shopify Shipping options in your country provide you with carrier packaging as an option, it's a good idea to select the packages that suit your products by selecting the packaging type in the Shipping and Delivery section of your Shopify admin. Figure 6-1 shows Australia's Shopify Shipping option through Sendle, which offers one package size; depending on which country you're in, you may see more than one option available. After selecting from the range of package types available, click on Add Package — the package types you have added appear next to your Default package type on the Shipping and Delivery page. You'll also see the packages available to choose from when you're ready to send out your orders.

FIGURE 6-1:
Click on the link to order carrier packaging in Shopify — in this case, Sendle's Unlimited Satchel.

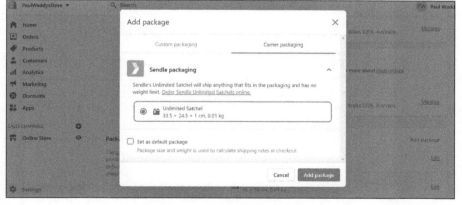

Source: Shopify

USING THIRD-PARTY CARRIERS IN SHOPIFY

If you intend to integrate a third-party shipping carrier, which is one of your two options (the other option is manual shipping) if your location country doesn't qualify for Shopify Shipping, this next section is applicable to you.

The next section is pretty technical, and I'm covering it for probably a small minority of new online retailers. Assuming you're early into your Shopify venture, I strongly recommend you use Shopify Shipping where available. If it's not available, you can always set up your shipping prices to display to your customers and take care of the shipping outside of Shopify. I cover a few additional options in Chapter 13.

If you have your own carrier account with a shipping carrier, you can display your negotiated shipping rates from that carrier to customers at checkout using an application programming interface (API) integration between Shopify and the carrier, which is known in Shopify as Enabling Third-party Calculated Rates at Checkout. You need to have the carrier-calculated shipping feature on your store's Shopify subscription plan to connect your own shipping carrier accounts to Shopify. This feature is included in the Advanced Shopify and Shopify Plus plans and can be added to any plan for a monthly fee. However, if you're on the Shopify plan or below and you switch from monthly to yearly billing, you can ask to get the third-party calculated shipping rates feature added for free.

For more information, contact Shopify Support, or visit help.shopify.com.

Shipping rates and profiles

Shipping profiles allow you to charge accurate shipping rates through product-based or location-based shipping rules, rather than using a one-size-fits-all approach to set shipping rates. Shipping profiles are not specific to any one of the three shipping methods you can adopt to ship your orders out (refer to the earlier section 'Shopify and shipping' for more on these), but rather are to do with how you charge your customers for shipping different products.

TIP

For businesses with simple products requiring a simple shipping set-up, your general shipping profile will be sufficient. For businesses with a complex shipping set-up (for example, an online florist that sells difficult-to-ship products like fresh flowers, which need to be shipped upright), an additional custom profile is helpful, which allows a florist to charge more for shipping delicate or fragile parcels.

You can use shipping profiles to set shipping rates for specific products, from fresh flowers to fragile items, which is known as *product-based shipping*.

Your Shopify store comes with a default shipping profile, which it calls a *general shipping profile*. (Shopify also gives you the option to create one or more custom shipping profiles.)

Your general shipping profile contains your *general shipping rates* — in other words, you edit this shipping profile to set up your typical *shipping price*, which is the price you charge your customer to ship their order. Most Shopify users only use this profile.

For businesses with a simple shipping set-up, general shipping rates are often sufficient. For businesses that manage products and locations that have different shipping costs and regional availability, additional shipping profiles help keep your shipping costs accurate and easy to manage. The chances are you fall into the first category and only require a simple shipping set-up.

Keep your shipping options simple. One of the main reasons for an online shopper abandoning their shopping cart is due to complex or prohibitive shipping arrangements.

Deciding on your shipping rates

Shipping rates are what you charge a customer for shipping their order, and you can set up shipping rates in your general shipping profile. The cost of shipping is added to a customer's order at checkout. The most common method of shipping in ecommerce is *flat rate shipping*, which is when specific shipping amounts are charged for every order regardless of which product has been ordered. An alternative is displaying shipping rates at checkout based on the weight and dimensions of the product a customer has ordered.

If you want to charge one fee for standard shipping and another for express shipping, then you set up two general flat rates, one for each option, which is probably the most common scenario in ecommerce. The two rates then appear as options in your customer's checkout. The next section shows you how to set up shipping rates, including flat rate shipping options.

Setting your shipping rates

Shopify enables you to charge whatever you want for shipping. In this section I show you how to do exactly that, although I recommend that online retailers charge a flat shipping rate (I discuss the flat rate shipping strategy in the earlier section 'Opting for flat rate shipping'). *Price-based shipping rates* allow you to offer different shipping prices depending on how much the customer is spending; for example, if they spend over $100 you may offer free shipping, and for orders under $100 you may instead charge a flat rate (such as $9.95) for shipping.

To set up price-based shipping rates for your location country, first you need to add a shipping zone. *Shipping zones* cover the countries that you ship to.

WARNING

If countries aren't included in one of your shipping zones, then customers in those countries won't be able to enter their delivery address in your checkout.

Follow these steps to add a shipping zone to your Shopify store:

1. **From your Shopify admin, select Settings → Shipping and Delivery.**

The Shipping and Delivery page appears.

2. **Click on Manage Rates, which appears next to General Shipping Rates in the top section of the page.**

The Manage Rates page appears.

3. **Click on Create Shipping Zone.**

4. **You are prompted to create a Zone Name. Start by creating a zone for your own country (which you're servicing domestically) — for example, Australia. When you have entered the Zone Name as prompted, turn to the list of countries below the Zone Name field and select the corresponding country (in this case, Australia).**

TIP

If you are creating a domestic shipping zone, you only click on one country here, but if you are creating an international shipping zone, you may select a range of different countries that you group together for shipping — or perhaps even simply select Rest of World if you only plan to have one international shipping zone.

5. **Click on Done in the bottom-right corner.**

You return to the General Shipping Profile page within your Shipping and Delivery page, which now shows the flag of the country or zone you just created underneath the Shipping To heading. All the countries and flags you see listed here will be the countries you are set up to ship to.

Repeat these steps if you want to add new countries to ship to.

Now that you have set up a shipping zone, you need to set up a price-based shipping rate for that zone. Continuing from the Shipping and Delivery page, follow these steps:

1. **Click on the Add Rate button, located below the shipping zone location you created in the preceding set of steps.**

   A dialogue box pops up that offers you two options: Set Up Your Own Rates *or* Use Carrier or App to Calculate Rates. If you qualify for Shopify Shipping or want to use third-party integrated shipping rates, you can click on Use Carrier or App to Calculate Rates. In this instance, however, you want to set up your own shipping rates.

2. **Select Set up Your Own Rates.**

TIP

   If you qualify for Shopify Shipping, you see a range of shipping carrier packages with prices here that you can simply select from, which passes the charges to your customer when they reach your site's checkout. In other words, if you want to pass on your Shopify Shipping costs to the customer rather than set up your own shipping prices, you can select this option. The advantage of choosing this method is that you're not going to lose any money on shipping — you simply pass the charges directly to the customer; however, the disadvantage is that you can't advertise one clear flat rate shipping price on your website, so customers may find it confusing to work out how much they are going to be charged for their order before they reach the checkout.

3. **The dialogue box extends to show a new section, Shipping Speed. You can select from Standard, Express or Custom Flat Rate — for this example, select Standard.**

   Typically, online retailers charge a flat rate for express and standard shipping, and it's rare to see more than these two shipping options. However, an example of a Custom Flat Rate may be a store choosing to offer same day delivery.

4. **Select Add Conditions, which is located at the bottom of the dialogue box.**

   A new section appears that extends the dialogue box. This is where you set up your price-based shipping rule (see Figure 6-2).

5. **Select Based on Order Price.**

   The other option is Based on Item Weight — use this to charge prices based on how heavy your products are, a delivery option that is pretty uncommon.

6. **You have the option to select a minimum and a maximum price. Enter the prices you require for your standard shipping rate.**

   If, for example, you want to charge $9.95 shipping for orders under $100, leave your minimum price at $0.00 and adjust your maximum price to $99.99. Then, enter $9.95 in the Price field, and click Done. Repeat the process of selecting Add Rate, Add Conditions, and then Based on Order Price, and this time put the minimum price at $100 and leave the maximum price empty, which means there's no limit.

7. **Click on Done, which takes you back to your General Shipping Profile page.**

FIGURE 6-2:
The Add Rate dialogue box, where you can add conditions.

Congratulations, you've just created shipping rates in your domestic market, for standard shipping on orders below and over $100! Follow the same steps if you want to create express or customized flat rate shipping rates — simply select Express or Custom Flat Rate in the Shipping Speed section, rather than Standard. For more on express shipping, refer to the earlier section 'Express shipping versus standard shipping'.

After you've set up your domestic shipping prices, your new rates appear in your general shipping profile, and a message appears at the bottom of the page telling you how many countries you're not shipping to.

TIP

If you wish to ship to additional countries, follow the steps earlier in this section to create a new shipping zone.

For international shipping zones, you may prefer to set up a zone for the rest of the world if they share the same shipping rate, or you may want to set shipping rates for specific countries or regions, such as the UK or Europe.

REMEMBER

Some countries may be easier and cheaper to ship to than others, which may mean you require a couple of different international shipping zones. For example, if you operate from the United States, shipping to Canada is a logical and straightforward option; equally, if you are based in Australia, shipping to New Zealand is feasible.

After naming your international shipping zone, select all the countries that fall into that zone from the list of countries provided. For example, if you want to set up one international shipping zone that covers the rest of the world, you can name the shipping zone Rest of World and tick the box that says Rest of World in the list of countries provided. Any customers who place orders outside of your home country will be charged the same shipping price that you set up for this shipping zone.

You'll see the options to select Standard International or Custom Flat Fee. Select Standard International, or create express international shipping by clicking on Custom Flat Rate. Name the rate Express Shipping when prompted to do so if you select Custom Flat Rate.

REMEMBER

Shopify doesn't specify an express shipping option for international zones by default, which is why you use Custom Flat Fee to set up express shipping for international express delivery.

Follow the same steps as earlier in this section to finish creating your basic but popular and effective shipping prices for all over the world!

Tax Time: Setting Up Tax Rates

Sales tax can be confusing for an experienced online seller, let alone someone just starting out. While you can set up your Shopify store to charge and collect sales taxes, Shopify will not remit taxes on your behalf.

REMEMBER

Make sure you get the right legal and accounting advice before starting any business, particularly if you plan to sell internationally. International taxation laws can be a minefield and may vary dramatically from country to country (or even state by state if you're selling within the United States!).

In Australia, 10 per cent GST (goods and services tax) applies to all imports, regardless of size. In the UK, VAT (value-added tax) must be charged on imports other than gifts under £39 (current at January 2021), while in Canada a 5 per cent GST applies.

This book isn't the place to discuss the intricacies of sales tax; however, it is the place to show you how to set your store up so you can collect sales taxes, and I cover the different ways you can do this depending on where you are based and where you are selling to.

TIP

While this isn't a book about sales tax, setting up your tax rates correctly can assist you with preparing reports and lodging your tax return.

WARNING

Getting sales taxes wrong when selling into certain countries can become a logistical nightmare if you aren't prepared. Overseas customers who are asked to pay unexpected fees when their parcel arrives are unlikely to return to your store, so it's important to develop a strategy that allows for the collection of the required taxes and fees to ensure frictionless trade through your online store. In my book *Selling Online For Dummies*, I go into more detail around international taxes for online sellers.

Setting up tax collecting in your store

If you're in the United States, Canada, the European Union, the UK, Norway, Switzerland, Australia or New Zealand, all of which use registration-based taxes, you can add your tax registration information to Shopify so you can collect tax.

As a merchant, you may need to charge taxes on your sales and then report and remit those taxes to your government. Although tax laws and regulations are complex and can change often, you can set up Shopify to automatically handle most common sales tax calculations. You can also set up tax overrides to address unique tax laws and situations.

Shopify uses many default sales tax rates, which are updated regularly. If you use the default rates, then you need to confirm that they are current and correct for your particular circumstances. You can override them whenever necessary.

The first step is to set up tax rates in the countries you'll be shipping to (in other words, your shipping zones), which you established in the earlier section 'Setting your shipping rates'. At the very least, you're likely to need to be collecting taxes in the country that you operate, so ensure you're collecting tax in your own country (if you're obliged to).

TIP

If you're in a country that collects registration-based tax and you're registered to collect tax, follow these steps to set up tax collection in Shopify:

1. **After you've set up your shipping zones (that is, the countries you want to sell to) in Shopify (refer to the earlier section 'Setting your shipping rates' if you still need to do this), head back to your Settings page in the Shopify admin and select Taxes.**

   The Taxes page appears. If you have already set up your shipping zones, you'll notice they appear here as Tax Regions (see Figure 6-3). You can expect to see your local country as one shipping zone, and one or more other zones, depending on where you're planning to ship to — for example, Rest of World (for the rest of the world).

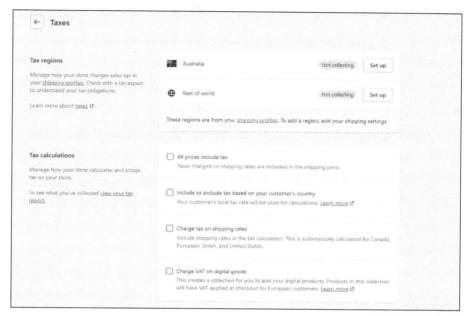

FIGURE 6-3:
The Taxes page,
which shows your
shipping zones.

At this stage, your shipping zones have a grey box next to them saying Not Collecting, which means you haven't yet set the countries/shipping zones up to collect tax.

2. **To the right of the grey Not Collecting box, click on the Set Up button for the first location you want to collect taxes for — for example, your domestic location, such as Australia.**

   You are prompted to enter your business or tax registration details, for example your Australian Business Number (ABN) if you're in Australia.

3. **Add your business or tax registration details as prompted and click the green Collect GST button to start collecting tax.**

   After hitting Collect GST or your country's equivalent (such as Collect VAT in the UK), you're taken to the Tax Calculations page of your Shopify admin.

4. **Select your tax calculation method from the options provided (see Figure 6-4).**

   Here you have four options that you can check or leave unchecked:

   - **All Prices Include Tax:** This means that the prices you create for your products include tax. If you leave this box unchecked, tax will be added at the checkout, on top of the price you have given each product.

     Prices usually include tax, so I suggest you check this box unless you know tax has not been included.

Tax calculations

Manage how your store calculates and shows tax on your store.

To see what you've collected view your tax report.

☐ All prices include tax
Taxes charged on shipping rates are included in the shipping price.

☐ Include or exclude tax based on your customer's country
Your customer's local tax rate will be used for calculations. Learn more ⧉

☐ Charge tax on shipping rates
Include shipping rates in the tax calculation. This is automatically calculated for Canada, European Union, and United States.

☐ Charge VAT on digital goods
This creates a collection for you to add your digital products. Products in this collection will have VAT applied at checkout for European customers. Learn more ⧉

FIGURE 6-4:
The Tax Calculations page.

Source: Shopify

- **Include or Exclude Tax Based on Your Customer's Country:** You can select some countries where your product prices include tax, and others where it does not include tax — however, I have rarely seen this used, so I don't suggest ticking this. You may need to tick this in the future if you want to change the first option (All Prices Include Tax) to be country-specific.

- **Charge Tax on Shipping Rates:** This option includes shipping rates in the tax calculation (which is automatically calculated for Canada, the European Union and the United States). Generally, you check this box, given that you are likely legally obliged to pay tax on any freight revenue received.

  I recommend you seek tax advice on whether or not you need to pay sales tax on freight revenue collected in your region.

- **Charge VAT on Digital Goods:** VAT (value-added tax) is the European Union's name for tax, and this option allows you to charge VAT on digital products such as courses or music.

  If you are in the EU, I recommend seeking advice on whether or not you need to collect tax on digital goods.

5. **Click the green Save button in the top-right corner to save your tax collection settings.**

6. **Repeat the preceding steps for each country/location where you are obliged to collect tax.**

REMEMBER

If you aren't registered for tax, you shouldn't collect tax. If you're not registered to collect tax for any of the countries you are shipping to, then leave them listed as Not Collecting on the Taxes page (Figure 6-3). In a country like New Zealand, where taxes are charged on online sales into that country, you can either register with the New Zealand government to collect tax, or you can send your orders as normal, with the awareness that your customer will be asked to pay tax in New Zealand when the order arrives.

WARNING

Always get the right legal advice around sales tax before proceeding. This book isn't designed to tell you whether or not you need to collect and pay tax — every business and location is different. This book is focused instead on showing you how to use Shopify to collect taxes from your sales where required.

Including tax in your product price

When you've set up tax collection correctly in your Shopify store, you need to make an additional decision — whether you want your product prices to include or exclude tax.

TIP

Most online stores display their pricing including tax because it avoids confusion at the checkout.

To include or exclude tax from product prices after you have completed the initial tax collection set-up (refer to the preceding section):

1. **In your Shopify admin, go to Settings → Taxes.**

   The Taxes page appears.

2. **Scroll down to the Tax Calculations section.**

3. **To exclude tax from your product prices, uncheck the All Prices Include Tax checkbox. To include tax in your product prices, check the All Prices Include Tax checkbox.**

   You may already have this box checked or unchecked as a result of any initial decisions you made when setting up tax collection (refer to the preceding section).

The Fun Part: Getting Paid

Show me the money, right? Well, sort of — at least show me how to get the money when a customer comes to my store and places an order!

Payment processing is way more interesting in ecommerce than you may think — payments can even help increase your revenue, as payment providers or banks often block good orders if they suspect they may be fraudulent. For example, only

80–90 per cent of all cross border (international) credit card transactions are approved by banks due to the higher risks of fraud in international transactions, whereas local transactions are approved at closer to 90 or even 95 per cent. A more fraud-aware system leads to more sales!

Over time, consumers have evolved from cash, cheque, money orders, and credit and debit cards, through to PayPal, paying on your smartphone and buy now pay later (BNPL) options — and don't even get me started on cryptocurrencies! There's a lot of different ways you can get paid and different reasons for using these payment methods on your online store.

The good news is, Shopify has its own payment gateway (Shopify Payments), so you don't need to sign up to and integrate a third-party payment solution — unless you want to, of course. Shopify Payments is available on all Shopify plans, so you can start transacting as soon as you're ready to launch your store.

Payment gateways provide a gateway for payments. When I sat down to think of an eloquent way to explain what a payment gateway is to an ecommerce business, I ended up considering the name to be a pretty accurate description of the service — albeit one that is not very imaginative on my part, so here is a better definition. A *payment gateway* is a service that processes credit or debit card transactions, sending money from a customer's bank to the merchant's bank — in other words, to you. When you go ahead and enter your credit card details at your favorite online store, it's a payment gateway that's processing your credit card payment and sending the funds from your bank to the online store's bank.

If your store has Shopify Payments enabled, then you receive payments through Shopify Payouts, which are transferred to your bank account every two or three days (on average, depending on where you're located).

REMEMBER

If customers pay using third-party payment gateways, you won't see your payout information in your Shopify admin, and your payouts will be dependent on their payout terms.

In the following sections, I unpack some of the payment methods you can accept in Shopify, along with how to accept foreign currencies (in case you're thinking of selling internationally) and add a third-party payment provider to your store.

Setting up Shopify Payments

Shopify Payments is available in the following countries:

- ≫ Australia
- ≫ Austria
- ≫ Belgium
- ≫ Canada
- ≫ Denmark
- ≫ Germany
- ≫ Hong Kong SAR
- ≫ Ireland
- ≫ Italy
- ≫ Japan
- ≫ Netherlands
- ≫ New Zealand
- ≫ Singapore
- ≫ Spain
- ≫ Sweden
- ≫ UK
- ≫ United States

If you're operating outside of the countries on this list, you need to integrate a third-party payment provider. Shopify supports over 100 payment gateways, so you have plenty of options.

To get started with setting up Shopify Payments, you need to have your bank account details ready, along with your business registration number (depending on the business registration requirements in your location).

TIP
If you don't have a business registration number yet, it's optional at this point — but make sure you get the right legal advice and that you find out at what point you need to register your business. Typically, customers want to see your business registration information on their tax receipts.

To set up Shopify Payments, go into your Shopify admin and click through Settings → Payments → Complete Shopify Payments Setup (see Figure 6-5). Go ahead and complete your company and personal information as prompted. You'll be asked for your legal business name, business registration number and your business type, along with personal information (such as your name, address and date of birth, and the industry you operate within). You'll also be asked for your bank account details, which is important if you want to get paid!

Click on Complete Account Setup when you're done, and voilà — you're all set up to receive payments from Shopify.

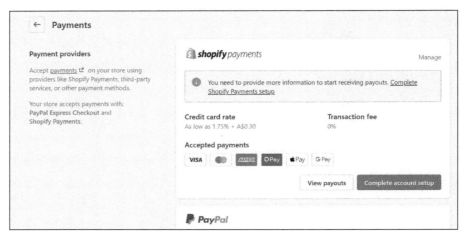

FIGURE 6-5:
The Shopify
Payments
setup page.

Source: Shopify

Accepting other payment methods

Offering alternative payment providers has never been more important, as consumers move away from typical payment methods like credit cards and towards other tech or convenience-based payment methods, many of which you're already able to accept through Shopify Payments. Simply click on Choose Alternative Payment Providers on the Payments page in your Shopify admin Settings, and a page appears with a long list of payment methods (see Figure 6-6, which shows the first few of many options), including most of the well-known BNPL options, such as Afterpay and Klarna.

EXAMPLE

Imagine you want your customers to be able to pay using Afterpay on your site. To add Afterpay as a payment option, simply type Afterpay into the search bar at the top of the Alternative Payment Providers page, and then click on the word Afterpay when it appears in the search results. You'll be prompted to enter a Merchant ID and Secret Key to add Afterpay, both of which will be provided to you by Afterpay when you create an account with them (which will be the case for all the alternate payment methods you want to add to your store).

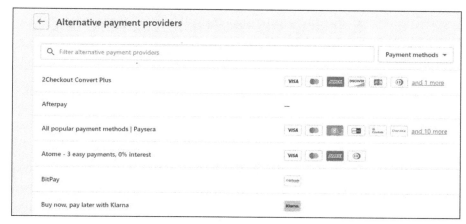

FIGURE 6-6:
The Alternative
Payment
Providers page.

Source: Shopify

TIP

I recommend starting with accepting Visa, Mastercard, PayPal and one BNPL option, as a minimum. Choose the BNPL option that dominates your local market or demographic.

Viewing your Shopify Payouts

From time to time, you or your bookkeeper may want to view the Shopify Payouts that are due to be processed (or have already been processed). To do this, follow these steps:

1. **From your Shopify admin, go to Settings → Payments.**

The Shopify Payments page appears.

2. **In the Shopify Payments section of the Payments page, click the View Payouts button.**

The Payouts page appears. It displays your previous and next Shopify Payout. If you have scheduled your payouts, you will see the estimated date that you get paid. You can see the available balance for your next payout and any funds held in reserve.

The All-payouts section of the Payouts page lists all your payouts and their current status:

- **In Transit:** The payout is in the process of being sent to your bank account.

- **Paid:** The payout has been sent to your bank. This does not mean that you have the funds in your bank account. Your bank may still need to process and deposit the funds into your account.

- **Failed:** Your bank failed to successfully process the payout so the funds have not been deposited.

Setting up multiple currencies in Shopify Payments

If you're using Shopify Payments, you can sell in multiple currencies. If you're using a third-party payment provider, you need to check with them if you can set up multiple currencies.

TIP

Look at adding extra currencies to your online store if you're getting regular orders from a certain country, or countries, or if you're planning to sell into other countries, as customers feel safer paying in their own currency rather than having to try and work out conversion rates or pay credit card fees associated with cross-border transactions.

If you're planning to add other currencies to your online store, you need to have a theme with a currency selector — or you can add an app to your store that allows customers to switch between currencies. It's also a good idea to add Shopify's Geolocation app to your site — it detects where a customer is shipping from and suggests they switch to their local currency (unless you're on Shopify Plus, in which case your store automatically detects where the customer is located from their IP address). You can set the exchange rate yourself or choose to display a market rate.

TIP

Some themes, such as Debut or Brooklyn, include a currency selector in the most recent versions. If you're using an older version, you can update your theme to automatically add a currency selector to your storefront.

To set up Shopify Payments to accept multiple currencies, follow these steps:

1. **From your Shopify admin, go to Settings → Payments.**

   The Shopify Payments page appears.

2. **In the Shopify Payments section, in the top-right corner in blue font, click on Manage.**

   The Manage Payments page appears, which displays Shopify Payments' processing fees and rates.

3. **In the Countries/Regions section of the Manage Payments page (about halfway down the page), click on Add Country/Region.**

   A new dialogue box appears with a list of countries and their currencies — for example, United Kingdon (GBP).

4. **Select the country or region's currency that you want to enable from the list of supported countries and regions by selecting the checkbox next to that country and currency.**

5. **Click on Add Country/Region, which saves your changes for you.**

TIP

While you can now sell in GBP (or whatever currency you have enabled), you still need your customers to be able to see their local currency when they shop on your site, which the steps above do not facilitate. You can use the Shopify Geolocation app (available in the Shopify App Store) to enable your pricing to be shown in other currencies — visit apps.shopify.com.

Setting up a third-party payment provider

You can bring your own relationship with a payment gateway to your Shopify store if you so choose. If you go to Settings → Payments, simply scroll down to the Choose Third-party Providers section, search for your payment provider in the list that appears and click on it. You need to have your merchant details on hand to set your payment provider up in Shopify — your merchant details are the banking details provided to you when you registered with your chosen third-party payment gateway.

WARNING

Shopify Payments activity is temporarily disabled on your site while you are in the process of adding a third-party provider.

Fraud prevention

Fraud attacks in ecommerce are a daily occurrence. If you have an online store that is making sales, you're likely going to be targeted at some point. Fraud occurs when a credit card or credit card information has been stolen and used to purchase goods. Chargebacks occur when the card holder realizes that their card has been used without their knowledge, and they ask their bank to retrieve the funds, which they do — from you, the seller.

Fortunately, Shopify has a robust approach to fraud and so can help you identify fraudulent orders and process chargebacks.

Investigating suspicious orders

Shopify has its own inbuilt fraud detection capability that analyses transactions and alerts you when it identifies that a suspicious transaction may have occurred, so that you can then take appropriate action.

To view the fraud analysis of an order, follow these steps:

1. **From your Shopify admin, go to Orders.**

A list of all the orders that your store has received appears, from newest to oldest.

2. **Click on the order number of the order that you want to review.**

TIP

You may have numerous orders appear, which can be difficult to wade through, so consider searching for particular orders using the search bar at the top of the orders page. You can search for orders using a variety of parameters, including customer name or email address, but you need to click on the order number to access the order details page.

The order details appear. You see the customer's details, including delivery address, phone number and email address.

Suspicious orders are flagged with an exclamation mark beside the order number.

TIP

Fraud analysis typically happens straight away, but if you see an order stating that fraud analysis is not yet available, hit refresh after a few minutes. It's best not to send the order until it's been passed as safe.

When an order has been flagged as suspicious, Shopify suggests several ways you can check the legitimacy of the order:

TIP

>> **Verify the IP address.** Is the customer's IP address located in a different general area from where they claim to be?

You can use free online tools like What Is My IP Address (https://whatis myipaddress.com) to check the location of an IP address.

If the answer is yes, try and email or call the customer — consider asking for a form of ID to be emailed to you, and explain to the customer that the security of your store is paramount in order to protect your customers. If you get no reply, you can be 99 per cent sure the order is a fraud attack on your store.

>> **Call the phone number on the order.** The majority of the time an order is fraudulent, the phone number on the order never connects or there's no answer. If you've called the number a few times over a day or two, the chances are you're dealing with a fraudulent order, so you can cancel it.

>> **Search for the email address.** Using the same principle as calling the phone number, try emailing the customer, or even searching for the email address in a search engine, to see if it's linked to any businesses or social media accounts.

>> **Verify that the billing and shipping addresses match.** Often in fraudulent orders, the billing address and delivery address are significantly far apart, which is a key indicator of potential fraud (generally, a customer is reasonably close to the location of their billing address).

Another red flag is when you have multiple orders for the same shipping address but each with different billing addresses, meaning numerous cards have been used to send orders to the same address — which is where the fraudsters collect their orders from before selling on the goods.

>> **Review high-value orders.** Fraudsters often get greedy and place orders with unusually high values — and if the fraudulent order slips through undetected, their windfall is significant. If you see an unusually high-value order come through, it's a good idea to verify the customer before you send out the items, using one or more of the strategies outlined in this list.

Following these steps can make a meaningful difference, reducing fraud and saving you money. You may wonder why I'm saying it saves *you* money (and not the poor person who's had their credit card details stolen), and the reason for that is one of the banes of an online seller's existence — chargebacks, which I explain in the next section.

Processing chargebacks

Chargebacks occur when a person believes their card has been used without their permission, so they dispute the charge with their bank — which then requests more information from you, the merchant. If the bank deems that the order has been placed without the cardholder's permission, it reverses the charge, taking the money off the merchant, who then has the indignity of losing the sale and the product that's already been sent!

Here's the typical chargeback process in Shopify:

1. The cardholder disputes a credit card charge with their bank.

2. The cardholder's bank sends a chargeback request to the credit card company.

3. The credit card company asks you for evidence that the charge was valid, such as a signature on the order.

4. You and Shopify gather evidence to figure out whether the charge was valid.

5. **Shopify sends a response to the credit card company.**

   If you use Shopify Payments, Shopify collects evidence and sends a response to the credit card company for you on the due date. You can add additional evidence to the response before the due date. The due date is 7 to 21 days after the chargeback or inquiry is filed. If you're using a third-party payment provider, you'll need to refer to its chargeback process.

6. **The credit card company reviews the evidence. The review can take up to 75 days after the response has been submitted.**

7. **The credit card company resolves the chargeback by either allowing the charge to be processed, or reversing the charge and giving the funds back to the cardholder.**

You won't be sent a bill for the chargeback — it will be taken directly from your next Shopify Payments payout (or other payment gateway if you don't use Shopify Payments) or settlement.

WARNING

In my experience, 99 per cent of the time the merchant loses rather than the customer, which places further emphasis on the importance of reviewing your potentially fraudulent orders before you send them. Chargebacks typically sit at 0.3–0.5 per cent of total orders, which is a potentially huge loss as your business starts to scale.

3

Curating the Customer Experience: The Customer Is Always Right

Understand the difference between customer service (CS) and customer experience (CX).

Set the scene to welcome loyal customers back to your store time and time again.

Ensure your user experience (or UX) is hassle-free.

Add a personalized touch to your online store.

Chapter **7**

What's the Difference? Customer Service and Customer Experience

Customer service (sometimes referred to as CS) forms part of your online store's overall customer experience (or CX). *Customer service* relates specifically to the way in which a business communicates with its customers, particularly when an enquiry or issue needs to be resolved, while *customer experience* relates to every interaction a customer has with a business. The overarching goal of an ecommerce business is to continuously strive to improve its customer experience as this leads to the acquisition and retention of customers.

By the end of this chapter, you'll have a good understanding of the different channels of communication that Shopify allows you to add to your store, and how to add them. You'll also discover how to set up customer service metrics (otherwise known as key performance indicators, or KPIs) to help you optimize the quality of the service that you're offering your customers, and use customer satisfaction (CSAT) surveys to help you better understand your customers' feelings about the service you provide them with.

You also consider how to offer your customers a more personal service using customer service software (CSS). In an ideal world, when a customer contacts you with a query, you want to know as much about that customer as possible so that you can help them find exactly what they're looking for.

Customer Service 101: Communicating with Customers

Customer service can be broken down into two parts of the customer journey: pre-purchase and post-purchase. The way to build a strong customer service position pre-purchase is to makes sure that your site is clear on frequent issues that arise when running an online business, such as your shipping and returns policies. With thoughtful planning, you can stop an influx of customer service enquiries about things that can be answered through clear online store policies.

Post-purchase, customers may reach out to you to track an order or query a delivery, to initiate a return, or to ask for more information about how to use the product they have purchased.

Regardless of what part of the purchase journey a customer or visitor to your site is on, providing clear, timely and accurate information to customers is essential when it comes to running a successful ecommerce store. In the following sections, I look at effective ways to communicate essential information to your customers to minimize confusion, as well as some customer service channels you can use to connect with customers about their purchases.

Creating clear policies and product information

You can achieve a few easy customer service wins to help reduce customer service enquiries when you're setting up your website. Consider

>> Providing clear return and shipping policies that you are prepared to uphold.

>> Adding pages with frequently asked questions (FAQs) and information about your business to your online store.

>> Updating your customers about new products using an email newsletter.

>> Giving your customers a place to tell you (and others) what they think of your products and customer service.

>> Offering multiple channels for your customer to contact you.

>> Providing sufficient product information on your product pages. Turn to Chapter 4 for more on creating pages that offer this kind of information for your customers.

REMEMBER

Good clear policies and up-to-date customer information can deflect needless customer service queries, which in turn saves you the time (and money) involved with replying to them.

TIP

Some of the most important things your store's webpages need to cover include:

>> **Answering repeat questions:** You can create a page for FAQs to answer any questions that your customers frequently ask, such as questions about shipping, returns and refunds. FAQs provide a self-help knowledge base for customers, which hopefully aids in their decision-making process and reduces the amount of contact a customer needs to make with the store.

>> **Telling your story:** Create an About Us page that tells the customer who you are and what your store or brand aims to achieve. Consider using a video here to provide some authenticity around your brand, which helps to build trust.

>> **Informing your customers about your products:** Many of your pre-purchase customer service enquiries will be from customers asking for more information or further clarity on certain products you're selling, so it's important not to get lazy with product descriptions. One of the most common product questions I've seen is customers asking what the dimensions of a product are, so remember to provide that sort of detail when you're creating and describing your products.

>> **Clarifying your shipping information:** Shipping information should be clearly available on a Shipping Policy page in your store. You need to show the time it takes for you to deliver to certain areas, and the price. Be as specific as possible, but don't go on and on — a clear table is a good way to display your shipping policy. You also want to tell customers how they can track their orders on your Shipping Policy page, as well as on your FAQ page.

>> **Explaining your returns and refunds policies:** Not only will customers email you if they're unhappy or unclear about your returns policy, they may leave public reviews. If there's one thing that really grinds the gears of an online shopper it's a poor returns experience. Choose a policy that is both competitive and financially responsible for your business, and make it very simple and clear to understand. Don't hide this crucial detail, particularly if you have a good policy — it can help you acquire and retain customers.

>> **Displaying clearly how to contact you:** Add a Contact page to your footer menu so customers know how to reach you. Be sure to display all your contact details, and your typical response times, including your standard business hours.

You can offer customers different ways to contact you (see the next section for more on these), but one useful addition to your site may be a contact form, which you can add after the rest of your contact details on your Contact page.

To create a Contact page and add a contact form to the page, follow these steps:

1. **From your Shopify admin, go to Online Store → Pages.**

2. **Click on Add Page.**

   A new page appears, with some text boxes for you to complete.

3. **In the Title text box, type a title for your contact page, such as Contact Us or Get in Touch.**

4. **In the Content text box, type any text that you want to appear above the contact form.**

TIP

   If you only want to include a contact form, you can leave this section blank. However, you may want to add some welcoming text and a reassuring note, such as 'We will get back to you as soon as we can!'

   Other useful information you may like to add includes:

   - Your store's address (if you have a retail location)
   - Your store's phone number (if you want customers to be able to reach you by phone)

5. **In the Theme Template section to the right of the page, choose Contact from the Template Suffix drop-down menu.**

   Choosing this means you use the Contact page template from your selected theme.

TIP

   Check the Contact page of your selected theme to see what you can expect this to look like.

6. **Click on the green Save button in the bottom-right corner to save your new Contact page.**

Customer service channels to consider

You can communicate with your customers in numerous ways, whether it be face to face, through direct channels like phone and live chat, or by providing clear information on your website — the more the merrier. The goal is to make it easy for the customer to get a resolution to any queries they have as quickly as possible.

The following sections cover some of the customer service channels you can add to your Shopify store.

Email

Also known as a support ticket, email is still the most common form of customer contact in ecommerce. Your customer service email is likely to be something like info@youronlinestore.com, customersupport@youronlinestore.com or help@youronlinestore.com — and you can clearly display that on your Contact Us page (the link to which is typically displayed in the footer of your homepage).

When a customer emails you, you don't really want to be accessing your Outlook or Gmail but connecting your email to a CSS, or customer service software.

REMEMBER

A CSS is a platform that connects all your customer service channels, such as emails, chats and social media messages, into one platform, so you can view and reply to all your messages from the same place.

I've used various CSS platforms over the years, but my favorite one to use with Shopify is Gorgias, mainly for its ease of use and the fact that it integrates with your Shopify store in minutes. Once a customer reaches out to you, Gorgias imports that email, chat, phone call or social media message into its platform, and brings up any associated order information for that customer so you can quickly check or amend their order details, track their shipment or refund their order — all without leaving Gorgias.

CSS platforms give you far more options than your normal email inbox, including being able to tag emails, or support tickets, into categories automatically, such as 'Shipping', 'Complaint', 'Product Enquiry' and 'Order Tracking' — which is useful intel to help you understand where your customers tend to have issues with your website or business in general.

A CSS also provides you with an easy-to-use inbox that shows you your emails, from oldest to newest — from here, you can check if anyone has responded to the email, or assign it to a team member.

TIP

Because your CSS integrates your live chat function (see the next section), your social media channels and phone channels so that all points of contact are brought into one platform. if you find that Cranky Johnny has messaged you across three different channels you can merge his communications into one support ticket, with all the issues pulled into one thread, which saves you time (and energy!) when responding to customers.

Live chat

Definitely my favorite customer service channel, *live chat* is when a customer is able to open a chat box and chat directly to customer service representatives, rather than having to send an email and wait for a reply. Live chat is a fast two-way conversation with an online store.

In my experience, 15–20 per cent of all customers that use live chat go on to make a sale. That conversion rate is worth a second, and third, look. Sure, some of those customers may just be checking a price, or asking a basic question, but many of them are sold by the service the agent gives quickly via live chat.

REMEMBER

Fifty per cent of online customers bounce and most sessions only last a few minutes — and people are not always patient enough to wait for an emailed reply. Shopping can be an impulsive activity, so you need to strike while the iron is hot, and live chat is a great weapon of choice!

I'd go as far as saying that live chat is an expectation now for most customers, so I recommend you get it on your site as soon as you can. Remember, though, that if your live chat option is always offline, it might look a little unprofessional, so make sure you download the live chat app and start jumping online whenever you can (I like Gorgias live chat).

TIP

As your business grows, and if you have a customer service team (rather than just you doing every role!), consider placing your live chat operators next to your product team in the office as they can feed back information on the products. For example, they pass on useful information such as 'I have a customer here who says their bag doesn't fit the 13-inch laptop', or ask questions such as 'Does anyone know if the red gumboots come in a size 12?' This sort of talk gets both teams involved but also passively teaches other team members about your products, and any related pain points for your customers. Answering customer queries then becomes all about teamwork.

Chatbots

Chatbots are a type of software that can provide automated responses that appear as though they're from a company customer service agent. Chatbots typically ask the visitor a series of questions aimed at guiding the customer through a bunch of pre-existing answers from an internal knowledge base. Chatbots can appear on live chat and Facebook Messenger — and really any channel that offers two-way chat between a company and a customer.

Bots can be segmented to talk to different customer groups in different ways, for example segmenting customers by those that shop sale items versus those that shop full-price items. They tend to start with a leading question, such as 'What brings you here today?' Next, they propose several answers, such as 'Shipping query', or 'Looking to buy a product'. Depending on which response the customer clicks on, routing rules kick in to show various options, such as 'Great, are you looking for black shoes or white shoes?' The bots can actually act as sales assistants, or gather leads to be followed up.

Chatbots such as Intercom can be integrated into your Shopify store through third-party apps that are found in the Shopify App Store. Given they operate as bots and not actual people, they don't need breaks and can work 24/7 for you across multiple languages. Chatbots are a great way to serve your customers, as they increase your response times greatly.

WARNING

Putting up too many layers of artificially generated responses can be a real turn-off — you have to know when to let C-3PO hand over to Derek from Customer Service.

TIP

You may not need chatbots during the early stages of your ecommerce career, but it's useful to familiarize yourself with them as your business develops. If it's just you when you're starting out, a robotic friend may be exactly what you need.

Phone

I love the good old telephone, and I think too many online stores hide their phone number — as if they're scared to actually talk to their customers. I say embrace the humble phone — get your customers on the line, even the grumpy ones! I often advise companies who want to go to the next level with their customer service (who actually *want* to be customer-focused, rather than just have it in their mantra in a pretty font) to call rather than email a customer when they see a testy message come through their CSS platform. Most of the time, a friendly phone call (with a friendly resolution) can turn that customer around. I can guarantee you they won't be expecting your call, and many customers apologize for the tone of the message they sent!

REMEMBER

One of the main pain points an online retailer faces is the lack of personalization. The phone gives you the opportunity to talk to, relate to and empathize with your customers.

TECHNICAL STUFF

Most online stores' phone systems are powered by VOIP (voice over IP, or 'internet protocol' if you want to get really technical) and can be integrated with a good CSS platform, where the calls are converted to support tickets, which gives you good, clear reporting on that channel. You may consider getting a professional number (as opposed to a typical household phone number), but I have seen no evidence of this having any impact on customer service or sales.

Social Media, SMS and WhatsApp

Depending on your target demographic, you may get a lot of customer service enquiries through social media platforms, especially through Instagram and your Facebook ads (chapters 16 and 17 cover Instagram and Facebook marketing in more detail). A good CSS system will integrate with the big social media channels and pull the messages in, creating support tickets out of them, so you won't need to scan each of your channels for messages.

TIP

Many CSS platforms seem to struggle with picking up comments on Facebook ads, so it's worth asking your potential provider about how this works to check the CSS is fit for purpose.

REMEMBER

Social media messages have to be treated as a priority because they're public facing, so you can be sure other people, and potential customers, are watching. Be on your best behavior and don't respond with an attitude to Cranky Johnny — instead, give him your best virtual smile and make it clear to all readers that you're ready to help (and make sure you respond quickly). It can be very easy for social media users to pile onto a brand, so you need to make sure you're watching your social media messages with an eagle eye.

Three different messaging channels to watch out for include:

REMEMBER

>> **Facebook Messenger** is a beast of its own. Using this channel is a no-brainer for your store. It integrates easily into Shopify, or most CSS platforms; it's free; and it's got some great capabilities. Assuming you, like the rest of the ecommerce world, are going to use Facebook as a marketing channel, then you can expect your customers to chat on Facebook Messenger with you.

Facebook Messenger is easy for the customer to use, and your message history sits there waiting for your next connection (in case the user drops off, and comes back online later). You can set up chatbots in Messenger, and as a bonus, you can push marketing information through Messenger as well. Even if you don't add one of the big CSS platforms like Gorgias to your store right away, Shopify allows you to integrate with Facebook Messenger via Shopify Inbox, so you can allow customers to chat to you using Facebook Messenger while they're on your website (see the next section for more on Shopify Inbox, which also has its own chat feature in case you want to add live chat to your store).

>> **SMS** (which stands for *short message service*) is a platform that isn't widely used for customer service, and I wouldn't say it's a must-have, but I do like it to communicate with customers on things like items coming back into stock or shipping notifications. SMS is supported through third-party applications in Shopify, but they're mostly geared towards marketing communications rather than customer service.

Before you send SMS messages, make sure you have the consent of the recipient.

>> **WhatsApp** is less popular, but I wouldn't discount it as it dominates messaging apps globally like no other platform. It makes sense that with so many users of the platform, the service might eventually trickle into a form of customer service that users may want to be contacted on.

You may have trouble integrating WhatsApp with your CSS, although it would be on the roadmap of most of them. You can, however, integrate it into your Shopify store directly through third-party apps such as WhatsApp Chat + Abandoned Cart by Pushdaddy.com.

TIP

You're unlikely to need SMS and WhatsApp in your early days of selling online with Shopify.

Shopify Inbox

Shopify Inbox creates a single mailbox for all your online customer interactions. It allows you to manage your customer conversations, customize the chat appearance on your online store, create automatic responses and view conversation analytics from your Shopify admin.

Using Shopify Inbox means you can easily add live chat to your online store — more easily that integrating a third-party CSS platform — allowing customers to message you while they shop. You can also receive Inbox messages from customers using other messaging channels like Facebook Messenger. Shopify Inbox lets you view and respond to these messages from your desktop and mobile device.

TIP

Shopify Inbox is a good option for beginners due to its ease to install, and the fact that it's free.

You can also use Shopify Inbox to send text or images to your team members who have a staff login for your Shopify store.

The good news is that Shopify Inbox can be set up directly from your Shopify admin. Visit shopify.com/inbox to get started, or to find out more. Shopify Inbox can be downloaded on iOS and Android mobile devices.

In Figure 7-1, you can see some of the customer service insights that Shopify Inbox provides you with, such as first response times, which is one of the most important KPIs in customer service. It indicates how long it takes, on average, for you to reply to a customer's first enquiry. A good benchmark to aim for is one hour.

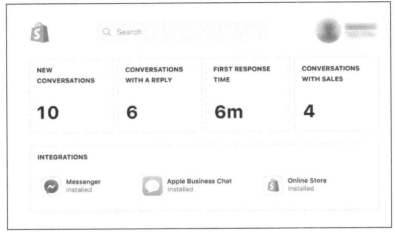

FIGURE 7-1:
Shopify Inbox.

Source: Shopify

Using Customer Service Metrics

Customer service performance can be measured using *key performance indicators* (KPIs), which are an important way to track how happy your customers are. Shopify Inbox offers some of these important metrics, such as first response time, which helps you keep on top of the quality of your customer service.

Here are the typical customer service KPIs that relate to all customer service channels:

>> **First response time:** First response times are a key metric for any customer service team, regardless of the channel that's being used, and they indicate the amount of time taken to respond to a support ticket (any email/chat/call/social media message in your CSS). A good KPI here is no more than one hour for email and social messages, and one minute for live chat. This is not a usual KPI for phones, which should be answered within 30 seconds of ringing, although most CSS platforms don't show this metric for phone calls.

You can set this KPI in some CSS platforms to only include business hours, unless you are running 24-hour customer service.

>> **Resolution time:** This is the time it takes to resolve a ticket in total, from the time it is opened to the time it is closed. You can expect your live chat resolution time to be around 10 minutes, whereas your email resolution time might be around 4–5 hours to allow for some back and forth.

Try to avoid resolutions going into the next day.

>> **One touch tickets:** Reported as a percentage, this is a ratio of the number of tickets completed with one response; that is, 'one touch'. Over 50 per cent is good here — the goal is not to be fast at all costs and hurry the customer along, but to answer the customer's question with one great reply so they don't need to ask you anything else.

It can be so annoying to get a reply after a few hours, only to find the customer service agent has forgotten to answer one of your questions or they still need to check something for you. Go and check it now, and get back to the customer quickly!

>> **Tickets created versus tickets closed:** This metric helps you check you're closing (completing) as many support tickets as you're receiving, which essentially means you're keeping on top of your customer service.

I suggest running customer service KPIs from day one because they're an easy, cheap way to start to improve your business.

Maximizing Customer Experience

Customer experience, or CX, is the sum of all parts, if you like. It's the overall feeling the customer experiences when they browse, shop, interact with or finish shopping on your store. It's the customer's everything!

Good customer experience in ecommerce leaves the customer feeling positive about your brand or business, and everything associated with it.

User experience (or UX) deals with how the user (the visitor to your site) interacts with the website. User experience is about the interaction with the website, whereas customer experience is about the customer's interaction with all parts of the business. Chapter 9 explores the user experience in more detail.

Customer experience is holistic — there are many cogs in the wheel, and some of those rely on third parties, like couriers, so as a retailer you need to try and own the experience as much as you can. Check out the nearby sidebar 'Falling short of a great experience' for an example of how pivotal customer experience can be to long-term sales success.

EXAMPLE

FALLING SHORT OF A GREAT EXPERIENCE

Mary starts a new job next month, so she is looking for a new work bag that fits her backpack. She is fairly brand agnostic and is open to looking at new brands, but she knows what she is looking for in a bag. Mary googles 'Women's Work Bags' and finds a site that sits up nice and high in the search results, 'xyzbags.com'. So far so good — the site ranks high in Google Ads and has a clear text description in the ad. After clicking the ad, the homepage pops up quickly, in around 1.5 seconds — so far, this has been great. Mary likes the look of the homepage banner and notices there's free shipping on orders over $100 — a nice clear offer that catches Mary's eye, so on she goes.

Next, Mary navigates through the menu and selects 'work bags' from the drop-down menu under the 'bags' category. There are so many bags to choose from, so Mary quickly filters for 'black bags', and then 'leather', which leaves around 10 bags to choose from. Mary has managed to narrow down a selection of potential bags in less than a couple of minutes.

Mary finds a bag that looks great, although she can't locate the measurements so she isn't sure if it fits her 13-inch laptop. None of the photos show what sort of laptop might fit in the bag, and nothing in the product description talks about the bag's size. Mary starts a live chat and is greeted quickly by a representative from the company.

Unfortunately, the agent isn't able to answer Mary's question right away, instead telling Mary that it 'should' fit her laptop. Mary isn't filled with confidence but she trusts the agent, and notes that the website offers free seven-day returns for a change of mind. So, Mary goes along to the checkout and smoothly completes the purchase using Afterpay — another great result, as she doesn't even have to pay for the item upfront!

So far, Mary's experience has been great while using the website — it's been fast, with clear info and an easy to navigate menu, though she acknowledges that the product description could have been better and the agent less vague. Despite this, Mary eagerly awaits her new bag, which will be with her in two or three days according to the shipping info on the website.

The next day, Mary hasn't received any email regarding tracking, which is a little strange — Mary regularly shops online and knows that it's normal to get tracking updates. Mary reaches out over the live chat again, but this time she doesn't get a reply. She looks for a phone number, but she can't locate one in the Contact Us section of the website. She sends an email, and by this time she's getting a little impatient.

The next day she still hasn't received a reply to her email. It's been three days since she placed her order. She manages to get hold of someone on the live chat, but they tell her that it's still within one to three days and so she should wait. That afternoon, to her surprise, a courier delivers Mary's parcel, and she unpacks it to find that it looks pretty good, and fits her laptop well! Mary asks the courier if it's normal that tracking numbers don't get sent, and the courier remarks that there has been an issue with tracking lately but that the online store usually sends tracking numbers.

Mary shows her bag to her friends, who remark how nice it looks, and how good the leather is. They ask her where she bought it, and if she'd recommend that they shop there as well. Mary sums her experience up as 'great product but poor communication and shipping', and says that if she could find the bag at another retailer, she'd probably try them instead.

Although Mary felt that she would recommend the product and the website, her overall experience meant she ultimately decided not to return to the store in a hurry.

While Mary's user experience was good — the website was easy to navigate, fast, and the categories and filters worked well — the customer experience was less than adequate, so the good user experience was undone by the poor customer service and delivery experience. Mary got the product she wanted but not the experience she wanted, and as such she was unable to wholeheartedly recommend the website to her friends.

REMEMBER

Customer service and customer experience go hand in hand in building a successful and sustainable online store. It's cheaper to retain a customer than it is to acquire a customer, and one of the key factors in whether or not a customer will come back to you is how you treat them when they need something from you.

The following sections explore why it's so important to prioritize customer experience — and how you can measure customer experience to help you strive for better outcomes as your business evolves.

Providing an excellent customer experience

Customer experience is everything. Without the customer, you're going to find it hard to make a living, so put the customer at the center of everything you do. You'll have noticed by now that I keep recommending you do things that your customer would want, not necessarily that you would want, although they don't always have to be mutually exclusive. The point is to gear your operation around the customer.

The goal is to gain your customer's loyalty by giving them an exceptional experience across all their interactions with your business. A key metric in your business will be customer lifetime value (CLTV), which is driven by the predicted value of the future relationship with your customer. I talk about how to calculate and measure CLTV in Chapter 8.

Measuring customer experience

You often read articles about different ways to measure customer experience, and people will talk about this survey or those reviews, but the best way I've seen to benchmark your customer experience is a good old Net Promoter Score (NPS). If you want to take your customer experience seriously, and really benchmark yourself against your industry, and strive to improve, then NPS is the way to do it.

The *NPS* is an all-encompassing scoring system used to assess how customers feel about their overall experience shopping with a store. It's a universal ecommerce metric that is generally sent to customers via a survey, which asks them to score their overall satisfaction in their dealings with a business out of 10. Respondents are divided into three groups: promoters, passives and detractors. *Promoters* are customers that score the business a 9 or a 10 rating; *passives* are customers who score the business a 7 or 8; and *detractors* score the business between 0 and 6.

A *detractor* isn't a large piece of machinery used on a farm; instead, it's someone who wouldn't recommend your online business (as opposed to a *promoter*, who would, or a *passive*, who is satisfied with your business but isn't someone who would recommend your business to a friend). Your *NPS* is the percentage of customers that would recommend your business to a friend or another person.

The NPS score is calculated by subtracting the percentage of detractors from the percentage of promoters:

NPS = Percentage of Promoters – Percentage of Detractors

Imagine you've collected 150 responses to your NPS question, and the scores look like this:

>> 80 customers gave either a 9 or 10 rating

>> 30 customers gave either a 7 or 8 rating

>> 40 customers gave between a 0 to 6 rating

This means you have 80 promoters, 30 passives and 40 detractors. To calculate the percentage of promoters and the percentage of detractors:

Percentage of Promoters or Detractors = (Number of Promoters or Detractors / Number of Respondents) × 100

To calculate the percentage of promoters:

(80/150) × 100 = 53% Promoters

To calculate the percentage of detractors:

(40/150) × 100 = 27% Detractors

Subtracting the percentage of detractors from the percentage of promotors give you the Net Promoter Score:

53 – 27 = 26

An NPS of 26 isn't particularly high, but results can vary widely between businesses. The highest NPS score I have seen is 85, whereas typically a score in the 60s and 70s is considered good.

The general question asked in an NPS survey is: 'How likely are you to recommend (your business) to a friend?' So essentially, an NPS survey is measuring the loyalty of your customers. NPS is considered to be the benchmark in overall satisfaction with a business, in ecommerce.

NPS cuts through the noise, post-purchase, and simply asks your customers, 'How likely are you to recommend us to a friend?' Which takes us back to our friend Mary (see the nearby sidebar 'Falling short of a great experience'), who ultimately decided she couldn't wholeheartedly recommend the business — which makes her a detractor.

TIP

In the early days, you can use NPS to gauge how your customers feel about your business, and as you get more staff you can strive to increase your NPS through improving your customer service and user experience, as well as looking into where you might be falling down. Down the track, you might have a data team that can pull the data on where your detractors' scores have let you down (for example, do customers who select same day delivery have a lower NPS than those that select economy delivery?), and you would then dive into trying to rectify the issue.

In the absence of a data team, I suggest you reach out to detractors to find out what they didn't like — you'll often find you win the respect of the customer and discover how to improve, and a good online business should strive for continuous improvement.

Checking Customer Satisfaction

Customer satisfaction (CSAT) surveys are a customer service metric used to score a customer's satisfaction levels when speaking with a customer service agent. I tend to use the NPS to score a company overall (refer to the preceding section), but I use CSAT to score the level of support that the company has provided to its customers.

Customer satisfaction surveys (CSAT) won't generally be an out-of-the-box report in your CSS analytics or insights, but a CSS worth its salt will offer it for you. CSAT results are gauged from surveys sent to their customers, usually from the CSS or other platforms, which asks the customer to rate their interaction with the business, or the customer service, providing you with a score out of 100.

TIP

To assess a customer's satisfaction with their service, you can create a question on a CSAT survey that asks: 'On a scale of 1 to 10, how satisfied were you with your experience with our customer service representative?' Be sure to call out the customer service agent, not the business (and not the product) because you have other ways of scoring those facets of the business, such as the NPS. Remember, the CSAT metric is designed to specifically measure the quality of the customer service your team gives.

CSAT scores are presented as ratios, or percentages, and are calculated by taking all the customer service agents' scores out of 10 and dividing them by all the maximum possible scores. A good CSAT is over 90 per cent.

EXAMPLE

Imagine you send out 10 surveys, with each being scored out of 10. The maximum score is 100. To calculate your CSAT, you tally all your actual scores. If you end up with 80 out of 100, you can take 80 and divide it by 100, and then multiply it by 100 to get a percentage — so in this case, your CSAT is 80 per cent.

CSAT is one of the best training tools for customer service teams. CSAT systems tend to show a leaderboard of customer service agents, from highest to lowest, and serve as a great rewards program for high-achieving customer service agents, as well as a way to help train customer service agents who may be scoring poorly. You can filter through your low-ranking CSAT tickets, and train up on how the customer service agent might have handled that better next time.

Chapter **8**

Reviews, Customer Loyalty and User-Generated Content

I f you're building an online store, you've probably shopped online before too — and if you've shopped online before, there's a good chance you've read an online store's reviews prior to making a purchase from them, particularly when you're shopping with them for the first time. Reviews are one of the best ways to achieve organic growth of an online brand — if they're positive. An unhappy customer is more likely to tell people about their experience than a happy customer, so while it's important to try and keep customers happy, it's equally important to follow up on unhappy customers.

Loyal customers are what every business wants, because not only will they keep coming back, but they'll also tell their friends. While ultimately, customers will decide if they're going to pledge their allegiances to a certain brand, there's plenty you can do to influence them.

In this chapter, I unpack some strategies for building customer loyalty, both organically and through loyalty programs, specifically using Shopify. I also tackle how to collect and utilize reviews, as well as consider how you can get some form of control over public reviews. Carrying on the theme of letting the customer do the talking (and the marketing) for you, I also look at the rise of user-generated content. Finally, I consider the different customer reports you can use in Shopify.

Having a site that's busy with lots of reviews, and a multitude of different people using your products, is going to give shoppers the perception that your store is thriving, trustworthy and authentic. An online store that launches with no reviews or user-generated content, and just a few edited marketing images, is going to take longer to gain traction as it can look a bit like a ghost town. In many ways, shoppers are led by trends — or by one another. Where there's a crowd, others will follow — if your store looks deserted, customers may be inclined to stay away.

Why Reviews Matter

When I write about *customer reviews*, I'm referring to reviews left in public online forums (such as Google Reviews) about the overall experience a customer has with an online store (offsite reviews). When I write about *product reviews*, I'm referring to reviews left on your website from customers about specific products (onsite reviews).

As an ecommerce business operator, you have to carefully manage your online reputation and harness the power of reviews for good. Positive reviews and testimonials can build *social proof* (elements on a website that build trust) for your business, so if you're genuinely offering a good product or service, you should be happy to ask people to review it.

REMEMBER

Almost everything you do as online retailers should be aimed at what the customer wants or expects from you, not what you want or expect from the customer. The same logic applies when understanding the perception of your store in the market — the perception of your brand is dictated by what your customers think of you, not what you put up on the vision board in your office. A customer is going to read your Google Reviews before they read your About Us page, which is a reality that's out of your control.

Customers trust one another to be authentic, much more than they do a business — it's why platforms like Trustpilot, Yotpo and Google Reviews exist, because customers want to read about what really goes on when you interact with a business. Collect as many reviews as you can, and be sure to publicly reply to them.

TIP

Select a Shopify theme that already has reviews or testimonials included, or integrate a third-party application that can collect reviews and allow you to respond to them. You can then use these reviews for marketing purposes.

Reviews are the lifeblood of many sellers on eBay and Amazon, so it's no surprise that most serious online retailers offer some form of reviews on their sites. Off your site, it's up to the customer where they leave reviews, but in the following sections I help you work out how to reply to reviews — even when they're off your website — and I consider your review platform options in Shopify.

Onsite product reviews

You collect product reviews from customers who have ordered a certain product, which you then match to that product on the front end of your website — but don't worry, there are some great platforms that integrate with Shopify to automate this process. These platforms send an automated email to each customer after they have placed an order, asking them to rate the product, usually out of five stars. Customers who leave reviews may also have the opportunity to leave a photo or video with their written review, and you then have the chance to moderate the review before it's published on your website. The average number of stars out of five (if this is the scale you're using) is then shown on the product page of each product, as well as the more detailed text, photo and video reviews.

EXAMPLE

Zappos.com has a review feature that indicates the number of reviews that customers have left for each product, along with an average star rating out of five. When you click on the stars, you're taken to a page where you can read individual reviews on that product. You'll also notice that Zappos uses its product reviews to inform customers about certain features of its products, such as shoes, breaking the review categories out into sections: in this case, Overall, Comfort and Style. Zappos also provides a useful key diagram, where customers can rate the sizing, such as whether the fit is small, true or large.

Zappos is not just asking customers how they feel; instead, it is using its reviews to build a product information library from its most trusted source — actual customers. Zappos wants you to review the shoes it stocks, even if the review isn't five stars, because you can be sure it has tested the impact of reviews and the company knows that informative and positive reviews lead to an increase in conversion rates.

Zappos also incentivizes its customers to leave reviews by offering them the chance to earn Zappos VIP points. This is a strategy employed by thousands of online retailers, because giving away a small discount or special membership to gain a review, which can lead to higher conversion rates, is often a small price to pay. I talk more about customer loyalty programs in the later section 'Why Loyalty Matters'.

Don't send your review request email before your order has been received. Consider allowing two weeks after the order has been placed to send a review request email so you can ensure that the product has been delivered successfully.

Offsite customer reviews

Offsite reviews occur when customers decide to leave a review of your business on Google, or other third-party platforms that facilitate reviews. Now, you may think that because these reviews are being left independently, often unprompted by you, that you have no control over them — but you do. Most third-party review platforms allow businesses to claim the business name and therefore have the right of reply to reviews.

Google Reviews is an important source of business information. Claim your business name on Google so you can take charge of your offsite Google Reviews.

To set up Google Reviews, follow these steps:

1. **Sign in to google.com/business, or register a new account.**

    Sign up by clicking on the Manage Now button — a new page appears with the option to Find and Manage Your Business, along with a search field.

    Sign up with your business email domain, since this account will be for your online store.

2. **Enter the name of your business in the search field.**

    A list of business names appears — identify yours and click on it.

3. **Under your business name, you'll be asked to select a category, such as Retail. Select the appropriate category and click on Next.**

    A new page appears asking if you want to add a location for customers to visit.

4. **Given you're opening an online store, select No and click on Next.**

5. **In the new page that appears, you're asked if you would like to select an area that your store serves — this section is optional, and given your online store is potentially going to serve customers all over the world, I generally leave this blank and click on Next.**

6. **You're then asked to select a region where your store is based — enter the country you are based in, and select Next.**

7. **The next page asks you to add your phone number and website, to be shown in Google. Both are optional; however, given you are opening an online store, you should enter the website address at least. Click on Next.**

8. You are then asked if you want to receive updates from Google about recommendations, which is optional. Select Yes or No and click on Next.

9. The next page asks you to enter your mailing address to verify that you are the business owner. This will be private; it will not appear in Google search results. Enter your business address and then click on Next.

10. You are then taken to a page that asks you to select whether you would like to receive a postcard to that address from Google, which allows you to verify that you are the business owner.

You can do this now, or select Verify Later (although you'll need to verify your business before you can edit it, so it's worthwhile doing it at this stage).

In this case, I select Verify Later and am taken to a new page where I can select my business hours.

11. Select the days of the week, and hours of the day, that your business is open from the options provided, then click on Next.

12. Google asks if you would like to accept messages. Select Yes or No, then click on Next.

Selecting Yes allows customers to message you through your Google listing.

A new page appears asking you to enter a business description.

13. Enter a description of up to 750 words about your business. This will help customers find out more about what your store sells or offers. Click on Next.

14. A new page appears where you can upload photos — this is optional.

You may like to upload photos of some of your marketing material, or of your office if you have one.

TIP

Photos are a good way to build trust — to prove that you're a real business with real people. Showing photos of your team, for example, has been shown to help improve your conversion rate, so I recommend uploading a photo here.

15. Skip to the next section if you don't want to upload any photos, or select Next when you've finished uploading.

16. Google then offers you a $10 Ad Credit. You can accept this and use it later (see the chapters in Part 5 for more on marketing and advertising), or select Skip.

A message appears telling you that your business profile is nearly ready.

17. Select Continue.

You are now taken to your My Business page, where you can see a menu on the left that includes a section called Reviews.

Any reviews left by customers will appear here, and you can click on them and reply publicly to them. You will need to verify your store before you can be notified about any reviews (refer to Step 10 for more on verifying your store).

Review the information you've entered before you request verification to ensure it's correct.

Collecting and replying to Google Reviews is a great, free way to start building trust with potential customers. I recommend that you set this up from day one. The greater the reviews, the greater the trust; the greater the trust, the greater the sales!

Selecting a review platform to use with Shopify

Shopify realizes that collecting reviews is a huge part of ecommerce, and so not only does it support third-party applications (which you can find in the Shopify App Store) that can use to request and add reviews to your store, but Shopify also has its own review platform, Product Reviews, which can be found in the Shopify App Store.

Product Reviews is free to use, and provides online retailers with a quick, cheap way to start collecting product reviews. You'll be able to collect reviews, display them on your product pages and reply to them, but you won't be able to pass them through to your Google Ads or paid media marketing campaigns. Product Reviews by Shopify doesn't have all the bells and whistles of the other reviews platform, but it's worth looking at for a quick way to get started with collecting product reviews.

Product Reviews by Shopify is a great, affordable way to get up and running with product reviews quickly. It is limited in what it offers compared to some of the other paid platforms I talk about in this section — for example, it doesn't have the ability to accept images and video along with reviews — but it's a nice app that's worth checking out as you get started with product reviews.

The following list covers some of my favorite review platforms, supported by Shopify, which can help you take control of your online reputation out there in cyberspace (I consider platforms that cover both onsite reviews and offsite reviews, as well as product reviews and general business reviews):

>> **Yotpo:** Yotpo is one of the dominant companies in the field of reviews, and handles both product reviews and general brand reviews. If you're using Yotpo, it's pretty much your one-stop-shop for reviews. You can get started for free with Yotpo and do cool things like send your customers automated review requests. You'll also be able to reply to reviews and share the good ones across your social channels, while flagging negative reviews for you to follow up. You can display widgets (another form of social proof) on your website to show customers how many great reviews you have, or your overall score out of five. The next plan up charges a monthly fee, and you'll be able to incentivize customers to leave reviews by offering discounts or special offers.

TIP

When you're up to 2,000 orders a month or more, you'll be able to push your reviews through to your Google Ads, which shows a star rating in your Google Ads and so can help your click-through rates (CTRs).

>> **Trustpilot:** Trustpilot integrates with Shopify and can be found in the Shopify App Store. Although slightly fiddlier than Yotpo to get set up on Shopify, Trustpilot is a solid platform and is one of the other major players in this space — it's also free to get started.

A lot of customers use Trustpilot to read reviews by other customers — it says over 529,000 businesses have been reviewed on their platform! If you search for one of your favorite brands, there's a fair chance there will be a review page dedicated to them. This is important, because it means a lot of people are reviewing businesses without the business needing to request the review — in other words, I can go to Trustpilot and review any company I want.

TIP

Taking ownership of your profile page on Trustpilot is a good idea, and can be done for free. This allows you to push people to leave reviews, but also to reply to them.

Trustpilot also offers a product review component as an add-on, so you need to pay for that. Their free plan is a good way to get started, with similar features to Yotpo, and the paid-for Standard Plan allows you to use more widgets on your site, plus it gives you greater review analytics and more personalized support through its Customer Success team.

>> **Reviews.IO:** This is another app available in the Shopify App Store, and it's very highly rated. What I like about Reviews.IO is that it integrates with a lot of my favorite Shopify apps, including Klaviyo, Gorgias and LoyaltyLion — and, of course, Google. Reviews.IO promotes its video reviews heavily, which I think is a great tool for an online retailer.

The one downside is that there's no free plan available, although the value in its cheapest plan is pretty impressive, with widgets, video and text reviews, and both brand and product reviews, available.

>> **Okendo:** Okendo is a great app available in the Shopify App Store and one that I use a lot. It's very simple to integrate with Shopify, and its support in onboarding is excellent — you have someone to talk to on the phone if you have any issues getting started. Okendo is geared towards collecting and showcasing product reviews and has excellent features, with my favorite probably being their video reviews. After your customer has left a video or an image, you can push this user-generated content across your social channels, as well as showcasing it on the corresponding product page. You can also create ads across social channels using the user-generated content captured through Okendo (for more on user-generated content, turn to the later section 'Utilizing User-Generated Content').

You can start on a free trial with Okendo, and then after 14 days move to the Essential plan for a monthly fee.

Free offsite review platforms to use

Many online review platforms are free for you to use off your site, and you can be sure your customers will use them to leave public reviews. It's a good idea to take ownership of the profile page of your company and respond to the reviews weekly. You can also create a spreadsheet where you track the number of positive and negative reviews, and maybe select a reason for the review, as a way of collecting data about what people like or don't like about your business or products.

These sites are a great way to build your business's profile overall, and over time you'll see your reviews appearing higher and higher in Google's search results, so you'll want to get a handle on them quickly. Above all, it's a cheap and easy marketing and brand information tool, which is always nice when you're starting out.

Here's a few review sites customers will be inclined to use and that you can reply on for free:

>> Sitejabber.com

>> Productreview.com.au

>> Trustpilot.com

>> Support.google.com

REMEMBER

If you're using a review platform, make it engaging by providing answers and comments to feedback left and using the Q&A feature, if available — this will help build trust with prospective customers, as well as providing more information on your brand or your products being reviewed.

Why Loyalty Matters

Ultimately the purpose of a loyalty program, or marketing efforts geared towards customer loyalty, is to increase customer lifetime value, or CLTV (sometimes shortened to LTV). So while it's nice to have happy customers, it's nicer to have profitable ones. Loyal customers increase profitability — according to Forrest Research, it costs five times more to acquire a customer than it does to retain one. Put simply, you may have two almost identical online stores, selling the same type of products, spending the same money on marketing, and acquiring the same customers, but the company focusing its efforts on customer loyalty will end up with the greater revenue and profitability.

TIP

Loyalty and customer reviews go hand in hand; it's more than just launching a loyalty program, it's putting customer satisfaction at the heart of everything you do in your business.

One of the people that inspired me to start my first online business was Tony Hsieh, former CEO of Zappos, whose mantra was to always put the customer first, sometimes even at the extent of short-term sales. The idea behind that is that the customer will eventually pay you back with their loyalty.

REMEMBER

Loyalty is an organic feeling that a customer has for a brand, which is driven through goodwill towards the customer in almost every interaction. Loyalty is the key to a long-term, sustainable business because of the impact that it has on CLTV.

TIP

LoyaltyLion, one of the main loyalty platforms used by Shopify merchants, talks about the growing number of businesses using ethically minded loyalty programs in its blog (www.loyaltylion.com/blog). It uses the example of fourstate.co.uk, which offers its customers a range of charitable options to contribute to, including planting trees and donating meals, rather than discounts or cash back. This can be a nice way for your online store to stand out and make a positive difference.

In the following section, I consider customer loyalty and how loyalty programs can help boost your business.

Understanding the lifetime value of a customer

CLTV is one of the most important metrics in ecommerce because it doesn't just factor in the value of one order, it also forecasts the future value of your customers — which is incredibly useful in forecasting how much revenue you'll make in the future, as well as how much to spend acquiring a customer in the first place.

You can calculate CLTV a few different ways, but the formula I like to use is the same way that Glew do it (my favorite ecommerce business intelligence platform you can check out at `go.glew.io/paul-waddy`): your store's average order value (AOV) multiplied by the number of purchases in the lifetime of your average customer. You are calculating the amount of time they are a customer of your store before they lapse:

Average Order Value (AOV) × Number of Purchases a Customer Makes in Average Customer Lifetime = Customer Lifetime Value (CLTV)

EXAMPLE

Imagine you own an online store selling tennis equipment. Your average order value is $50, and the average shopper comes back twice a year, therefore spending $100 per year. The average customer stays a customer for two years, so you can find your CLTV as follows:

$50 × 2 × 2 = $200 (the CLTV)

TIP

If you're a new business and don't know the average lifespan of a customer yet, you can set a time period of three years for planning purposes. Look at how many times a customer on average purchases in your store over a year, then multiply that by three.

The logic behind striving to increase CLTV is that you're able to spend more on acquiring a customer, with the knowledge of how much they will eventually spend in their lifetime with you. Understanding and focusing on CLTV can be one of the levers to rapid growth.

TIP

Some applications like Glew (available in the Shopify App Store) can calculate CLTV for you, and your average customer lapse point, but it's a good idea to familiarize yourself with the metric anyway.

EXAMPLE

Kate runs an online store that sells pharmaceuticals online. She knows that her AOV is $100 and that her profit margins allow her to spend 15 per cent of on her cost per order (or CPO) on acquiring a new customer while still making a profit. In other words, to get a $100 sale, Kate can safely spend up to $15 on advertising.

Kate decides to focus on developing a loyalty program and gathering as many positive reviews as she can, with her goal being to increase purchase frequency and keep her customers for longer. As a result, she's able to get her customers shopping twice a year instead of once a year, thus increasing her average purchase frequency.

Not only has Kate doubled her CLTV (as her AOV of $100 is now multiplied by two purchases instead of one per year), but she's found that when customers shop the second time, she's not having to spend marketing dollars on them due to her loyalty program offering free delivery.

So, if Kate now spends 15 per cent of her CLTV on marketing, instead of 15 per cent of one sale, she can actually spend 15 per cent of $200, not $100, meaning she can profitably spend $30 instead of $15 to acquire a customer, knowing they will come back and shop the second time without her having to spend marketing dollars on them. As a result, because her marketing activity has ramped up, so has her customer acquisition and her business! (The nearby sidebar 'RFM analysis' expands on this example further.)

TIP

Put the metrics of CLTV at the heart of all your marketing activities: AOV, purchase frequency and customer lifespan are all worthy projects that result in a fast-growing ecommerce business.

Loyalty programs are membership or incentive-driven programs that reward customers for being loyal. Customers can hit a certain level of reward through spending a certain amount, being a customer for a certain length, or referring a friend, plus a variety of other reasons. A *referral program* is considered part of a loyalty program. It specifically depends on a customer's social circles to be influenced by a customer's referral, and it focuses on your customers referring you new customers. Some loyalty programs have a referral component as part of the overall offering; however, they'll drive revenue opportunities across a variety of strategies, including incentivizing higher spend, more frequent shipping, social shares and things like birthday rewards.

Referral and loyalty programs provide a host of flow-on benefits to your online store, including:

>> Increasing repeat purchases by encouraging shoppers to use points and rewards for shopping

>> Acquiring new customers

>> Growing social audiences by rewarding social follows, likes and shares

>> Incentivizing reviews and user-generated content

>> Accessing your loyalty program's customer insights and data

TIP

Here's a list of some apps in the Shopify app store that can help you segment out your highest CLTV customers:

>> **Reveal: Customer Data Platform** by Omniconvert SRL

>> **Everhort** by Lifetime Analytics

>> **Segments Analytics** by Tresl Inc.

RFM ANALYSIS

Going back to the example of Kate's online store (from the section 'Understanding the lifetime value of a customer'), if Kate wanted to get a little more advanced, she could segment her customers into different CLTV based segments, from low to high, rather than just working on the average CLTV. The way to do this is through Recency Frequency Monetary value modelling (or RFM analysis), which ranks customers based on the three RFM metrics (recency, frequency and monetary value) individually, and then combines their scores, with the highest scoring customer being the most valuable. The idea here is to then look after that customer and seek feedback from them when making key decisions, such as developing new products.

On the flipside, you can identify the infrequent, or low-value, customers and try to engage them into shopping more frequently with you. Glew is a great program that takes the calculator out of your hands here, and provides you with segments of customers based on CLTV.

When you know who your top customers are, the key is to treat them like VIPs!

Glew is a great app for when you're a little bigger (see the nearby sidebar 'RFM analysis'), as it spits out a variety of customer segments that you'll be able to use in your marketing, but if you're new to ecommerce then CLTV is probably enough to get you started.

REMEMBER

In business, there's something called the Pareto Principle, which means that 80 per cent of results come from 20 per cent of actions. In this case, it's often true that 80 per cent of your sales come from 20 per cent of your customers. As well as finding your CLTV, try and segment your customers to find the group with the highest CLTV — and never, ever let them go.

Loyalty, referral programs and Shopify

Shopify has some great customer loyalty apps in the Shopify App Store, but it's important to choose the right ones for your business. It's important to understand what drives and motivates your customers to purchase, so I'd recommend asking your customers what drives loyalty for them. Typical loyalty and referral programs offer rewards in the form of accumulated points that can be exchanged for discounts, and I have seen programs like this improve key metrics, particularly purchase frequency.

In my experience, members of a good loyalty or referral program do have a higher CLTV than average customers. In the following sections, I look at some of the major loyalty and referral programs that you can integrate with your Shopify store.

LoyaltyLion

LoyaltyLion is one of the more popular loyalty and referral applications used by Shopify merchants. It has a broad suite of features, including rewards in the form of:

>> Discounted/free shipping

>> Percentage/money off vouchers

>> Early access to VIP sales

>> Free products

>> Custom rewards

LoyaltyLion can also reward customers across a variety of actions, including:

>> Purchases

>> Sign-ups

>> Site visits

>> Reviews

>> Referrals/refer-a-friend

>> Social follows, likes and tags

>> Birthday rewards

What I like most about LoyaltyLion is that it integrates with a lot of my favorite Shopify third-party apps, like Okendo (a review platform) and Klaviyo (an email marketing platform). I also like that it comes with a free plan, which is great for new online retailers.

LoyaltyLion has good customer support to help you during the *onboarding phase* (which is what a lot of tech-type companies will call the phase where you're getting up and running), when they can help you optimize your loyalty programs post-launch.

TIP

You may need a developer to use LoyaltyLion to its full extent, including extracting more from the look and feel of your store (your loyalty program will have its own page on your website, so you'll want to design it to fit in with the rest of your theme); however, you can certainly get started without needing one.

ReferralCandy

ReferralCandy is another widely used referral program app on the Shopify App Store, with over 1,000 reviews. I like ReferralCandy's look and feel, and it's important that any of these third-party apps don't look tacky when they sit on your site — they have to fit seamlessly into the style of your online store. There's no free plan unfortunately, although you can trial it for free for 30 days.

ReferralCandy is probably sneaking into affiliate marketing territory, which I touch on in Chapter 17, as it offers cash payments for successful referrals to your business.

ReferralCandy's suite of products isn't as extensive as LoyaltyLion's, but I think it's a good tool for some aggressive customer acquisition — although if you're going to give cash discounts, or cash back, this can become a slippery slope. As always, make sure your profit margins allow for it.

Yotpo Loyalty

Formerly known as Swell, if you've decided to trial Yotpo for your reviews, it might make sense to add on Yotpo Loyalty. Yotpo Loyalty has a free plan, through which you can offer 14 different kinds of loyalty campaigns, including reward pop-ups, birthday rewards and points for spend. It integrates well with Shopify and can be found in the Shopify App Store, and it also integrates with a lot of the other Shopify apps that go hand in hand, such as Klaviyo and, obviously, the Yotpo reviews platform.

TIP

Visit yotpodemostore.myshopify.com to find a nice demo store that shows off Yotpo's features.

Utilizing User-Generated Content

User-generated content is content produced by real-life customers that brands can use to promote their business or products.

User-generated content comes in a variety of formats, but generally refers specifically to media provided by customers, such as product reviews that include a photo of the customer using the product. User-generated content can be collected when requesting reviews, such as the way Okendo allows you to provide incentives for customers to leave a photo or video review, or through a loyalty program that offers points or rewards for content or simply requests that users provide content to be shared across your business.

According to research from TurnTo Networks, user-generated content tops marketing tactic options by influencing 90 per cent of shoppers' purchasing decisions, outranking search engines (87 per cent) and email (97 per cent). An impressive 63 per cent of people surveyed responded that user-generated content provides a more authentic shopping experience — and it's hard to argue with that, given the content is produced by actual customers, not models in a studio.

You only have to turn back time a decade or two to remember early forms of user-generated content on TV, through programs such as *Funniest Home Videos*. These days, think about YouTube, Snapchat, TikTok and just about every other social media platform under the sun, as well as the emergence of reality TV — they thrive on people's fascination with each other. People have an insatiable appetite to see what other real people are doing, wearing, saying or thinking, and examples are everywhere.

Brands are adopting user-generated content more and more, and I for one am thankful because user-generated content has lowered the barriers for ecommerce start-ups, like yours, to gain traction against traditional online retailers with bigger budgets. For next to nothing, a smart ecommerce operator can fill their boots with content.

Seeking user-generated content should be one of the key focuses of your post-purchase activity, for two key reasons:

1. To help other shoppers in their decision-making process

2. To provide your business with marketing content

A happy customer is a marketing tool (I talk more about marketing in Part 5), and your customers can be used to grow your business. Here are the top ways you can use user-generated content in your new online store:

>> **Use the content:** It sounds obvious, but when a customer leaves you a review with a great image, use it. Platforms like Okendo allow you to collect reviews and turn them into advertising.

Other platforms like Foursixty can grab user-generated content from your social platforms and bring it into your website, linking it to the relevant product page on your website. You can find Foursixty in the Shopify App Store.

- » **Monetize the content:** When a user posts content on social media, you can make that content shoppable, so that if someone browsing it likes it, they can click through to your product page and buy it. Foursixty is again my preference for this.

- » **Utilize user-generated content to grow your social media channels:** When you're stuck for content for your social media channels, user-generated content is a great, authentic option that often gets good engagement (likes, comments and interactions). Use your social media channels to grow your library of user-generated content through competitions or giveaways. With the growing popularity across social media, and ecommerce, of video, it might be a clever idea to launch a contest to find the best user-generated video content.

EXAMPLE

Imagine you're selling monogrammed leather wallets, which allow your customers to get their initials stamped on their wallet. To gather user-generated content through your social media channels, ask followers to post a photo of the most interesting location they've taken their wallet to. For example, a customer might take a photo of their wallet sitting on the table of a café outside of the Eiffel Tower in Paris. The photo with the coolest location, or the most likes or comments, wins a $500 gift voucher, or something similar. Create a special hashtag for the entrants, and collect the content that is created, reposting it across your channels, and using it (with permission) on your website through Foursixty.

- » **Mine the data:** This also applies for customer reviews. You need to be reading your customer reviews and categorizing the problems. I suggest a weekly KPI that tallies negative reviews, and puts them into categories: for example, Quality Issue, Tracking Issue and Returns Issue. I also like to have a weekly KPI that monitors reviews across all the major review platforms, tallying the average rating and making sure it doesn't decrease. In terms of social media user-generated content, it's a matter of analyzing what products customers are posting about, and the engagement levels of certain customers, who may end up becoming influencers.

TIP

I'd encourage you to spend as much time obtaining user-generated content (and reviews) as possible, right away. That may even start with family and friends who use your product before you launch your website, so that you can use the content and reviews on your site at launch.

If you aren't starting out with a loyalty program, at least foster loyalty by treating your customers well, particularly those with a high CLTV — at the very least know who your VIP customers are. The chances are you won't have the marketing budget of your better-known competitors, so use the great equalizer — user-generated content. It's free, it's real, and it provides a large catalogue of images for you to use, with permission.

I caution you against launching your online store without at least a loyalty program or user-generated content on your site. If I had to choose one, I would go for user-generated content as your first priority as it's likely to have a greater impact on sales, in the shortest space of time, and can save you money on costly photo shoots.

TIP

Engage with the customer in every way you can. Every time you communicate with a customer, you are doing business with them, and people want to engage with the brands they do business with. Try and set yourself a target of obtaining a certain number of user-generated content pieces per week, and another goal of replying to every single public comment or review that your brand receives. It's free, and it pays off in the long run by fostering trust and loyalty.

Customer Reports: Loyal and At-risk Customers

The Pareto Principle in business refers to 80 per cent of your results coming from 20 per cent of your actions, and you see this time and time again, whether in revenue from your bestselling products or from your top customers. It's not unusual to see 80 per cent of an online store's revenue come from 20 per cent of its loyal customers.

By the same token, it's good to get on the front foot and spot any customers that your store might be about to lose (also known in Shopify as *at-risk* customers). Once a customer has stopped shopping with you, they're usually known as a *defector*.

TIP

In Chapter 16 I look at email marketing, which is one of the tools that you can use to bring back customers who no longer shop with you. Most good email marketing platforms, such as Klaviyo, offer an out-of-the-box 'win-back' segment, which automates emails to customers who haven't shopped in a certain time period.

In the following sections I show you how to use and customize customer reports in Shopify to gain insights into who your best customers are and who might be an at-risk customer.

Using customer reports in Shopify

If your store is on the Shopify, Advanced Shopify or Shopify Plus plan, then you have access to some useful reports about your customers. Using the reports listed below, you can find insights into your customers' purchase patterns, including their average order count, whether they're at risk of leaving you as a customer, or how much they're predicted to spend in the future. Using that information, you can take certain actions to give a more personal service to these customers:

>> Customers over time

>> First-time vs returning customer sales

>> Customers by location

>> Returning customers

>> One-time customers

If your store is on the Advanced Shopify or Shopify Plus plan, then you also have access to reports that identify:

>> At-risk customers

>> Loyal customers

TECHNICAL STUFF

Reports may not show activity from the past 12 hours, although the First-time vs Returning Customer Sales report is up to date to within a few seconds and can be refreshed constantly.

Customer reports are limited to 250,000 customers. If you have more customers than that, give yourself a pat on the back — you're doing fine. You can, however, export all your customer details from the Customers page in your Shopify admin, in case you want to use your own reporting system (perhaps in Google Sheets or Excel), upload customer data into email marketing campaigns, or create Facebook audiences (I talk more about Facebook and email marketing in chapters 16 and 17).

REMEMBER

Even if you're using a selected time frame to view reports, take note that the data in the reports will be based on the customer's entire order history. For example, if you retrospectively look at a customer report for a previous month, and a new customer who placed an order in that month has since placed an order in a subsequent month, they will be classified as a repeat customer, as Shopify is taking into consideration their entire order history.

To get started with customer reports, start by navigating to the reports section of your Shopify admin:

1. **From your Shopify admin, go to Analytics → Reports.**

2. **In the Customers section, click on the report that you want to see.**

The following sections run through the customer report options you can utilize in Shopify.

Customers Over Time

The Customers Over Time report shows how many customers overall have placed orders with your store since you started it.

You can select a unit of time in the Group By drop-down menu, located under the report title (see Figure 8-1), to control how the data is grouped. For short periods of time (say one month's worth of data), I tend to group by day, and for longer periods of time I tend to look at the data grouped by week or month.

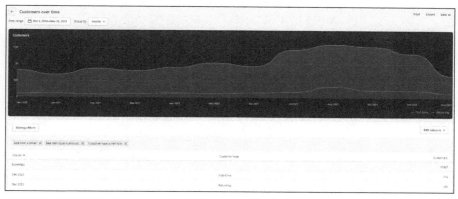

FIGURE 8-1:
The Customers Over Time report.

TIP

Checking by hour is also useful in determining when to send marketing campaigns or when to staff your customer service channels, such as phones or live chat.

The report shows both first-time and returning customers for each time unit selected. A *first-time* customer is a customer who has placed their first order with your store, and a *returning* customer is a customer who has placed an order, and whose order history already includes at least one order.

For each time unit, you can see the following data:

TECHNICAL STUFF

>> The number of new (first-time) customers who placed an order during that time

In ecommerce, customers who are placed into groups or segmented in this fashion are often referred to as *cohorts*.

>> The number of returning customers who placed an order during that time

This report is useful for keeping an eye on the growth of both new and existing customers. As online stores seek to grow, sometimes existing customer can be forgotten, so it's important to see the returning customer number growing each month — it's a good health check for your business's longevity.

First-time Vs Returning Customer Sales

The First-time Vs Returning Customer Sales report shows the value of orders placed by first-time and returning customers.

You can click on Group By under the report title to select the time unit that you want to view the total sales by in the graph: Hour, Day, Week, Month, Quarter, Year, Hour of Day, Day of Week or Month of Year. The results in the report are then grouped according to the time unit selected.

The report table again shows two rows for each time unit when there are both types of customer: one for first-time customers, and one for returning customers. The main difference between this report and the Customers Over Time report is that this report shows order quantity and sales figures, whereas the other one tallies the actual customer numbers.

For each time unit, you can see the following data:

>> The number of orders placed by each group of customers

>> The value of orders (total sales) placed by each group of customers

It's a good idea to check this report from time to time to make sure you're growing your revenue from returning customers, and not just focusing on acquiring new ones.

Customers by Location

The Customers by Location report shows data for new customers organized by their geographical location, according to their default address in your Shopify admin.

For each geographical region, you see:

>> The number of new customers who placed their first order during the selected time frame

>> The total number of orders that those customers have placed since their first order

>> The total amount that they have spent, including taxes, discounts, shipping and any refunds

REMEMBER

The Orders to Date and Total Spent to Date totals are based on the entire order history of the new customers in the report, not only the orders that were placed during the selected time frame.

This report is useful to track international sales, including for those wanting an idea on which countries to target in their marketing.

Returning Customers

The Returning Customers report shows data about all your customers whose order history includes two or more orders. Remember your CLTV calculations (refer to the earlier section, 'Understanding the lifetime value of a customer') when you read through this report — the key metrics are found here.

You can see the following details for each customer:

>> Their name

>> Their email address

>> Whether they agreed to accept marketing when they placed their most recent order

>> The date of their first order

>> The date of their most recent order

>> The number of orders that they have placed

>> Their average order value

>> The total amount that they have spent, including taxes, discounts, shipping and any refunds

You can use this report to send emails to existing customers (as long as they have opted in to receive marketing, which you can see in the Accepts Marketing column in Figure 8-2 — Yes indicates they have signed up to receive your marketing; No indicates they would not like to receive your marketing). For example, you might email them special offers or thank you emails, or use the list to create ads in Facebook.

FIGURE 8-2:
The Returning
Customers
report.

One-time Customers

The One-time Customers report shows data about all your customers whose order history includes only one order. These are the customers you should be focused on bringing back.

You can see the following details for each customer:

>> Their name

>> Their email address

>> Whether they agreed to accept marketing when they placed their most recent order

>> The date of their first order

>> The number of orders that they have placed (that is, one)

>> The value of their order, including taxes, discounts, shipping and any refunds

REMEMBER

It's cheaper to retain a customer than it is to acquire one. Don't underestimate the value of a personal phone call to one-time customers to thank them for their business and ask if there's anything you can do to help them with their next purchase.

At-risk Customers

REMEMBER

You can only access the At-risk Customers report if your store is on the Advanced Shopify or Shopify Plus plan.

Shopify uses a machine learning model to determine the likelihood that a customer will return to purchase an item in the next 90 days, which determines whether or not a customer is 'at-risk'. A customer is at-risk if they haven't ordered from your store in a while and you don't anticipate that they will return to place another order.

In the report, you can see the following details for each customer:

>> Their name

>> Their email address

>> Whether they agreed to accept marketing when they placed their most recent order

>> The date of their first order

>> The date of their most recent order

>> The number of orders that they have placed

>> Their average order value

>> The total amount that they have spent, including taxes, discounts, shipping and any refunds

You can use this list to email customers with a special offer or promotion, to bring them back from the edge of disappearing as a customer. In Chapter 16, I look at email marketing, so you may want to refer back to this report when I take you through how to set up email marketing.

Loyal Customers

You only have access to the Loyal Customers report if your store is on the Advanced Shopify or Shopify Plus plans.

A customer is loyal if they're estimated to have a high probability of returning to place another order with your store, and they've placed more orders than the average customer.

You can see the following details for each customer in the Loyal Customers report:

>> Their name

>> Their email address

>> Whether they agreed to accept marketing when they placed their most recent order

- » The date of their first order

- » The date of their most recent order

- » The number of orders that they have placed

- » Their average order value

- » The total amount that they have spent, including taxes, discounts, shipping and any refunds

Your loyal customers are the customers you want to keep as happy as possible, and it's great to reward them. You can use this report to phone or email customers to thank them for their business, or add them to a VIP marketing list if they have opted to receive marketing from you. It's also useful to check this list when you're handling customer service enquiries so you can see if the customer is a big spender and in need of extra attention.

TIP

Don't underestimate the impact of small tokens of appreciation to loyal customers, and don't take them for granted — your competitors will be doing everything they can to win them over! (Chapter 10 has some tips on ways to wow your customers.)

Customizing your customer reports

If your store is on the Advanced Shopify or Shopify Plus plan, then you can use the filtering and editing features to customize the reports about your customers. This is useful when you're trying to sort through certain groups of customers.

EXAMPLE

As an example, you may want to email all your at-risk customers who have subscribed to your newsletter, so you navigate to the At-risk Customers report and select Manage Filters in the top-left corner. In the dialogue box that appears, you see a filter that says, 'Is At Risk', with a grey box under it that says, 'Is Yes' (see Figure 8-3). Under that you can add a new filter by clicking on the Add Filter box, then selecting Accepts Marketing in the Select Filter field, then typing Yes in the search field. Click on the green Apply Filters button in the bottom-right corner of the dialogue box and all your at-risk customers who have opted to receive your marketing will appear — which is great for Chapter 16, when I show you how to send marketing emails.

You'll find the Manage Filters option in the same spot for all your Shopify reports.

Table 8-1 shows some of the filters and columns that you can use to customize your reports.

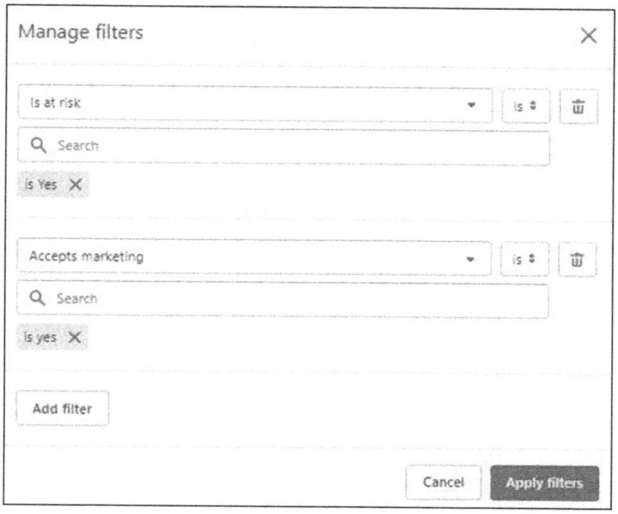

Source: Shopify

FIGURE 8-3:
Filtering your
reports to identify
at-risk customers.

TABLE 8-1 **Shopify Report Filters and Columns**

Filters you can adjust in your customer reports	
Customer email	The email address associated with a customer.
Customer name	The first and last names of a customer.
Customer attributes	**Accepts marketing:** Whether customers agreed to accept marketing when they placed their most recent order.
	Is one-time: Customers whose order history includes only one order.
	Is returning: Customers whose order history includes more than one order.
Customer segment	**Is at risk:** Customers who are a repeat customer and estimated to have a medium probability of returning, but who have not placed an order in a while.
	Is dormant: Customers who have a low probability of returning to make another purchase.
	Is loyal: Repeat customers who are estimated to have a high probability of returning, and have placed more orders than the average customer.
	Is promising: Customers who are estimated to have a high probability of returning and becoming a loyal customer.
Location	The city, country and region of customers, based on their default address in your Shopify admin.

(continued)

TABLE 8-1 *(continued)*

Filters you can adjust in your customer reports	
Columns you can utilize in your customer reports	
Customer email	The email address associated with a customer.
Customer name	The first and last names of a customer.
Customers	The total number of first-time and repeat customers who placed an order during the selected timeframe.
Customer attributes	**Accepts marketing:** Whether customers agreed to accept marketing when they placed their most recent order.
	Is one-time: Customers whose order history includes one order.
	Is returning: Customers whose order history includes more than one order.
Customer segment	**Is at risk:** Customers who are a repeat customer and estimated to have a medium probability of returning, but who have not placed an order in a while.
	Is dormant: Customers who have a low probability of returning to make another purchase.
	Is loyal: Repeat customers who are estimated to have a high probability of returning, and have placed more orders than the average customer.
	Is promising: Customers who are estimated to have a high probability of returning and becoming a loyal customer.
Location	The city, country and region of customers, based on their default address in your Shopify admin.
Order	**First order:** The date of a customer's first order.
	Last order: The date of a customer's last order.
	Average order value: The average value of customers' orders since their first order. It's calculated by dividing the total value of new customers' orders by the total number of new customers' orders. The total order value includes taxes and shipping, and is before refunds. The total number of orders does not include orders that consist only of gift cards.
	Total spent to date: The total amount that a customer has spent, including taxes, discounts, shipping, and any refunds. For example, let's suppose a customer ordered two $50 items from your store, paid no tax, received 10 per cent off one of the items, spent $10 in shipping, and received a $7 refund for a shipping delay. In this example, the Total spent to date is 50 + 45 + 10 − 7 = $98.
	Orders to date: The total number of new customers' orders since their first order.
Time	The day, month and week of the order.

Being able to play around with filters in reports is going to help you find out more about your customers, such as who's at-risk, who's loyal, how much they spend and more. As you discover more about marketing in ecommerce, you'll realize the value of segmentation — grouping together similar customers and setting up marketing automations for them, such as the marketing emails I cover in Chapter 16.

TIP

Leveraging Shopify's customer reports is something I do almost every day. It's essential that as a store owner, you get familiar with your customers, both loyal and at-risk. In this spirit of personalization, treating your VIPs well is a great place to start. Of course there are clever marketing tools that you can use to automate some of this, but I'm a big fan of personal service, and as such I'm an advocate of surprise and delight strategies, which are a great, old-fashioned way to give your customers a more personal experience (for more on these, turn to Chapter 10).

Chapter 9

Understanding the User Experience

The user is the person using your website — in other words, the shopper or hopeful customer. When a user lands on your website, there's a gap that both you and your customer are trying to fill, a common ground where you're both hopeful of landing. Your customer wants to find something to buy from your site, and you want them to find something to buy from your site. An optimal user experience brings those two together as smoothly as possible, with as few clicks as necessary.

Online stores are not 'set and forget' type businesses, despite what those ads on YouTube tell you — they're proper businesses that need nurturing and constant attention. Think of your online store as a flower — it needs to be watered, fed and maintained to fully blossom. User experience does these things, and more, because it deals with the people interacting with your digital product — your website.

User experience (often abbreviated to UX) is something we have had a few sneaky looks at within the book already, but it's a topic that deserves its own chapter. (As a reminder, customer experience — also known as CX — deals with the user's entire journey within your online business, from the point that they land on your website to the point where they receive delivery of their order, whereas UX is about the experience of using your website specifically. Chapter 7 explores customer experience in detail.)

It's hard to make sales without the user, so you need to spend time analyzing them — asking them questions, as well as showing them different versions of your website — to see which version of your store they engage with the most. In this chapter I'm going to introduce you to some user experience fundamentals, including user research, AB testing and observing the user — all of which can be achieved using Shopify.

Understanding the Basics of a Good User Experience

User experience is all about the on-site experience — how a user interacts with your website. You want it to be fast and frictionless, and you want to keep the customer moving towards the checkout.

REMEMBER

Specifically, user experience focuses on the design and navigation of the website — the elimination of friction and the ease of use for the website visitor — and ultimately plays a large part in the overall layout of the website, and therefore impacts key metrics like conversion rate and cart abandonment. Your website's users can be a fickle bunch, and even great websites can have a bounce rate of greater than 40 per cent, so you need to know where your users are dropping off, and therefore which pages of your website require further work.

TECHNICAL STUFF

A user experience hire is called — surprise! — a user experience (or UX) specialist (or something along those lines). You often find these people mapping out the various journeys a user takes while on your website, identifying problems and blockers, and working on designs to improve them, with those designs then going to the developers to implement. You're unlikely to be hiring a UX specialist in your early days, and I aim to give you plenty of tips as to how you can take a DIY approach to optimizing user experience.

UX specialists also run (or suggest) AB tests, as well as create designs for AB tests. AB testing is one of, if not the best way to increase conversion rates in ecommerce, and I cover this in more detail later in this chapter in the section 'Implementing AB Testing'.

Getting to know how users behave

Methods to identify problems on your website include surveys that ask specific or open-ended questions, such as: 'What can we do better?' However, by far the most fun way of gaining user experience data is through watching screen recordings of users navigating your website, using applications like Hotjar or Lucky Orange (which are both available in the Shopify App Store).

These recordings can be set to have various parameters or triggers as to when they will start recording, and you can filter the recordings and view them using a range of useful filters, including 'Which Exit Page'. For example, if I find that my product pages have a high bounce rate, I can sit and watch recordings of users who abandon the website at the product page to see if I can identify where the friction occurred. In a recent, real-life example, I could see that the product page was simply taking too long to load — and users were leaving the page in droves.

TIP

Recordings are legal — they don't display any sensitive information or anything outside of your website, and they are a great way for you to get to know your website better. Everyone should use recordings, not just UX specialists, as I guarantee no matter how experienced you are, you'll discover something about your website that you can improve.

Conducting user research is a fantastic way to get to know your customers and their needs. Turn to the later section 'Conducting user research' to discover some helpful tools you can use to get to know the visitors to your online store.

Considering the theory

Creating a good user experience incorporates marketing, research, the digital product and psychology, with the end goal being to design a user experience on your website that engages the customer, informs them of the problem you're trying to solve, and gets them into your checkout and beyond. If you're an online seller you're competing against bricks and mortar, and even digitally against marketplaces and other places your potential customers can go and shop. You need to give your customers a reason to shop with you, and part of that reason has to be the experience — it can't just be the product and the price.

When it comes to online store design, I often refer to Louis Rosenfeld and Peter Morville, who created the three circles of information architecture model. Although specifically designed for information architecture, it's useful for explaining user experience when you set up your menus and site navigation, and serves as a great reference point whenever you're looking to create a new feature or design on your website — even more so when you're starting from scratch.

Rosenfeld and Morville defined the key points in each of the three circles (which they call the *information ecology*) as:

>> **Users:** Audience, tasks, needs, information-seeking behavior, experience

>> **Context:** Business goals, politics, technology, funding, culture, resources, constraints

>> **Content:** Content objectives, volume, governance and ownership, funding, culture

**TECHNICAL
STUFF**

THE USER EXPERIENCE HONEYCOMB

To further illustrate the need to create a user experience that provides value to the user, Peter Morville also created the 'user experience honeycomb', where six key elements of customer experience all contribute to creating a valuable user experience. In the user experience honeycomb, 'valuable' sits at the center, surrounded by these six points.

He sums up the six points in what I consider to be the clearest outline of what good user experience aims to achieve if it wants to add value:

- **Useful:** Your content needs to be original and fulfill a need.

- **Usable:** Your site needs to be easy to use.

- **Desirable:** Your image, identity, brand and other design elements need to evoke emotion and appreciation.

- **Findable:** Your content needs to be navigable and locatable on-site and off-site.

- **Accessible:** Your content needs to be accessible to people with disabilities.

- **Credible:** Your users need to trust and believe what you tell them.

When you consider all of the bells and whistles that a website can have and some of the incredible technical advancements over time, it's important to remember that good user experience principles are about providing an easy to use, simple experience for the customer. A good user experience comes before worrying about some of the tech that exists around ecommerce, like augmented reality or artificial intelligence.

The three circles cross over, like a Venn diagram, with information architecture — or in this case, user experience — at the center of the circles. Defined simply, user experience needs to factor in these three key components. To refine it further, your online store layout, and design, need to take into consideration the *user* first, and how smooth the experience of navigating your website is, followed by your business goals (the *context*) — for example, is the purpose of the function you are designing to get sales, to get newsletter sign-ups or to provide information (such as a Shipping page)? Finally, the *content*, which includes the culture and ideology of the brand, but also ensures the content fits in with the user and context components. Content that stands alone, in its own bubble, serves no purpose. Content needs to be useful and simple, and to lead the user to perform the desired action.

Improving Your User Experience

Your navigation and information architecture are key factors in determining whether or not your website is conducive to a good user experience, but the reality is you'll be constantly creating, editing and changing content within your website.

You're unlikely to be hiring a UX specialist at this stage of your ecommerce career, and that's okay, because the good news is there are plenty of basic user experience principles that you can apply yourself, along with some useful tools that Shopify can help you with.

REMEMBER

Managing your user experience is a never-ending task, and you should always be seeking to improve your user's experience on your website.

You can do certain things every day to ensure your store is not leaking users. Small improvements across your online store can add up over a year to bring your business forward in leaps and bounds, as Tom O'Neil explains in his book *The 1% Principle*.

O'Neil's 1% principle is based on the idea that if you do just a little more than you normally would, every single day of the year, you're left with a significantly greater result over the course of the year than if you didn't otherwise. So although the 1% takes relatively little effort each day, the result over the course of the year is significant.

TIP

Certain aspects of user experience are non-negotiable for a successful online store. At this point, I suggest going back through your website's design (refer to chapters 4 and 5) to ensure that you have considered user experience fully, and if you haven't already got some of the basics, such as a fast site or a search function, it's a good idea to pick this low-hanging fruit now by making any changes you require so that you maximize your conversion rate. If you make improvements to your website every single day, one day you might wake up and realize you're running a successful ecommerce store!

In the following sections, I share some user experience essentials that will hold you in good stead for the entirety of your ecommerce journey.

Conducting user research

Interviewing, surveying and recording customers and users, and generally finding ways to monitor their behavior while on your site to find pain points and information about them or potential customers, is incredibly value and not that hard to do. In my opinion, user research never ends as there are always improvements to be found.

The outcome of user research is to take the data and apply it to the design and function of your store. You'll also be able to find out other useful bits of information when doing user research, particularly around brand perception.

As for which method to use in gathering data, aim for a range of techniques to give you a good mix of attitude and behavioral research techniques, because what people *say* they do, and what they *actually* do, are often two very different things.

On the behavioral side, you've got tools like Shopify's Analytics page (within your Shopify admin) and Google Analytics to provide the data, and Hotjar or Lucky Orange to help you observe the user; and on the attitude side you have surveys and focus groups you can use to ask questions around attitudes, such as, 'What did you think of the website overall?' There's definitely a place for both. I encourage user research as often as possible, because research and development (R&D) is an age-old, proven concept.

R&D comes in the form of research first, development second — what good is guessing what to develop when the answers are so easy to discover from your site's users?

As you get bigger, you may consider AB testing (for more on this, turn to the later section 'Implementing AB Testing'), but there's nothing stopping you from commencing some user research from day one. You're never too small to start optimizing your website.

Here, I highlight some methods and tools you can use to gather research so you better understand your users and their requirements.

Analytics tools

Analytics in ecommerce typically refers to different forms of data dashboards that show an online retailer how their visitors and customers are behaving on their site.

Shopify merchants use two main analytics platforms:

>> Shopify Analytics (the Analytics section of your admin page)

>> Google Analytics (or GA as it's sometimes known)

Google Analytics dives a little deeper into the behaviors of visitors on your site, and while used primarily by marketing teams to attribute sales to marketing channels, it's also an incredibly valuable user experience tool. Google Analytics can give you key performance metrics such as bounce rate, but you'll be able to check bounce rate at a page level, which is useful for showing you which pages aren't performing and may need revision. It also shows you your highest and lowest sales-converting pages. GA will also show you page view data, including which pages are being viewed the most, and which pages people tend to exit on, and on what device the user is browsing on. All pretty good insights for someone looking to improve their website.

However, Shopify's analytics are excellent as well, and you don't need to install anything — it's already inside your Shopify admin (Figure 9-1 shows the analytics and reports you get with each Shopify plan).

REMEMBER

To access your Analytics dashboard, go to your Shopify admin, click on Analytics in the left-hand menu, and then click on Dashboards from the drop-down menu that appears. You're taken to the Overview dashboard, which provides a whole bunch of useful insights into your store's performance.

The Overview dashboard shows sales figures, orders and online store visitor data. You can quickly see how your store is performing, and easily adjust date ranges to see how your store is (hopefully!) growing.

Some of my favorite things about the Overview dashboard include:

>> You can check your recent sales and compare them to a previous time period — for example, were your sales this month higher than last month?

>> You can monitor the number of visits your store is receiving.

>> You can track your average order value (AOV).

Analytics and reports (for details, click the links)	Shopify Lite	Basic Shopify	Shopify	Advanced Shopify	Shopify Plus
Overview dashboard	✓	✓	✓	✓	✓
Finances reports (including taxes and payments)	✓	✓	✓	✓	✓
Product analytics	✓	✓	✓	✓	✓
Live View	-	✓	✓	✓	✓
Acquisition reports	-	✓	✓	✓	✓
Inventory reports	-	✓ (4 of 5)	✓	✓	✓
Behavior reports	-	✓ (5 of 6)	✓	✓	✓
Marketing reports	-	✓ (1 of 5)	✓	✓	✓
Order reports	-	-	✓	✓	✓
Sales reports	-	-	✓	✓	✓
Retail sales reports	-	-	✓	✓	✓
Profit reports	-	-	✓	✓	✓
Customers reports	-	-	✓ (5 of 7)	✓	✓
Custom reports	-	-	-	✓	✓

FIGURE 9-1: The Shopify Analytics reports available for your Shopify plan.

Source: Shopify

>> You can see where your visitors are coming from — by region or by social media source.

>> You can check your conversion rate (the rate that site visitors go on to purchase from your store).

The Overview dashboard is a place where Shopify merchants like to dwell. It shows the most valuable metrics that give you insight into the performance of your store and the behavior of your customers. The metrics are shown in numeric format and also as graphs where appropriate. For all the metrics, the percentage change from the previous date range can also be shown; for example, if your online store's sales have grown by 20 per cent versus the previous period.

TIP

When you click on Analytics in your Shopify admin, you also see a drop-down menu option called Live View — this shows you how many visitors are on your store right now, and where they're from! You also get a snapshot of your store's performance that day. Figure 9-2 shows the Live View page.

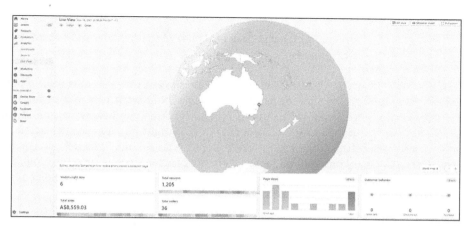

FIGURE 9-2:
The Live View
page.

The other option from the Analytics drop-down menu is Reports. Shopify has plenty of reports across just about every aspect of your store. It's a good idea to familiarize yourself with some of the reports, as they can be useful to help you see what's selling, how your marketing is performing and all sorts of other data.

TECHNICAL STUFF

To sign up to Google Analytics, visit `marketingplatform.google.com/about/ analytics`. You're likely to need a developer to install Google Analytics, who you can find in the Shopify Experts marketplace (`experts.shopify.com`).

Observation and usability tests

In the early days, you may not have that many visitors to your site, but observing them is a great way to find improvements. You can watch session recordings of what your visitors do using programs such as Hotjar and Lucky Orange.

TIP

Both of these platforms can also show you heatmaps of your store, which shows where visitors are clicking and scrolling, and how far down the page they scroll. You may find, for example, that some of your best products aren't being seen because visitors are exiting the page before they scroll that far down.

Here's a few ways you can get to know how users behave when visiting your online store to ensure you're staying ahead of their needs.

SURVEYS

I love a good survey. R&D is essential for building anything good, in my opinion. That goes for the products you sell, the people you hire and the digital product you sell on — that is, your website. The research part of R&D can come in the form of surveys, which can then be analyzed to provide insights into the changes you may need to make.

When creating surveys, the key is to ask the right questions. So rather than asking generic questions, try and think about what you're wanting to achieve with the question. For example, in user research you may want to find out why people are abandoning the checkout, so you might pop up a survey when someone exits the checkout page, but instead of broadly asking, 'Why are you leaving?', which opens up non-digital, product-related issues such as price or product, you want to ask about the user experience. So, you might instead ask, 'Did you face any challenges when using our website?'

You then want to collate the responses and look for themes that need work, such as 'site speed too slow'. This then forms the basis of the user experience projects that you need to focus on.

TIP

Surveys can be easily added to your Shopify store. Lucky Orange has a survey component, or you could try the Zigpoll Customer Surveys app.

USER (OR FOCUS) GROUPS

These groups involve structured interviews with small groups of your website's users that seek to uncover how your users feel about your website. Remember, in the context of user experience, these focus groups can uncover how site visitors feel about the usability of your website overall. I like this method because it's free, and no matter how small you are, you should be able to get a group of family and friends together to form feedback on your website. Focus groups are an underrated tool that even larger online retailers ignore.

USER INTERVIEWS

Much like focus groups, one-on-one interviews can be a meaningful and cheap way to gather information. Start with family and friends, and remember to look for common themes, such as site speed or image quality, so you can go away with an action plan.

Monitoring and maintaining your page speed

According to a 2017 Think with Google article ('Find out how you stack up to new industry benchmarks for mobile page speed'), 53 per cent of mobile visitors leave a page that takes longer than three seconds to load. If your pages take longer than that to load, there's a good chance you are losing around half of your visitors!

The Shopify App Store has some apps to help increase your site's page speed, such as:

>> Booster: Page Speed Optimizer by Booster Apps

>> Page Speed Booster by RoarTheme

To check your page speed in Google Analytics, go to Behavior → Site Speed → Page Timings. Run any slow pages through Google's PageSpeed Insights page for tips on how to improve certain pages on your website (go to the web page pagespeed. web.dev).

Fixing broken links

Broken links can arise if the page you are directing people to has either moved or doesn't exist anymore. An error message will appear to inform your site visitors, which is definitely not conducive to a positive user experience!

Here are some helpful apps in the Shopify App Store that can detect and fix broken links for you:

>> Redirectify by Kelsey Judson

>> Broken Link SEO 404 Redirect by Giraffy

You can also find broken links using Google Analytics via the Behavior → Site Content → All Pages report. Search for the page title of your 404 page (that is, '404 Page Not Found') and select Page Title as your Primary Dimension in the top left-hand corner.

Running your own device analysis

Test your website speed and function on every device you can get your hands on. You may find the site is converting well on iPhone but poorly on an older model smartphone, or, worse still, it looks great on your desktop but horrible on your mobile.

As well as testing your site on different devices, remember to test it in as many different browsers (such as Google Chrome and Safari, among others) as you can in case you find one that isn't performing well. You can test this in Google Analytics by going to Audience → Technology → Browser & OS, or by using a third party such as BrowserStack (browserstack.com).

Optimizing your website's internal search

If you have a search function on your website (and you should), this is a gold mine of data. Not only can you use this information to research what products to source, but you can also see how well you're serving people what they're searching for.

The Shopify App Store has plenty of apps to help with this, including the one I usually use: Product Filter & Search by Boost Commerce.

You can also use more advanced platforms such as Nosto.com that tend to cover a broader range of personalization.

TECHNICAL STUFF

To find search terms in Google Analytics, navigate to Behavior → Site Search → Search Terms. Not only can you rank search terms from most popular to least popular, but if you look at the Time After Search in the reporting that appears you can see how long the customer stays on the site after searching for their product. If the time is short, you aren't showing the customers what they want, so you need to improve your search parameters.

TIP

Not sure which page to start working on? Start with the page with the highest traffic and lowest conversions, which you can find using Google Analytics.

Implementing AB Testing

AB testing is one of the biggest levers you have to improve your conversion rate at the lowest cost. It requires little to no marketing dollars, and little more than good ideas, a good testing framework and the ability to take action on the insights. What it does require though, is decent amounts of traffic, so you might need to wait until your traffic is a little higher before commencing AB testing.

So, what is AB testing, and how can you do it in your Shopify store? *AB testing*, also known as split testing, is essentially showing two different versions of a web page or features on a website to different segments of visitors, with the goal being to see which variation performs better. The main KPI of a successful AB test is usually conversion rate, but it can also be average order value (AOV), overall revenue or simply clicks.

EXAMPLE

Say you have an online shoe store, and you keep getting returns due to incorrect sizing. A UX specialist, or designer, might come up with an alternative sizing chart, which is then loaded into an AB test, so that half of the users see the current or 'control' version of the size chart (option A) and the other half see the new option (option B). After a period of time, when there is sufficient data to determine a winner, you can adopt the size chart resulting in the lowest return rate as the new normal.

In my opinion, AB testing is a must for any ecommerce business with significant traffic, and using Shopify it can be cheap and easy to get started. Let the data decide what you need to do with your online store — rather than making sweeping design changes, test them first to make sure your ideas deliver as they should.

Sometimes untested design changes go wrong and it's hard to know why. For instance, I've seen checkout page redesigns that look great but where sales tank and checkout abandonment soars, costing that business tens of thousands of dollars. Had that design been AB tested, the business would have seen that it was better to stick with the original design, also known as the *control*, as opposed to the *variant*. (You can also test more than one variant against the control.)

On the flip side, I have seen many AB tests deliver huge conversion rate increases, resulting in increased revenue, such as one displaying buy now pay later (BNPL) options on the homepage, above the fold (Chapter 4 explains this crucial web page real estate in more detail). Winning AB tests don't have to be huge projects, either, as small incremental improvements often achieve more growth than one or two big changes hitting the mark.

TIP

Keep an AB tests spreadsheet, where you log your ideas for AB tests. Work your way through them, taking note of the results in a comments field. Try not to have more than one AB test running at a time, in case the results get muddied.

When can I start running AB tests?

You may feel frustrated if you don't have enough traffic to AB test yet, because it sounds fun — and it is! But you need to wait until you've got enough traffic on your site, so if you're just getting started then you may have a little longer to wait. How much is enough? The answer is, enough to get a statistically significant outcome from the test, and generally, the more the merrier.

TECHNICAL STUFF

In the Shopify blog article 'The complete guide to AB testing', Shanelle Mullin references an AB test calculator from Evan Miller that estimates the sample size needed to run a successful AB test. Miller's calculator asks for your regular, or baseline, conversion rate, and the minimum detectable effect, which is the smallest acceptable improvement for the test to be a clear winner. A 15 per cent relative improvement in conversion rate is what is suggested, meaning you want your conversion rate to be lifted by greater than 15 per cent for the variant to be considered statistically significant — therefore, a win. Any improvement on conversion rate that has a relevant improvement of less than 15 per cent isn't worth it, or at least you can't be sure it's a clear winning test. To be clear, a relative improvement of 15 per cent on a 5 per cent conversion rate is not 20 per cent, it is 5.75 per cent. You're not talking about changing the conversion rate from 5 to 15; instead, you need to *improve* the conversion rate by 15 per cent.

So, if I'm running an online store with a conversion rate of 5 per cent and I want to detect if an AB test can deliver greater than a 15 per cent improvement on conversion rate, I need traffic of 13,533 during the AB test.

The length of the AB test is ideally a full business cycle — let's call it 30 days. This allows for various activities to be normalized — such as the general time it takes for a customer to browse, browse again and then purchase; or external factors, such as positive or negative press, and sale periods.

TIP

Miller's AB test sample size calculator can be found here: `evanmiller.org/ab-testing/sample-size.html`.

I've got the traffic, so how can I AB test in Shopify?

The big tools for AB testing are generally:

>> `VWO.com`

>> `Optimizely.com`

>> `Optimize.google.com`

These are probably the most widely used AB testing platforms, but you'll likely need some help from a developer to integrate them into your store. There are some third-party apps in the Shopify App Store that also may be worth a look, but given the importance of AB testing, and making the sure the results are accurate, I recommend going with one of these three.

REMEMBER

You can't run an AB test for forever and a day — until it reaches the right amount of traffic, you're polluting the test, as visitors may delete their cookies and come back to your website as a new user. But fortunately, you can take action in Shopify to improve your user experience while you're waiting for AB testing to become an option (check out the earlier section 'Improving Your User Experience' to find out more).

Chapter **10**

Getting Personal: Personalizing Your Website

Traditional retailers and anti-online shoppers used to say online retail would never work because you lose the personal touch found in stores through face-to-face contact with salespeople. In this chapter I'm going to show you how to curate your customers' experiences, making their shopping journey unique to them. I look at how to offer some personal, one-to-one experiences to regular visitors to your site, but I also consider how personalization techniques can increase the chances of a visitor becoming a customer.

Website personalization comes in many forms. In this chapter, I focus in particular on how to bring your customers closer to the products that you know they're interested in using machine learning, or artificial intelligence (AI).

Creating a Personalized Shopping Experience

In ecommerce, *personalization* is the practice of dynamically showing or curating content, such as products or offers, to specific targeted shoppers based on useful customer data, such as their previous shopping or browsing behavior, and the products they've purchased or viewed before. Personalization can range from changing the order your products are shown in on your collection pages based on what the visitor last viewed, to adding a layer of AI that takes into consideration the weather in your shopper's region (which can be useful, for example, if you're selling things like heaters or air conditioners, or even winter and summer clothing ranges).

EXAMPLE

Still not sure what personalization means? Picture walking into a clothing store, and the friendly sales assistant offers you a T-shirt that they promise will look great on you. You know it's hideous, but you politely pretend to consider it anyway, before meandering through the store to find what you're looking for. Now imagine that you walk into a store and a sales assistant appears at exactly the right moment, showing you five T-shirts that you absolutely love, in the right size. You buy two and stroll happily out of the store to get on with your day. This is something online retailers can offer their customers when they use data to show the right products to a shopper at the right time, which brings them closer to purchasing exactly what they want.

A well-executed personalization strategy is proven to increase conversion rates. How come? Research from marketing firm Epsilon.com indicates that 80 per cent of customers are likely to make a purchase when brands offer personalization, while Google (via Think with Google) claims that 90 per cent of leading marketers say personalization significantly contributes to profitability.

Although it's true that online retailers need to find ways to compete on a personal level with traditional bricks and mortar retail stores, it's now also true that online retailers need to find a way to make the overall customer experience special — and personalization tools offer a way to do that. Personalization brings the shopper closer to your checkout, in as few clicks as possible, by leading them down the path to purchase.

Another great reason to use personalization on your online store is to gather customer data. Customers are often willing to hand over useful data in order to get added value, which can arise in a multitude of ways, including:

>> Saving the customer time

>> Offering discounts at the right time

>> Displaying the right product

Almost every touchpoint on your website is an opportunity to gather behavioral data on prospective customers, from the product pages they look at to the collections they browse or the items they search for on your site.

REMEMBER

It can be confusing trying to work out the best ways to personalize your site, and the answer may be different depending on the product, industry or lifecycle stage of your business. Not all customers are the same, so you can't give them the same shopping experience.

One of the great benefits ecommerce retailers have is that they can showcase a huge range of products. They're not limited on space by the physical constraints of a shopfront or showroom — and because they don't pay per square meter, they're always able to expand. Yet, in a great paradox, too much choice can drive customers away — and online shoppers can be an impatient lot, bouncing off a site when they don't find what they're looking for within the first few pages. According to consultancy firm Accenture.com, 40 per cent of online shoppers have left one site and bought from another, simply because they have felt overwhelmed by too much product or content. The clever personalization tools I look at in this chapter help narrow your product range down to the products most likely to be purchased by specific shoppers.

TIP

I recommend using some form of personalization on your site from its earliest stages. If you're also carrying a large product range, personalization tools can help customers sift through your products as your site gets to know their preferences (using their previous browsing and purchasing data).

REMEMBER

Machine learning is the key to personalizing your online store. Machine learning is a form of AI. AI uses data and algorithms to learn the way humans perform functions — like their browsing and shopping behaviors on websites — and then develops a way to improve the process.

For example, an AI platform in ecommerce might learn that you keep browsing the same pair of blue jeans, so when you come back to the website, it may feel like those jeans are being shown to you quite a lot — and that's because they are. The AI on the website has determined that you keep looking at those jeans, and so it assumes that if it keeps showing you the jeans, you will eventually buy them — the AI is making it easier for you to purchase them too, because you don't have to dig through the whole catalogue again before you find them. In other words, it makes shopping more convenient, and more personal — hence the term personalization.

MAKING SENSE OF MACHINE LEARNING

Machine learning sounds like something out of *Terminator 2*, but it's far less scary. We depend on machine learning more than what most people think, and the reason we do is because machines can process data quickly, taking data from many sources and offering back meaningful insights in real time — for instance, showing an online shopper the items of most interest in an online store's product range. Performing tasks with this sort of speed and efficiency is simply not feasible for humans.

Outside of an ecommerce setting, an example of machine learning that results in a personalized service is Google Maps, or your navigator of choice. Not only will your map show you the route from A to B, it will also take into consideration the speed that you're travelling, providing you with a more accurate estimated time of arrival. For instance, I could be a slow walker, while my friend might be a faster walker, which makes our arrival times different, so we're offered a personalized time of arrival.

Inside of an ecommerce environment, personalization from machine learning is everywhere. If you visit a large online retailer, you may notice that over time their homepage starts showing you the products or brands that you looked at, and their email marketing might start to look the same. To extend the idea, imagine that these website homepages are filled with blank grey squares, waiting for the data they need to populate the pages with relevant content to appeal to an individual. It might sound like rocket science, but the logic is simple — put products in front of the people that are mostly likely to buy them, and they will buy more than if you did not.

It might sound complex, but you can easily use Shopify to apply forms of AI just like the biggest ecommerce brands. The nearby sidebar 'Making sense of machine learning' provides some additional examples that explain how helpful machine learning can be!

Tailoring Your Store to Suit Your Customers

If you think about the parts of your site where a customer might benefit from personalization by being served some form of curated, selective content, the obvious places that spring to mind are when they're searching for a product in the site search, when they're browsing collections or when they're reviewing product pages.

The good news is your Shopify store is already a hub of relevant data — every time a user visits your site, they're leaving behind valuable insights into how they prefer to shop, and it's those insights you can use to bring them back time and time again, and eventually snag them as a customer.

REMEMBER

The goal of your first foray into personalization is to use tools to predict what your customer will buy next. You don't have to reinvent the wheel, nor do you have to roll out personalization on an Amazon-esque scale in order to compete and gain loyal customers. In chapters 7, 8 and 9, I spoke about techniques to increase customer loyalty and optimize your store for a great user experience — personalization flows on nicely from there, as it achieves both of these objectives.

Personalization comes in many forms, and the growing rate of AI being used to personalize and carefully curate a shopper's digital experience can't be ignored. However, it's easy to forget the easy wins that can be had in this area.

I use the ICE score methodology created by Sean Ellis, which is a project prioritization tool, to look at three main factors when deciding what personalization projects to focus on. The ICE score ranks each factor out of 10 points, with the end result being a score out of 30 points. The higher the score, the higher priority the personalization project should be.

The ICE score method measures:

>> The **I**mpact of the project

>> The **C**onfidence you have in the expected outcome

>> The **E**ase of the project, or how much effort is required

To determine the impact of the project, I generally ask myself how much in yearly sales or cost savings the project is likely to deliver. For example, is the project worth $100,000 a year if executed correctly? If so, I deem that to be a 10/10, high-impact project. A project worth $100 a year might score 1/10 and therefore be a low-impact project.

To determine a confidence score, I score anything that is a sure-fire home run a 10/10 for confidence — for example, if I was sure that adding a wishlist to my store would achieve my desired impact, I would rate it a 10/10 for confidence. If I was new to machine learning and wanted to try a complex AI app on the store, I might rate it as 1/10 in confidence, as I am not 100 per cent sure that the impact will be achieved. Often you need to score complex projects low on confidence, as you won't have the experience to determine if they're a home run or not.

To determine an ease score, I simple score the project out of 10 based on how many days it takes. If it's a simple one-day job to deploy a wishlist onto my store, I rate it as 10/10 in ease. If it involves the slow, tedious deployment of a complex piece of tech, I might rate it as 1/10 in ease.

The combined scores out of 10 give you the highest-impact projects, which are easy enough to implement, with the most confidence. Moving through projects in this manner has helped me and my clients to move through projects that take the online business forward quickly, while operating within our skillset, a set budget and a reasonable time frame.

Some of the simplest ideas often require the least effort for some pretty impressive results, so I'd consider picking some of the low-hanging fruit available to build personal relationships with your customers before charging into some of the more complex possibilities.

You can find plenty of wishlist apps in the Shopify App Store — it's a great, low-effort way to try and get customers across the line to purchase from you. Try Wishlist by Zoomy — it's free, and is a favorite of mine.

No two shoppers are the same, and in ecommerce you have the machines on your side to help you learn from previous customer behaviors in order to predict future actions — so put them to work and start reaping the rewards!

In the following sections, I introduce you to some easy wins to be had in your Shopify store through personalizing the experience for your customers. The advice I give here is based on what I believe is suitable for an early-stage online business.

Personalized banners

Believe it or not, the banners that you see on your favorite online store's homepage may not be the same ones that I see. I'm not being cryptic — some of those banners are there just for you. What's the point of showing me a banner with a stylish new cut of skinny jeans, if I only wear straight leg jeans? So, while you may see the skinny jeans, I'll see the straight leg jeans, and *click*, off I go down the path to purchase — instead of bouncing off the other way.

A *dynamic banner* in ecommerce is generally a grey box of nothing that is populated by different images, depending on the user's shopping or browsing behavior — as opposed to a *static banner*, which always remains the same.

TIP

Personalization solutions like DataCue allow you to showcase dynamic banners and inform you which banners are most popular and getting the most clicks, which is useful for making creative decisions. DataCue: Personalized Homepage by DataCue is available in the Shopify App Store and offers a free trial before you have to start paying a monthly fee.

Product recommendations

Product recommendations provide a way for your store to direct customers towards the products they want to buy while they're browsing your store. To do this, you use a product recommendation engine (many of which are available in the Shopify App Store), which predicts the products a user is likely to purchase by analyzing their previous browsing behaviors.

Product recommendations are a must for your Shopify store, unless you only have one or two products. They're a known conversion winner and are typically used on the website homepage or product page.

On the homepage, a strip of recommended products running across the homepage is one way to provide personalized product recommendations — and rather than selecting any old products to place there, it's a good idea to let an algorithm determine the best products to showcase. For example, when I go to a website, I may see one set of product recommendations based on my browsing or shopping behaviors, and when you visit the same site, you may see something entirely different based on your shopping and browsing experiences.

TIP

You can purchase apps that add product recommendations (such as DataCue: Personalized Homepage by DataCue, Wiser Personalized Recommendations by Expert Village Media Technologies or Recomatic Related Products by Wordsense), but Shopify also offers out-of-the-box solutions through the following free themes:

>> Boundless

>> Brooklyn

>> Debut

>> Express

>> Minimal

>> Narrative

>> Simple

>> Venture

People also bought

Adding a 'people also bought' feature to your store is essentially another form of product recommendation, and a powerful upselling and cross-selling tool because it targets products of potential interest towards customers. You can see this feature in action under statements such as 'People who bought this product also bought . . .', with the additional recommendations listed on the product page.

The algorithm that runs this simply identifies products that are usually bought together. The idea is to sell an additional product; if your store sells shoes, the algorithm may suggest shoe polish products to your customers.

TIP

Plenty of apps in the Shopify App Store and companies offer this feature as either part of their suite of AI-driven products — for example, they might offer product recommendations, provide an AI-powered search and show items frequently bought together. A nice app in the Shopify App Store is Also Bought by Code Black Belt, which is geared towards product recommendations powered by AI. It has a free plan and hundreds of five-star reviews from happy Shopify merchants.

Product quizzes and guided selling

You can add features to your site that ask shoppers questions to determine their needs, and identify the most suitable products based on their answers. Such features are particularly useful for stores that have large product ranges, but also for products where there may be certain specific needs, such as mattresses — some customers like a soft mattress, a hard mattress or a king-sized mattress, so you can ask all these questions in a quiz-like format and show the most relevant products in your store that may be a good match. I've seen this increase conversion rates; it can also be used to minimize customers abandoning their browsing session, because often a customer can't work out the right product for them without a nudge in the right direction. Using a product quiz takes the shopper to the closest matched product to their needs.

EXAMPLE

Many online fashion brands do this well, such as when they ask visitors to tell them a bit about their style, taste or budget. A personalized wardrobe can be curated, showing the customer products they're more inclined to buy using the data they have volunteered.

TIP

Two good examples of product quiz tools may work well in your store: the Product Recommendation Quiz by RevenueHunt, which is available on the Shopify App Store and has a free plan, so provides a nice starting point for new stores; and Preezie (preezie.com), which isn't in the Shopify App Store but does integrate nicely with Shopify (its entry-level plan suggests it targets online stores with turnover starting at $1 million, so it's a good one to consider as you grow). If you're in fashion, Dressipi (`dressipi.com`) is a great one for curating wardrobes for users based on their personal preferences, although it's not available in the Shopify App Store, and you'll need to contact them for information regarding pricing and plans — again this is another one for when you join the million-dollar-a-year club.

Recently viewed items

Showing returning shoppers products that they recently viewed is another easy way to bring them closer to purchase, simply through saving them the time they would have otherwise spent going back through pages of products. It also serves as a reminder to shoppers, which can then often prompt them to buy the product.

Recently viewed items are typically shown on the homepage or on product pages, but this tool also works well on the cart page. You'll find plenty of app options in the Shopify App Store, such as Recently Viewed Items by QeRetail, which has a small monthly fee, and Simple Recently Viewed Product by Tech Dignity, which has a free plan available and has an encouraging 4.9 star rating from Shopify merchants.

Bestsellers

Similar to the product recommendations feature on the homepage, this feature usually presents a horizontal row of popular bestselling products on your homepage. Although not catered to an individual (rather, it displays the bestselling items on your store), I include this here because many of the apps I mention in this chapter include this as part of their suite of services. For example, the Wiser Personalized Recommendations app by Expert Village Media Technologies is a great personalization app that also includes a bestsellers feature. People are drawn to popular things — think about music charts, or trending streaming shows — so you'll likely be interested in the bestsellers before selecting something from further down the list.

You can use different parameters to define your bestsellers — they might be the bestselling products over the last week, or the last 24 hours, or whatever time frame you like. For a more personal experience, you can also segment bestsellers by region (see the next section for more on this), which is useful if your product sales vary depending on location — an example may be winter clothes selling in the southern hemisphere, while summer clothes are selling in the northern hemisphere.

TECHNICAL STUFF

Getting to this level of segmentation isn't available out of the box with all Shopify themes or apps, so you may need to engage a more specialized personalization platform (such as Nosto). Nosto is available in the Shopify App Store, but you're likely to need some help from the Nosto team, and possibly a developer, when it comes to integrating Nosto into your Shopify store.

Personalize by location

Seasonal or regionally themed shopping, such as for clothes, is a great way to target products towards your customers, but location-based personalization comes in many forms. If you're getting visitors from overseas, it's imperative that your store recognizes where they're browsing from, either by asking or through the use of *cookies* (cookies are files that contain data used to identify users, which is valuable in online retail as it improves the browsing experience).

Where this matters most:

>> **Currency:** Detect where the customer is from and show them their local currency, if you've set it up — refer to Chapter 6 for help setting up foreign currency on your online store. Allowing people to shop in their own currency is a guaranteed conversion-rate winner.

>> **Language:** As per currency, simply having your website translated into a local language can have a meaningful impact on conversion rate. While it's unlikely that this is going to be your lowest hanging fruit, as you get bigger and find your store getting significant traffic (in the tens of thousands per month) from a certain country whose language differs from your store's native language, it may be worth getting your store translated and presenting that language automatically to shoppers from that country.

Shopify Settings allow you to set up your store in multiple languages:

>> If you're a Basic Shopify, Shopify or Advanced Shopify merchant, then you can sell in up to five languages.

>> If you're a Shopify Plus merchant, then you can sell in up to 20 languages.

TECHNICAL STUFF

To sell in multiple languages, you need a third-party app, which you can search for in the Shopify App Store — for example, Translate Your Store by Weglot, which is a widely used and positively reviewed app that can translate your store into one language, with a maximum of 10,000 words. You also need a theme that's compatible with selling in multiple languages.

All the free themes from Shopify are compatible with selling in multiple languages. If you're using a third-party theme, then you can contact your theme developers to check if it's compatible.

You also need a theme that has a *language selector*, which provides users with the option to select the language they would like to browse the website in. Only the newest versions of the Debut, Brooklyn and Express themes have built-in language selectors. If you're using another theme or an older version of the theme, then you can add a language selector using the Geolocation app by Shopify.

Location-based sizing

I've experienced first-hand the inconvenience of a lack of universal sizing in clothing and footwear. If you plan on selling within these two categories, or any product that has size variants, be aware that sizes can vary between countries. For example, in footwear, US sizing is different to UK sizing, and European sizing is different again. In China, a medium-sized shirt is often different to a Western-style medium.

One way to combat the location-based sizing issue is to identify when a visitor is coming from a certain country and show them that particular size chart. To be even more personal, your store can remember the size that a visitor last browsed or purchased, making it easier for them to remember and select their correct size next time.

The Gift of Giving: Creating and Fulfilling Gift Cards

Everyone has a fussy friend or relative that's just too hard to buy for — and that's where gift cards come in. Online stores can sell digital gift cards at a certain value that can be used on their stores to pay for products and services. The gift card feature is currently available on all Shopify subscription plans.

Gift card sales always boom around Christmas time, so it's a good idea to display them prominently in the lead-up to Christmas. And because they're delivered digitally (by email), the recipient gets their gift right away — which is great for last-minute shoppers like me!

Before you can sell gift cards, you need to activate the gift card feature — which is easy to do in Shopify. Gift cards don't need to be fulfilled manually, as they're sent to your customer automatically.

You can access everything you need to know about creating and issuing gift cards in your Shopify admin by clicking on Products → Gift Cards, which appears as the last item on the drop-down Products menu. On the Gift Cards page that appears, you have the option to sell or send gift cards.

You can perform two main functions on this page:

>> Issue a gift card.

>> Create a gift card as a product for your online store.

In the next two sections I take you through the steps to perform these functions in your online store.

Issuing a gift card

Issuing a gift card (as opposed to selling a gift card as a product and receiving payment for it) can be a useful customer service tool. You may decide to send a gift card to an unhappy customer, or perhaps offer a customer a gift card instead of a return (this is effectively a *store credit*, which is when a customer returns a product and wants store credit to buy something else — Shopify suggest using gift cards as store credits).

When you issue a gift card in this way, it's a simple process — it's functional rather than designed to look pretty.

To issue a gift card:

1. **From the Gift Cards page (which you access from your Shopify admin by clicking on Products → Gift Cards), select Send Gift Cards.**

   The Gift card page appears.

2. **Click on the green Issue Gift Card button in the top-right corner.**

   A dialogue box appears (see Figure 10-1), which shows an automatically generated Gift Card Code and asks you to set an Initial Value for the gift card, along with the option to set an expiry date or leave it open-ended.

   The customer will be able to enter the Gift Card Code into your checkout as payment for future purchases.

FIGURE 10-1:
Issuing a gift card.

Source: Shopify

3. **You can copy and paste the Gift Card Code and send it to your customer or desired recipient, or you can search for and select a customer in the Search Customers field to the right inside the dialogue box. You can also create a new customer — this pops up a new dialogue box, where you can enter their name, number and email and issue the gift card directly to them from your Shopify admin.**

   You can add a note that will be emailed to the customer, or leave it blank.

4. **Click on the green Save button.**

   By saving the gift card, your Shopify admin sends an email to the selected customer (if applicable) and activates your gift card.

Making gift cards available for purchase

A more gift-oriented way to make gift cards available to your customers is to make them available for purchase as a product on your online store.

TIP

Try to offer denominations for gift cards that are close to your average order value and give a variety of options, as your customers won't be able to edit the amount themselves.

To create a gift card for purchase:

1. **From the Gift Cards page, select Add Gift Card Product from the menu in the header.**

   When you click on this, you're taken to the Create Gift Card product page, which looks a bit like the normal Add Product page (refer to Chapter 5).

2. **Fill out all the fields, including the card's Title (for example, Paul's Gift Card) and a brief description in the Description field (for example, 'Offer your friends and loved ones a gift card to spend on anything at Paul's Online Store').**

3. **Click on Media, and then Add File to upload a nice image of a gift card.**

   It's a good idea to add an image to create a better visual effect for your customers, and to make sure your gift cards stand out on the page. This is purely for the benefit of the customer purchasing the card — the recipient of the gift card won't see this image as they will receive an image by email that looks more like Figure 10-2.

TIP

   Visit burst.shopify.com to get access to free, high-res images sourced by Shopify, just for you. This is helpful if you don't have ready-made images of gift cards of your own.

FIGURE 10-2: What the gift card recipient sees when they receive a gift card.

Source: Shopify

4. **Select the denominations that you want to offer your gift card in. The defaults are $10, $25, $50 and $100. Hit the trash can next to each denomination to delete it, or click on Add Denomination to add a new amount to offer on your gift cards.**

You can come back to the Search Engine Listing Preview after you've found out more about SEO in Chapter 16. For now, the details you see on the right-hand side under Organization are optional; however, if you enter Gift Card in the Product Type field it can help you filter products when you're looking at your products in your Shopify admin.

5. **Skip the Vendor field (but you can enter your own business name if you would like).**

6. **You can add the gift card to a collection manually by searching for the collection in the Search for Collections field (you can add these randomly throughout any collections so customers can find them, rather than creating a collection purely for Gift Cards — although you can if you want), and you can add tags to help customers find your gift cards through your online store's search, or to automatically add the gift card to a collection.**

Chapter 5 talks about all these elements of creating products and collections in more detail.

7. **Click on the green Save button in the bottom right to create your gift cards in all the denominations that you have selected.**

To find the gift cards you have created, go to Products → Gift Cards and you will see them all listed on the page. Open a particular gift card to make any edits. At the top of the page, click on Preview to see what it will look like. Figure 10-3 shows a gift card created through the free Shopify theme Debut.

When a customer clicks on View Gift Card from the email they receive delivering their gift card, they are taken to a new page, where they can copy the gift card code and paste it into your store's checkout. If a customer uses part of the balance, the gift card balance is updated to the customer's digital gift card and in your Shopify admin.

FIGURE 10-3:
A gift card in the Shopify theme Debut.

Source: Shopify

Giving Little Unexpected Extras

I find that with the impressive rise of AI and machine learning, some of the old faithful selling traditions have been left behind. But good old-fashioned personalization strategies still have their place, such as surprise and delight, or giving little unexpected extras (GLUE — ecommerce loves an acronym!).

To give each customer on your website a personalized experience, you need to treat them as if they're unique. This isn't a new concept, but it's become dominated by the evolution of new technologies.

TIP

Getting personal with customers forges trust and loyalty, so taking this sort of personal strategy may sit comfortably in a customer service, customer experience, loyalty or customer retention strategy.

GLUE refers to giving customers a little something special that goes beyond the product they've ordered. You may choose to adopt this strategy for all your customers in a small way, or on a grander scale for some of your most loyal customers.

The following sections provide a few ideas for non-machine-learnt, old-fashioned ways you can get personal with your customers.

Handwritten notes

An oldie, but a goodie. You may be surprised how far a nice handwritten note, written to a customer and sent with their order, will get you, particularly if it comes from you, the business owner.

I've used this strategy and love it. You see customers share the notes on social media or in public reviews, and it's a very small investment to buy some nice, branded cards for you to write on. A simple note thanking a customer for their order is an option, or if that gets too difficult to maintain perhaps consider offering handwritten notes as a free option for birthday gifts, Christmas presents or special occasions that resonate with your customers. You might also start small and target five orders a day to write handwritten notes for random customers.

TIP

Don't just save personal notes for loyal customers. If a customer has a difficult experience with your store and reaches out through your customer service channels, you can often turn that experience around by posting out a card to them (along with offering a resolution to the problem), specifically mentioning the experience they had so they know it's a personal card, not a generic one.

Gift with purchase

Sending a gift with purchase can be used as a marketing tool to increase your conversion rate, but in this context, I suggest trying it as a means of standing out, where you treat the customer as a unique person, not a number.

A little gift, like a small sample of a complementary product, such as a spare set of laces for shoes, or a sample of a leather conditioner with leather goods, or even just a packet of sweets, can put a smile on a customer's face and make them feel special. Again, you may see happy customers posting reviews or feedback on your store, or sharing their experience via social media!

Personalized video

Video in general is more personal than text, and a nice touch can be to automate your order emails to include a video of you or a team member thanking the customer. You might also take the time to record a video for VIP customers rather than building a generic video into your post-purchase email flows.

Using video as part of your customer service offering is also a nice touch. Think about a customer with a product enquiry who, rather than seeing an email, receives a video demonstrating the product or showing off the feature that the customer had asked about.

EXAMPLE

Canadian leather goods company Popov Leather's founder sends a personal, seemingly unscripted video to new customers, thanking them for their business, which is a great personal touch.

Show off your personal side

Let the customer in. Don't be afraid to show a nice video of you and your team talking about your business and why you started it. The same goes for your customer service team — consider adding a video to your customer service team's email signatures.

EXAMPLE

The team at Wistia tried this and found that their email signature videos had a whopping 80 per cent engagement rate and 87 per cent play rate! What a great way to get personal with your customers and let them in to your brand a little more. Read about their experience at `wistia.com/learn/sales/video-email-signature`.

4

Taking Stock of the Situation: Inventory, Logistics and Orders

IN THIS PART . . .

Organize and store your inventory.

Process orders, capture payments and minimize fraud.

Fulfill your customers' orders.

» **Receiving stock into your online store**

» **Adding stock to your sales channels**

» **Keeping track of your stock levels**

» **Using Shopify inventory reports**

Chapter **11**

Stocked Up: Buying, Receiving and Managing Inventory

t's time to look at the stuff that pays the bills — your inventory. Inventory management in general can be a difficult beast to tame if you don't know what you're doing, and getting it right from the start is important because it can be very difficult to go back and unwind mistakes in your inventory, such as over-ordering or misplacing inventory items.

Treating your inventory buying, storage and general management incorrectly can cause errors in your profit numbers; can cause you to over- or under-order stock, which dries up your cashflow; and can cause your orders to be delayed due to messy inventory management. On the flip side, managing your inventory well can generate more sales with less money through better demand forecasting, which frees up cash for use in growing your business. Good inventory management is also good for your customers, who reap the rewards through speedy delivery and accurate fulfillment of orders.

In this chapter, I take you through managing your inventory — including the nitty-gritty of raising purchase orders and receiving stock into your online store, both physically and into your product information on Shopify. I also talk about storing your stock and updating your stock levels through your sales channels, as well as the crucial role of tracking and monitoring your inventory levels to minimize wastage.

By the end of this chapter, you'll have a solid understanding of why inventory management is crucial to the success of your online business, and how to put good processes into practice so that you're running a tight ship when it comes to your inventory.

Defining Inventory Management

No matter what stage you're at, inventory management is always going to play an important part in your online business. *Inventory management* (the way you store, manage and keep track of your stock of products; that is, your *inventory*) has a direct flow-on impact to your customer — a well-organized storeroom or warehouse leads to faster fulfillment of your orders, which leads to happy customers. When it comes to fulfillment, speed and accuracy are key, and anything that slows down the pick, pack and dispatch process is going to hurt your business.

An *inventory management system* (IMS) is the master of your inventory. You use your IMS to raise purchase orders (POs), receive POs and feed inventory into your sales channels.

Do you really need an IMS? Well, yes — eventually, you do. But do you need one right now, while you're in the early days of your Shopify journey? Probably not, unless you're planning to commence with tens of thousands of units of stock or a wide breadth of sales channels, in which case you might consider it.

REMEMBER

Stock should never leave your business, or come into your business, without your stock levels being updated in your IMS; however, an entry-level Shopify merchant doesn't need an IMS as Shopify can manage your inventory quite well on all its plans. Most importantly, Shopify allows you to edit your inventory quantities manually and track inventory as it sells, which you can then use to monitor fast-moving or slow-moving products, as well as giving you basic information you need to run a business, like the value of your stock on hand.

Shopify has a scalable inventory management function inbuilt to your Shopify admin — it can be found under Products → Inventory (which you find in the drop-down menu that appears). It is rare for a new Shopify merchant to need more than what's on offer here; however, if you have more than one warehouse (for example, one in the US and one in Australia), you may find it helpful to use an IMS to separate the inventory for each warehouse and raise purchase orders for each warehouse.

The typical process or flow of inventory through an IMS is as follows:

1. Create and draft the purchase order (PO).

2. Approve the PO and send it to the supplier.

3. Pay for the PO, with any foreign exchange (FOREX) and shipping fees applied.

4. Receive the PO, in full or partially.

5. Adjust inventory from the PO to update your stock on hand (SOH).

6. Feed inventory data into the appropriate sales channels.

An IMS can often double as a warehouse 'pick-and-pack' system, which will also print barcodes and store the location of inventory in your warehouse, so that as you get bigger, you can easily find the location of each unit of your inventory. An IMS also enables you to scan stock, which makes stocktaking easier.

TIP

As your warehouse starts to get busier and busier, you may find that an IMS helps you keep track of your inventory a little better than Shopify's inbuilt features. Your IMS will become a favorite on your desktop when you reach a certain point — when you're either handling 50 or more orders a day, selling on more than three sales channels or holding more than 15,000 units of stock, you might consider an IMS. If you run an *omnichannel* business (a business that has multiple sales channels, such as online, wholesale and physical retail stores), a good IMS will provide you with sales data, including profit margin, sell-through rates, inventory levels and more. A good IMS also gives you this data by customer, sales channel and geographical location.

REMEMBER

An IMS is the name for the tech platform that handles your inventory management. So while Shopify has an inventory management feature, it is not an IMS — but it offers enough inventory management support to get you to a good size. When you graduate to a third-party IMS (not Shopify's inbuilt feature), your IMS will play a crucial role in managing your inventory from start to end.

In this chapter, I show you how Shopify can get you started with inventory management. When you start needing to handle blending your shipping or currency conversion costs into your cost prices, or running large-scale stocktakes, you may need to consider an IMS.

However, these needs are one of the reasons why Shopify went ahead and bought its own IMS, Stocky. *Stocky* is an inventory management app that's included with Shopify POS Pro subscriptions. Shopify POS is for physical retailers, not for online retailers. You would use this if you had a Shopify online store as well as physical stores that you want to connect to Shopify.

Like any system or software, you can get different levels of sophistication in an IMS. Stocky is a great tool; however, if you're not using Shopify POS Pro, you can still add some alternatives to your Shopify store in the early days to give you deeper insights into your stock movement and when you need to replenish (reorder) stock.

Stocky used to be available for online retailers, not just POS users. Stocky also used to be available on other Shopify plans, and merchants who subscribed to Stocky before it moved to Shopify POS are still able to log in and use Stocky.

If you're planning on using Shopify POS Pro (because you have physical shopfronts), then the nearby sidebar 'Managing your stock with Stocky' has some more information on using Stocky.

Stocky is a good place to start with using an IMS if you have physical stores and want to use Shopify POS, if only for the demand forecasting tool (which is a feature of most good IMS products). If you're an online-only store looking for some help with your demand forecasting, I recommend you try a new app called StockTrim, which offers a paid-for monthly plan, or Cogsy, which is in the Shopify App Store and starts with a free plan. Alternatively, you can utilize old-fashioned demand forecasting. For example, if you want to buy enough stock for three months (in other words, three months' worth of inventory cover), then you can look at your sales of each product for the last 30 days and multiply it by three to tell you how much stock you need to buy to maintain sales for three months. You can also use the Average Inventory Sold Per Day report in Shopify to tell you how many of each product you have sold per day and in total for the past 30 days (or any other time period you choose). To access this report, go to Analytics → Reports → Average Inventory Sold Per Day.

TIP

When you're ready to upgrade, look out for an IMS that integrates with all and any sales channels you're wanting to add to your store, such as Amazon or eBay — this will save you time later.

MANAGING YOUR STOCK WITH STOCKY

Stocky helps you manage your inventory by tracking your inventory levels, forecasting the inventory that you need and suggesting which products you ought to order. To adjust your inventory levels, you can perform inventory counts and create inventory transfers.

Stocky doesn't have all the bells and whistles of a more specialized IMS, but it is a useful tool for beginners as it has a very easy-to-use demand forecasting feature. In other words, it will tell you when you're going to sell out of stock before you do — prompting you to place an order. Where it falls down is its inability to hold the location of your inventory in your warehouse or adjust the cost of goods sold (COGS) of a particular product. For example, if you buy a batch of a product, such as 100 units of blue jeans, and then a month later you place another order when you're close to running out, you may be buying the blue jeans on two separate purchase orders at two separate prices (maybe due to currency fluctuation). A more sophisticated IMS handles the two different costs using a FIFO (first-in, first-out) model. This means the stock units bought first are sold first. So, if you have 100 pairs of jeans at a cost price of $10 each, and a second order of 100 pairs of jeans at a cost price of $12 each, an IMS will record the COGS as $10 for the first 100, and $12 for the second 100, whereas in Stocky you can only enter one cost price.

Stocky is probably too basic for helping with the physical organization of inventory in a large warehouse, which is where a more sophisticated IMS such as Cin7, Unleashed, TradeGecko or DEAR Systems may be more suitable.

Starting from Scratch: Your First Purchase Order

A *purchase order* (or *PO* as it's commonly shortened to) is an official document generated between a buyer and a seller, which confirms the details of an order, including product type, quantity and price. Many retailers neglect the PO, instead relying on the supplier to send an invoice (or pro forma invoice, sometimes shortened to PI). The problem with this is that it's the first step to losing control of your inventory.

TIP

Raising a PO yourself forces you to cross-check the finer details, such as pricing and quantities, against previous orders, whereas a lazy operator may decide to pay a PI from a supplier, only to later find that the quantity, price or finer details (like SKUs — stock-keeping units — or colors) were actually incorrect. (I put my hand up here, as this has happened to me!)

REMEMBER

A PO isn't only used to create orders, it's also used to receive and check orders when they arrive at your premises. When your first shipment of stock arrives, you should have your PO in hand so you can count what has been delivered, ticking it off as you count it. Standing with pen in hand counting stock as it arrives may sound a little old-fashioned, but unless you're using a third-party IMS, it's perfectly acceptable to start like this.

Creating a purchase order

A PO can be created through an IMS that is connected to your Shopify store and any other sales channels you have, or it can simply be created in a standard platform such as Google Docs, Google Sheets, Microsoft Excel or Microsoft Word.

TIP

If you're raising your first order through a platform like Alibaba, you'll notice it's a lot like shopping online, where you simply select items and add them to your cart — and so a PO isn't usually required. However, as you get bigger, or if you're designing your own products, you'll find yourself negotiating with your regular suppliers outside of those platforms, and instead via email or other forms of communication like Zoom or even WhatsApp — this is when I recommend you start using POs.

If you're not using an IMS (and for most newly established online stores, I would guess that you're not), then here's the key information that a PO needs to include:

>> The date

>> A PO number

>> The name of the SKU you are ordering

>> The quantity

>> The unit price

>> The grand total (in the correct currency)

Figure 11-1 shows an example purchase order containing one item.

If you're using an IMS, it's likely that you'll have the option to record payments on the PO as you make them, so you can keep track of what you've paid and what you owe. This is a really useful feature, as it's universally expected that a buyer will pay some form of upfront deposit to commence the production of an order, especially if the objects are customized or there is a large order quantity.

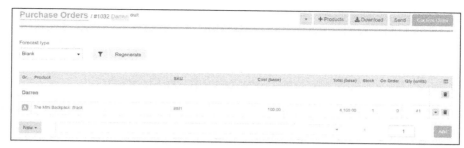

Source: Shopify

FIGURE 11-1:
An example
purchase order.

TIP

Keeping track of deposit and balance payments can be a nightmare, so I encourage you to record the payments on your purchase orders as you make them, whether you are using an IMS or managing your inventory manually.

Receiving a purchase order

In the same way that ordering or buying stock is sometimes known as *raising a purchase order*, receiving stock is also known as *receiving a purchase order*. Receiving a PO has two components:

1. Physically taking receipt of stock

2. Receiving inventory into your online store or IMS

Physically taking receipt of stock

When a delivery of stock arrives at your door, there's more to inventory management than just hiding it away in your garage or spare room (for more on stock storage, see the later section 'Storing Your Inventory'). You need to ensure that the order you raised and paid for has been accurately received before you update your stock quantity.

When you get your stock, count it against your PO to ensure that the delivery matches what you have ordered. Any discrepancies need to be reported to your supplier, in which case you can either ask for a refund or ask for the correct order to be sent.

TIP

I advise you to do a *quality control check* (known as a QC check). This means opening up every item in your order and checking that the item's quality is the same as you ordered and that it meets your expectations. As you progress further into your ecommerce career, you might only randomly QC your products as it may not be feasible to check every product, but in your early dealings with suppliers, I recommend checking each product — after all, it's going to impact both sales and your online store's reputation if your products aren't up to scratch.

(If you're using an IMS, you generally hit Receive on your POs, which updates Shopify with the new stock quantities of each product.)

Receiving inventory into Shopify

Landed stock is stock that has landed in your warehouse, as opposed to being in transit; *stock on hand* (SOH) is stock currently in your warehouse ready to be sold (so not in transit — although stock in transit is still owned by you if you've paid for it, and therefore it should be in your total inventory count). To receive inventory into Shopify means entering the details of your landed stock, or SOH, into Shopify so you can begin to sell it through your online store.

At this point, you may recall that in Chapter 5 I showed you how to create products in Shopify — now it's time to add inventory quantities to the products that you have created.

One way you can do that in Shopify is through the Transfers function in the Products section of your Shopify admin. The *Transfers* function enables you to record, track and receive incoming purchase orders and inventory from suppliers. You can even use this function to create purchase orders at a basic level — essentially, you're transferring stock from your supplier to your business.

Transfers can help you manage your purchase orders and inventory in several ways:

>> You can record incoming inventory after you've submitted and confirmed your purchase order (PO) with your supplier.

>> You can indicate whether you've received full or partial inventory, which allows you to process inventory at your own pace.

>> Your product inventory updates automatically after you receive the items from your supplier.

>> You can see the number of incoming items and their expected arrival date in the product's details.

To receive items using Shopify's Transfers function, you first need to create a stock transfer. To create a stock transfer, follow these steps:

1. **From your Shopify admin, go to Products → Transfers.**

    All your transfers are displayed on the page that appears.

2. **Click on Create Transfer.**

    The Create Inventory Transfer page appears.

3. **If you want to enter the name of your supplier, then select one in the Supplier section.**

TIP

You can add a new supplier by clicking on Create New Supplier, which is located on the Create Inventory Transfer page — click on Select Origin at the top of the Create Inventory Transfer page and then enter your supplier's contact and location information.

4. **If you use multiple locations and want to change the location for the transfer, you can change it in the Destination section, which is next to the Origin section at the top of the Create Inventory Transfer page.**

REMEMBER

Using the Origin and Destination sections at the top of the Create Inventory Transfer page, you can create any *origin* (supplier you order stock from) or any *destination* (location you want stock delivered to).

5. **In the Shipment section, enter a date in the Expected Arrival field.**

6. **If you want to assign a reference number or tag to the transfer, then enter it in the Additional Details section. Tags can have up to 255 characters.**

REMEMBER

These tags are not the same as product or collection tags, but they're a nice way to easily keep track of your shipments. For example, if you create a tag called 'Wholesale', you can search for all your wholesale purchases by typing Wholesale in the search bar on the Transfers page.

Using tags enables you to search for and find Transfers quickly. You can use reference numbers and tags to filter and organize your transfers on the Transfers page.

For example, you can create an Urgent tag to show that this is an urgent request, which is helpful because after you've created multiple transfers, they all appear on the Transfers page.

7. **In the Products section, either enter the name of the product that you want to add to your transfer, or click on Browse Products to view a list of your store's products and collections. Use the checkboxes to select individual products or variants.**

TIP

If you need to add a new product to your transfer, then you can do so by opening another browser tab and creating a new product in Shopify there. When you return to the tab with your transfer, you can search for the product that you just created and add it to your transfer.

8. **After you've used the checkboxes to add the products that you want to include in the transfer, click on Add Products.**

9. On the Add Transfer page, enter the quantities for each product that you are expecting to receive from your supplier.

WARNING

Make sure that you've added the correct number of items as you cannot edit the quantities after you begin receiving inventory.

10. Click on Save Transfer.

After you create a transfer, you can view incoming inventory amounts on the product details page for each of your products in Shopify.

After you have created your stock transfer, you are ready to receive items into Shopify.

To receive inventory into Shopify, follow these steps:

1. From your Shopify admin, go to Products → Transfers.

2. Click on the transfer number — this number is generated each time you create a transfer.

3. Click on Receive items.

The items you have transferred will be received into your inventory, making them available to sell (assuming you enabled the product for sale when you created the product).

TIP

If you don't need to review inventory line by line, you can click on Mark as Complete as a quick way of indicating that you've received, rejected or cancelled all the remaining items on the transfer.

WARNING

Inspect each unit of stock you receive as it's unfortunately common to have issues with purchases of stock, especially with new suppliers — whether it be poor quality, incorrect sizes or overall issues with quantity. I suggest that you review your inventory line by line before marking the transfer as complete.

4. For each item, click on All or enter the number of items that you've received in the Accept column.

For example, if you order 50 pairs of blue jeans but only receive 49, then you need to enter 49 so that you don't oversell. *Overselling* is when a customer orders the stock but you don't have the stock on hand to fulfill the order.

5. Click on the '. . .' button and enter the number of items that you need to reject (damaged items, for example) or cancel. The quantity of the items adjusts accordingly.

For example, if 10 pairs of jeans arrive with water damage, you need to reject these so that they're not added to your inventory and sold — and so that you can raise the issue with your supplier.

You can always manually enter stock numbers; for example, if you've received extra items from your supplier that you're willing to accept, you can specify a greater number of items than you expected in the Accept column.

6. **Click on Save.**

7. **To finish the transfer, click on Archive.**

   Only transfers that have a Completed status can be archived.

You can see all Pending (open), Partial, Completed and Archived (which shows as a greyed out Completed status) transfers on the Transfers page of your Shopify admin. If you need to update a transfer at a later time, you can click on its transfer number to open and edit the transfer.

When you receive inventory from your supplier, Shopify updates the products in your admin with the number of units you have received, which means that you don't need to update it manually. For this to work, you must enable Shopify's inventory tracking option for your products and variants — refer to Chapter 5, where I talk about how to add products to your store and set up the inventory section of your product pages.

You can enable inventory tracking by clicking on Products → All Products, finding the name of your product, and then clicking on Track Quantity in the Inventory section.

If you don't fancy using the Transfers function, you don't need to, although I do recommend moving to some form of automated PO creation or stock transfer system sooner rather than later. If you're looking for a shortcut, however, you can manually adjust your inventory in Shopify — you just need to have set up inventory tracking in the product or variant you want to adjust.

Follow these steps to adjust inventory quantities for your products:

1. **From your Shopify admin, go to Products → All Products.**

   A list of your products appears.

2. **Click on the product that you want to track.**

   The Product page appears.

   If the product has variants, then click on the variant that you want to track. For example, if you've received an order of jeans, and you have 10 in Small, 10 in Medium and 10 in Large, you need to click on each size variant and edit the quantity of each.

3. **In the Inventory section, which appears partway down the Product page, select Track Quantity.**

   Set the quantity by entering in the number of units of stock that you have available to sell.

4. **Click on the green Save button in the bottom-right corner.**

Turn back to Chapter 5 if you've forgotten how to enter your retail and cost prices — which you can edit at any time.

Everyone loves a shortcut, right? To update your stock quantities quickly, follow these steps (also see Figure 11-2):

1. **From your Shopify admin, go to Products → Inventory.**

   A list of all your store's inventory appears, along with the quantity available.

2. **On the left-hand side of the headings, where it says Edit Quantity Available, change the inventory count as follows:**

   - To adjust the count, click on Add and enter a number.

     You can use a negative number to subtract from the inventory.

   - To set a new total inventory count, click on Set and enter a number.

   The new total is shown under Quantity.

3. **Click on Save (the option to save appears for each row that you are editing, directly next to the Edit Quantity Available box).**

FIGURE 11-2:
Adjust your stock quantities quickly from the Inventory section of your Shopify admin.

Source: Shopify

Storing Your Inventory

There's absolutely nothing wrong with the quintessential 'I started in my garage' story — it's how some of the very best online businesses got started. I advocate for staying as lean as possible, especially when you're getting started, so if you have a spare room, a garage or a small storage facility you can use then that's a great place to start storing your products.

REMEMBER

You will need easy access to your storage facility to pick your orders, so try and keep it at home if you can when you're starting out.

After your shipment has arrived, the last thing you (or your partner) wants is to have storage cartons all over your house. Order is important in a warehouse or indeed in any storage facility, and any time you waste tracking down your stock can be better spent on growing your business.

BARCODES AND SKUS

A *SKU* (or stock-keeping unit) is a unique identifier for a product or variant. If you connect a marketplace like Amazon or eBay to your Shopify store, in most cases you need to enter your SKU name into the marketplace for each product you want to list, so that you're your inventory updates, or an order comes in, the marketplace knows which item from your store it needs to be adjusting or selling. Think of a SKU as a common thread that ties your products to multiple sales channels — including warehouse and inventory management systems.

Although most entry-level ecommerce merchants won't need to use barcodes, Shopify does support their use. A *barcode* is a label that holds information on a product, including the SKU. If you want to use a barcode number when you're adding a product to your Shopify store, you can, you'll just need a barcode scanner.

For example, if I'm selling shoes on my Shopify store and a supplier or manufacturer sends them to me with barcodes, I can enter the barcode numbers from the barcode label on each product into the Shopify barcode field in the Add Product section of my Shopify admin. I can then use an app in Shopify — or my inventory management system (IMS) or warehouse management system (WMS) — to scan those shoes when I pick them off a shelf for an order, which will adjust the inventory quantity and update the order status, which (depending on the app you use) can also trigger the printing of the shipping label. As your Shopify store grows, all these helpful time-saving strategies can help make things easier.

You can do other cool things with barcodes and barcode scanners, including stocktaking and receiving inventory into your Shopify store, although in the early days of your Shopify store it's unlikely you'll need these advanced approaches.

If you wish to further explore using barcodes and barcode scanners with Shopify, check out the EasyScan: SKU and Barcode app by 506, or the Quick Scan — Barcode Scanner app by Stock Sync in the Shopify App Store. You can also find plenty of other barcode scanner apps in the Shopify App Store.

Although not strictly a Shopify-specific issue (as anyone who holds stock needs to find an efficient, economic way to store it), the following sections provide a few tips on how to store your inventory and optimize it for quick and easy fulfillment of orders. I talk about the ideal layout for your makeshift home or small-scale storage space — something suitable for a product that's about the size of a bag or item of clothing, or that's any size smaller than, say, a washing machine.

Shelving equipment

Shelving, also known as racking, is going to become a core part of your online business — whatever the size of your storage space. Unless you're in the business of selling large, bulky goods, it's not typical to use *pallet racking* (large steel frames that hold pallets, typically accessed using a forklift rather than by hand — not that it would fit in your garage anyway), but even in a fully fledged warehouse you will typically see what is known as RET shelving.

RET (rolled edge type) shelving, sometimes known as long-span shelving, consists of steel frames, with timber boards for shelves. Dimensions can range but, for your home, you may be looking at something 1,500cm wide, by about 54cm deep, with room for about four or five rows of shelves. The shelves clip out of the frames easily and can be adjusted in height, making them perfect for adapting to different-sized products. Brand new, these shelves can cost $100–200 per shelf but a shrewd buyer can pick them up second-hand for $20–30. A great way to find this equipment is to look out for when another warehouse is closing down or doing a *makegood*, which is when a tenant is leaving a warehouse and dismantling their equipment to leave it in its original state.

TIP

Make sure the top row isn't above hand height so you can pick your orders easily — without needing a ladder.

Locations

Your shelves hold your *locations* — the plastic or cardboard boxes, tubs or totes in which you store your products. I have seen some pretty creative locations in home storage set-ups, from shoeboxes to shipping cartons, with a square cut out of the front, for easy access when picking items. The purpose of these locations is to hold your products, also known as *stock-keeping units* (SKUs), which are short serial numbers used to identify your products and which include variations in your products, such as different colors and sizes (see the nearby sidebar 'Barcodes and SKUs' for more on SKUs).

Only have one SKU per location, so your *pickers* (those people designated to pick your orders from the shelves — which in the early days, is probably going to be you) don't get confused by having to sort through various different products.

Keeping one SKU in each location also helps you avoid picking errors — where possible, you want to eliminate the risk of human error in order fulfillment. The goal is to make your warehouse as user-friendly as possible for your picking and packing processes.

Layout and design

It may only be a small space at home when you get started, but good practices that will serve you well throughout your ecommerce journey have to start from somewhere — and starting them early is a great way to hone your ecommerce skills without huge risk. This is as true for the layout and design of your storage space as it is for picking the right products. I always say 'start small, act big' — it will hold you in great stead for scaling your business.

Even if you are starting with one bay of shelving, you can begin the habit of naming each bay, shelf and location (this is really important for efficient order fulfillment, which I cover in Chapter 13). A *bay* is another name for a group of shelving — one RET system equates to a bay. Again, the logic behind the labelling of each and every location in your space is to save time, and therefore money, in the long run.

The best large-scale example of an effective storage layout and design can be found in every IKEA store. Those guys are so clever; anyone can simply go and pick their own order by following the code on the product display label. An IKEA-style approach is a tried-and-tested method of inventory management, and it's a great way to get started, even for a small business.

Imagine you have your eye on the Waddydorf Study Table in Beige Timber. You check the product label and see that it's located in Aisle A, Bay 3, Location 32. When you make your way down to the warehouse area, you simply follow the enormous signs that say Aisle A, and once inside Aisle A, you can locate Bay 3, which, lo and behold, has a Location 32, where your trusty new table awaits you.

Consider laying out your shelving in a similar way to IKEA. Many shelving providers out there sell smaller, cheaper versions of RET shelving that are perfect for an online seller. Some companies have even copied the steel-based concept of a RET shelving unit and made them from cardboard, producing shelves that can be set up as needed while taking up minimal space in the meantime — very clever!

TIP

If your stock has already arrived and you don't have your shelving set up, you can use the same principles with your cartons. Stack them one on top of the other (weight permitting), cut a hole in the front of each carton (like a letterbox, but where you can reach in and pull your orders out), and label each carton as a location.

WARNING

Beware of taking on too many fixed costs too soon. Before you look at moving into a warehouse, forecast your inventory holdings over the course of any proposed lease you're going to take. If you take a warehouse hoping to grow into it, you can often end up losing a lot of money. It's much easier to take a short lease, outgrow it and move, than it is to be stuck in a long lease in a space that is double the size of what you need.

Wherever you store your products, at home or in a warehouse, you need to know the point at which you are going to hit capacity and begin thinking about your next space six months before you reach that point.

Putting Your Stock to Work: Listing Inventory Across Sales Channels

Sales channels in Shopify are the sales platforms that your Shopify store is connected to and that you're able to sell on. Your very first sales channel will be your online store!

If you then add other sales channels, such as eBay or Amazon, they are considered to be new sales channels, and so they will appear in two places:

>> In your Shopify admin, under Sales Channels

>> In your product pages, on the right-hand side of the page, under Product Status

Now that you have created your products (refer to Chapter 5) and have your inventory quantities set up, you're ready to set your products free into various sales channels. To make your products available to sell, you can change their status.

The following sections talk about how to make products available across certain sales channels — for example, you may have some products you want to sell on eBay, and others you don't.

Changing a product's availability status

Product *availability* enables you to control the status of your products and the sales channels in which they appear. A product's *status* determines if a product is available in your store.

REMEMBER

In Shopify, the product status of newly created products is set as Draft by default.

You change a product's status in a two-stage way:

1. Switching your product from Draft to Active — which makes your product live and visible on your online store's front end.

2. Selecting the sales channels in which you want your product to be available to purchase; for example, if you're selling across marketplaces in addition to your own online store.

You can set the following product statuses in the product page of each product by navigating to the top-right corner of the product's page, to Product Status, and selecting Active or Draft:

>> **Active:** The product details are complete and the product is available to be displayed in the sales channels.

>> **Draft:** The product details need to be completed before it can be displayed in your sales channels.

Making products available to your sales channels

You can control where you are selling a product by making it available to your active sales channels. If you decide not to make a product available to a particular sales channel, then it will be hidden from that channel's product catalogue.

You might hide a product from a sales channel for a variety of reasons:

>> You have seasonal products that you want to display for only part of the year.

>> A product is out of stock but you will have more in stock at a later date.

>> You don't want to sell a product right now, but you might offer it again later.

>> You want to offer online exclusive, or in-store exclusive, products.

>> You don't want to sell a product through a particular sales channel.

Follow these steps to adjust a product's availability across your sales channels:

1. **From your Shopify admin, go to Products → All Products.**

   A list of your products appears.

2. **Click on the product you want to make available to open the product's page.**

   The product is available to the sales channels listed in the Product Status section to the right of the page.

3. **Change the product status from Draft to Active.**

   An Active status makes your product available to sell and visible on your store's front end (the customer-facing part), whereas the Draft status keeps your product in draft mode.

4. **Below Product Status in the top-right corner of the product's page, click on Manage, located next to the Sales Channels and Apps section.**

   Note: before you click on this, you will see a list of any sales channels you have already added to your store directly under the Sales Channels and Apps heading (see Figure 11-3), along with a green circle (if your product is active across that channel) or an orange circle with white inside (indicating that the product has not been activated on that particular sales channel yet).

   A dialogue box appears with options to select which sales channels or apps you want to activate.

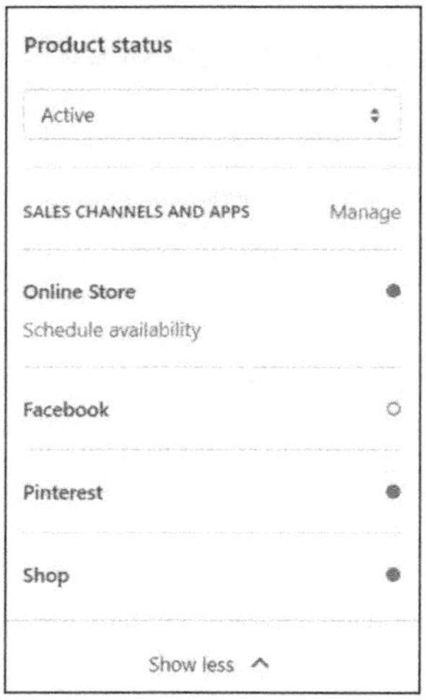

FIGURE 11-3: The Sales Channels and Apps section.

Source: Shopify

5. **Select the sales channels and the apps you want to make the product available to.**

   In Figure 11-4, you can see that my store has five sales channels or apps installed (for more on these channels and apps, check out Part 5 of this book), with four out of five activated:

   - **Online Store:** My Shopify online store.

   - **Google:** The Google marketing channel.

   - **Facebook:** Facebook's Shopify app allows you to create Facebook ads.

   - **Pinterest:** Another app that allows my store to create shoppable Pinterest pins.

   - **Shop:** This is Facebook's own sales channel, which allows me to create a Facebook shop and sell across it. I also look at this briefly in Chapter 17.

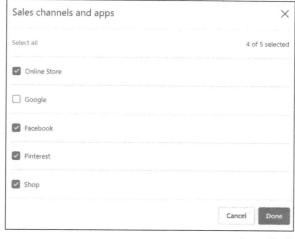

FIGURE 11-4: Select the sales channels and apps you want to activate in your store.

6. **Click on Done.**
7. **Click on Save.**

REMEMBER

If you're wondering which extra sales channels are good to start with, you can link your Shopify store to popular channels such as eBay or Amazon, plus many other marketplaces, using apps in the Shopify App Store. Refer back to Chapter 3 where I explore different sales channels you can add to your store.

Catch Me If You Can! Tracking Stock Movement

Understanding the costs that go into your landed cost per unit underpins the success of your business, but it's equally important to keep accurate records of the total cost of your inventory, also known as your stock on hand (SOH).

I've seen companies turning over $50 million plus per year that don't have a good handle on their inventory costs and stock movement. For example, a friend running a fashion brand once uncovered $1 million worth of inventory they didn't know they had when it moved from one 3PL (third-party logistics provider) setting and into a new one!

Maintaining accurate inventory levels also impacts the financial side of your business. Your inventory is an essential part of your COGS (cost of goods sold), which is a key component of your *gross profit* (sales − cost of sales = gross profit).

The formula for calculating your COGS is:

> Opening stock (at the beginning of a period) + Purchases (stock you buy in a given period) − Closing stock (at the end of a period) = COGS

REMEMBER

Your opening stock, or SOH, includes all the costs associated with landing the goods, such as freight and duties. This term is referred to as the landed cost. By the same token, your purchases figure should also include the same associated costs.

If your opening or closing stock figure is wrong, your COGS will be wrong, meaning you can be overstating or understating your profitability.

Using Shopify, you can accurately check your SOH at any time, plus run a profit margin report, which shows your COGS and your profit margin (sales less tax, less COGS). In the next section of this chapter. 'Using Inventory Reports', I run you through the key inventory reports you can run in Shopify.

TIP

The Profit by Product report is not strictly an inventory report, but I find it to be a very useful report in relation to gross profit. It shows you your overall gross margin, so it's a report I monitor closely.

To run a Profit by Product report in Shopify, go to your Shopify admin → Analytics → Reports. Around halfway down the new reports page that opens, you'll see a section titled Profit Margin, and under that, a subheading titled Profit by Product. Click on Profit by Product and the Profit by Product report appears.

In this report (see Figure 11-5), you see a list of all your store's products that have sold, within an adjustable time frame of your choice. Alongside each product you see the Product Vendor name, Product Type, quantity of stock you have sold (Net Quantity) and the amount of *Net Sales* (sales – tax) for each product. You will also see the Cost (in other words, the COGS) and the Gross Margin, along with the Gross Profit.

FIGURE 11-5:
The Profit by
Product report.

Source: Shopify

You can use this report to ensure that the pricing and margin structures you set up for your products are being achieved. For example, in Figure 11-5, the gross margin of the first product listed is 29.91 per cent — which is a pretty low gross margin. Good gross margins are a little subjective, in that some businesses can make a good overall net profit with a low gross margin by running their business extremely lean when it comes to things like marketing, rent, wages and other operating expenses. On a day-to-day basis, this is the report you use to see if you are realizing your projected gross profit.

Using Inventory Reports

Using reports in Shopify is going to save you a lot of time and help you make better decisions around how much inventory to order and what products to order. If your store is on the Basic Shopify plan or higher, then you have access to a bunch of great inventory reports right away.

To view your available inventory reports:

1. **From your Shopify admin, go to Analytics → Reports.**

   A list of Shopify reports appears.

2. **In the Inventory section, click on the report you want to see.**

Here, I take a look at the inventory reports you have access to and offer tips on how to use them.

Month-end Inventory Snapshot

This report gives you a snapshot of the quantity of each product variant you are holding at the end of each month.

If you notice a negative number in the quantity of any of your products here, it may be for one of these two reasons:

TIP

>> **You have inventory tracking available enabled, and you oversell a variant or product.** *Overselling* means to sell more stock than what you have available. For example, if you have five units of a product in your inventory but you sell eight units, you will be oversold by three units, so you will see –3 as your quantity.

Overselling does serve a purpose — I use it for putting items on presale, and when I know that stock is on the way I sometimes allow customers to purchase the product, informing them in the product description as to when that product will be sent to them.

>> **You don't have inventory tracking enabled.** If this is the case, your default inventory is always set to 0, and each time you make a sale, your quantity drops below 0.

TIP

To allow overselling of a product, tick the box in the product's page in the Inventory section that says Continue Selling When Out of Stock (see Figure 11-6).

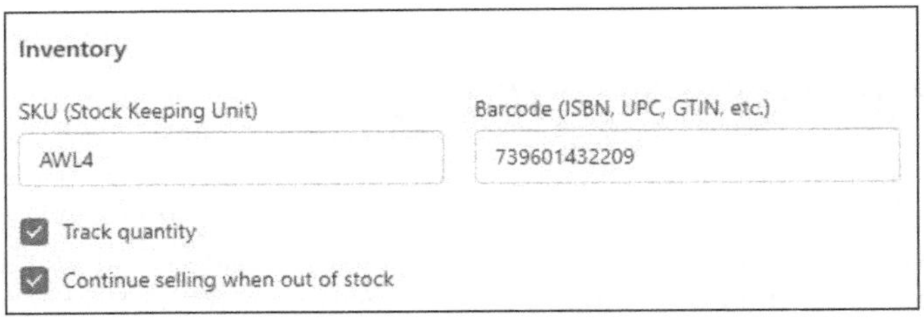

Inventory

SKU (Stock Keeping Unit)

AWL4

Barcode (ISBN, UPC, GTIN, etc.)

739601432209

☑ Track quantity

☑ Continue selling when out of stock

FIGURE 11-6:
Enabling overselling of a product.

Source: Shopify

Average Inventory Sold Per Day

This report, as the title suggests, tells you how many units of each of your products you're selling each day. I love this report because it's useful in helping you decide how many units of certain products you need to reorder (also known as replenishment). It also helps tell you when you're likely to sell out of products.

For example, if you've decided that your aim is to always hold 90 days of inventory cover (meaning enough inventory to sell for 90 days), then you can use this report to see how many units you need to order. If you're selling one unit of a certain product on average per day, then you need to order 90 units to last for 90 days. Likewise, if you have 30 units of that product on hand and you're selling on average one per day, then you will be sold out in 30 days. If your supplier takes more than 30 days to manufacture and send you your order then you're at risk of running out of stock before the next batch lands!

REMEMBER

Mastering simple replenishment is a huge lever for growing an online business, so I suggest you keep a keen eye on this report, make sure you aren't over-ordering or under-ordering, and never, ever order based on gut feeling — let the data decide!

Percent of Inventory Sold

Another favorite of mine, this report's great for monitoring your *sell-through* (the percentage of units sold per product, divided by the number of units received into your store, expressed as a percentage).

The percentage of inventory sold is important to see if your products are on track to sell as well as you planned. For example, if your goal is to hold 90 days cover, then you want your percentage of inventory sold to be 100 per cent after 90 days, and so if you've sold 50 per cent of that stock after 45 days (the halfway point to 90 days) then your product is on track to sell-through within 90 days. If your product is not on track to meet your target cover period, it either means you're ordering too much stock or your sales are too slow, so you need to either order less or sell more, which isn't as easy as it sounds — welcome to the world of buying!

ABC Analysis by Product

ABC Analysis by Product is another of my go-to reports. This report tells you what your most valuable and least valuable inventory is, according to the contribution it makes to your store's overall revenue.

The grading system works on the Pareto principle — that 80 per cent of your revenue comes from 20 per cent of your products (which are your Grade A products). If you're finding that you have less than 20 per cent of your products marked as Grade A, it may be a warning that too much of your revenue (80 per cent) is coming from a very small group of products (less than 20 per cent), which means you need to do better with your buying as you are dependent on so few products.

The grading system for the ABC Analysis by Product report looks like this:

>> **A-grade:** Your top-selling products that collectively account for 80 per cent of your revenue

>> **B-grade:** The products that collectively account for the next 15 per cent of your revenue

>> **C-grade:** The products that collectively account for the last 5 per cent of your revenue

Never, ever sell out of your A-grade products, unless it's deliberate, such as deliberately trying to remove a product from your range. Sticking to this simple rule can drive significant growth to your business.

If you need to run a sale, start by looking at your C-grade products — they're only contributing 5 per cent of your total sales so they probably haven't made a positive return on your initial investment, so you won't miss their revenue.

» **Capturing payments**

» **Contacting customers about their orders**

» **Refunding orders and initiating returns**

» **Checking orders for fraud**

Chapter **12**

So, You've Received an Order — Now What?

t's important to know your way around your customers' orders, because speedy, accurate order fulfillment is one of the key factors in determining whether or not a customer will return to your store. In this chapter, I'm going to introduce you to the three stages of an online order in Shopify — receiving an order, being paid for an order and fulfilling an order (Chapter 13 covers how to fulfill orders).

I also run through how to recognize when you've got orders to send out, how to check an order's details (such as the delivery address) and how to make any changes (such as editing the delivery address). I also show you how to search for old orders, find customer contact details, and create refunds or returns.

From time to time, your online store will be subject to fraudsters trying their luck with stolen credit card numbers, and it's important to know what to look out for and what to do if you're targeted, so I finish the chapter with some additional tips for handling fraudulent orders.

Receiving and Confirming Orders

When a customer places an order in your online store — or any of your other activated sales channels, such as Amazon or eBay — it appears in the Orders page of your Shopify admin.

REMEMBER

To view your orders at any time, go to your Shopify admin and navigate to Orders in the sidebar on the left of the screen.

Don't worry, you won't have to keep checking the Orders page every 20 minutes! You'll receive an email when you get an order — and if you've downloaded the Shopify app, you'll hear a delightful 'cha-ching!' sound each time you receive an order.

TIP

You can create and edit email notifications to let you and/or your staff know when a customer places an order. You need the Orders permission on your account to make changes to order notifications.

To add a recipient who will also get emails when a customer places an order, follow these steps:

1. **From your Shopify admin, go to Settings → Notifications.**

   A list of notifications appears.

2. **In the Staff Order Notifications section, click on Add Recipient — this is located towards the bottom of the page, on the left-hand side of the Notifications page menu.**

   The Add an Order Notification window appears.

3. **From the first drop-down menu that appears, select the email address for the notification from the following options:**

   - Select Email Address, and then enter a new email address that you want to send the order notification to, such as a team member who is fulfilling orders. (This option is to email people not set up with an account within your Shopify admin.)

   - Select a staff member so you can send notifications to their email address. If the staff member is already registered as a user on your store, you will be able to select their email address when you click on Email Address under Notification Method.

4. **Click on Add an Order Notification.**

TIP

After you've set up a new order notification for an email address, you can test it by clicking on Send Test Notification, which is the last item in the Notifications menu, near the bottom of the page.

As well as you or your team receiving an email confirmation of a new order, so too will your customers. You can edit the style of your order confirmation email, or add an SMS notification, by navigating to Settings → Notifications, and then selecting Order Confirmation from the list of available notifications. You may want to hire an expert from the Shopify Experts marketplace to help you style your order confirmations, or you can click on Customize, which is the very first option that appears in the Notifications section, and do some basic style editing, including adding logos, and changing colors and messaging.

TIP

When you click on the Orders section of your Shopify admin, you see a heading called Abandoned Checkouts. These are customers who reached the checkout but didn't follow through to a completed sale. An absolute must for any ecommerce store is to have an abandoned checkout email flow that sends customers who abandon their checkout an email reminding them to complete it, with a link to the items they added to their cart. I look at automated abandoned checkout emails in Chapter 15.

The Three Stages of an Online Order

Orders go through three stages in your Shopify admin:

Order State	Action You Need to Take
1. Order placed	Capture payment
2. Order paid for	Fulfill the order
3. Order has been paid for and fulfilled	Archive the order

The following sections look at different ways to take action to process orders through each stage.

Order placed: Capture payment

Most merchants set their stores to capture credit card payments automatically, which means that payment is charged to the customer's credit card straight away rather than the merchant needing to go into each order and manually capture payment. This saves time and also ensures that money flows into your business promptly.

A situation where you may not automatically capture payment may be if you're unsure about whether or not you have the stock to fulfill an order, or if you're taking pre-orders and you don't want to charge the customer until you fulfill the order. Another possibility is that you want to accept part payments; for example, if you have one but not all of the ordered items in stock.

If you don't automatically capture payments, you need to manually process each payment.

TIP

Chapter 6 covers payment set-up if you need to refer back to getting started with processing payments.

Capturing manual payments in Shopify

I don't usually recommend this approach, because it means you don't get paid straight away — and if you're selling in a foreign currency, the exchange rate may change between the time the order is placed and the time you process the payment.

However, if you feel manual payment processing is for you, then follow these steps to get set up:

1. **From your Shopify admin, go to Settings → Payments.**

   The Payments page appears.

2. **In the Payment Capture section, click on the Manage button.**

   The Payment Capture Method dialogue box appears (see Figure 12-1).

   Two options appear in the dialogue box:

   • Automatically Capture Payments for Orders

   • Manually Capture Payments for Orders

3. **Select Manually Capture Payment for Orders.**

4. **Click on the Save button.**

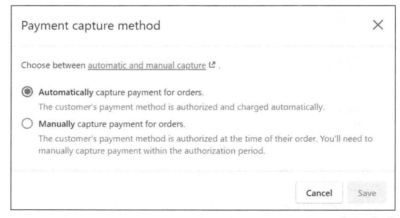

FIGURE 12-1: The Payment Capture Method dialogue box.

Source: Shopify

Capturing automatic payments in Shopify

Most online merchants will capture payments automatically, because it means you won't have to take action, which saves you time and brings money into your bank account faster.

To ensure your store is set up to automatically capture payments (which I recommend you enable), follow the steps in the preceding section, selecting Automatically Capture Payments for Orders rather than Manually Capture Payments for Orders in Step 2. This option is already ticked, as it is Shopify's default payment capture option, so you simply leave it ticked.

WARNING

If you're capturing payments automatically and you don't have the product the customer ordered in stock, you'll need to issue a refund because you've already taken the customer's payment. I talk about processing refunds later in this chapter in the section 'Refunding a customer'.

Order paid for: Fulfill the order

Fulfillment is a word you hear a lot in ecommerce. It means to pick, pack and send the order, thus completing it, or fulfilling it.

After payment has been captured, your customer will want their order quickly; however, there are numerous ways Shopify can handle order fulfillment, so I dedicate Chapter 13 to exploring all your order fulfillment options.

Order has been paid for and fulfilled: Archive the order

After the order has been paid for and fulfilled, the next action is to archive the order. *Archiving an order* means to close it, meaning no further action is required, so you can clearly see how many *open* orders there are in the Orders section of your Shopify admin — in other words, orders that have not been fulfilled.

You can elect to either archive orders manually or automatically.

Manual archiving

I rarely see any online retailers manually archive their orders, although you may want to do this at the start of your Shopify selling career so you can get familiar with the ins and outs of each order, and check them before they're archived.

To manually archive orders in Shopify, follow these steps.

1. **From your Shopify admin, go to Orders.**

   The Orders page appears, which lists all of your store's orders, with the most recent orders appearing at the top.

2. **From the Orders page, click on the checkbox to the left of the orders that you want to archive.**

3. **Click on More Actions, which is an option that appears in the header, above your order list, after you select an order, and then click on Archive Orders from the drop-down list that appears.**

   Your order is now displayed as Archived.

You can also print packing slips using the same steps — a good tip to remember when you start dispatching orders.

Automatic archiving

Automatic archiving is the most common way to archive your orders due to its simplicity and the little effort required.

Orders can be set to automatically archive after they've been marked as fulfilled (when you see your orders in the Orders page, the status is displayed alongside each order; you also see an order's status at the top of the Order Details page when you click on an order on the Orders page) — I look at how to fulfill orders in Chapter 13.

To automatically archive your orders, follow the below steps:

1. **From your Shopify admin, go to Settings → Checkout.**

   The Checkout page appears, which enables you to customize your store's checkout — the page where your customers pay you.

2. **Scroll down to the Order Processing section of the Checkout page.**

3. **Under the heading titled After an Order Has Been Fulfilled and Paid, you have one option: Automatically Archive the Order, which directs Shopify to automatically archive an order after it has been paid and fulfilled. Select this feature if you want to automatically archive all orders.**

4. **Click on the Save button.**

Creating Draft Orders for Customers

From time to time, you may need to create an order *for* a customer. This actually happens more than you might think, and it can be a useful selling point. For example, if you're selling a product that might be well-suited to you offering phone support, you may want to take orders over the phone to save the customer any hassle. This is particularly helpful if you're selling things that are technical, such as computer parts, or products that might be geared towards older people, who may be more used to phone or store sales — don't underestimate the personal touch!

Other reasons you may find it helpful to create draft orders, sometimes called *backend orders*, might be for taking wholesale orders either in person or over the phone, or if you're selling at a physical location, such as a trade fair.

To create a draft order:

1. **Go to your Shopify admin and click on Orders, then click on the green Create Order button.**

    The Create Order page appears (see Figure 12-2).

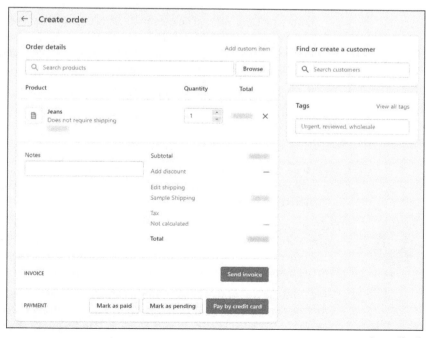

FIGURE 12-2: The Create Order page.

Source: Shopify

2. **Add the order details in the following sections:**

- **Order Details:** In this search field, you can search for products already added to your store, or you can add a new product that isn't in your online catalogue by clicking on Add Custom Item, located just above this field. This will be a quick product set-up, useful for selling items like one-off samples that don't need to be shown on your website. You will be prompted to enter an Item Name, a Price and a Quantity, then you can click on Done to finish adding the product.

- **Find or Create a Customer:** Here you can select the customer that you're placing the order for by searching for them in the Find or Create a Customer search field — if they have already been a customer of your store, you'll see their information pop up as you begin typing their name. If it's a new customer, just select Create a New Customer from the Find or Create a Customer search field and enter their details as prompted.

- **Tags:** Tags are used a little differently here to the way I showed you to use them when creating products and collections in Chapter 5. Here, you may like to add a tag to help you easily find an order in your list of orders, such as using the tag 'wholesale' — you can then search for orders tagged with 'wholesale' on your Orders page (to access this page, select Orders from your Shopify admin, then Orders again from the list that pops up).

- **Notes:** You have an optional field to add any notes, such as 'call customer before fulfilling order'. The person fulfilling this order will see the notes when they're looking at the order details. Notes are also useful for when a customer calls to tell you special information about the order, such as, 'Item is a gift; please remove invoice from order.'

3. **Edit the price, shipping costs and tax information.**

When you enter a product into Shopify, a new section pops up in which you can manually edit the price of the item you're selling and add a shipping cost. You can also elect to charge tax or charge no tax.

4. **Click on the green button labelled Send Invoice. Shopify then asks for your customer's email address, along with space for a message to be included in the email.**

TIP

If the customer is on the phone, or in front of you, you can select the other green button Pay by Credit Card, which brings up a section for you or the customer to enter payment details in, followed by pressing the Charge button at the bottom of the screen, which processes the payment.

5. **After the payment has been made, finish the process by selecting Mark as Paid (at the bottom of the page) or, if you're waiting for the customer to pay an emailed invoice, select Mark as Pending until the customer pays — this ensures your order isn't accidentally sent to the customer before their payment has been captured.**

Managing Orders

From time to time, you may need to check certain information in an order, or even make changes to an order. You'd be surprised how often a customer enters their shipping address incorrectly, only to call or email later to update it.

In this section, I show you how to access, edit and manage your customers' orders, including discovering how to contact customers about their orders, update them on their order or check the status of an order — for example, checking if an order has been sent or not.

Viewing an order

REMEMBER

You can view your orders, and view the details of specific orders, by following these steps:

1. **In your Shopify admin, click on Orders in the left-hand menu.**

   A list of all your store's orders appears, in order of newest to oldest (see Figure 12-3).

2. **Click on the order number of the order you wish to view, and the order details will appear.**

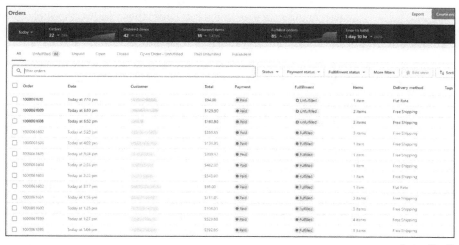

FIGURE 12-3:
The Orders page
in Shopify.

Source: Shopify

You can search for a customer's order using a number of parameters, including name, order number and email address. Simply enter the search details in the Filter Orders field at the top of the Orders page.

You can also filter orders at the top of the page in the same section, by clicking on the Filter option in the header, where you will see various parameters, including an order's Status — for example, you may like to check all your unfulfilled orders each morning so you can get round to sending them! (To do this, click on Fulfillment Status → Unfulfilled.)

When you click inside a customer's order, on the right-hand side, under the Customer heading, you can see their complete history with your store, including how often they've ordered from you and how much they have spent with you. It's always nice to acknowledge your VIP customers, and noticing your VIPs in this way gives you a nice opportunity to write a message to your customer, give them a little extra love when you send their order or swiftly handle an enquiry from them.

In the same right-hand side of the customer's order page, you see a section called Conversion Summary. A *conversion* is an ecommerce term for a sale, or transaction. If you click on View Conversion Details, a dialogue box will pop up displaying information about how many times the customer visits your store before placing their order, and how many orders they've placed with your store overall. It also tells you their traffic source — in other words, how they found you (for example, direct — meaning they typed your website into their browser directly — or via a search engine such as Google). I cover these traffic channels in Part 5, which covers attracting customers through your marketing efforts.

Viewing an order's Timeline

When you're in an order, you can see the details of the order, including the product the customer ordered, along with their shipping address and contact details (see Figure 12-4). (You can also create shipping labels from this page, but I come to that in Chapter 13, when I talk through fulfilling orders.)

At the bottom of the order page, you see a section called *Timeline*. Here, you can see the sequence of events that occurs after the order has been placed, including when the customer was sent their order confirmation email (along with a button giving you the option to resend an order confirmation email to a customer), and when the money from the order will be added to your Shopify Payout (Chapter 6 covers Shopify Payouts in more detail). You can also add notes for other team members to see in the order's Timeline, which is useful for noting things like customer address changes or notes for the warehouse.

FIGURE 12-4:
The Order
Details page.

TIP

With Timeline, you can view detailed histories and write notes and comments for orders, draft orders, customers and transfers in Shopify. All notes and comments are internal and will not be visible to your customers. If you use the Shopify app, then you can receive notifications whenever you're mentioned in a Timeline comment (you can @ mention any team members who are users on your Shopify store, which notifies them of your message).

Editing an order

Customers may contact you after they've placed an order to make changes, such as adjusting the delivery address, changing sizes or colors, or even selecting an entirely new product that costs a different amount to what they initially chose!

Here's a chance to provide a great customer experience (commonly called CX, and which I explore in Part 3). Log into your Shopify admin and navigate to Orders, then select Orders again in the drop-down menu of the sidebar. Search for the customer's order in the Filter Orders field using parameters such as their order number or email address, and click on the order number when it appears.

When you're inside the order you wish to edit, you'll see three options in the top-right corner: Refund, Edit and More Actions. Click on Edit and the Edit Order page appears. To adjust the product quantity in the order, click on Adjust Quantity; to remove the item altogether, click on Remove Item; or to add a completely new item to the order, click on Search Products to Add. When you're done, click on Update Order to save your changes.

You can add a reason for the edit, if you wish, at the bottom of the page. If you're adding an item, or increasing the price of the order, you then need to hit the Send Invoice button on the right when it pops up — this sends an email with an invoice to the customer, allowing them to pay the difference. Once done, click on Update Order in the top-right corner to save your changes.

Contacting a customer about their order

If you need to contact a customer about their order — for example, if you're out of stock of an item they bought, or you need to clarify their address details — you can access their order details to do so.

On the right-hand side of the Order Details page, you see a section called Contact Information, followed by the customer's email address. Click on the email address and a pop-up box appears, prompting you to email the customer directly from the Order Details page. You can enter the email text here — and add other email recipients as well, if needed. Click on Review Email to check you have covered everything, and then click on Send Notification if you're happy to send the email.

If you want to call the customer, the phone number (if supplied by the customer) can be found in the Customer Information block on the right-hand side of your Order Details page.

TIP

Customers often claim they haven't received an order confirmation email (which may be due to their email service's spam settings). In the order's Timeline, you're able to see when that email was sent, along with a button labelled Resend Email — click on that to resend a copy of the order confirmation to the customer.

Checking an order's status

To check the status of an order in your store, you or your customers can use the Order Status page, which keeps a customer informed of where their order is up to — for example, whether it has been fulfilled (picked, packed and shipped), or whether it's yet to be processed.

The customer will be sent a link to their order status page, which helps them to feel comfortable about their order while they wait for it to be delivered.

You can also check an order's status by following these steps:

1. **From the Order Details page, click on More Actions in the top-right corner, and from the drop-down menu that appears select View Order Status Page.**

   The Order Status Page appears with the customer's order details, along with updates as to where the order is up to. For example, the first stage of an order status will be Order Confirmed, and once it's been shipped, the Order Status Page updates to reflect the tracking number (I talk more about shipping orders in Chapter 13).

2. **Update your customer and/or take action (such as organizing shipping) if required.**

Refunding a customer

If a customer requests a refund — and you've decided that as part of your Returns policy, you'll offer refunds — or if a product you sell is faulty and the law in your country requires you to offer a full refund, then you're able to quickly issue a refund in the Order Details page of the customer's order.

Navigate to the top-right corner of the Order Details page inside the order that you're refunding. You'll see three options, including Refund.

Click on Refund and you'll be taken to a new screen (see Figure 12-5) that gives you the chance to confirm the items you're processing for refund, including being able to select how many items you want to refund (along with the option to refund, or not refund, shipping, depending on your Refund and Shipping policies).

TIP

You may sometimes want to offer a partial refund — for example, if a customer is unhappy because their delivery was late, you may decide to take $10 off the order as a gesture of good will. You do this by editing the Refund Amount field on the right-hand side of the Refund page.

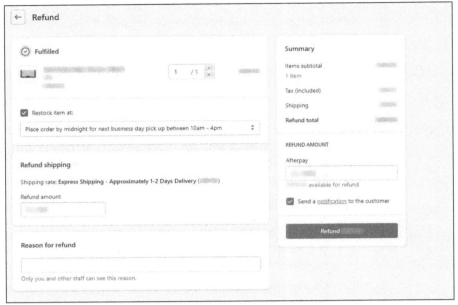

FIGURE 12-5:
The Refund page.

Source: Shopify

Enter a refund reason if you'd like to, at the bottom of the page, such as 'faulty item', and then select whether or not you would like the item to be added back to your inventory. For example, if the customer has sent the product back and you can resell it, tick the box that says Restock Item At. If the item is damaged or faulty, or the customer is keeping it, then you don't need to add it back to your inventory as you can't sell it, so leave the box unticked.

TIP

Tick the box labelled Send a Notification to the Customer if you want the customer to be emailed confirming their refund, and click on the word Notification to edit the messaging inside the email.

Finally, check that the amount in the Refund Amount section is correct, and then click the green button labelled Refund (which also shows you the amount you're refunding).

Creating returns

If a customer wants to send an item back to you for a refund, or for any other reason (such as requiring a different size), then select Return Items, which is located in the top-right menu, right alongside the Refund option. Note: You only see this option on orders that have been fulfilled.

You're taken to a new page that looks similar to the Refund page — the Return Items page (see Figure 12-6). The first section of the page asks you to Select a Return Reason, such as 'size too small' or 'unknown' (you don't need to enter this, but it's useful to keep track of why customers are making returns).

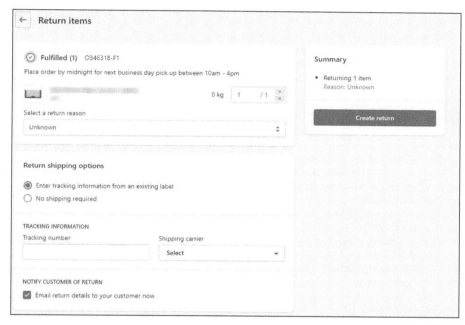

FIGURE 12-6:
The Return Items page.

If the customer has sent the item back to you, you can request a tracking number and enter it in the Tracking Information field further down the page; otherwise, select No Shipping Required if you don't need to track the package on its way back to you.

TIP

Select the checkbox under Notify Customer of Return to send an automated email to your customer, confirming their return.

REMEMBER

Returns can be hairy! Slow return processing leads to very cranky customers, who are unlikely to return to your online store. Try and keep your returns neat and tidy — using features like the ability to enter tracking numbers into a returned order can make life much easier for you in the long run.

Checking an Order for Fraud

Unfortunately, where there is ecommerce, there is fraud. The good news is that Shopify has some inbuilt tools to help prevent fraud. Failure to recognize a fraudulent order can result in a chargeback, which is when a customer disputes a transaction that occurred on their credit card, often because it's been stolen and used on an online store like yours. (Chapter 6 shows you how to process chargebacks.)

If your store is on the Basic Shopify plan and you don't have Shopify Payments, then fraud analysis includes the following:

>> Fraud analysis indicators

>> Support for third-party fraud prevention apps

If your store is on the Shopify plan or higher, or you have Shopify Payments on any plan, then fraud analysis includes the following:

>> Fraud analysis indicators

>> Support for third-party fraud prevention apps

>> Fraud prevention recommendations

Although I've provided an overview of fraud investigation strategies in Chapter 6, the Order Details page offers some further information that you can use to examine potentially fraudulent orders within the process of confirming your orders — as explored in the following sections.

Fraud analysis indicators

Shopify's fraud analysis provides indicators for each order. The indicators can be used to investigate an order that you think may be fraudulent.

The fraud analysis indicators include information such as:

>> **Whether the credit card used for the order passes address verification service (AVS) checks.** These checks compare the address entered in your store's billing address field when a customer places an order against the billing address that the bank has on file for the credit card being used.

>> **Whether the customer provided the correct CVC code.** The CVC code is the three- or four-digit code on the back of your credit card, near the signature panel.

>> **Details about the IP address used to place the order.** IP stands for Internet Protocol, and the IP address is used to provide the address of the device being used to place the order. If an IP address is very far from a billing or delivery address, there's a chance the credit card may have been stolen.

For example, if you see an order placed with an IP address in Dubai but the billing address provided is in Los Angeles, then that's an order worth checking for fraud — also known as a high-risk order.

>> **Whether the customer tried to use more than one credit card.** Another high risk-factor! Shopify can identify if multiple credit cards have been used to try and pay for an order, which is a sign that a fraudster may be cycling through stolen credit card numbers.

The full analysis for an order lists all the indicators. These indicators are marked with green, red or grey icons to help you highlight different behavior types (see Figure 12–7):

>> Green indicators show information about the order that is usually seen on legitimate orders.

>> Red indicators show information about the order that is usually seen on fraudulent orders.

>> Grey indicators give you additional information about the order that may be useful.

Indicators

Characteristics of this order are similar to non-fraudulent orders observed in the past

Card Verification Value (CVV) is correct

Billing street address matches credit card's registered address

Billing address ZIP or postal code matches the credit card's registered address

There was 1 payment attempt

Payment was made with 1 credit card

Billing country matches the country from which the order was placed

The IP address used to place the order isn't a high risk internet connection (web proxy)

Location of IP address used to place the order is Ottawa, Ontario, Canada

Shipping address is 520 km from location of IP address

Source: Shopify

FIGURE 12-7: Shopify's fraud analysis indicators.

To view the fraud analysis of an order, follow the below steps:

1. **In your Shopify Admin, click on Orders in the left-hand menu.**

   A list of all your store's orders appears, in order of newest to oldest.

2. **Click on the order number of the order you want to investigate.**

   The Order Details page appears. You see a section titled Fraud Analysis on the Order Details page. If your store is on the Basic Shopify plan or higher, then you see a list of indicators and a button you can click on to view the full analysis.

3. **Review the fraud analysis indicators (as shown in Figure 12-7).**

   If your store is on the Shopify plan or higher, or you're using Shopify Payments, you also see a fraud prevention recommendation.

TIP

At the start of the chapter, I looked at manual payment capture as an option. If you want to allow time to investigate orders before you accept payment for them, you can set up manual payment capture for your store.

How to handle potential fraud in your store

If an order is flagged as high risk, or even if you think it's suspicious, you have three options:

1. **Verify the order.**

   Reminder, go back to Chapter 5 to review how to verify whether payments from customer's are legitimate or not.

2. **Cancel the order.**

   To cancel an order in Shopify, go back into the Order Details page of the order you wish to cancel, and navigate back to the More Actions button in the top right. Click on Cancel Order.

TIP

If you want to add the stock back to your inventory (which you would, in the case of spotting a fraudulent order before you've sent it out), then leave the box labelled Restock Items ticked before you click on Cancel Order. As with most actions that affect customers, you can select whether you want to notify the customer or not, in the same way you do for processing refunds.

3. **Refund the order (if you have already accepted the payment).**

   Refer to the earlier section 'Refunding a customer' for how to refund an order.

Order refund and order cancellation actions are slightly different. You can only cancel an order if payment has not been accepted, or if payment has been accepted but the products have not been shipped. If you cancel an order that has been paid for, then a refund is issued as part of the cancelling process. If you cancel an order that has not been paid for, then you only need to cancel the order, as there's no payment to refund.

TIP

If you've placed a test order and want to delete it so as not to impact your sales reports, first cancel the order and then click on Delete This Order at the bottom of the Order Details.

» **Printing shipping labels**

» **Offering click and collect, or local pickup**

Chapter **13**

From Here to There: Fulfilling Your Orders

The good work you've done in finding great products and building your new Shopify store can be undone in a heartbeat through a poor logistics offering, or sloppy fulfillment.

In ecommerce, when a customer places and pays for an order in your store, the order is recorded in Shopify and you are then notified of the order so you can find the product and send it to the customer — in other words, *fulfilling* the order by ensuring the customer receives what they ordered. *Logistics* refers to the physical movement of goods that is involved when you fulfill an order, sending them from your storage space or warehouse to the customer.

The key word when it comes to fulfillment and logistics is speed. Customers who shop online expect their orders to come quickly, so it's no longer okay to deliver in a week or two — in my experience, speeding up your delivery times, and reflecting those improved speeds on your website's Shipping Information page, can lead to an increase in conversion rate. On the other hand, I have also seen slow delivery, and slow processing of returns, lead to a drop in repeat customers.

In this chapter, I show you how to ship orders manually (the simple way) and automatically (as you get braver and braver). I also consider your shipping options, from fulfilling orders yourself to using a fulfillment service to store and ship your orders. Finally, I look at how you can make life easier for your customers by offering click and collect options to suit their needs.

There's a shipping option for every online store, and by the end of this chapter you'll be equipped to fulfill orders like a pro!

Fulfill Your Own Orders

Fulfilling your own orders is likely going to be the best option for you if you're an ecommerce beginner or you're new to Shopify. You simply receive an order, then pack and ship that order in whichever way you like. Fulfilling your own orders allows you to save money on using a fulfillment service (which I talk about in the later section 'Using a Fulfillment Service') and enables you to take extra care with packaging and presenting your orders, which can contribute to a nice, personalized customer experience.

Shopify defaults to manual order fulfillment, which means you have to update each order as Fulfilled manually in your admin, but you can also fulfill your orders automatically, which means that the status of an order changes to Fulfilled automatically. The following sections explore your different fulfillment options in Shopify.

Fulfilling your orders manually

Manually fulfilling your orders is the ideal way to get started with fulfilling an order in Shopify, primarily because it minimizes errors (and it's easy). If you opt to fulfill an order manually, it forces you to go and check that you actually have the stock before you manually fulfill the order and update the order status to Fulfilled. It's also useful for when a customer orders two items, but only one is in stock — manual fulfillment allows you to partially fulfill the order by first sending the item that you have in stock, and then sending the second item when it is available.

Manual fulfillment is also a great option when you make products *to order* (producing or manufacturing the product after the order has been placed), as it may take you a few days to be ready to fulfill an order. When an order has been fulfilled, the order's Fulfillment Status changes from Unfulfilled to Fulfilled on the Orders page. Your customer receives an email when an order's status changes, so you don't want to fulfill the order in Shopify (that is, change the status to Fulfilled) until you're ready to ship the item to the customer.

When you're fulfilling an order manually and you're not using Shopify Shipping, you won't see an option to buy a shipping label through Shopify, so you need to arrange your own shipping, including buying your own shipping labels from whichever carrier you use. In your early days, you may simply take your orders to your local post office. When you book an order through your own shipping carrier, you need to take the tracking number that your carrier gives you and enter it into the order in Shopify, which then sends an email to your customer with their tracking number in it. When you use Shopify Shipping, the tracking number process is automated, so you won't need to enter it manually.

You may want to create a few practice orders through your admin so that you can test your fulfillment process on them before you get started with fulfilling real-life orders.

The following sections run through how you fulfill orders manually using Shopify.

Fulfill entire orders manually

Manual order fulfillment can apply whether you're using Shopify Shipping or not — it means that you're picking, packing and sending your own orders, rather than using a fulfillment company, such as a 3PL (third-party logistics provider) to fulfill your orders.

Shopify's default position enables manual order fulfillment, so if this is your preferred process then you're not required to do anything to get set up — you're ready to go!

To manually fulfill an order, follow these steps:

1. **From your Shopify admin, go to Orders.**

   A list of your orders appears.

2. **Click on the order number of an unfulfilled order (see Figure 13-1).**

   You can sort your unfulfilled orders in the Orders section by clicking on the Unfulfilled option in the header (after 'All').

   The Order Details page appears.

3. **If you're using Shopify Shipping (for stores based in the United States, Canada or Australia) to buy a shipping label for your order, then select Create Shipping Label (see Figure 13-2).**

FIGURE 13-1:
Unfulfilled orders
on the Orders
page.

Source: Shopify

FIGURE 13-2:
Creating a
shipping label
using Shopify
Shipping.

Source: Shopify

4. **If you're using a carrier other than Shopify Shipping — for example, you're planning to take your orders to your local post office — click on Fulfill Item(s), which is located on the order details page, next to the Create Shipping Label button.**

   You're taken to a new page titled Fulfill Item(s).

5. **Enter the tracking number provided to you by your shipping provider in the field labelled Tracking Number.**

   The tracking URL will appear in your customer shipping confirmation and shipping update emails.

6. **Select your shipping carrier from the Shipping Carrier drop-down menu, or if it doesn't appear, select Other, which then prompts you to enter a URL from which your customer can track their order.**

Shopify may recognize the tracking number format and choose a shipping carrier for you. If it doesn't, or if it chooses incorrectly, then select your shipping carrier from the Shipping Carrier drop-down menu.

7. **If you want to send a notification email to the customer right away, then select Send Shipment Details to Your Customer Now, which is a checkbox located below the Tracking Number field.**

8. **Click on Fulfill Items to mark the order as Fulfilled. If you're using Shopify Shipping, select a shipping carrier and click on Buy Shipping Label.**

You're returned to the Orders page, where the order's fulfillment status will have updated to Fulfilled.

Fulfill partial orders manually

Fulfilling orders partially occurs when a customer orders more than one product, or more than one unit of a product, but only some of the products or units in the order can be fulfilled — the rest may be on pre-order or need to be made to order, or they may be out of stock completely.

You can only partially fulfill orders when you're using manual fulfillment rather than automatic fulfillment.

If you're using Shopify Shipping to buy labels, (for stores based in the United States, Canada or Australia) then you can print a label after you've marked the order as fulfilled (as noted in the preceding section, 'Fulfill entire orders manually'). I talk more about printing labels in the later section 'Printing Shipping Labels and Customs Forms'.

To partially fulfill an order in Shopify when your store uses Shopify Shipping, follow these steps:

1. **From your Shopify admin, go to Orders.**

2. **Click on the number of an unfulfilled order.**

The Order Fulfillment page appears (Shopify calls this a Fulfillment Card).

3. **To buy a Shopify Shipping label for your order, click on Create Shipping Label.**

The Create Shipping Label page appears (see Figure 13-3, which shows an Australian example — different carriers aside from Sendle appear for the United States and Canada).

Source: Shopify

4. **Change the number of products that you want to fulfill for each item in the Items section.**

For example, if a customer has ordered two pairs of jeans but you're only fulfilling one pair right now because you're waiting for the second to arrive in stock, you need to adjust the number of products being fulfilled to one rather than two.

5. **Select the shipping method in the Shipping Service section — here, you see your Shopify Shipping carriers.**

6. **If you want to send a notification email to the customer right away, then tick Send Shipment Information to Customer Now, which is located in the Shipping Date section of the Create Shipping Label page.**

This option is available only if you have an email address for the customer on file.

FIGURE 13-3: Creating a shipping label in Shopify when you're using Shopify Shipping.

7. **Click the green Buy Shipping Label button in the bottom-right corner.**

The Order Details page updates to display the order's Fulfilled and Unfulfilled items. At this point, you've booked your shipment through Shopify Shipping, so you need to make sure you have your order picked, packed and ready to send to your customer.

REMEMBER

When you create a shipping label using Shopify Shipping, you incur a charge because you're also booking a courier when you create the label, which is added to your Shopify store's billing. You'll be shown where to drop the parcel off or how to arrange collection when you create a label — information you can find just under the Shipping Service section, after you click on Create Shipping Label.

To partially fulfill an order in Shopify when your store is not using Shopify Shipping, follow these steps:

1. **From your Shopify admin, go to Orders.**

2. **Click on the number of an unfulfilled order.**

The Order Fulfillment page (or Fulfillment Card) appears.

3. **If you have multiple locations (meaning you hold stock in more than one location) and you want to change the location that you're fulfilling your order from, click on the name of the location on the Order Fulfillment page, and select Change Location. Select the location that you want to use, and click on Save.**

4. **Click on Marked as Fulfilled.**

REMEMBER

At this point, you should be 100 per cent sure you have the products to fulfill the order. You need to have either posted your order to your customer, or booked a courier to come and pick up the order before updating an order to the Fulfilled status.

5. **Change the number of products that you want to fulfill for each item in the Items section.**

6. **Enter the tracking number from your shipping provider in the Tracking Information section.**

The tracking URL will appear in the customer's shipping confirmation and shipping update emails.

TECHNICAL
STUFF

You can customize the look of these emails by going to Settings in your Shopify admin and then clicking on Notifications. Navigate to the Shipping section and click on Shipping Update. You may need to hire a Shopify expert from the Shopify Experts marketplace as the design is written in code.

7. **If you want to send a notification email to the customer right away, then select Send Shipment Information to Customer Now.**

   This option is available only if you have an email address for the customer on file.

8. **Click on Fulfill Items.**

   The Order Fulfillment page updates to display the order's Fulfilled and Unfulfilled items.

9. **If you want to review the order's fulfillment details or add a tracking number, click on Add Tracking in the Fulfilled section of the order, which is also on the Order Fulfillment page.**

TIP

In Step 7, you're able to email tracking updates to customers when they use an email address to place their order and your store has their email address on file (for more on tracking, see the nearby sidebar 'Where is my order?'). You can allow customers to check out using an email address (which then adds it to their file), or you can choose to allow the customer to check out using either a phone number *or* an email. Shopify's default is to allow the customer to choose between checking out with a phone number or an email address.

To adjust these settings, go to Settings → Checkout in your Shopify admin. When the Checkout page appears, in the second block of text labelled To Check Out, you can select either option.

WHERE IS MY ORDER?

'Where is my order?' is one of the top reasons that I see customers create a customer service ticket (enquiry) with an online store. Tracking is such an important part of the overall customer experience that I always recommend sending tracking numbers to customers. Customers are usually understanding when an order is running late if they are informed along the journey; however, a customer may become suspicious — with new stores in particular — about whether they can trust a store that doesn't communicate with them through post-purchase emails, such as those providing order tracking updates.

Order tracking is so important in ecommerce that some companies have built successful business models around offering order tracking platforms that connect multiple carriers into one platform. For example, AfterShip is a technology business that only focuses on tracking shipments as a service. A great post-purchase experience is a good way to increase purchase frequency, and therefore customer lifetime value (CLTV), which is one of the holy grails for ecommerce merchants — a high CLTV means customers are happy and will come back for more.

By selecting several orders at once in the Order page, you can use the Fulfill Orders button to fulfill them at the same time. This applies to stores that manually fulfill orders. If you aren't using Shopify Shipping, you need to manually add tracking numbers to the orders.

Fulfilling your orders automatically

Setting your orders to fulfill automatically means that the order status updates to Fulfilled immediately after it's been paid for.

Automatic fulfillment triggers an email to the customer telling them their order has been fulfilled as soon as payment has been made, so make sure you're in control of your inventory before setting up automatic fulfillment — it can be a poor customer experience for a customer to be told their order is on the way, only for the store to then tell them it's out of stock!

Automatic fulfillment works well if you offer digital products, such as digital gift cards. I explain how to create digital gift cards in Chapter 10.

You can capture payments automatically with automatic fulfillment when you don't have any physical products available for pre-order. In other words, you're confident that all the stock listed on your store is actually in your warehouse, so you don't believe you need to check the stock before accepting payment; you're selling digital downloads; or you're using a fulfillment service. (I cover capturing payments in Chapter 12.)

You can change your store's order processing settings to automatic fulfillment by following these steps:

1. **From your Shopify admin, go to Settings → Checkout.**

   The Checkout Settings page appears.

2. **Find the Order Processing section, which is about halfway down the page.**

3. **Under the heading After an Order Has Been Paid, select Automatically Fulfill the Order's Line Items.**

4. **Click on Save.**

Setting your orders to be fulfilled automatically doesn't apply to local pickup orders — you must fulfill local pickup orders manually. I show you how to set up local pickup in the later section 'Using Local Pickup'.

Using a Fulfillment Service

A *fulfillment service* is a third party that stores your goods and fulfills your orders for you. A new online business typically starts by storing its own products; however, if you don't have the room, consider searching for a 3PL (third-party logistics provider) in your target market. This is also generally cheaper than renting a warehouse of your own, as a 3PL only charges you per product for storage, or sometimes not at all, in some instances only charging you a fee to send an order, which is a highly cost-efficient way to start your online business if you're holding large volumes of stock (or bulky items that you can't store at home). Chapter 11 talks more about storing your inventory.

Larger businesses sometimes use fulfillment services to save money and time, particularly as they grow — they take away the stress of needing to find bigger warehouses and more staff, as well as the fear of taking a long lease on a warehouse, only for order volumes to change, with the space no longer being suitable.

TIP

You can use fulfillment apps that will sync with Shopify, which Shopify calls a Fulfillment Service with an App — these services update your order's status within Shopify as the fulfillment service picks, packs and ships your order. Fulfillment by Amazon is one example, and dropshipping apps tend to do this as well.

The other fulfillment service that Shopify supports is what's known as a *custom fulfillment service*. Shopify considers a 3PL with a Shopify integration (or app) to be a fulfillment service, and a 3PL that doesn't have a Shopify integration to be a custom 3PL. Using a 3PL with a Shopify integration is a more automated process, where orders are sent automatically to be fulfilled; however, you need to customize the way you send orders to a custom 3PL.

If you use a custom fulfillment service that does not have a Shopify app, you can enable Shopify to send emails to the fulfillment service every time you receive an order so that your custom fulfillment service can fulfill each order for you.

REMEMBER

Because there's no app being used, your Shopify admin doesn't automatically update with the progress of the order, so you need to update the order status to Fulfilled yourself using the manual fulfillment method I covered in the earlier section 'Fulfilling your orders manually'.

If you decide to use a fulfillment service, here's how you can integrate this with Shopify, whether the service uses an app or is a customer fulfillment service without a Shopify app or integration.

Activating a custom fulfillment service

You can use any fulfillment service you like with Shopify, as long as it can accept orders by email. If the fulfillment service you're using doesn't have an app with Shopify, you can also build a custom integration or app, using a web developer, although this is probably not something I would recommend in your early stages, plus so many fulfillment centers have pre-existing integrations with Shopify.

To add and activate your chosen custom fulfillment service, follow these steps:

1. **From your Shopify admin, go to Settings → Shipping and Delivery.**

   The Shipping and Delivery page appears.

2. **In the Custom Order Fulfillment section (which is the last section on the page), click on Add Fulfillment Service.**

   The Add Custom Fulfillment Service dialogue box appears (see Figure 13-5).

3. **The dialogue box has two fields, asking for:**

   - The name of your custom fulfillment provider
   - The email address of your custom fulfillment provider

   When you receive an order, in your Shopify store, the fulfillment service is sent an email to the email address you set up in the previous steps, with all the order information so that they can fulfill it for you.

4. **Click on Save.**

The next step is to select the products that you want to be fulfilled by this fulfillment service. You can set up multiple fulfillment services — for example, you may have more than one fulfillment service that your stock is held at, or you may have some of your products at a fulfillment service and the rest with stored with you.

TECHNICAL STUFF

If you're dropshipping, apps like Oberlo help with integrating dropshippers as a kind of fulfillment service, but if your dropshipping supplier doesn't have an integration with Shopify you can set up each of your dropshipping suppliers as a fulfillment service and allocate each one to their respective products using the following steps (so that the supplier gets sent an order email to fulfill every time someone places an order).

For example, if I am selling furniture through a dropshipping model and my tables come from supplier X and my lamps come from supplier Y, I can set up suppliers X and Y as fulfillment services, who will each receive an email with the delivery details to fulfill their respective orders. I talk more about the merits of dropshipping in my book *Selling Online For Dummies*, and I also talk about dropshipping as a sales channel in Chapter 3 of this book.

Follow these steps to assign a fulfillment service to a product (remembering that you first need to add the fulfillment service as per the earlier steps in this section):

1. **From your Shopify admin, go to Products.**

   The Products page appears, which lists your store's products.

2. **Select the product that you want the custom fulfillment service to fulfill.**

   The product's page opens.

3. **In the Inventory section of the product's page (which is about halfway down the page), select the fulfillment service that you want to use from the Inventory Managed By drop-down menu (see Figure 13-4).**

4. **Click on Save in the top-right or bottom-right corner to save your changes.**

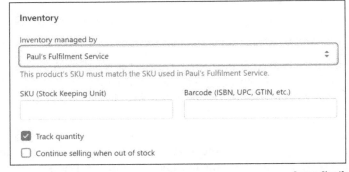

FIGURE 13-4:
The Inventory section of a product's page.

Source: Shopify

TIP

You can add a custom fulfillment service when you add a new product (refer to Chapter 5 for the process involved), or you can edit an existing product after it has been created.

REMEMBER

When you're using a custom fulfillment service, the act of marking an order as Fulfilled is what sends the email with the order details to the fulfillment service. You can set your store to either manual or automatic fulfillment when using a custom fulfillment service.

Deleting a custom fulfillment service

If you'd like to delete a custom fulfillment service you have added to Shopify, follow these steps:

1. **From your Shopify admin, go to Settings → Shipping and Delivery.**

   The Shipping and Delivery page appears.

2. **Scroll down to the bottom of the page and find the Custom Order Fulfillment section.**

   Here you'll see a list of any custom fulfillment services you've added.

3. **Next to the fulfillment service that you wish to delete, click on Edit.**

4. **In the Edit dialogue box that appears, click on the red Delete button. You'll be prompted to confirm that you want to delete the fulfillment service, so hit Delete again if you're sure you want to proceed.**

   You'll be returned to the Shipping and Delivery page, with the fulfillment service now deleted.

REMEMBER

If you have any inventory set to the service you're deleting, activate the new location that will inherit the deleted service's stocked products by following the steps in the earlier section 'Activating a custom fulfillment service'.

Using a fulfillment service with an app

Apps are what separates non-custom fulfillment services from custom fulfillment services, because the apps sync with Shopify so you can make changes to and receive updates about your fulfillments from your Shopify admin. A custom fulfillment service needs to be manually added to your Shopify store, along with an email address, so that it receives the order details every time an order is received for stock it is holding on your behalf.

Some 3PLs have apps available in the Shopify App Store, while others may have what's known as a *Shopify integration*, meaning they have a simple, out-of-the-box solution that connects your Shopify store to their internal system so that orders can flow into their systems automatically. Usually, tracking numbers can be sent to your store when the order has been fulfilled. If you're choosing a 3PL, it's going to make your life a lot easier if they have an existing Shopify integration.

EXAMPLE

One example of a fulfillment service with an app is Fulfillment by Amazon (FBA), which can be used to fulfill orders for your products placed via Amazon but also for orders placed on your store, using Amazon's MCF service (multi-channel fulfillment). Some other 3PLs I've used that have an integration with Shopify include ShipBob and ShipHero — both have apps in the Shopify App store.

When you're looking for a fulfillment center to work with, ask 'Do you have an integration with Shopify?' Most good ecommerce fulfillment services do, and this means you can set up automatic order fulfillment, which saves you time and helps you process orders quickly.

TIP

Printing Shipping Labels and Customs Forms

So far in this chapter, I've covered what to do when it's time to fulfill an order that has come into your online store. Now it's time to look at how you can print shipping labels using Shopify Shipping (and also when you're not using Shopify Shipping), as well as printing custom declaration forms and packing slips when required.

Figure 13-5 shows a typical shipping label.

Source: Shopify

FIGURE 13-5:
A typical shipping label.

I recommend that you use Shopify Shipping if it's available in your country (you can use this in the United States, Canada and Australia). For the rest of you, it's not a big issue if you don't have Shopify Shipping — you'll just have to either manually ship your order or use a fulfillment service.

Creating and printing shipping labels

In the earlier section 'Fulfilling Your Own Orders', I look at how to fulfill orders manually and automatically, and buying a shipping label is part of the fulfillment process for Shopify Shipping. After you've bought a shipping label using Shopify Shipping, the order is updated to the Fulfilled status, and you then need to prepare the order for collection or drop off. If you're not using Shopify Shipping, but rather you're manually fulfilling your own orders, then you still need to prepare the order in much the same way.

Preparing the order includes packaging it and attaching a shipping label that contains the customer's name and address to the outside of the package so that the courier or postal service can deliver it accurately. Additionally, in the case of international orders, you may be required to print a customs declaration form (for more on this, see the later section 'Printing a customs declaration form').

Shopify Shipping labels and label price adjustments are charged to the credit card that is on file for your Shopify account. All Shopify Shipping charges are billed in US dollars. If you're in Canada or Australia, shipping label prices are shown in your local currency when you purchase the label but the charge on your invoice will be in US dollars.

BUYING A SHIPPING LABEL PRINTER AND LABELS

Before you get started with anything that involves technology, it's important that you've got the right tools for the job. Nobody wants to be fiddling around with a printer that doesn't seem to be working — we've all been there, right?

Shopify recommends a range of label printers and label bundles to get you started (find out more and purchase recommended labels through hardware.shopify.com.

You can also use a standard desktop printer to print shipping labels that you can buy through Shopify. To install your printer, follow the instructions that came along with it. If you're using a standard desktop printer, then make sure that you select the 8.5 × 11-inch (21.59 × 27.94cm) paper option when printing the label.

You can view your shipping label charges in the Bills section of your Billing page in your Shopify admin (go to Settings in your Shopify admin, then click on Billing).

In the following sections, I show you the steps to printing shipping labels with and without Shopify Shipping.

Printing Shopify Shipping labels

After you buy a label using Shopify Shipping within the order fulfillment process (refer to the earlier section 'Fulfilling Your Own Orders' for more on this), you can either print it and attach it to your package, or void it — both occur within the Order page.

Here, I show you how to print a test label, print a purchased shipping label and void a shipping label when you're using Shopify Shipping.

PRINT A TEST LABEL

You aren't charged for printing a test shipping label, so it's a good idea to print one to make sure that your printer is set up properly.

To print a test shipping label, follow these steps:

1. **From your Shopify admin, go to Settings → Shipping and Delivery.**

   The Shipping and Delivery page appears.

2. **In the Shipping Labels section, click on Print Test Label next to the size that you want to print — for example, A4 or A6, depending on which label size is on offer.**

3. **If the label downloads to your computer, find the file on your computer and open it. If the label opens in a new tab in your browser, then go to the tab.**

4. **Click on the Print option for your computer.**

   The Print dialogue box appears.

5. **In the Print dialogue box, select the printer that you want to use to print the label.**

6. **Select the paper size that matches the printer you want to use to print the label.**

7. **Click on Print.**

PRINT A SHOPIFY SHIPPING LABEL

After you buy a shipping label through Shopify Shipping, you need to print it and attach it to the outside of the package you want to ship.

To print a shipping label, follow these steps:

1. **From your Shopify admin, go to Orders.**

   A list of all your store's orders appears.

2. **Click the order number of an order that you've purchased a shipping label for.**

   The Order Fulfillment page appears.

3. **Click on Print Label, which appears in the top half of the Order Fulfillment page.**

   The Print dialogue box appears.

4. **In the Print dialogue box, select the printer that you want to use to print the label.**

5. **Select the paper size that matches the printer you're using to print the label.**

6. **After you've chosen the correct printer and paper size, click on Print.**

VOID A SHOPIFY SHIPPING LABEL

You may need to void a shipping label if you've purchased a shipping label and then the customer cancels the order, or you cannot locate the stock to fulfill the order.

You can void a shipping label if it meets the following requirements:

>> It has been less than 30 days since you purchased the label.

>> There have been no tracking events on the label, such as the shipping carrier accepting the shipment.

After you void a shipping label, the cost of the label is credited to your account. This amount is applied to the cost of any shipping labels that you buy in the future.

WARNING

If the package has already been shipped, you need to contact the carrier for help.

To void a shipping label, follow these steps:

1. **From your Shopify admin, go to Orders.**

   A list of all your store's orders appears.

2. **Click the number of the order with the shipping label that you want to void.**

   The Order Details page appears.

3. **In the Fulfilled section, click on the . . . icon → Void Label.**

4. **Enter a reason for voiding the label, such as 'order cancelled', or 'out of stock'.**

5. **Click on Void Label and Insurance to confirm.**

Printing a label without Shopify Shipping

If your fulfillment locations aren't based in the United States, Canada or Australia (so Shopify Shipping isn't available), you can use a shipping label app to print shipping labels instead. Your shipping carrier may request that you attach shipping labels with barcodes, so this can be quite important.

Plenty of label-printing apps can be found in the Shopify App Store (www.apps.shopify.com). Here are some of my favorites:

>> Shipstation

>> Shippit

>> Starshipit

>> Easyship

TIP

These apps do more than just print labels — they can also integrate third-party carriers with your Shopify store, a concept I introduce in Chapter 6.

Printing a customs declaration form

If you're shipping to an international destination, then you need to complete a customs declaration form. A *customs declaration form* is used by international customs teams to check the contents, components and value of products being shipped.

Some mail types require that you print a separate customs form for your shipment, and others include the form on the standard shipping label:

>> If you use the international shipping services Priority Mail International or Priority Express Mail International, then you need to print a separate customs form as well as the shipping label and attach them both to the outside of your package.

>> If you use First Class Package International Service, Priority Mail Flat International flat rate envelopes or Priority Mail International small flat rate boxes, then the customs declaration is included in the shipping label itself.

To print a customs declaration form, follow these steps:

1. **From your Shopify admin, go to Orders.**

   Your store's orders appear.

2. **Click on the order number of an international order that needs a customs declaration form.**

   The Order Fulfillment page appears.

3. **In the Unfulfilled section, click on Create Shipping Label.**

4. **In the Items section, click on Edit Customs Information (see Figure 13-6; you won't see this for domestic orders, only international ones).**

   A Customs Information Form dialogue box appears.

5. **Fill out the Customs Information Form information, then click on Save.**

   Typical information that international customs ask for include a description of the goods, such as leather shoes, or cotton dress, as countries often impose a tax, or duty, on imported goods, which can be classified by the type of product being sent across the border.

6. **When you're ready to purchase the label, click on Buy Shipping Label.**

   Optional: On the Print Shipping Labels page, tap Change Format and choose the correct shipping label size.

7. **Click on Print Label.**

   The customs declaration form is printed with the shipping label.

Source: Shopify

Printing packing slips

Packing slips are pieces of paper that are similar to a tax invoice, in that they detail what a customer has ordered. The person packing the online order will often print a packing slip and place it inside the package so that the customer has a record of what they ordered when it arrives. The packing slip can also be used when you're *picking orders* (finding them in your warehouse) — it acts as a sort of online order shopping list. You can tick each item on the packing list as you pick it, and then place the packing list inside the order.

THE SHOPIFY FULFILLMENT NETWORK

The Shopify Fulfillment Network (SFN) delivers orders to your customers (it is only currently available in the United States and Canada). You can store your inventory close to customers in fulfillment centers across the United States and Canada for fast, affordable shipping. With SFN, you can manage all business data in one place, including shipment tracking, customer data and inventory levels.

Review the following criteria to check if SFN is the right fit for your business:

- Your business sells in the United States or Canada.

- You ship a minimum of three orders per day.

- You don't sell any regulated or perishable products.

After you prepare and send your inventory to this network of fulfillment centers, they pick, pack and ship your products to your customers when an order is placed, freeing up your time to focus on growing your business.

To apply to use the Shopify Fulfillment Network, visit shopify.com/fulfillment.

To print a packing slip, you click on Print Packing Slips in the top-right corner of the Order Fulfillment page (from your Shopify admin, go to Orders, click on an unfulfilled order and then click on the Fulfill Order button inside the Order Fulfillment page). You can also print a packing slip by going to Orders, then checking the box next to the order you want to print a packing slip for and selecting More Actions from the header of the Orders section, and then clicking Print Packing Slips.

TIP

If you're fulfilling your own orders, a good idea is to go to Orders in your Shopify admin and filter your orders by Unfulfilled (by default, Shopify shows you your most recent orders first). Check the box next to all your unfulfilled orders, selecting More Actions then Print Packing Slips. This allows you to print packing slips for all the orders you need to go and pick, effectively giving you a picking list.

Using Local Pickup

Local pickup — or as it's also known, click and collect or curbside pickup — has grown in popularity, particularly as COVID-19 placed strain on delivery networks.

Click and collect, local pickup and curbside pickup are much the same, but there are some subtle differences in the terminology, although for Shopify's purposes, they are the same thing. For click and collect and local pickup, you tend to get out of your car and go to a reception or collection point, whereas with curbside pickup you don't have to get out of your car (grocery stores are starting to offer this service now). Whatever you call local pickup, the concept is the same — your customer collects their order from you, the retailer.

Customers who live close to the online retailer don't need to wait for delivery, which is a bonus for many customers who are happy to collect to suit their need for the product. The benefit for the retailer is that there are no delivery costs, and giving customers the flexibility to collect their items is a nice trait for a store hoping to deliver a positive user experience.

The following sections take you through setting up local pickup options for your online store.

Setting up local pickup

Local pickup can be set up directly from your admin settings. Local pickup is always free; you can't charge for it.

REMEMBER

When a customer comes to collect a local pickup order, you need to manually change the order status within Shopify from Unfulfilled to Fulfilled. This signals to you and your staff that the order has been picked up and no further action is required. Do this by checking the checkbox next to the order that is being collected in the Orders page, and selecting Mark as Fulfilled from the options in the header of the Orders page.

You can add pickup delivery instructions by managing the preferences for your pickup locations. For example, after a customer places an order online and arrives to collect it, you can add instructions that tell the customer to call you and then you can bring their order out to them.

You need to set up the local pickup option for each location where customers can go to get their orders (in case you have more than one pickup location).

To enable local pickup, follow these steps:

1. **From your Shopify admin, go to Settings → Shipping and Delivery.**

   The Shipping and Delivery page appears.

2. **Under Local Pickup, click on Manage beside the location that you want to enable, which at this stage is likely to be your only pickup address. If you have several locations, then click on Show More to display all your locations.**

   REMEMBER

   You must have a location set up already before you can select it. Chapter 6 explains how to add a new location to your online store.

3. **Select This Location Offers Local Pickup.**

4. **Under Information at Checkout, change the settings to meet your needs.**

   Optional: Under Order Ready for Pickup Notification, enter any pickup instructions to assist your customers — for example, 'call phone number upon arrival'.

5. **Click on Save.**

Managing local pickup locations

You can edit certain settings for your local pickup locations in your admin, including the following:

>> Enabling or disabling local pickup.

>> Specifying any instructions or information related to local pickup, such as store hours or a reminder to the customer to bring a copy of their order confirmation. The information is included in the notification that you send when you prepare an order for pickup.

>> Choosing the estimated pickup time to show when the customer checks out. For example, you might choose Usually Ready in 2 Hours.

To manage your local pickup location's settings, follow these steps:

1. **From your Shopify admin, go to Settings → Shipping and Delivery.**

   The Shipping and Delivery page appears.

2. **Under Local Pickup, click on Manage for the location that you want to edit. If you have several locations, then click on Show More to display all your locations.**

   You must already have added a location to your store before you can select it.

3. **Update the settings you want to change.**

4. **Click on Save.**

Customizing pickup notifications

It's a good idea to send a customer a notification when their order is ready for collection. In that email notification you can provide your address and phone number plus any extra instructions, such as asking the customer to park in a particular spot or wait for someone to come to the car.

To edit your pickup notifications, follow these steps:

1. **From your Shopify admin, go to Settings → Shipping and Delivery.**

   The Shipping and Delivery page appears.

2. **Under Local Pickup, click on Manage beside the location. If you have several locations, then click on Show More to display all your locations.**

   You must already have added a location to your store before you can select it.

3. **Under Order Ready for Pickup Notification, which is a text box located within the Local Pickup section, enter any additional pickup instructions for your customers, such as 'call on arrival'.**

4. **Click on Save.**

5

Attracting Attention: Sales and Marketing

IN THIS PART . . .

Assess your sales prices and create special offers to win over customers.

Utilize digital marketing to help you discover new potential customers.

Pay your way to success with paid advertising through Google and Facebook.

Discover the influence of social media marketing.

» Identifying when the time is right for a sale

» Creating a reduced sale price

» Offering discounts and free shipping

» Saving time by taking some discounting shortcuts

Chapter **14**

Pricing, Discounts and Promotions: Creating Eye-Catching Offers

Your pricing is crucial to the success of your online business, and depending on your strategy, attractive pricing could be your point of difference; alternatively, you could be selling at a higher premium, and offering a higher quality product or a superior service. Some businesses use discounts to attract new customers or retain customers who haven't shopped in a while. However you approach it, discounting should be used strategically rather than you handing out price reductions to customers here, there and everywhere.

In this chapter, I show you how to price your products and run sales and promotions. I also show you how to create discount codes that offer a certain percentage or dollar discount, and how to create offers that provide free shipping or allow customers to buy one get one free.

Pricing Your Products

Pricing isn't a 'feel' thing; it's more science than art. When you price your product, you need to ensure two things:

1. That the price you set is profitable now (in the early stages of your ecommerce journey, when the chances are you are operating alone or have a very small team)

2. That the price you set is profitable when you're a bigger business with higher expenses

TIP

I always recommend budgeting (and operating) as though your business is already a larger scale operation, otherwise the danger is that you will never have enough margin in your profit to allow for hiring staff, accelerating your marketing spend and all the other costs that come with a growing business — including paying yourself! All these factors need to be considered when you price your products.

REMEMBER

The *profit (or product) margin*, or mark-up (the mark-up on the *cost price* of your products — the price you paid for them), is the percentage profit you make, factoring in only the cost price of your product and the sales price you are selling at — not the other costs of sales. Your *gross profit margin* includes your costs of sales (such as shipping costs and merchant fees), not just the product costs, and so it is lower than the profit margin.

While I recommend aiming for a 70 per cent profit margin on the product's cost price, I try and run my businesses by the 50/30/20 rule — aim for a 50 per cent gross profit margin, where 30 per cent covers operating expenses, leaving a 20 per cent *net profit margin*.

EXAMPLE

Johnny orders 100 new dog beds from Alibaba for $10 each. Landed, they come in at $15 each. Johnny has decided to sell the beds on his website for $25 because another seller on Amazon has sold over 1,000 units of a similar style at the same price. Johnny is looking at a profit margin of 40 per cent, and he's pretty excited.

Johnny launches his website, but no sales come in. He picks up this book, flips to chapters 15, 16 and 17 to review marketing techniques, and realises he's going to need to spend about 15 per cent of his projected revenue on marketing, or what's known as a CPO (cost per order) of 15 per cent. In other words, he will need to spend 15 per cent of the sale price of $25 to get that sale. Johnny is then left with 25 per cent profit — so he doesn't cancel the lease on his new BMW yet.

Johnny makes a few sales and posts them, only to realise he needs to allow 8 per cent for shipping, so he's left with 17 per cent. Johnny's bank wants 3 per cent of that sale for merchant fees, so he's left with 14 per cent profit. Johnny dreams of having an online business with 50 staff, so he realises he's got to budget at least around 8 per cent for wages, including his own, which means he's down to 6 per cent. Johnny's wife is a little sick of the sight of dog beds piling up in the unit, so he's got to get a storage space — there goes another 5 per cent, and suddenly Johnny is down to 1 per cent. Now Johnny's cancelled the seafood dinner, and he's navigating the drive-through at McDonald's.

Poor old Johnny has 1 per cent of that $25 sale left, and I haven't even listed half of the expenses of a typical ecommerce business. Every business is different, but you can use common benchmarks when budgeting for your online store. If you don't know your expected net profit, let alone your gross profit, it's time to take a step back before you get started.

So, how do you price your goods to allow for all those expenses?

REMEMBER

In my experience, a profit margin of 70 per cent or more on your products for a direct to consumer (D2C) business is a reasonable target.

In other words, if you are creating a new brand or a new product, you should target a 70 per cent profit margin on your products when you set your retail price, so your landed cost price should be 30 per cent of your retail price. This gives you enough of a buffer to allow for fixed expenses so you don't end up like Johnny.

If you're a business to consumer (B2C) seller, the profit margin on your products is typically smaller, as you're likely to be the person in between the customer and the manufacturer. A B2C profit margin could be as low as 45 per cent but you would not want to see it any lower than that, and you are likely to have less control over the retail price as the manufacturer may not like seeing you heavily discount a product. Equally, if you over-price the product the customer may look elsewhere if you're stocking a well-known brand. (I explain the differences between D2C and B2C sellers in Chapter 3.)

EXAMPLE

Here is an example of how to calculate your retail prices using these target profit margins when you're launching a new product or brand.

Landed cost: $30

Target margin: 70%

$30/0.3 = $100

In other words, your landed cost divided by 0.3 equals your retail price, not including tax. Add your country's tax — for example, 10 per cent — and round your pricing to a round number (for example, $110 including tax).

To test the margin, you can reverse the equation as follows:

(Retail Price, excluding tax – Landed Cost Price)/Retail Price = Profit Margin

($100 – $30)/$100 = 70%

If you take your retail price less tax, deduct your landed cost price, and then divide that total by your retail price, you are left with your profit margin.

TIP

If you are currently selling products, you can check your margin by following the same process.

The number that comes out is your product's profit margin, which is hopefully above 70 per cent! Anything below 70 per cent means you are at risk of not being able to spend healthily on marketing, wages and the other things you'll need as you grow. A bigger business with a margin of 70 per cent, selling in-demand products, should end up with a net profit margin of greater than 20 per cent — even as high as 40 per cent if it really catches fire.

Your net profit margin could be much higher in your early days if you take this approach to pricing as your expenses generally start lower — for example, if it's just you and a couple of helpers in the business, or you are running it from home and not paying rent. However, if you really want to accelerate your sales and increase the sum of your net profits, you will need to spend more money, which will decrease your profit margin but put more money in your pocket — a smaller slice of a bigger pie! Pricing for a healthy profit margin sets you up to scale your business.

REMEMBER

A good pricing model allows you to take a handsome profit in the early days, but it also sets you up to become a much bigger company, with higher sales, while still maintaining a healthy profit. If your goal is to stay small rather than think big, you could probably drop that margin down to 60 per cent or so, but anything less than that, for a new brand, leaves very little money for the typical ecommerce expenses you encounter.

Preparing to Run Sales and Promotions

So, when to go on sale? It's a question I've been asked by retailers who are turning over tens of millions of dollars, as well as those just starting out. There's no one-size-fits-all approach to discounting and promotions — although I do look at tactical promotions to win back lost or at-risk customers, as well as to acquire new customers, when I look at marketing techniques in chapters 15, 16 and 17.

Most online retailers go on sale at least once or twice throughout the year. It's probably a customer expectation that around the Black Friday/Cyber Monday period just after Thanksgiving in the United States, most online retailers will be on sale, as well as on Boxing Day and around the end of the financial year (which varies by country).

Sales and promotional periods begin sooner than you might think. For example, Christmas occurs on 25 December every year; however, look at Figure 14-1, which depicts Google's search volume in the United States for the search term 'Christmas Gift Ideas' — it starts trending up at the end of August!

FIGURE 14-1: Google search results for the term 'Christmas gift ideas'.

Source: Google Trends

WARNING

If your margin doesn't allow for discounting, there's little point in making sales a part of your strategy. If you do plan on using sales and discounts, now is a good time to rethink your profit margins on your products and make sure they pass the stress test.

TIP

It's a good idea to pencil the key promotional periods into your diary and to always plan at least three months in advance.

The following is a list of key promotional periods where online stores typically run sales and promotions:

>> **Christmas:** The build-up may begin long before 25 December (see Figure 14-1), but you have a few opportunities for promotions over Christmas:

- **Green Monday:** Green Monday is usually the second Monday in December and is usually the shipping cut-off for most postal outlets to get standard shipped packages to customers before Christmas.

- **Free Shipping Day:** Free Shipping Day is a one-day event held annually in mid-December. Merchants are encouraged to offer free shipping with guaranteed delivery before Christmas.

- **Super Saturday:** Super Saturday is the last Saturday before Christmas, a major day of revenue for American retailers, which marks the end of the shopping season they (and many customers) believe begins on Black Friday. Super Saturday targets last-minute shoppers. Typically, the day is ridden with one-day sales in an effort to accrue more revenue than any other day in the Christmas and holiday season.

- **Boxing Day:** Post-Christmas sales begin from Boxing Day onwards. Traditionally used as an opportunity to clear last season's stock, you can continue this sale through January to help boost what is often a quiet sales month.

» **Black Friday/Cyber Monday:** A huge few days for online retail, this Thanksgiving holiday weekend is celebrated with mass promotions across most online verticals. Held on the fourth Friday of November, many retailers extend to Cyber Monday, three days later, to form what has become known as Cyber Week! Many retailers start cyber sales one or two weeks before Cyber Week to get a start on the sales.

» **Halloween:** Big in the US, Halloween sales are commonplace, although they're not as big in Europe or the Southern Hemisphere.

» **Singles Day:** Singles Day started in China as an unofficial holiday to celebrate those that aren't in relationships. It is always held on 11 November. Singles Day has gone on to become the largest physical retail and online retail shopping day in the world.

TIP

Many of these dates are fairly universal, but there may be key dates and times in your region or country that work well for promotions too. Do some research to find out the key dates for celebrations and events in your local religious and cultural calendar!

Setting Sale Prices for Products: The 'Compare At' Price

In Chapter 5, I looked at how to enter a price into your products as you add them to your Shopify store. In this chapter, I'm going to show you how to mark down your price when you want to put your products on sale. In Shopify, this is called the *Compare At* price.

When you set a Compare At price, the product listing updates on your online store to show that the item is on sale. The way that a sale price is shown depends on the theme that you're using; for example, you might see a Sale label on the product image, or you might see nothing at all in the product image, and just see the original price, crossed out, with the new sale (or Compare At) price in red text next to it.

Typically, the way that sale prices are shown depends on whether:

>> Your product has variants at different prices

>> The item is a single-variant product, or its variant prices are identical

REMEMBER

A *variant* is an extension of a product, for example a size or color of a product. Sometimes stores have variants at different prices — for example, if a store is selling shoes and the red leather shoes are more expensive than the black variant, there are two prices within the same product; or, when one variant is put on sale and the other variant is left at full price, you have two prices listed for the same style. The important point to get right is which price gets shown when a customer is browsing your shoes collection!

For a product with variants whose prices are not identical, the lowest sale price is indicated at the collection level. So, the variant with the cheapest price is what will appear in that product when the customer is browsing through your collections. As a customer changes sizes or variants while on the product page, the displayed price changes accordingly.

For a single-variant product, or a product whose variant prices are all identical, the original and sale prices are shown as a comparison when a customer is browsing your collections, usually with the original price crossed out and the sale price next to it (the appearance of this depends on your theme — Chapter 4 covers choosing a theme for your online store).

Here's how to set a Compare At (or sale) price for a product:

1. **From your Shopify admin, go to Products → All Products.**

   A list of all your store's products appears.

2. **Click on the name of the product you want to put on sale.**

   The product's page appears.

3. **In the Pricing section, set the Compare At Price to be the same as the product's original price (see Figure 14-2).**

   For example, in Figure 14-2 you would add 299.00 to the Compare At Price field.

4. **In the Price field, change the price to reflect the sale price you want to sell the product at in your sale.**

   For example, you might reduce the sale price of the product in Figure 14-2 from 299.00 to 150.00.

5. **Click on Save.**

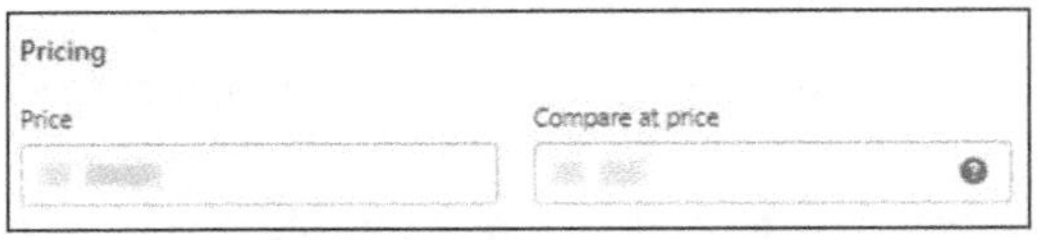

FIGURE 14-2: Setting a Compare At price on the product's page.

Pricing		
Price	Compare at price	
		❓

Source: Shopify

For another example, if a pair of jeans retails for $100 but you want to put them on sale for $80, you delete $100 from the Price field and enter it into the Compare At Price field, and then you enter $80 into the Price field and click on Save.

Here's how to set a Compare At (or sale) price for a variant within a product:

1. **From your Shopify admin, go to Products → All Products.**

   A list of all your store's products appears.

2. **Click on the name of the product you want to put on sale.**

   The product's page appears.

3. **Scroll down to the Variants section of the product's page.**

4. **Find a variant you want to put on sale, such as a size or color, and click on Edit.**

5. **In the Pricing section, set the Compare At Price field to be the same as the product's original price.**

6. **In the Price field, change the price of the product to the sale price you want to sell the product at in your sale.**

7. **Click on Save.**

REMEMBER

The value in Compare At Price must always be higher than the value in Price to show a sale price.

Delivering Discounts

Many online retailers view discounting as a necessary evil, although some hang their hats on it and make it a part of their core offering. The online retailer that discounts because everyone else is doing it is a lazy online retailer. It's also not true that you can simply emulate what everyone else is doing because every business has its own strategy. I work with businesses who discount their products 365 days of the year because it's a part of their strategy, and I also work with retailers who only go on sale twice a year. The upside for the high-discounting business is that conversion rates are very high; the downside is that gross margins are very low, meaning there is less money to spend on things like marketing and wages.

WARNING

Heavy or frequent discounting can do irreparable damage to your brand, as customers may start to question the quality of your products — or they might wait for your next discount, without ever wanting to pay full price.

The challenge is to price your products optimally, ensuring you're leaving enough wiggle room for running your business and taking a wage. Discounting can eat into that if you're not careful.

REMEMBER

Discounting is fine if it's profitable and a deliberate part of your overall business strategy, including being factored into your profit margins. If you find yourself only getting sales when you run a discount, you may be discounting too frequently and training your customers to wait for your discounts. Resist the temptation to discount because you think everyone is doing it; only discount if it works for you — profit pays bills, not sales.

So, when to discount? The answer is to discount when your business can afford to do it as a means to increase profits, not just sales, and when it doesn't have a negative impact on your brand. What is the point of driving heavy sales — putting a strain on your fulfillment and incurring high shipping costs with your increased volumes — if you haven't actually increased your net profit?

REMEMBER

Automatically increasing your revenue by discounting does not mean your profits go up, as many of your costs increase accordingly, such as shipping and staff, and you also need to factor in what you originally paid for your stock — something many retailers forget about.

Earlier in this chapter (in the section 'Setting Sale Prices for Products: The 'Compare At' Price'), I looked at marking down the price of individual products. In the following sections, I'm going to show you how you can offer your customers a fixed amount, percentage or shipping discount on products, collections or variants. You can also offer more creative offers, such as 'buy X get Y' discounts to encourage customers to buy more items or spend more than they typically would (because they are rewarded with a discount for doing so).

Before diving further into discounting, you might want to go back to the earlier section 'Pricing Your Product' to ensure you have a healthy margin to begin with — one that actually allows you to discount as a means to drive higher profits.

Creating discount codes

All Shopify plans offer discount codes as part of their subscription, so you can get creative with discounting from day one.

You can specify the following rules for discount codes in Shopify:

>> The dates for which the code is valid

>> The numbers or letters in a code, for example 'WELCOME10'

>> The number of times that a code can be used

>> A minimum order amount before the code can be used

>> Which products, collections or variants the discount can be applied to

Some things to consider before creating a discount code

>> **Extent:** You are limited to 20,000,000 unique discount codes for each store — I hope you don't need more than that!

>> **Usability:** Make the code easy to use — remember, to provide a good user experience, you always want to reduce friction between the customer and the website.

Avoid using special characters in the name of the discount code, such as &, * and %. Keep it simple as you don't want customers to abandon the checkout because they can't enter the code correctly.

>> **Timing:** If you create a discount with a start and end time, then the time is based on the time zone for your store (which you select in your Shopify admin when you set up your store). For example, if your store's time zone is Eastern Standard Time (EST) and you select a start date of 26 November, then your discount starts at 12.00am EST on 26 November.

You can create four kinds of discounts with a discount code in Shopify, and three when you elect to create an automatic discount that is auto-applied at checkout:

>> **Percentage:** Choose this option when you want your discount code to give customers a percentage discount — for example, 20 per cent off certain products, collections or your entire store.

» **Fixed amount:** Choose this option when you want your discount code to give customers a fixed dollar amount discount — for example, $20 off certain products, collections or your entire store.

» **Buy X get Y:** Choose this option when you want your discount code to give customers a discount when they either buy a certain quantity of products — for example, 'buy one get one free' — or when they spend a certain amount — for example, 'spend $200 and get 20 per cent off'.

» **Free Shipping:** You can elect to run a free shipping discount when you create a discount code; however, this option drops off when you elect to create an automatic discount that is applied at checkout.

Percentage or fixed amount discount codes

To create a percentage or fixed amount discount code, follow these steps:

1. **From your Shopify admin, go to Discounts, which is in your main menu on the left-hand side.**

   The Discounts page appears.

2. **Click on Create Discount — the green button in the top-right corner.**

   The Create Discount dialogue box appears (see Figure 14-3). You're presented with two options: Discount Code and Automatic Discount.

   Clicking on the Discount Code option requires the customer to physically enter a discount code into your store's checkout to get the discount, whereas Automatic Discount is applied automatically in the checkout, so the customer doesn't need to enter anything.

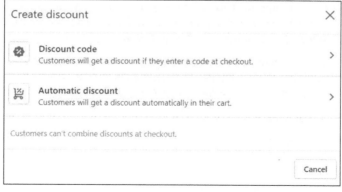

FIGURE 14-3: Creating a discount in Shopify.

Source: Shopify

3. **Select Discount Code or Automatic Discount.**

The Create Discount Code section appears.

In the Discount Code option, you're prompted to create a discount code at the top of the page, such as VIP20, which customers can enter into the discount code box in your checkout (see Figure 14-4).

If you select Automatic Discount, you're asked to enter a name ('Title') for your discount, where it is a good idea to describe the discount on offer — for example, if you use VIP20, your customers will see this when they're in the checkout and know that the code they're expecting to see has been applied, but they won't need to enter a code as the discount has already been automatically applied.

Source: Shopify

FIGURE 14-4:
Creating a
Discount Code
in Shopify.

4. **For both options (Discount Code and Automatic Discount), in the Types section (which is the next section down the page — see Figure 14-4), select the discount type that you want to create.**

You have four options when you select create a Discount Code, and three options when you create an Automatic Discount (the Free Shipping Discount drops off when you select Create Automatic Discount):

- Percentage

- Fixed Amount

- Buy X Get Y

- Free Shipping

I look at Buy X Get Y and Free Shipping discount codes in the next two sections of this chapter.

5. **If you select Percentage or Fixed Amount under Types, you see a Value box in the next section (below Types). Enter a monetary or percentage value for the discount in the box, depending on whether you selected Percentage or Fixed Amount (for example, 20% or $20).**

TIP

This step applies whether you are creating a Discount Code or an Automatic Discount.

6. **In the Applies To section that appears next in the dialogue box, select what this discount applies to: All Products, Specific Collections or Specific Products.**

- If you want your discount code to apply to all products in your store, then select All Products.

- If the discount applies to specific collections or products, then use the search field or the Browse button to add them to the discount. For example, as you type your collection name into the search field it should appear, so you can then click on it (see Figure 14-5).

- If you want to remove a collection or product from the discount, then click on the 'X' next to the collection name or product name to delete it from the list.

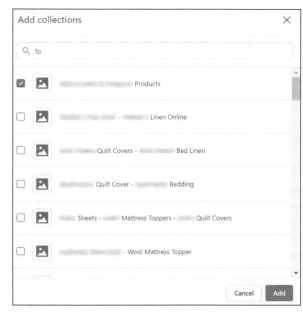

FIGURE 14-5:
Adding a collection to your discount code.

Source: Shopify

7. Optional: **If you want to set a minimum requirement for the discount, then select one in the Minimum Requirements section.**

Select from the following options:

- **Minimum Purchase Amount:** This requires customers to spend a minimum amount to qualify for the discount.

  If the discount applies to a specific product or collection, then only these items contribute to the minimum purchase amount.

- **Minimum Quantity of Items:** This requires customers to order a minimum number of products to qualify for the discount.

  If the discount applies to a specific product or collection, then only these items contribute to the minimum quantity amount.

8. **In the Customer Eligibility section, select who this discount applies to: Everyone, Specific Groups of Customers or Specific Customers.**

Usually you would select Everyone and just distribute the discount code to whoever you like; for example, you might create a discount code that you email to your VIP customers, but you can still select Everyone and rely on the email to ensure it reaches the customers you are targeting.

Use the search field to choose the individuals or groups that you want to receive the discount. Customer listings show the email used to register for your store. If no email was provided, then the listing shows the customers' phone numbers.

To remove an individual customer or group of customers from eligibility for a discount, click the X next to the customer's or group's name.

9. **If you want to limit discount usage, then check one of the options in the Usage Limits section.**

You can limit discount use in two ways:

- **Limit Number of Times This Discount Can Be Used in Total:** This option allows you to set a total number of times that a discount can be used. For example, setting a limit of 200 allows the discount code to be used 200 times across your customer base. If you choose this setting, then customers can use the discount multiple times.

- **Limit to One Per Customer:** This option tracks a customer's email address or phone number to limit the discount to one use per customer. *Note:* This only applies to fixed value discounts.

10. **Use the calendar in the Active Dates section to set the start date for the discount.**

If you want to set an end date for the discount, then click on Set End Date and use the calendar to choose when the discount ends.

REMEMBER

If you don't want to choose an end date for your discount, then it doesn't expire. If you want the discount to be valid for only one day, then select the same calendar day for both the start date and the end date.

11. **Click on Save Discount.**

TIP

If you're setting up an automatic discount, you see Save Discount, whereas if you're setting up a discount code, you see Save Discount Code.

Your new discount appears in the Discounts tab in your Shopify admin. To distribute this discount, you can send the code to your customers by email, use it in other forms of marketing (which I look at in chapters 15, 16 and 17) or display it on your online store in the announcement bar or on a homepage banner.

REMEMBER

If your discount is set to discount all products, then the discount is applied proportionally across all items in the cart. For example, if you have a $50 discount applied to a cart with a $50 and a $100 item, then the first item is discounted by $16.50 and the second one by $33.50. If the total price of the order is less than $50 and you have put no limit on the minimum spend/quantity of products ordered, then the value of each item is discounted to $0 because the order value can't go below $0 (which is a good reason to set minimum requirements for the use of your discount code!).

TIP

If you're at the top of the Create Discount Code page (because you've selected Discount Code and not Automatic Discount), and you're stuck for ideas on what to enter as a discount code, click on Generate Code, right next to the Discount Code box, and Shopify will create a discount code for you.

Buy X get Y discount codes

The name of the discount is a good description of the functionality it provides: What does the customer have to buy, and what do they get for free, or at a discount, for buying it? Typical promotions that work here are ones like buy a T-shirt and get a free hat, or buy one water bottle and get a second one free.

TIP

If you're going to offer a Buy X Get Y discount code, consider trying a minimum spend that's just above your average order value (AOV) so that your customers have to spend more than normal to access the deal. For example, if your AOV is $100, you might offer 20 per cent off when a customer spends $120 or more. Setting the price threshold too low can often result in giving away a discount or a product to customers who were going to spend that amount anyway.

To create a Buy X Get Y discount code, follow these steps:

1. From your Shopify admin, go to Discounts.

The Discounts page appears.

2. Click on Create Discount.

The Create Discount dialogue box appears (refer to Figure 14-3). You're presented with two options: Discount Code and Automatic Discount.

TIP

The steps for both options are the same, with one exception. If you select Discount Code, you're asked to create a code for the customer to enter at checkout; however, if you select Automatic Discount, you won't need a discount code so you get to skip that step.

Here, I show you how to set up this promotion when you select Discount Code.

3. Select Discount Code.

4. In the Discount Code section, enter a name for the new discount code — for example, 'buyonegetonefree'.

5. In the Types section, select Buy X Get Y from the options provided.

6. In the Customer Buys section (see Figure 14-6), configure the following settings (to confirm the product the customer needs to 'buy', or the amount the customer needs to spend, in order to trigger the 'get' promotion):

- Choose Minimum Quantity of Items or Minimum Purchase Amount.

  Set the number of items that the customer must buy or the amount of money that the customer must spend to be eligible for the discount (for example, if you're offering the customer a third item free if they buy two, then the customer needs to buy two items; if you're offering a 'spend X and save' promotion, then the customer may have to spend $100 to get the discount). These are the triggers that will activate the discount.

- In the Any Items From section, choose whether you want to include products or collections to limit where the qualifying items come from (that is, if you only want to apply the promotion to certain products or collections, as opposed to your entire product catalogue).

  Use the Search Products field or the Browse button to add products or collections to the promotion. If you want to remove a product or collection from the discount, then click on the X next to it to delete it from the list.

7. In the Customer Gets section (see Figure 14-6), configure the following settings:

- Set the number of items that the customer will get as part of the discount or promotion, and select the product they will get for free, by searching for it in the 'Search Products field'.

- In the Any Items From section, choose whether you want to include products or collections for where the discounted items may come from (that is, if you want to add selected products or collections to the promotion as the 'get' for the customer, as opposed to offering products from your entire product catalogue).

- Use the search field or the Browse button to add products or collections. If you want to remove a product or collection, then click on the X next to it to delete it from the list.

- In the At a Discounted Value section, choose the discounted value that customers receive when they buy the set number of items. If you want to offer a percentage discount, then select Percentage and enter a rate. If you want to offer items for free, then select Free.

- Optional: Check the Set a Maximum Number of Uses Per Order box and then enter the maximum number of times that this promotion can be applied to a single order.

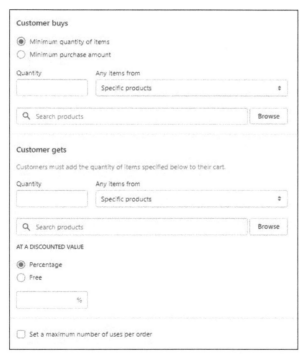

FIGURE 14-6:
Setting up a Buy X
Get Y code in
Shopify.

Source: Shopify

If you want to create a create a Buy One Get One Free offer on a specific product, you can enter 1 in the Quantity field of the Customer Buys section, and then search for the product in the Search Products field, and then in the Customer Gets section that follows, you can enter 1 in the Quantity field and search for the product that will be given for free. Remember to select either Free under the section At Discounted Value or, if you would rather offer a discount (such as 50% off the second item), check the Percentage option.

8. **In the Customer Eligibility section, select who this discount applies to: Everyone, Specific Groups of Customers or Specific Customers.**

   Use the search field to choose the individuals or groups that you want to receive the discount. Customer listings show the email used to register for your store. If no email was provided, then the listing shows the customer's phone number.

   To remove an individual customer or group of customers from eligibility for a discount, click on the X next to the customer's or group's name.

9. **If you want to limit discount usage, then check one of the options in the Usage Limits section.**

   You can limit discount use in two ways:

   - **Limit Number of Times This Discount Can Be Used in Total:** This option allows you to set a total number of times that a discount can be used. For example, setting a limit of 200 allows the discount code to be used 200 times across your customer base. If you choose this setting, then customers can use the discount multiple times.

   - **Limit to One Per Customer:** This option tracks a customer's email address or phone number to limit the discount to one use per customer. *Note:* This only applies to fixed value discounts.

10. **In the Active Dates section, configure the date settings.**

   Use the calendar to set the start date for the discount. If you want to set an end date for the discount, then click on Set End Date and use the calendar to choose when the discount will end.

   If you don't choose an end date for your discount, then it doesn't expire. If you want the discount to be valid for only one day, then select the same calendar day for both the start date and the end date.

11. **Click on Save Discount Code.**

Your new discount appears in the Discounts tab in your Shopify admin. To distribute this discount, you can send the code to your customers by email or display it on your online store. Your customers need to add the items to their cart and then enter the code during checkout to receive the discount.

Create a free shipping discount

If you want to offer free shipping, then you can create a free shipping discount, which can be useful for *flash sales* (short promotions at random times, outside of typical promotional periods, that usually last 24–48 hours) or as a reward for spending a certain amount.

Free shipping discounts can only be created when you select Discount Code; you cannot offer them when you select Automatic Discounts.

To set up a free shipping discount code, follow these steps:

1. **From your Shopify admin, go to Discounts.**

   The Discounts page appears.

2. **Click on Create Discount.**

   The Create Discount dialogue box appears (refer to Figure 14-3). You're presented with two options: Discount Code and Automatic Discount.

3. **Select Discount Code.**

4. **In the Discount Code section, enter a name for the new discount code, such as FREESHIP (or select Generate Code if you're feeling lazy or uninspired).**

5. **In the Types section, select the Free Shipping discount type.**

6. **In the Countries section, leave All Countries selected or choose the countries that you want the discount to apply to.**

7. **If you want to exclude free shipping for shipping rates over a certain monetary value, then check Exclude Shipping Rates Over a Certain Amount and enter the amount in the field.**

   This discount applies to shipping rates only and is unrelated to order amounts.

   Optional: In the Minimum Requirements section, select Minimum Purchase Amount or Minimum Quantity of Items, and then enter the dollar value or number of items that need to be added before the discount code applies.

   Cast your mind back to Chapter 6, where I looked at free shipping as a possible means for driving sales: here's where you can experiment with free shipping before making any permanent changes to your free shipping threshold. For example, try offering free shipping on all orders, and watch the uptick in sales to see if it offsets the cost of you absorbing the shipping fees.

8. **In the Customer Eligibility section, select who this discount applies to: Everyone, Specific Groups of Customers or Specific Customers.**

Use the search field to choose the individuals or groups that you want to receive the discount. Customer listings show the email used to register for your store. If no email was provided, then the listing shows the customer's phone number.

To remove an individual customer or group of customers from eligibility for a discount, click on the X next to the customer's or group's name.

9. **Discount usage is unlimited by default. If you want to limit discount usage, then check one of the options in the Usage Limits section.**

   You can limit discount use in two ways:

   - **Limit Number of Times This Discount Can Be Used in Total:** This option allows you to set a total number of times that a discount can be used. For example, setting a limit of 200 allows the discount code to be used 200 times across your customer base. If you choose this setting, then customers can use the discount multiple times.

   - **Limit to One Per Customer:** This option tracks a customer's email address or phone number to limit the discount to one use per customer.

10. **Use the calendar in the Active Dates section to set the start date for the discount. If you want to set an end date for the discount, then click Set End Date and use the calendar to choose when the discount will end.**

REMEMBER

If you don't choose an end date for your discount, then it doesn't expire. If you want the discount to be valid for only one day, then select the same calendar day for both the start date and the end date.

11. **When you're finished, click on Save Discount Code.**

Your new discount will now appear on the Discounts page in your Shopify admin. To distribute this discount, you can send the code to your customers by email, or display it on your online store.

Discounting Shortcuts

Here's a few helpful discounting tips and shortcuts you can use to save time when managing discount codes in your Shopify store.

Promote a discount using a shareable link

A shareable discount link might be useful when you're starting out — for example, if you want to create a discount code for family and friends and share it around to get some traction for your new online store. You can also use a shareable link on social media, give it to influencers to share or use it in your email marketing.

Follow these steps to create a shareable link for a discount code:

1. **From your Shopify admin, click on Discounts.**

   The Discounts page appears.

2. **Click on the name of the discount that you want to promote.**

   For example, click on the FREESHIP code that you might have created to offer free shipping on all orders for a limited time.

3. **Click on Promote in the top-right corner of the discount you have clicked into, and then select Get a Shareable Link from the drop-down menu.**

   A dialogue box appears with a URL that you can use across your social media or marketing communications, which will automatically apply the discount to the checkout of customers that click on the link.

   The options available for you to link to depend on the specific products or collections included in your active discounts.

REMEMBER

4. **Click on Copy Link to copy the shareable link to your clipboard.**

5. **Click on Close.**

After you copy a shareable link to your clipboard, you can post or embed it wherever you want to promote your discount.

Filter discounts

You can filter your discounts in your Shopify admin so that you can check the discounts that are used most frequently, or check for all the enabled discount codes currently running in your online store.

To filter your discount codes, follow these steps:

1. **From your Shopify admin, click on Discounts.**

   The Discounts page appears, displaying all discount codes that have been created in your store over time (see Figure 14-7).

2. **Choose how you want to filter your discounts from the list of options you can see after the Filter Discount Codes search field.**

   You can filter by Discount Type or Status — or click on More Filters, where you can filter by the number of times a discount code has been used.

3. **Select a filter option, and the Discounts page will refresh to show you the discount codes that match your search.**

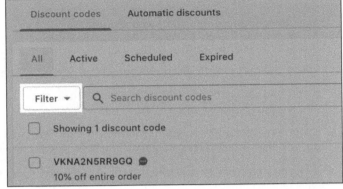

FIGURE 14-7:
Filtering your
discount codes
in Shopify.

Source: Shopify

You may not need to do this much in your early days as you won't have many discounts to filter through, but as you add more to your store this becomes a handy tool.

Edit a discount

From time to time you might get it wrong (you're only human!) and need to edit your discount code. Alternatively, you may need to adjust a discount for a specific purpose — for example, if you create a discount code that can only be used once, you may then want to edit it for additional one-off usage.

To edit a discount code, follow these steps:

1. **From your Shopify admin, go to Discounts.**

   The Discounts page appears.

2. **Click on the name of the discount that you want to edit.**

3. **Edit the discount's settings as required.**

4. **Click on Save.**

Disable a discount

You may occasionally need to disable a discount code — for example, if you create a welcome discount for new newsletter subscribers and it gets leaked across coupon sites, which means lots of people are using it without the desired intention of having them sign up to your newsletter.

To disable a discount, follow these steps:

1. **From your Shopify admin, go to Discounts.**

   The Discounts page appears.

2. **On the Discounts page, locate the discount that you want to disable and click on the discount's name.**

   A page showing the details of the discount appears.

3. **At the top of the page, click on Disable.**

   A dialogue box appears, asking you to confirm.

4. **Click on Disable to confirm.**

Re-enable a discount

Whoops – disabled the wrong discount code? No problem!

Follow these steps to re-enable a discount:

1. **From your Shopify admin, go to Discounts.**

   The Discounts page appears.

2. **On the Discounts page, click on the disabled discount that you want to re-enable.**

   The details of the discount appear in a new page.

3. **At the top of the page, click on Enable.**

   A dialogue box asking you to confirm appears.

4. **Click on Enable to confirm.**

» **Creating a marketing plan for your business**

» **Using marketing campaigns and automations in Shopify**

Chapter **15**

Getting Discovered: Finding New Customers

I n ecommerce, *marketing* is typically referred to as digital marketing. Two primary objectives are involved in digital marketing: acquiring customers (*acquisition* — the process of acquiring customers, usually through your marketing efforts) and retaining customers (*retention* — the efforts and strategy involved in marketing to existing customers in order to keep them). Finding a healthy balance between the two is ideal, although in the early days you're going to focus heavily on acquisition — otherwise you'll have no customers to retain.

In this chapter, I talk about the basics of digital marketing, including beginning to think about how to position your online store, and which customers you intend to target, across which marketing channels — also known as building a *channel mix*. I look at how to discover who your target market is, how to build a marketing plan and how to measure your plan's success. I also introduce you to setting up marketing campaigns and automations using some helpful Shopify apps and native features.

By the end of this chapter, you should have an understanding of the basics of digital marketing in relation to selling products online through a Shopify store, and be able to action several strategies geared towards bringing visitors to your website.

Introducing Digital Marketing

Digital marketing is a form of marketing that relies on digital, or online, channels; in other words, it's when you use the internet to market your business.

Digital marketing is not only reserved for online retailers; in fact, almost any business can use forms of digital marketing to find customers. The growth in social media (through platforms such as Facebook, Twitter and Instagram, which I consider further in Chapter 17) makes social media marketing a highly sought-after form of digital marketing. Two other popular forms of digital marketing involve search engine marketing (SEM) and search engine optimization (SEO), which I look at in Chapter 16.

REMEMBER

Although digital marketing generally refers to fairly specific, *below the line* marketing activities (marketing that's targeted towards specific groups of customers), such as SEM, I wouldn't discount using traditional *above the line* techniques (wider reach marketing, which is often untargeted), which involves building brand awareness through traditional media, such as outdoor advertising and print media. A combination of both creates an integrated approach to marketing that both builds brand awareness and gains wide reach, while still bringing in customers with a high intent to purchase who may be actively searching for the products you sell.

TIP

In the early days, you're going to want to put as much hustle as you can into spreading the word about your new online store; however, marketing can be expensive — it isn't uncommon to spend $1 for every click that you drive to your website. If you see a cheap and effective opportunity to market your business, you should explore it!

Building a Marketing Plan

Failing to plan is planning to fail, and I've seen this time and time again when it comes to online retailers throwing good money after bad, especially when it comes to *paid media* (paid advertising through channels such as Facebook and Google Ads, although technically paid media includes any paid marketing activity across similar online channels — I cover paid advertising in Chapter 16). You need to ensure that your pricing and your gross margin allow you to spend a reasonable amount on marketing while still achieving a good level of net profit; if you're unsure about how much gross margin you need then it may be a good time to review Chapter 14 before you proceed.

In the following sections, I take a look at what you need to know before you dive into marketing, focusing on six steps that you can consider before launching your store or undertaking any marketing activities.

REMEMBER

Think of the end goal, not the short-term outcomes.

Step 1: Define your unique value proposition

By being very clear in knowing what problem your product or online store is solving for a customer, it will be easier to promote the message to your audience. The two questions you want to ask before you bring a product to market are:

>> **Why is your product different to that of your competitors?** In other words, what makes your product special? If your product is being sold on other online or physical stores, then the same question should be posed about your actual online store: Why should people buy from your store instead of another store?

WARNING

If you can't answer this question for your products or your store, it means that to attract attention and visits to your site you will need to enter a bidding war with your competitors — and whoever spends the most money will win the customer, which is not a position most ecommerce start-ups want to be in. It's also common to *burn* (lose) a lot of cash in the early days using this strategy.

>> **What do you stand for?** More and more consumers want to know what a brand stands for as much as they want to know what it sells. Think about whether your product or store is doing anything that makes a stand on certain subjects — for example, are you donating a portion of your sales to charity, are you recycling your old products, are you carbon neutral?

After you fully understand your core offering, you will know exactly what your *unique value proposition* is, or *unique selling points* are (in other words, your answer to the question, 'What problem does your product solve for your customers?').

TIP

Run a strategy planning session where you and any business partners or co-founders think about the above questions to determine a list of value propositions. Aim to use keywords to represent them — for example:

>> **Value:** 'We aim to sell products cheaper than our competitors.'

>> **Quality:** 'We sell products that may be a little more expensive, but they use superior materials that our customers can clearly see.'

>> **Sustainable:** 'We only use recycled packaging, and all our products are ethically sourced.'

When you have your list of keywords, they can become part of your brand messaging that you take forward into your marketing communications (often shortened to 'comms'). For example, your Facebook adverts may contain the keyword 'sustainable', which helps you target a particular audience that is drawn to sustainable products.

Keywords are the name of the game when it comes to SEO and SEM, as I explain in Chapter 16.

Step 2: Know your customer

When you're launching a new business or product, it's important to know exactly who your customer is and what problem you're solving for them. It's a very familiar story for online store owners to think they know who their customer is, without actually taking the time to get to know who they are — and getting it wrong can cause your business fail. In Chapter 8, I look at the analytics and reporting available from your Shopify admin, which is a good way to monitor user behavior — for example, how many of your sales are from repeat customers, and how much they spend on average (average order value, or AOV).

TIP

Google Analytics (also known as GA) is a popular platform that online retailers can use to monitor the behaviors of their customers. Find out more about Google Analytics at `analytics.google.com/analytics`.

WARNING

Who you *think* your customer is — versus who they actually are — can often be two very different things. Take the time to survey your customers/potential customers to understand their motivation for buying from you (and to understand why they didn't buy from you). This is one of the cheapest, most effective ways to grow your online business.

Part 3 of this book covers the customer's experience in more detail to help you better understand your customer — the target audience for your marketing.

Step 3: Choose a marketing strategy

The next step is to choose a strategy for your marketing. A *marketing strategy* is a top-level plan to gain customers and sell your products. The goal here is to identify the tactics you can use in your marketing efforts and some of the channels that you can target.

EXAMPLE

If you're selling pet toys, you might consider a grassroots marketing campaign that sponsors the local dog park's Christmas party, or you might start a video series with a dog trainer to provide useful tips to your target market — both of these serve as tools to grow your brand presence and establish a community of your own.

If you've decided that your core offering is to provide a certain product at very competitive pricing, and you know that your customer is a bargain hunter, then your tactic may be to use discount codes and *flash sales* (a promotional strategy where you discount all or selected products for a short period of time, typically 24 to 48 hours, to build urgency) as part of your marketing strategy. I cover discounting in Chapter 14.

Some examples of marketing tactics you might use to improve your marketing include:

>> **Getting to know your customers:** Conduct more user research to find out what your customers want from you, and who else they shop with. Part 3 is all about understanding your customers and their experiences on your site.

>> **Researching competitor pricing:** Find out if your product is priced competitively. Refer to Chapter 14 for more information on how to price your products.

>> **Organizing your social media:** Draw up a content plan that outlines how often you'll send emails and post on social media, generally looking a month ahead, as well as outlining all the content you need to create to service your channels. I look more at social media marketing content in Chapter 17.

>> **Focusing on customer service:** Consider how you can use customer service to build loyalty — could your business become known for going above and beyond for your customers? Chapter 7 goes deeper into customer service.

>> **Advertising:** Not every business engages in paid advertising, but paid media or advertising is likely to form part of the tactics you use to acquire new customers. Chapter 16 dives deeper into paid advertising.

Step 4: Consider how to measure the success of your marketing

A question I ask myself often when reviewing projects I need to work on in an online store is: 'How will I measure it?' When I work with online businesses, we often meet for a planning session every three months to determine the projects that we believe will result in profitable growth, and I encourage business owners to put a definitive measurement on each project.

TIP

Another way of framing the question is: 'What does success look like for this project?'

By putting a definitive measurement on the project or marketing effort, it does two things:

>> **It forces you to *analyze* the project's impact.** This helps you choose the right projects or marketing efforts to focus on.

>> **It forces you to *review* the project or marketing effort, and evaluate its success.** This helps you confirm whether the project was a worthwhile use of your time and money, which informs future marketing efforts.

Some examples of measuring success in marketing include:

>> One hundred new email subscribers within the first three months of trading

>> A new website design targeting a conversion rate uplift from 2–2.2 per cent

>> Social media followers growing by 20 new followers each week

>> Facebook Ads generating a ROAS (return on ad spend) of four times the initial investment

Most marketing platforms, such as Facebook Ads or Google Ads, will report on their platform's ROAS — in other words, how much you spend on your ads in relation to how much you make from your ads. It's also a good idea to track your *blended ROAS*, which is how much you've spent across all advertising platforms, over a certain period, versus how much you've made in your online store, in total, during this time.

TECHNICAL STUFF

Google Analytics can be used to track and measure certain website metrics, such as *conversions* (transactions) and *web traffic* (people visiting your site). It uses UTM codes (UTM stands for Urchin Tracking Module) to track the performance of ad campaigns. *UTM codes* are snippets of code that are added to the URL of your campaigns, such as email or Facebook marketing campaigns, which then show up in Google Analytics, so you can see how much traffic or revenue has come from the URL associated with the marketing campaign. Although it may be too early in your ecommerce journey for you to be thinking about Google Analytics and UTM codes right now, I recommend you look into using Google Analytics as your business grows because its insights will become increasingly valuable as your revenue increases.

Step 5: Create a marketing channel plan

You can use many different marketing channels to bring customers to your store, from outdoor billboards and bus ads through to paid digital media via Facebook and Google Ads, so developing the right *channel mix* is important. If your strategy is to only use one marketing channel, you're probably putting too many eggs in one basket, so think about diversifying a little (just as with any investment!).

When you develop your marketing channel mix, it's also a good time to think about a budget for each channel (by now you may have already started to think about how much you're comfortable spending on marketing as part of developing an overall marketing strategy).

TIP

A profitable online business with a gross margin of over 50 per cent (or a product margin of over 70 per cent) would be wise to invest 15–20 per cent of its net online revenue back into marketing. In your first 6–12 months, you may elect to spend more to gain traction in the market, as you're unlikely to have any *organic revenue* (revenue derived from free marketing channels, which I talk about in Chapter 17). However, remember that you may break even (or even make a loss) at first, so try and build a plan to gradually improve your marketing efficiency, allowing you to reduce marketing spend and build profit.

Some marketing channels you may consider helpful include:

>> Social media marketing, primarily through Facebook and Instagram (see chapters 16 and 17)

>> Google Ads (see Chapter 16)

>> SEO (see Chapter 16)

>> Email marketing and SMS marketing (see Chapter 16)

Step 6: Review performance

Analyzing the performance of your marketing efforts is essential if you want to understand if, how and why you've achieved your desired outcomes (and if you haven't achieved them, what went wrong?).

TIP

I suggest checking in on your marketing metrics once a week (Monday may be a good day for this) so that you can pull back if you need to, or hopefully increase spend as you see your performance outrunning your projections. Log the performance in a spreadsheet so you can monitor the trend over time. Trending is very important in marketing, and in ecommerce, as it tells you the trajectory that you're on — which can be encouraging when you're just starting out — and identifies if sales, or visits to your site, are quite low, which you can aim to improve.

A common mistake I see in online businesses is for store owners to leave paid marketing channels that are not performing switched on, draining the company of marketing funds because they haven't properly thought about the outcome they need for the marketing to be considered a success, and they haven't bothered to close the loop by evaluating its performance.

Implementing Marketing Campaigns and Automations

Marketing campaigns and automations are effective ways of growing your audience and reach (the number of people that see your ads or marketing content).

Marketing campaigns are usually directed at a specific promotion, such as a Boxing Day or Black Friday sale, and are therefore generally active within a set time frame — for example, a Boxing Day sale may launch on 26 December and run until 1 January. In this case, you might group your marketing activities together across social media, Google Ads and email to advertise a certain offer in your marketing communications within that time frame, such as 'Boxing Day Sale — take 25% off!' In other words, you're marketing towards a specific event or campaign.

Marketing automations are marketing activities that are triggered by certain events, aimed at capturing online sales on an ongoing basis as opposed to during a specific time frame. For example, you could send targeted ads to your customers on Facebook that show them the products they've previously viewed on your store, or set up abandoned checkout emails to automatically remind visitors to return to your store and complete an order. (Email automations are also known as *flows* in ecommerce.)

A good online store runs a series of automations across multiple marketing channels at all times, from the time you welcome a customer to your email marketing database (possibly by offering them a discount upon signing up) to the time you email or SMS them a reminder to come back and visit your store if it's been a while. Automations are an essential part of a successful ecommerce business.

Campaigns and Automations are listed in your Shopify admin under Marketing. Your store needs to be on the Basic Shopify plan or higher to create marketing activities and automations.

In the following sections, I show you how to get started with creating marketing automations and campaigns using Shopify.

Automating your marketing with Shopify

By default, your store has one marketing automation already turned on — Abandoned Checkout Emails by Shopify (see Figure 15-1). You can find this automation by going to your Shopify admin → Marketing → Automations. This is a great automation that enables you to send emails to customers who commence a checkout in your online store but fail to complete their purchase (it may seem surprising, but this is very common). I show you how you can set up this automation to remind customers to come back and complete their purchase in the upcoming section, 'Creating your first automation: Abandoned Checkout Emails'.

Aside from this existing automation, you need to install an app to create another marketing automation, such as Google Channel to create automated Google Ads, or SMSBump (SMS Marketing by Yotpo) to send automated marketing messages, including sending abandoned checkout notifications via SMS (see Chapter 16 for more on SMS marketing).

TIP

You may notice that Google Smart Shopping is offered as a suggested app when you set up your automations (see the next section for the steps to do this). Google Smart Shopping is a great addition to your Abandoned Checkout Email automation, and I look more at Google Smart Shopping and Google Ads in Chapter 16.

Otherwise, there's plenty of good automations to choose from that work well within Shopify's marketing offering. You can browse the Shopify App Store, but also look out for suggestions for suitable apps when you are on the Marketing Automations page (see Figure 15-2).

Creating your first automation: Abandoned Checkout Emails

To get started with marketing automations, I suggest setting up the automation that's ready by default — Abandoned Checkout Emails by Shopify.

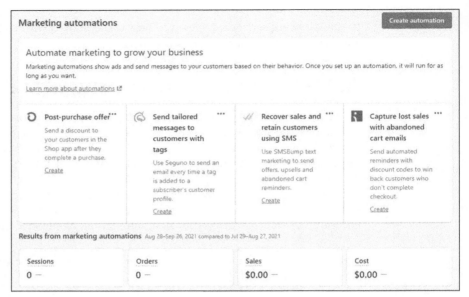

FIGURE 15-2:
The Marketing
Automations
page, showing
recommended
automations.

Source: Shopify

REMEMBER

Abandoned Checkout Emails by Shopify is probably the most popular of all ecommerce automations. You're targeting customers who have initiated a checkout in your online store but who failed to complete their purchase; by setting up this automation, you're sending out an automatic email reminder to try and get the customer to come back and finish their purchase.

To set up the Abandoned Checkout Emails automation:

1. From your Shopify admin, go to Marketing.

Three options appear: Overview, Campaigns and Automations.

2. Click on Automations.

The Marketing Automations page appears (refer to Figure 15-2).

3. Scroll down the Marketing Automations page to the Abandoned Checkout Emails by Shopify automation, and click on it.

You're taken to the Abandoned Checkout Emails by Shopify page, where you see a summary of sales generated through the Abandoned Checkout Emails automation (you won't have any results here yet as you haven't sent any emails yet).

4. To set up your Abandoned Checkout Email automation, click on Edit Settings in the top-right corner of the Abandoned Checkout Emails by Shopify page.

You're then taken to a new page called Checkout, so don't be alarmed if you see a whole bunch of options that don't seem to relate to marketing.

5. **Scroll to the bottom of the Checkout page, where the third to last section is titled Abandoned Checkouts (see Figure 15-3).**

   By default, Automatically Send Abandoned Checkout Emails will be checked, meaning every customer who abandoned their checkout (as per the parameters you select from in the next step) will receive an email from your store, reminding them to complete their purchase.

FIGURE 15-3:
The Abandoned
Checkouts
section of the
Checkouts page.

Abandoned checkouts

Send an email to customers who left products in their cart but didn't complete their order. Learn more about abandoned checkouts.

Customize email

☑ Automatically send abandoned checkout emails

Send to
○ Anyone who abandons checkout
⦿ Email subscribers who abandon checkout

Send after
○ 1 hour
○ 6 hours
⦿ 10 hours (recommended)
○ 24 hours

Source: Shopify

6. **Select between sending to Anyone Who Abandons Checkout or Email Subscribers Who Abandon Checkout.**

   I generally opt for the 'anyone' option as it increases the likelihood of generating sales.

TIP

7. **In the Send After section, choose the time that you want to elapse between the checkout being abandoned and your email being sent to the customer.**

   You can choose between 1 hour, 6 hours, 10 hours (which is recommended by Shopify) and 24 hours.

8. **Click on the Customize Email button to the left and the Preview page appears, written in developer code (see Figure 15-4).**

9. **Click on Preview in the top-right corner (see Figure 15-4) to preview the email that will be sent to your customer. If you're happy with the email's content, close the Preview box.**

   You don't need to click on Save (unless you have changed the code — which I don't recommend doing unless you know your way around developer code).

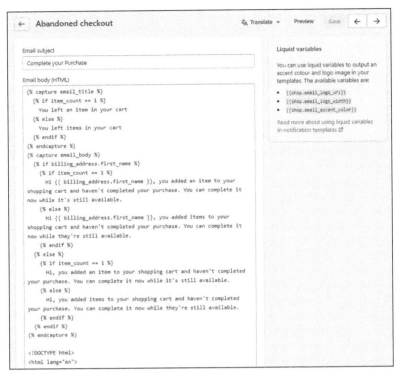

```
←   Abandoned checkout                    ℤA Translate ▾    Preview    Save   ←   →

Email subject                                        Liquid variables

Complete your Purchase                               You can use liquid variables to output an
                                                     accent colour and logo image in your
Email body (HTML)                                    templates. The available variables are:

{% capture email_title %}                            •  {{shop.email_logo_url}}
  {% if item_count == 1 %}                            •  {{shop.email_logo_width}}
    You left an item in your cart                     •  {{shop.email_accent_color}}
  {% else %}
    You left items in your cart                      Read more about using liquid variables
  {% endif %}                                        in notification templates ⬀
{% endcapture %}
{% capture email_body %}
  {% if billing_address.first_name %}
    {% if item_count == 1 %}
      Hi {{ billing_address.first_name }}, you added an item to your
shopping cart and haven't completed your purchase. You can complete it
now while it's still available.
    {% else %}
      Hi {{ billing_address.first_name }}, you added items to your
shopping cart and haven't completed your purchase. You can complete it
now while they're still available.
    {% endif %}
  {% else %}
    {% if item_count == 1 %}
      Hi, you added an item to your shopping cart and haven't completed
your purchase. You can complete it now while it's still available.
    {% else %}
      Hi, you added items to your shopping cart and haven't completed
your purchase. You can complete it now while they're still available.
    {% endif %}
  {% endif %}
{% endcapture %}

<!DOCTYPE html>
<html lang="en">
```

FIGURE 15-4:
The Abandoned Checkout Email Preview.

Source: Shopify

TECHNICAL STUFF

You can customize these emails, but I suggest that you hire a Shopify Expert to do this (the Shopify Experts marketplace is a good place to find an expert) as you can see the code isn't for beginners. The Preview option is useful to check, but save the coding for the experts unless you're a coding whizz!

10. **Click on the left-facing arrow next to Abandoned Checkout, which indicates a 'back' button.**

You're taken to a Notifications page — which is a useful page for looking at all the customer emails and notifications you can send.

TIP

Browse the notifications page to see what sort of emails you can send your customers automatically after they place an order — also known as *post-purchase emails*.

Exploring other automations

Shopify offers four default email marketing automations with prebuilt templates for you to use (the fifth option here — 3rd Party Automations — is an overview of the third-party automations your store is running, such as Google Smart Shopping). Figure 15-5 shows all these automations:

>> **Welcome New Subscriber:** This is also known as a Welcome Series, and is a chance to email your new subscribers, telling them a bit about your online store and its story. Use this email to be as engaging and authentic as possible, and remember to try and let the subscriber into your journey, perhaps by showing them a brand video or photos of your team behind the scenes.

TIP

With this email automation, you could include a discount code to incentivize new subscribers to make a purchase.

>> **First-purchase Upsell:** This automation sends an email to a customer after their first purchase. Statistically, if a customer is likely to purchase a second time, it's likely to be shortly after the first (depending on the products you sell, of course). For example, you could use this email automation to showcase your other products to new customers and drive future sales by offering a 15 per cent discount if customers shop again within 30 days. Bringing customers back to your store and increasing purchase frequency are two of the core drivers when it comes to increasing each customer's lifetime value (the CLTV, or LTV — for more on this, refer to Chapter 8).

>> **Customer Winback:** When a customer no longer shops with you, don't wave at them nostalgically as they sail off into the sunset — use this Customer Winback email automation (and perhaps also an SMS automation) to remind them that you miss them and encourage them to shop again.

TIP

Given lost customers are probably ignoring your email campaigns, you may want to use discounts to lure them back — a strategy I approve of because they're already lost, so they aren't coming back of their own accord.

>> **Custom Email Automation:** Shopify provides you with lots of other opportunities to send automated emails, such as when a customer creates an account, receives a refund or receives an order. These aren't really marketing automations, but they're important touch points for communication nonetheless.

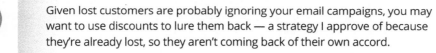

TIP

Communication is an important part of the overall customer experience, so it's helpful to use email automations for events such as order confirmation, courier or shipping tracking, any refund or return actions, or other key events, such as when a customer signs up to your newsletter or creates an account. Go through the list of automations carefully, selecting the ones you think may be useful when you're dealing with your customers.

>> **3rd Party Automations:** This is where you see any other automations that have been connected to your Shopify, such as Google Smart Shopping (you can also commence Google Smart Shopping ads by clicking on this section — I cover Google Ads in Chapter 16). Essentially, any marketing app from the Shopify App Store that connects with Shopify will display here (or can be connected here).

When you click on this section, you see a dialogue box pop up, with a Visit the Shopify App Store link — clicking on this link takes you to a section of the Shopify App Store that shows you third-party apps that can be used to create marketing automations. One of my favorites is SMSBump by Yotpo, which can be used to create automations that are delivered by SMS (see Chapter 16 for more on SMS marketing).

REMEMBER

The first three options in this list are must-have email automations — they're guaranteed money-makers, so I suggest you turn them on.

To view these Create Automation options you can access through Shopify:

1. **From your Shopify admin, go to Marketing.**

   Three options appear: Overview, Campaigns and Automations.

2. **Click on Automations.**

   The Marketing Automations page appears (refer to Figure 15-2).

3. **Click on the green Create Automation button in the top right.**

   The Create Automation dialogue box appears (see Figure 15-5).

   You see five sections that you can click on: Welcome New Subscriber, First-purchase Upsell, Customer Winback, Custom Email Automation and 3rd Party Automations.

To activate these email automations:

1. **From your Shopify admin, go to Marketing → Automations → Create Automation.**

2. **Click on the tile image of the automation you want to enable (refer to Figure 15-5).**

   A dialogue box appears that asks if you want to use the template you have clicked on — for example, the default template for the Customer Winback automation.

3. **Click on Use Workflow to begin setting up the automation you want to enable, or Close to go back to the list of available automations.**

   A dialogue box appears showing an automation workflow (see Figure 15-6).

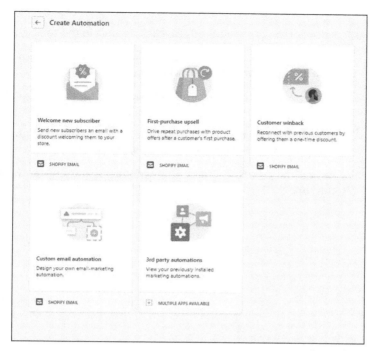

FIGURE 15-5:
The Create
Automation
dialogue box.

FIGURE 15-6:
The email
automation
workflow.

4. **In the image of the workflow, click on the icon that reads Send Marketing Email.**

A dialogue box appears that previews the email marketing template, which you're able to edit.

5. **Click on the green Edit Email Content button at the bottom of the dialogue box.**

A new page appears, where you can edit the email's design, copy and general style.

TIP

6. **Edit your email as required and click on Save in the top-right corner.**

   You can also click on the white Send Test button next to the Save button if you want to preview your new email template.

   When you click on Save, you're taken back to the automation workflow dialogue box.

7. **Click on the green Turn On Workflow button in the top-right corner of the dialogue box to enable your first email automation.**

8. **Repeat the process for each of the four email automations you wish to turn on.**

Chapter 16

Advertising and Promoting Your Online Store

Marketing and advertising play an important role in ecommerce, and it's useful to diversify your marketing rather than tie yourself to only one channel.

Chapter 15 introduced you to marketing strategy and how you can start using digital marketing to promote your online store. In this chapter, I look at some of the marketing and advertising channels and strategies that play nicely with Shopify — namely Facebook, Google Ads, search engine optimization (SEO) and email marketing.

I show you how to set up Facebook marketing and place Google Ads through your Shopify store so you can target new and existing customers. I also look at how you can ensure your online store appears on page one of Google's search results for certain keywords, using both a paid Google Ads strategy, and through using a more organic, non-paid approach, via SEO.

Email subscribers are like gold for an online store; they often provide your business with the highest LTV (lifetime value) of any of your marketing channels, and the marketing cost is very cheap given that they have already subscribed to your email marketing list — so they tend to have a high intention to purchase again. By the end of this chapter, you will know how to capture email subscribers and send marketing emails to them in order to generate sales.

Getting Started with Facebook Marketing

At last, I hear you say. Facebook is certainly a channel that is used widely by online retailers, and it can be an effective means to grow your business. Shopify integrates very well with Facebook, so you can get up and running pretty quickly.

TIP

To advertise through Facebook, you need to have a Facebook Page for your business and create a Facebook Business Manager Account — go to business.facebook.com to register. (In 2021, Facebook changed its name to Meta — however, for all intents and purposes, it's still good old Facebook, for now at least.)

You can create Facebook ads and Facebook campaigns and automations directly from Shopify by using Shopify's Facebook sales channel, which can be found in the Shopify App Store.

Follow these steps to add Facebook as a sales channel in Shopify for your online store:

1. **From your Shopify admin, click on the + icon next to Sales Channels.**

2. **In the dialogue box that appears, click on the + next to Facebook, and then click on Update Sales Channel to install the Facebook channel (see Figure 16-1).**

TIP

If you can't see Facebook as an option, then click on the blue Visit Shopify App Store text at the bottom of the dialogue box (you'll need to scroll down to see this) and search for Facebook in the Shopify App Store. Click on the Facebook icon, and then click on Add App. The Facebook sales channel is then added to your Shopify store and is available in your Shopify admin under Sales Channels.

After you have installed the Facebook sales channel, you see a range of options owned by Facebook that you can use within Shopify to market your store (see Figure 16-2).

FIGURE 16-1:
Adding Facebook
as a sales channel
in Shopify.

3. **Click on Start Set-up on the feature that you want to install first.**

   You can choose from:

   - **Facebook Shop** (see Chapter 17)

   - **Instagram Shopping** (see Chapter 17)

     Facebook bought Instagram in 2012 for US$1 billion, which is why you can set up Instagram marketing within the Facebook sales channel.

   - **Facebook Marketing**

   - **Facebook Messenger** (see Chapter 17)

   Figure 16-2 shows a Shopify store that has started but not completed the set-up of its Facebook Shop and Instagram Shopping (Shopify saves your progress so you can go back and complete it later). It also shows that Facebook Marketing and Facebook Messenger have not been set up yet.

   A new Set Up page appears, which includes the name of the platform you're setting up (for example, 'Set Up Facebook Shop').

TIP

FIGURE 16-2:
Different ways
you can use
Facebook to
market your store
using Shopify.

Source: Shopify

4. **Click on Connect Account.**

   You are diverted to Facebook and prompted to log in.

5. **Sign in to your Facebook account.**

6. **Connect the Facebook assets that are required to set up the features that you want — for example, your Facebook Page or Instagram account.**

   Follow the prompts provided to complete set-up.

7. **Accept the terms and conditions.**

8. **Click on Finish Set-up.**

After you add the Facebook app to your Shopify store, it appears in your Shopify admin, in the left-hand-side menu under Sales Channels (see Figure 16-3).

TIP

After you've configured your Facebook and Instagram settings, you'll be able to create Facebook and Instagram campaigns directly from the Marketing section of your Shopify admin (Marketing → Overview; see Figure 16-4).

FIGURE 16-3:
Facebook added
as a Sales
Channel in the
Shopify admin.

Source: Shopify

FIGURE 16-4:
The Marketing
Overview page.

Source: Shopify

After you set up Shopify's Facebook channel, you can create the following Facebook marketing activities in Shopify:

>> **Facebook audience building ads** can increase the traffic to your online store.

>> **Facebook dynamic retargeting ads** can help your customers find products they've previously viewed on your website.

>> **Facebook Page posts** can make your existing Facebook audience aware of store promotions or new products.

The following sections go into the first two of these in more detail. I talk about Facebook Page posts and social media in Chapter 17.

Audience building ads in Shopify

Facebook is a great tool for building an audience for your online store. You can create *audience building ads* (that are aimed at growing brand awareness, with a wide reach of new potential customers) in Shopify that appear as *carousel ads* on Facebook (ads with multiple images that appear on your Facebook feed that you can scroll through, as opposed to one single image on an ad).

TECHNICAL STUFF

When you create Facebook audience building ads in Shopify, Facebook automatically determines the best placement for the ad across its audience network. Your ad may also appear on another 'Facebook family' platform, such as Instagram.

WARNING

When you buy Facebook ads, you pay for them through your Facebook Ads account. Make sure you understand Facebook's advertising policies before you create a Facebook Ads campaign.

Creating your first audience building ad

If you have connected your Facebook account to Shopify and added Facebook as a sales channel, you can now create ads in Facebook and Instagram through Shopify.

Follow these steps to create your first audience building carousel ad in Facebook:

1. **From your Shopify admin, click on Marketing → Overview.**

   The Marketing Overview page appears.

2. **Click on the green Create Campaign button in the top-right corner.**

   The Build Your Campaign by Adding a Marketing Activity dialogue box appears (see Figure 16-5). The dialogue box contains a list of marketing options that you can run.

3. **Click on the first Facebook-related activity, Facebook Audience Building Ad.**

   The Facebook Audience Building Ad page appears — this is where you'll create your first Facebook ad.

4. **Name your activity in the Activity name field, under the Activity Details heading.**

   Use something that relates the activity to the campaign you are running, such as Men's Jeans Sale.

5. **Scroll down to the Products section and select Browse next to the search bar labelled Search Products. Start entering the items in the list of products from your store that you want to appear in the ad, such as products in your Men's Jeans range.**

   Add a checkmark next to up to five products from the list that appears in a new dialogue box as you search for your products.

   You can only add up to five products per ad.

REMEMBER

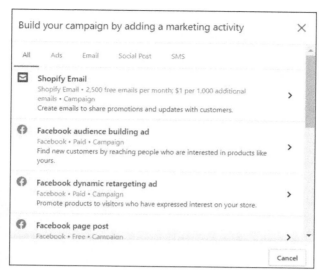

FIGURE 16-5:
The Build Your
Campaign by
Adding a
Marketing Activity
dialogue box.

6. **Click on the blue Add button in the bottom-right corner.**

You're taken back to the Facebook Audience Building Ad page.

A preview of your ad appears on the right-hand side of the section you're now in (see Figure 16-6).

7. **Scroll through the images on the preview to see all the images of the products you uploaded to create your carousel ad.**

TIP

You can see the preview to the right of the ad you're creating, so there's no need to leave the page. You can also view your ad preview in mobile view, by clicking on Mobile (this option is next to Desktop, above the preview of the ad).

8. **Click on Browse in the Discount section, which is the next section below Products, if you wish to add a discount code to your ad as a way of incentivizing customers.**

When you click browse, the Add Discounts dialogue box appears, with a text box prompting you to Search Discounts. As you begin to type, your options appear — click on any of the discount codes you have previously created and click on Add in the bottom-right corner of the dialogue box. You're then taken back to the Facebook Audience Building Ad page.

9. **To include the discount in your ad's text, tick the box under Discount Placement (Optional).**

10. **Customize the Ad Details section, which is the next section down, by editing the text inside the Ad Text box.**

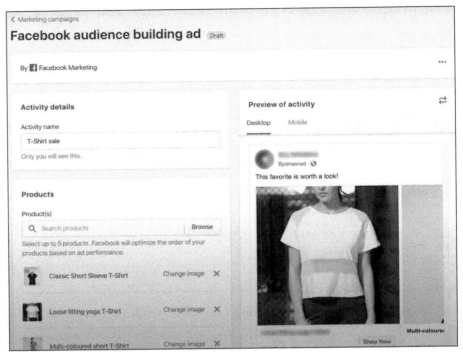

FIGURE 16-6:
A Facebook
Audience Building
Ad preview.

Source: Shopify

This is the text that appears in your ad, so refer to your unique value propositions/
unique selling points and your target audience (refer to Chapter 15 for more on
these) to remind yourself how you want to communicate with them.

TIP

Keep the text short and to the point, with a strong *call to action* (an attention-
grabbing headline that compels users to click on your ad).

11. **The next section down is called Audience — it's where you select the
audience that you intend to target with your ad (see Figure 16-7).**

Here, you can select either a Shopify Site Visitor Lookalike audience or a People
Who Have Specific Interests audience.

A Shopify Site Visitor Lookalike audience is a default audience; in terms of
Facebook advertising, it describes a target audience with similar interests and
in a similar demographic to your website's visitors. The other option, People
Who Have Specific Interests, allows you to enter keywords such as 'cycling' or
'rock climbing' so your ads can target people who share those interests.

The audience options here vary depending on traffic and the number of
followers your Facebook Business page has.

In Figure 16-7, you can see that the advert wants to target people who are into fitness (this ad is for athletic apparel), so the audience selected is people with specific interests that include CrossFit, Cycling, Running, Yoga, and Fitness and Wellness. The number next to each audience is the audience size.

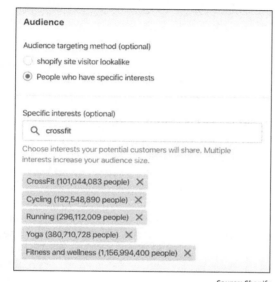

FIGURE 16-7:
The Audience
section.

Source: Shopify

TIP

If you select an audience based on Shopify site visitors (the first option in the Audience section), then you don't need to enter interests; however, you can add age and gender filters further down the Audience section.

12. **Set a daily budget for your ads, or a budget for the lifetime of the ad, in the Budget and Schedule section (charges are in USD so remember to work out the cost in your local currency).**

Start small and check in on your budget frequently.

TIP

13. **Next, select your start and end dates for your ads using the calendar selection options in the Budget and Schedule section.**

You don't need to set an end date if you want to keep your ad running.

REMEMBER

14. **Click on Publish in the bottom-right corner.**

Your ad will now appear in the Marketing → Campaigns section of your Shopify admin, where you can keep track of its performance, such as how much you've spent, how much you've made and how many visitors each ad has driven to your site. Keeping a check on performance means you can invest more in the ads that are performing well and stop the ones that are missing the mark.

Congratulations, you've created your first Facebook ad in Shopify!

Creating dynamic retargeting ads

Have you ever noticed that when you visit an online store, the products you look at seem to follow you around Facebook? Yep, that's what this section is all about.

Facebook's *dynamic retargeting ads* promote relevant products to customers who have visited your online store. Dynamic retargeting ads are shown as personalized Facebook carousel ads for each visitor and include the products they viewed or added to their cart.

TECHNICAL STUFF

Facebook tracks visitor behavior on your online store using the *Facebook pixel*, a piece of code that sits on your website and tracks the performance of your Facebook marketing (a little like the Urchin Tracking Module codes I mentioned in Chapter 15), and then builds an audience of visitors who have been active on your store in the last 30 days.

When you create a Facebook marketing activity with a dynamic retargeting ad, you can use the ad template that is provided by default (you'll see this when you create the campaign) to set up the ad. You can also preview your ad before you publish it. Because everyone's experience of this ad is personal to their behavior, the preview uses random products from your store so that you can get an idea of what the ad will look like.

To create a Facebook dynamic retargeting ad in Shopify, follow these steps:

1. **From your Shopify admin, click on Marketing → Overview.**

   The Marketing Overview page appears.

2. **Click on the green Create Campaign button in the top-right corner.**

   The Build Your Campaign by Adding a Marketing Activity dialogue box appears (refer to Figure 16-5).

3. **Click on Facebook Dynamic Retargeting Ad from the list of options that appears in the dialogue box.**

4. **Enter a name and the ad text for your activity in the same way you did for your Facebook Audience Building Ad (refer to the preceding section if you need a reminder).**

5. **Set the budget in the same way as for your Facebook Audience Building Ad.**

6. Set a start date and time. You can also choose to set an end date and time.

7. Click on Publish Activity.

TIP

Your ad appears in the Marketing section of your Shopify admin for you to monitor revenue, visits and cost of ads.

Trying Search Engine Marketing with Google Ads

Google Ads are a form of Search Engine Marketing (SEM), and they're one of the most popular methods of paid advertising for an ecommerce business. *SEM* differs from SEO (which I discuss in the later section 'Making the Most of Search Engine Optimization') in that it's a paid channel, meaning you can pay to have your business listing appear on the first page of Google when people type in certain keywords (as opposed to SEO, which is a free, or *organic*, keyword ranking strategy).

REMEMBER

When you advertise using Google Ads, you're trying to rank as high as you can on page one of a Google search for keywords that people might search for when they're looking for products like yours.

EXAMPLE

Imagine you're selling guitars online. People might Google the term 'buy guitars online' — Google Ads allows you to pay to appear as high as possible in the search results, in the sponsored section. Often the first couple of search results have the word Ad in front of the link, indicating that the advertisers have paid to appear at the top, whereas the rest of the results may not show as Google Ads — indicating that this company has good SEO and is placed in the top organic position (which is worth a lot of money in terms of traffic and sales).

Google Ads is by far the most popular SEM channel. Although you can advertise on most search engines, Google is used by most online businesses.

TIP

Keyword research is critical. I look at keywords in more detail in the later section 'Making the Most of Search Engine Optimization'.

Shopify allows you to add a Google sales channel, which is primarily used for running a Google Ads campaign. Google Ads can be set up directly within Google, where you link the ads to your store in order to drive traffic, in the form of potential customers, towards your products.

The Google sales channel in Shopify

Adding the Google sales channel to your Shopify store allows you to run ad campaigns through Google, primarily Google Shopping or Google Smart Shopping campaigns. If you visit the Campaigns and Automations sections under Marketing in your Shopify admin, you can see a list of marketing campaigns that you can run after you connect the Google sales channel to your store.

To set up the Google sales channel in Shopify, you need to have a Google account and a Google Merchant Center account. A Google Merchant Center account allows you to upload your store data (such as product listings) to Google and use this information in Google Ads and Smart Shopping campaigns.

TIP

Visit ads.google.com to find out more about Google Ads and to set up a Google Ads account. Visit google.com/retail/solutions/merchant-center/ to set up a Google Merchant Center account.

In addition to the above, Google requires your store to have a Refund Policy and a Terms of Service (or Terms and Conditions) page in your header of footer — refer to Chapter 4 for more on adding pages to your store. However, if you haven't added these yet then don't worry, as Shopify will remind you to add these during the process of setting up your Google sales channel. Google also requires your store to have two forms of contact information, such as a phone number and email address — again, if you haven't yet done this, Shopify will give you helpful reminders and instructions on how to complete the required set-up.

TIP

As well as prompting you to set up any missing information or pages, Shopify will also take you to the relevant page and provide you with an auto set-up option — which is to use one of their existing templates! You can skip ahead to that cool feature at any time — from your Shopify admin, go to Settings → Legal, and a list of legal pages suggested for your store will appear, including a template Refund Policy, Privacy Policy, Terms of Service and Shipping Policy. Each (except for your Shipping Policy) has a button underneath that says Replace with Template. Clicking on that button populates a template for each legal page that Shopify has prepared to make ecommerce easier for you (see Figure 16-8 for an example).

Before you set up your Google sales channel, you need to install the Google Channel app from the Shopify App Store. After you install the Google Channel app, you need to connect your Google account and Google Merchant Center account so that you can sync your Shopify products with Google.

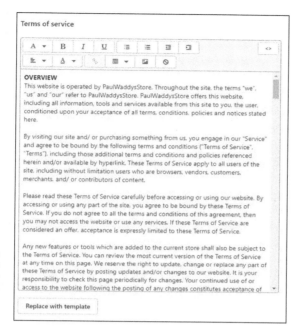

FIGURE 16-8:
A quick and easy
solution for your
essential policy
pages, such as
Terms of Service.

To set up your Google sales channel:

1. **From your Shopify admin, go to Sales Channels → Google, and click on Add Sales Channel.**

   A new page appears asking you to Connect Google Account.

2. **Click on Connect Google Account.**

   In the dialogue box that appears, the Google accounts that you have set up on your computer or device appear.

3. **Select a Google account (or create a new one if you haven't yet done so).**

   A new dialogue box appears, asking you to allow Google Channel by Shopify to access your Google Account.

4. **You need to allow Shopify to access your Google account information to set up the Google sales channel, so click on the Allow button at the bottom of the screen.**

   A new page appears, called Set Up the Google Channel (see Figure 16-9).

5. **Review the set-up requirements for your online store and make any required changes.**

   For example, here you'll be prompted to set up a Refund Policy page and a Terms of Service page if you haven't already done so (see Figure 16-9).

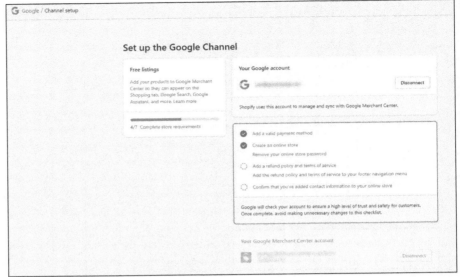

Source: Shopify

6. Select or create a Google Merchant Center account.

TIP

This may look different for each person, as you may have existing Google Merchant Center accounts associated with your account, which will appear in the drop-down list, or you may have none, meaning you're about to create your first one.

To select or create your account:

- Select a Google Merchant Center account from the drop-down list. The Merchant Center IDs listed are the ones associated with your Google account. To avoid approval delays, select the account that was connected to the old Google channel.

- If you don't have a Merchant Center account, then click on Create New and complete the account creation process.

7. In the next section down the page, you need to verify yourself as the Merchant Center account owner.

To verify your account:

- In the Verify It's You section, enter your phone number, select your country from the drop-down menu and click on Get Code to receive your verification code.

- In the Verify It's You section, enter the six-digit code that is sent by text message to your phone.

- Click on Verify.

8. In the next section down, you're asked to notify Google of your target country and language. Click on Select beside Target Market to set up where you want to sell your products, and then select a target market and its language.

Your store's currency settings determine the countries and regions available for you to target. The languages available are based on those supported by Google and depend on your target market.

9. If you're setting up for paid marketing on Google (and in these steps, you are), click on Select beside Shipping Settings, and then click on the drop-down menu to select how you want to configure your shipping rates.

You have two options:

- Select Automatically Import Shipping Settings to sync your shipping rates from Shopify, and then click on Save.

  If you've already set up your shipping settings in Shopify (refer to chapters 6 and 13), it's safe to select this option.

- Select Manually Set Up Shipping Settings in Google Merchant Center to set up your shipping rates on Google Merchant Center, and then click on Save.

  I've never selected the second option; I always select the first option as I set up my shipping rates within Shopify.

TIP

10. Read the terms and conditions at the bottom of the page, and then select the green button labelled I Have Read and Agree to the Terms to complete set-up.

After you complete set-up, you will be taken to the Google page in the Sales Channels section of your Shopify admin, where you can see the products that are available to your online store automatically beginning to sync with Google (see Figure 16-10). If you haven't added any products to your store yet, you will see zero results in the product listings (that is, products won't have a tick in the 'Available to Google' checkbox — when this checkbox is ticked, these products feed through to Google, meaning they can be used in your ads). You can access this page at any time from your Shopify admin by clicking on Google under Sales Channels.

FIGURE 16-10:
Google sales channel — product listing available to Google.

Source: Shopify

TIP

When you set up the Google sales channel for the first time, all the products that are available to your online store are automatically synced with Google. If no products are available at first, you may need to wait 3–5 days as Google can take that long to sync your products. However, at any time, you can click on the Manage Availability text in the top-right corner of your Google page in the Sales Channels section of your Shopify admin and be taken to a list of all your products, where you can manage products to be added or removed from your Google sales channel by ticking or unticking the Available to Google checkbox, and then clicking the green Save button in the top-right corner (the Save button only appears when you tick or untick a product — if there's no change, the Save button won't appear).

Create a Google Smart Shopping campaign

After you set up the Google sales channel, one of the marketing automations that you can set up in Shopify is a Google Smart Shopping campaign.

Google Smart Shopping campaigns are paid advertising campaigns through Google that can help you to promote your products and increase traffic to your online store. They can help you to *remarket* (show ads to previous visitors to your site) to existing customers, introduce your products to new customers, and connect with new customers across a variety of Google-owned platforms and ad formats.

Google Smart Shopping uses machine learning to create ads for your business by using product feeds submitted from your Google Merchant Center (a *product feed* is a data feed made up of your product information including images, attributes and pricing). Smart Shopping campaigns use insights from Google and your store to reach new buyers and remarket to existing users who have interacted with your online store before.

To create a Google Smart Shopping campaign from Shopify, follow these steps:

1. **In your Shopify admin, go to Marketing, and then click on Automations from the drop-down menu that appears.**

   The Marketing Automations page appears.

2. **Click on Create Automation, the green button in the top-right corner.**

   The Select an Automation dialogue box appears (refer to Chapter 15 for more on the various options at this stage).

3. **Click on the section titled 3rd Party Automations.**

   The Select an Automation dialogue box appears.

4. **In this dialogue box, you're presented with a Google logo and text that reads 'Google Smart Shopping Campaign'. Click on this text.**

REMEMBER

At this time, only the Google Smart Shopping option appears until you add other third party integrations.

Google can take 3–5 days to approve your products, so if you've made products available in Google but can't see them, they may still be syncing.

If you've already set up your Google sales channel in Shopify (refer to the preceding section), you can proceed to Step 5; if not, you're prompted to complete your set-up via a dialogue box that appears. Click on the green Finish Google Set Up button and follow the prompts to connect your Google account to your Shopify store before you move on to Step 5.

5. **Enter a name, such as Blue Jeans, or the name of the product or collection you're promoting.**

6. **Add the required details requested, following the prompts.**

   You can preview your marketing activities and automations before you save or publish.

7. **Save a draft or publish your campaign.**

   Click on one of these two options:

   - To save a draft, click on Finish Later.

   - To publish a campaign activity or automation, click on Publish.

Track the performance of your Google Smart Shopping campaign

Tracking the performance of your marketing campaigns is one of the most crucial parts of marketing. You can review the impact of your Google Smart Shopping campaign from the Marketing → Automations page in Shopify.

You can review the following information:

>> **Total sales:** The total number of sales from your Google Smart Shopping campaign

>> **Total impressions:** The total number of times a Google Smart Shopping campaign ad is shown on Google

>> **Total clicks:** The total number of clicks each ad receives

>> **Total orders:** The total number of orders from your Google Smart Shopping campaign

>> **Cost per click:** The average amount of money paid for a single click on each ad

>> **Cost per acquisition:** The total cost of ads divided by the total number of orders

You can also manually calculate your return on ad spend (ROAS) by dividing your total sales from the ad campaign by your total ad spend. If your ROAS is 2, it means your sales are 2 × more than your ad spend. ROAS can vary from industry to industry, but try and ensure that your ads are generating at least a 1 × ROAS, which means that sales are covering the cost of the ads.

TIP

All of the above is also accessible for review in your Google Ads account.

Making the Most of Search Engine Optimization

If you want to find something on the internet, you begin by using a search engine such as Google or Bing. *Search engines* take information and content from websites and rank them in their search results for a particular search query.

Search engine optimisation (SEO) is the art of optimizing a website so that Google or other search engines prioritize it in *organic* (non-sponsored) search results. It's not a form of paid media, but a technically complex process undertaken by SEO experts. Organic search results rely on organic rankings — advertisers cannot directly pay Google to appear higher in organic search results.

REMEMBER

Search engines rank websites in order of relevance to the term being searched and then display results based on that relevance. Making your website SEO-friendly means you're making sure its content is relevant for terms that your customers are likely to search.

Many factors can make your online store appear higher in search results:

>> The number of *natural* (not paid or social media) links pointing to your store from other websites (these are also known as *backlinks*)

>> The authority of the website based on engagement and other factors, also known as *domain authority*

>> The age of your domain name

>> Whether your website's structure and content is optimized for search engines

When you are new to selling online, it can be difficult to do much about the first three factors — it takes time to build a reputation for your brand and get other sites to link to yours. However, you can plan for the long term through your content strategy.

In the short term, the easiest way to get more traffic to your online store is to optimize your content so that a search engine recognizes it as relevant to queries related to your products. This is SEO — which is all about keywords.

Using SEO keywords in your Shopify store

Keywords are what people type into search engines to try and find relevant products or websites. For example, you might search for men's jeans in Canada. The keywords in this search would be 'men's jeans' and 'Canada'. To make your store appear higher in search results, you need to find out which keywords your customers might use to find your products, and add those keywords into your website's content — for example, in your product descriptions.

TIP

You can use online keyword research tools to get ideas on what keywords to use, find out the search volume of certain keywords and work out how many people search for these keywords each month (keyword research is also useful when thinking about which products to source as well). Google Trends is useful for keyword research (refer to Chapter 3), and Google also offers another free tool called the Google Keyword Planner, which you can access when you create a Google Ads account. Other keyword research websites offer both free and paid plans, such as keywordtooldominator.com and semrush.com.

Shopify allows you to enter keywords that can help improve your store's organic search results in numerous places. When you're entering keywords, try and keep them in natural sentences, rather than trying to force them into sentences where they don't belong.

EXAMPLE

If I'm selling Blue Jeans and one of my keywords is 'stretch denim' and another is 'comfortable jeans', then I can use these terms in my product description: 'Blue Jeans made from stretch denim, perfect for those that like comfortable jeans.' This description is informative to the customer, and it also uses search-engine-friendly keywords, helping to ensure that the website content is considered relevant by search engines when those terms are searched by shoppers.

You can add keywords in three main places in Shopify to improve the SEO for your online store:

>> Titles and meta descriptions

>> Alt text on images

>> H1 headers

Titles and meta descriptions

The title tag and meta description are two of the most important elements of SEO. They're shown in search engine results and provide information to people who are looking for things related to your products. A good title and meta description encourages customers to click the link in search results to visit your store. By *title* (or *meta title*), I mean the name of your page or collection that displays in your search engine results — as opposed to your H1 header, which is the name of your product, page or collection as your customers sees it on your website.

REMEMBER

A *meta description* is the brief bit of text that is shown in search engine results after the title tag. The meta description can be set for webpages, product pages, collection pages and blog posts in Shopify. Make sure each page has a unique meta description that uses plain, direct language. A good description encourages more people to click on the link to your store. Make sure to include relevant keywords to help new customers find your link, and to include your store name. Use natural, readable phrases rather than lists of keywords. You can enter up to 320 characters in the description.

You can edit titles and meta descriptions at a product page level (for example, for each product), and also at a store level.

EDIT THE TITLE AND META DESCRIPTION FOR A PAGE

Follow these steps to edit the title and meta description on a page (here I use a product page as an example, but you can also use a collection page):

1. **In your admin, go to a product you want to optimize for SEO, and click on it.**

   The product page appears.

2. **At the bottom of the page you will see the Search Engine Listing Preview section. Click on the blue text to the right of the page that reads Edit Website SEO.**

   The Search Engine Listing Preview Page appears as an extension of the product page (see Figure 16-11).

3. **In the Page Title field, enter a descriptive title for your product.**

REMEMBER

   The title is shown as a link in search engine results. You can enter up to 70 characters in the title (if you add more characters, the search engines may shorten your title).

   When writing SEO-friendly page titles:

   - Use a unique, descriptive title.

   - Include your most important target keywords for each product or collection near the beginning of the title.

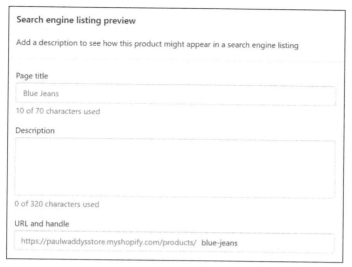

FIGURE 16-11:
The Search
Engine Listing
Preview page.

Source: Shopify

4. **Enter a description in the Description field (this is otherwise known as the meta description).**

5. **Click on Save in the bottom-right corner.**

The same rule applies for any pages on your store that you hope can bring organic traffic to your website (including collections pages and blogs, if you want to create one).

EDIT THE TITLE AND META DESCRIPTION FOR YOUR STORE

As well as pages, such as product or collection pages, you can also set a title and meta description for your overall online store. The logic behind doing this at a store level and not just a product level is exactly the same because search engines crawl through your site to compare the content on the site to that of your title and meta description to check that your store is relevant to a particular search.

To edit the title and meta description for your store, follow these steps:

1. **From your Shopify admin, go to Online Store → Preferences.**

   The Preferences page appears.

2. **Enter a title and meta description for your store in the first section of the Preferences page.**

3. **Click on Save.**

For tips on how to write SEO-friendly content, see the later section 'Keeping your online store SEO-friendly'.

Image alt text

Although search engines can't read your images, you can still use alt text (short for alternative text) as a way of helping search engines to find your content — which is great, as nobody wants to have too much text plastered all over their website. *Alt text* is a series of text used within HTML code to describe an image.

EXAMPLE

Alt text may look like this:

<img src="womanreadingpaulsbook.gif" alt="Woman Reading">

You won't need to enter all the fancy code — that's just how it appears when search engines are crawling the image.

The best format for alt text is to describe the image without going overboard with keywords. Picture yourself closing your eyes and having someone read the alt text out to you. Can you guess what's happening in the image?

TIP

Alt text is more than just a useful tool for your online store — it is used by visually impaired people to help them picture images.

You can set alt text for a product image, an image featured in a collection or an image featured in a blog post. The process is a little bit different for a product image.

To set the alt text for a product image:

1. **From your Shopify admin, go to Products → All Products.**

2. **Click on the product with the image that you want to edit.**

   The product page opens.

3. **Click on the image that you want to add alt text to.**

   The image enlarges in a new page.

4. **Click on Edit Alt Text on the right-hand side.**

5. **Enter descriptive alternate text for the image, such as 'men's blue jeans'.**

6. **Click on Save Alt Text.**

To set the alt text for an image featured in a collection or blog post:

1. **Click on the name of the collection or blog post that you want to edit from your Shopify admin, either by clicking on Products → Collections or finding the page or blog post by clicking on Online Store (located under Sales Channels).**

   For this example, you click on a collection called Men's Jeans.

   The Collection page appears.

2. **Next to the Collection Image, which appears on the right-hand side of the collection page you have entered, click on Edit (which is above and to the right of the image).**

   Three options appear:

   - Change Image
   - Edit Image Alt Text
   - Remove

3. **Click on Edit Image Alt Text.**

   The Edit Image Alt Text dialogue box appears.

4. **Next to the image of the product, you see a field called Image Alt Text (see Figure 16-12). Type in the alt text for this image.**

   For example, to enter alt text for the image of the bed sheets in Figure 16-12, you might type '100% 1000 count [insert brand name] queen bed sheet set'.

5. **Click on Save.**

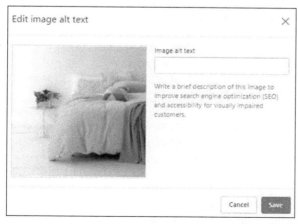

FIGURE 16-12:
The Edit Image
Alt Text
dialogue box.

Source: Shopify

The H1 header

The third area you can score some easy wins in SEO is in your H1 header, which you might also know as the title of your product or page.

An *H1 header* is the main heading at the top of a page. When you create a product page, collection page, webpage or blog post, Shopify uses the title that you use (such as Men's Jeans) to generate the H1 header for the page. The largest text size on a page is often the H1 header, and search engines use them to determine what the page content is about. When you enter a page title, include your main keywords so the H1 header automatically includes them.

To add or edit keywords to your H1 Header, follow these steps:

1. **Select the product, collection, webpage or blog post that you want to edit — go to your Shopify admin, then click on Products and select the product you're optimizing for SEO; go to Collections to find the collection you're optimizing; or for a blog post or other webpage, click on Online Store under Sales Channels and locate the webpage or blog post you're optimizing.**

   The selected item appears.

2. **In the Title field of the product, collection, webpage or blog post you've selected, enter a descriptive title that includes your keywords.**

3. **Click on Save.**

Keeping your online store SEO-friendly

Your website is (or should be) full of content. From the product and collection descriptions that you write to the blog posts you create, you have multiple opportunities to optimize your content for SEO.

When you write content for a product or collection description, webpage or blog post, use readable, unique phrases that include some of your keywords. Search engines compare a page's content with its headers to make sure that the page is about what it claims to be about.

TIP

When you write product descriptions, make sure that you don't copy text that's been provided to you by a manufacturer because that description may already have been used by other websites.

Focus on quality writing over quantity, but know that search engines use longer content to understand your page better. Make sure that every page has at least 250 words of descriptive text, and that informational pages and blog posts have at least 500 words.

SMS MARKETING

SMS (which simply means *short message service*) marketing is a form of text-message-based marketing that can be an effective marketing channel for an online store when used correctly. I use SMS sparingly — I might use two SMS campaigns a year to promote my two biggest sales campaigns of the year, and I might also incorporate SMS into my automations, such as sending out abandoned checkout SMS messages (Chapter 15 talks more about this type of automation). For example, I might include an SMS message at the end of an abandoned checkout automation, in case the potential customer hasn't checked their email or has entered the wrong email address (or the abandoned checkout email is going to their junk folder).

Typically, SMS messages have higher *open rates* (the number of recipients opening a marketing message) than marketing emails; however, SMS marketing is more expensive than email marketing.

Many SMS providers integrate with Klaviyo (an email marketing platform that is popular with Shopify merchants — including me!) so that your email marketing and SMS marketing are coordinated, but I generally prefer to use SMSBump (SMS Marketing by Yotpo), or Klaviyo's own inbuilt SMS function. I talk more about Klaviyo in Chapter 18.

It's important to check your country's laws around how you can use SMS marketing to engage potential customers. For example, SMS marketing laws are more relaxed in Australia than in the United States.

SEO is a slow burn. Don't be disheartened if you don't see your traffic or sales growing within the first few months — stick at it, in the long run it's likely to be one of your most profitable channels.

To track SEO traffic and sales, set up Google Analytics, with the *organic channel* (as it is known in Google Analytics) being the one to watch with regard to SEO traffic.

Experimenting with Email Marketing

Email marketing (commonly known as EDM, or electronic direct mail) is a must-have in your ecommerce marketing arsenal. Sending email marketing, or sending an EDM, is when your online store sends a marketing email, such as a regular newsletter, to your *subscribers* — people who have signed up to receive your email marketing material.

Send marketing emails only to people who have signed up to receive your marketing communications, and even then, try and send them only to engaged subscribers. An *engaged subscriber* is someone who has engaged with your email in the last 30 or so days by opening and clicking on its content. You can never have enough engaged email subscribers; they often have the highest lifetime value of any of your marketing channels.

Treat your subscribers like VIPs; after all, they've gone out of their way to sign up, so they want to hear what you have to say.

Email deliverability is how you measure whether or not your emails are reaching a subscriber's inbox, or whether they are being flagged as spam or bouncing back. Email service providers will flag your emails as spam if they think you're sending unsolicited emails, or even if they notice that a subscriber's email open rate is low — they may assume the subscriber is not interested in seeing your email, so they'll send it straight to spam. Sending too many emails to disengaged email subscribers results in fewer of them opening the email (resulting in a declining open rate) and fewer people clicking on the content (resulting in a declining click-through rate) — both of these declining metrics equal low deliverability and reduce the potential impact of your email marketing campaigns.

For legal and privacy reasons, you can send promotional emails only to customers who have agreed to receive marketing from your online store. Customers can accept marketing by adding their email address to a newsletter signup on your online store, or by checking a checkbox in the checkout. When you view a list of your customers, it will show you who has agreed to accept marketing. You can export this list at any time.

Shopify works nicely with many email marketing platforms, such as Klaviyo, Emarsys and Mailchimp, but it also has its own inbuilt email marketing features (such as the abandoned checkout email automation I covered in Chapter 15). In the following sections, I take you through getting Shopify Email up and running so that you can explore your online store's email marketing options.

Email marketing using Shopify

Shopify has its own inbuilt email marketing tool called, unsurprisingly, Shopify Email. This means you can send marketing emails directly from Shopify to your email newsletter subscribers.

Shopify Email lets you send up to five campaigns per week, which resets every seven days at midnight UTC. Each activity allows you to email up to 40,000 subscribers per campaign.

If you have more than 40,000 subscribers, you can split your email database into segments, such as men and women, or by country.

At the time of writing, all merchants with a paid Shopify plan have 2,500 free emails to send at the beginning of every month. Emails are counted based on each individual email address that an email activity is sent to. For example, sending one promotional email to 800 subscribers counts as 800 emails and one activity. Unused emails don't carry over to the following month. You can send additional emails beyond the 2,500 free emails at a cost of $0.001 USD per additional email. (For example, sending 1,000 additional emails would cost you $1 USD.) You aren't billed for the additional emails until the cost reaches $0.05 USD. There's no additional subscription plan, and Shopify Email only charges for what you send.

Shopify Email is only available for Shopify store owners, and you've got to be on a paid plan with a payment provider set up. If your account is on the trial plan, then you can create email messages and send test email messages to yourself using Shopify Email, but you can't send messages your subscribers (though you may not have many subscribers at the trial stage anyway!).

Consider changing the email address of the 'sending' email to something starting with 'info@' or 'news@' — it looks more professional than using your name or personal email address. This is the email address customers see when they receive your marketing emails. (Refer to Chapter 2 if you need a refresher on your domain name, web hosting and email hosting options, so you can secure and use email addresses associated with your domain.)

To change your email 'sending' address:

1. **From your Shopify admin, go to Settings.**

   The Settings page appears.

2. **Click on General.**

   The General Settings page appears.

3. **In the Store Details section, change your email address under Sender Email.**

4. **Click on Save.**

Installing the Shopify Email app

Installing the Shopify Email app is the first step towards sending marketing emails through Shopify Email.

To install the Shopify Email app, follow these steps:

1. **Go to the Shopify Email app page:** `apps.shopify.com/shopify-email`.

2. **Click on Add App.**

   If you aren't logged into your Shopify account, then you are prompted to log in.

3. **Click on Install App.**

   You'll now see this (and any other apps you've installed) in your Shopify admin under Apps, which is in the main left-hand-side menu.

Creating an email marketing campaign using Shopify Email

After installing the app, you're able to begin creating marketing email campaigns and sending them to your subscribers. For example, for your first email campaign you may decide to create an EDM announcing your new online store, and maybe offer a reward for early-bird email subscribers.

To create an email campaign, follow these steps:

1. **From your Shopify admin, go to Marketing.**

   The Marketing Overview page appears.

2. **Click on Create Campaign in the top-right corner.**

3. **In the dialogue box that appears, click on Shopify Email.**

TIP

4. **You're redirected to a new page entirely dedicated to Shopify Email, and I have to say, it's a fun page to be on. Here, you can browse email marketing templates and choose one you like. So, have a browse, and click on one that takes your fancy.**

   After you click on a template, a preview box of that template will appear.

5. **When you like the look of the template, click on the green Select button in the bottom-right corner to start creating an email campaign using this template.**

   You now see an entire email template on your screen, including a To field and a Subject field.

6. **Click in the To field to select from a list of your customer groups.**

   For example, you might select All Subscribers, which means this email campaign will go to all your email subscribers.

Shopify will by default start giving you three subscriber groups, also known as *segments*. You don't need to do anything — these customer groups will populate automatically: All Subscribers, New Subscribers (who haven't yet purchased), and Returning Customers (who have purchased in the past). As an example, you might create a campaign to customers who haven't purchased yet, offering them an incentive, such as a discount or promotion. Using more targeted email campaigns like this often yields results. Segmentation in email marketing is very important, as is personalization of the content, because what one person likes, another may not. (When you're ready to start looking at personalization, you might start to review email platforms such as Klaviyo and Emarsys, two of my favorites.)

You probably won't have any subscribers yet, so you can send this first email to yourself as part of your training!

7. **Enter a subject for the email, remembering not to spam your subscribers.**

Send engaging content with a strong call to action (CTA) in the subject line, and in the body of the email. The subject line is one of the most important parts of an email campaign, because without a catchy subject line, nobody will open the email, so they won't even look at the amazing content or offer you're presenting.

Subject lines should be short and clear, letting the subscriber know what they can expect inside the email. Avoid capitals in your subject line, and symbols such as *, @, !, $, ^ or ! If you can, try and use personalization in your subject line, such as using the subscriber's name in the subject. 'Hi Paul, here's a surprise from us for your birthday' is likely to get a higher email open rate than 'HOT DEAL NOW ON JUST 4 U!!!'.

8. **Optional: Enter Preview Text to customize the text that appears after the subject in your customers' email inboxes (remember, this isn't part of the main body of your email).**

For example, Your New Go-To For Jeans.

9. **After you set up the email activity details, you can customize the email body content as you like.**

In other words, you can enter your text (copy) or upload creative assets (images and videos and other forms of media). Most email templates in Shopify include the following customizable sections:

- **Header:** Enter image, store name and logo.

- **Text:** Enter text and links.

- **Image:** Select an image in your Shopify store, upload a new image or add an image from Burst (*Burst* is a free stock photo platform provided by Shopify to help your store look professional, offering you a range of great free photos to use — see more at burst.shopify.com).

- **Product:** Link to a product from your Shopify store.

- **Footer:** Include your shop address, phone number and social media links to customize the content at the bottom of the email.

To add social media links to your email, you need to use the Brooklyn, Debut, Kagami, Minimal, Narrative or Parallax theme.

10. **If you would like to test the email, click on Send Test. Alternatively, you may prefer to click on Review to preview the email (both options in the top-right corner of the page).**

11. **Click on Send when you are happy to send out your email marketing campaign.**

Always know your limitations. If graphic design isn't your thing, consider hiring an expert or using the Shopify Experts marketplace to bring the expertise you need in-house to make your emails look awesome.

After you've sent your email campaign, you can track its results in the Marketing Overview page (click on Marketing in your Shopify admin).

Don't send an email just because you can. If you don't have anything to say, don't say anything at all. I've seen online retailers send emails once or twice a week that have zero impact on revenue, and I watch their engagement steadily decline, to the point where not one person opens their emails. When you're dropping new products weekly, running regular promotions or have something genuinely exciting for a subscriber, then you might consider moving to weekly emails; until then, focus on building up your subscriber network and only communicating with them when you have a great offer or exciting news. Also, remember to ensure your email content looks amazing. Resist the urge to send emails that look 'good enough' — it's a jungle out there in online retail, so you need to stand out to be noticed.

Chapter **17**

Getting Social: Using Social Media to Grow Your Business

When I think about social media, the channels or platforms that come to mind are Facebook, Instagram, Twitter and, more recently, Snapchat and TikTok. In the 'old days', a business could get significant reach, or even go viral, simply by posting engaging content, which would be organically viewed by thousands, sometimes millions, of people. Over time, as people have flocked to these social media platforms, the corporations have made it harder and harder to give businesses organic reach, instead prioritizing paid placements or ads (such as the Facebook ads I talk about in Chapter 16).

While it is true that I've already touched on Facebook marketing, this chapter is primarily about *organic* social media, which means unpaid social media strategies that grow your business and enable you to communicate with your customers (as opposed to the paid media strategies from Facebook and Google).

The challenge for new online businesses is to understand the opportunities of social media but also its limitations, and to use this understanding to post engaging content that is likely to increase engagement (*engagement* is the one of the key metrics that determines success in the use of social media — basically, it's how many people are engaging with your content by liking, commenting on or sharing it).

In this chapter, I'm going to look back in time at the history of social media in ecommerce, and discuss the main platforms and how you can utilize them through Shopify to grow your audience and your business. By the end of this chapter, you should know how to post engaging content across suitable social media channels for your target audience in order to reach thousands of new potential customers.

All About Socials: The Rise and Rise of Social Media in Ecommerce

I don't think I need to explain to readers of this book what social media is, except to note that it is one of the incredible phenomena of the 2000s — and you are probably already using it (or have used it at some point) in your life. For many people, social media is their exclusive way of communicating, meeting people and being introduced to new brands. Depending on what product you're aiming to sell, and to which demographic, there's a very good chance that social media is going to play an important role in your online business.

In the early days of ecommerce, a digital marketing team probably consisted of search engine specialists (for the all-important search engine optimization, or SEO, that I discuss in Chapter 16). These days, it's at least as common for an online business to have a social media team, often actually split out from the marketing team altogether, as the marketers focus on paid advertising channels, whereas the social media team focus on building a community through delivering engaging content.

REMEMBER

Content in social media terms is one of the key outputs of a successful social media strategy. Content is generally visual assets, such as pictures or video. Very rarely does content refer to text (or *copy*) when it comes to social media — it's a highly visual channel.

REMEMBER

The purpose of using social media in the context of an online business is to build and engage with an audience, ideally within your target market or target demographic. When social media is used well, it can expand your reach through users sharing your content. The overarching objective of building an engaged audience on social media is to then convert them into paying customers.

Here are a few tips to help you maximize your store's social media strategy from the get-go:

REMEMBER

>> **Master the major platform(s) for your target audience.** Find out which social media platforms your target customer uses, and try and master those first.

You can't be all things to all people, so select the right channels and nail them.

>> **Always reply to comments.** Two-way communication is a great way to boost engagement on your social media platforms.

>> **Keep your posting consistent.** Not too often, not too little — once a day is plenty to begin with. Use a scheduling tool so that you can block out an hour or two a week to schedule all your social media content — that way, you're not doing it on the fly.

TIP

Good scheduling tools include Loomly.com, later.com and sproutsocial.com. They aren't available in the Shopify App Store as they connect to your social media channels directly, not to your Shopify store.

>> **Experiment and report.** Keep a reporting spreadsheet where you track your posts' audience engagement levels.

TIP

A good metric to monitor is to divide the total amount of likes and comments (engagement) per week by the number of posts. If you see your average engagement rising, you're posting content that your audience appreciates.

REMEMBER

Don't post on social media because 'all businesses have to these days'. Put thought into your content, and if it's not your strength, consider outsourcing your content creation to an expert.

Meeting the Social Media Marketing Channels

Social media may have exploded in popularity in recent years, but if you get to know a few of the key players you can become an expert social media marketer in no time — even if you don't use these channels already in your personal or professional life.

The following sections take a look at some of the main social media channels you can use to promote your business.

Facebook

Facebook used to be a platform that a business could use for free to find new customers. These days, Facebook is rarely used in ecommerce as a channel to post on — unless you intend to put advertising behind the post as well.

When Facebook first came out, brands could post content on Facebook, from images of new products to behind-the-scenes videos of photoshoots, funny videos and memes — anything really, in the hope that their *followers* (the people that like their Facebook Page) would like and share the comment, and potentially make it go *viral* (a term used to describe something that spreads to large groups of people online very quickly). In 2007, the Facebook Ads platform launched and was steadily promoted to Facebook Page owners as a marketing tool — to the point that Facebook has essentially become a pay-to-play platform.

In August 2021, social media channel management experts Hootsuite reported that the average reach for an organic (non-paid) Facebook post was down to 5.2 per cent — meaning only 5.2 per cent of that page's followers actually even saw the post (to read the article, type 'Hootsuite blog organic reach decline' into Google).

To test that theory, if you take a look at some of the largest online retailers on Facebook, you may be surprised to see that they have a rather small number of likes on their posts, even if they have thousands, if not millions, of followers!

REMEMBER

Facebook is a great platform, but it needs paid advertising to gain reach for your brand.

So, given this chapter is all about organic marketing channels, what else can you do with Facebook and Shopify to grow your business?

Facebook Shop

Facebook Shop is a feature that Facebook launched to allow businesses to showcase their products for free to users of Facebook and Instagram. Having a Facebook Shop doesn't replace Shopify, but it can be used as a nice additional channel to reach new customers.

Facebook Shop is free and simple to use. You can choose which products you want to display in your Facebook Shop, and customize its look and feel with cover images and colors. People can find a Facebook Shop on a Facebook Page, on an Instagram profile, or through their Facebook or Instagram stories or ads (*stories* are images or videos that appear as a slideshow and disappear after 24 hours — I talk more about stories in the later 'Instagram' section). A customer can then click on a product and be taken to the business's online store to complete the checkout process (although in the United States, a customer can complete the checkout within Facebook if they have the Checkout feature enabled).

Before you set up your Facebook Shop using Shopify, remember to ensure you have Facebook added as a sales channel in your Shopify admin. I cover this in Chapter 16.

To add a Facebook Shop to your online store, follow these steps:

1. **Click on Facebook in your Shopify admin, under the Sales Channels heading.**

   A new page appears prompting you to select a Facebook feature to set up.

2. **Click on Start Setup under Facebook Shop (or Continue Setup if you've already commenced at an earlier point).**

3. **Connect the required Facebook assets when prompted, including your Facebook account, Business Manager account and Facebook Page for your business.**

4. **Accept Facebook's terms and conditions and click on Finish Setup.**

It can take up to 48 hours for Facebook to review your products and approve your store. When the review process finishes, you're notified by email and in your Shopify admin. After the shop is approved, customers will be able to see your Facebook Shop and browse your products.

TIP

If your store isn't approved in this time, contact Facebook for more information. All Facebook accounts, pages, and products associated with Facebook Shop are subject to approval by Facebook. Your products in Facebook Shop aren't displayed to your customers until the Facebook review process is complete.

Facebook Messenger

Facebook Messenger is Facebook's native messenger or chat service that allows users to chat to each other. Facebook allows your customers to message you by connecting its Messenger service to your Shopify Inbox so you can receive and reply to messages in one place. With this interaction between Messenger and Shopify, customers can message you from your Facebook Business page using the Message Us button.

Find out more about using Shopify Inbox in Chapter 7.

To enable Facebook Messenger in your Shopify store, follow these steps:

1. **From your Shopify admin, click on Facebook → Overview.**

   A page appears with different Facebook options you can add to your store.

2. **In the Messenger section, click on Set Up to Start.**

   The Set Up Facebook Messenger and Shopify Inbox page appears.

3. **Click on Confirm to authorize Shopify Inbox to work with Messenger.**

4. **On the next page that appears, click on Go to Facebook to set up your Messenger button.**

   Your business's Facebook Page must have a Message Us button to complete this step — you can set this up in your Facebook Business page's settings.

   REMEMBER

   The Set Up Facebook Messenger page appears.

5. **Click on Go to Shopify Inbox to log in to Shopify Inbox to complete your Messenger set-up.**

6. **Click on Finish to complete Facebook Messenger set-up.**

When a customer messages you on Facebook Messenger, you can now respond through your Shopify Inbox, which saves you from monitoring lots of different messaging channels — all the Facebook Messenger messages will now appear in your Shopify Inbox.

Instagram

Instagram was created by Kevin Systrom and Mike Krieger in 2010 as a photo-only social media platform. It was reasonably popular at first, gaining a million users in its first year, and it was acquired by Facebook in 2012 for $1 billion dollars — during the same year, Instagram reached 80 million users. In 2013, Instagram added video to the platform so that users could use their mobile devices to post photos and videos directly to the platform to share with their followers.

Surprise! In 2013, Instagram announced that it was adding sponsored posts and videos to the platform — in other words, a person or business could now place advertisements on Instagram. In 2015, it added carousel ads to the ad platform, and in 2016 it introduced *stories*, which are photos or videos that can only be viewed by followers for 24 hours. In 2016, Instagram also introduced *Boomerang*, which is a feature that takes a burst of photos and turns them into a mini video that plays forwards and in reverse.

In 2017, Instagram announced that it had 15 million business profiles using the platform, with 2 million monthly advertisers and 800 million total users. In 2020,

Instagram launched a revamped Instagram Shopping, which allows brands to sell directly through the platform, and enables users to complete their purchase without leaving Instagram (using the Checkout feature).

So, is it possible that Instagram's reach will die the same death as Facebook's reach? It's more than possible, it's probable. It's owned by Facebook, its ads have been aggressively rolled out over the years, and, ultimately, if a business is trying to grow its ad revenue, then reducing the amount of organic reach that a business gets through its posts is an easy way to get that business to start paying for reach, if it values Instagram as a marketing (and sales) channel.

However, at the time of writing, there are still gains to be had from organic posting on Instagram, so I strongly recommend that you consider this channel as part of your organic social media strategy — if it's used by your target demographic (which, given the number of Instagram users, it probably is).

Here are some tips for improving your Instagram following, reach and engagement:

>> **Produce quality content.** Instagram's algorithm shows users more of what they have engaged with. So, if you're producing content that people aren't engaging with, there's really no point using Instagram as a tool to grow your business.

>> **If you're getting the engagement, then increase the number of posts you make.** The majority of your followers will not see your posts. If your posts are getting high levels of engagement, post more frequently in order to increase the chances of your posts being seen.

WARNING

Don't waste your time posting frequently if people aren't engaging with your posts; the Instagram algorithm will not prioritize your posts if your engagement is low.

>> **Review the performance of your Instagram account by using Instagram Insights (see the next section).** Instagram Insights is only available for business or creator accounts and only on the mobile app.

>> **Post at the optimal time.** There is no general right time, so you need to test your engagement levels at different times throughout the day and week to find the optimal time.

TIP

If you're tracking engagement levels (which I highly recommend, using Instagram's Insights feature), consider adding 'time of day' to your post-tracking.

>> **Encourage shares.** Consider posting a competition or giveaway that requires entrants to 'like, share and comment' which increases the reach of your post and your profile. Instagram's algorithm favors accounts that have high engagement, by giving them wider *reach* (the number of people who see the post).

Curious to know more about how to get the most from organic opportunities when using Instagram? Read on — in the following sections, I look at Instagram Insights and Instagram Shopping in more detail.

Instagram Insights

Planning and reviewing is important for all parts of your business, from budget planning through to pricing your products correctly, reviewing marketing performance and spend, and then resetting where you need to go next. The same goes for any strategy you adopt in business, including your social media strategy.

Given the decline in organic Facebook reach, there's a good chance you're planning to focus on Instagram as a free channel to post your content. Instagram Insights provides useful data on how you're going and how you can improve.

Instagram Insights is Instagram's analytics section that is made free to business accounts. It's accessible inside the Instagram app. You can use Instagram Insights to find out more about overall trends across your followers and your content's performance with your audience. You can also view Instagram Insights for specific posts, stories, IGTV (Instagram TV) videos, reels (short 15-second videos) and Instagram Live videos that you've created to see how each one performed and how much people engaged with them.

REMEMBER

Instagram Insights are free but are available only for business or creator accounts.

To access Instagram Insights:

1. **Go to your Instagram profile.**

2. **Tap on the Insights Action button.**

   You can also tap on the triple line icon (often called the hamburger icon!) in the top-right corner and tap on Insights.

3. **Tap the metrics under the Overview section to view key metrics such as reach, follower growth or number of content interactions, or tap on specific content you've shared for a more detailed breakdown of how that particular post has performed.**

Here's a list of the available Instagram Insights and how to use them:

>> **Recent highlights:** This section announces any notable increases in account performance over the last week, such as whether your content interactions were up or down compared to the previous week.

- » **Overview:** This section showcases the total number of accounts reached, content interactions, followers and approximate earnings (if applicable) for your selected preset or custom time frame within the past 90 days. You can tap on each of these metrics for a more detailed breakdown.

- » **Accounts reached:** When you tap on this metric, you see the total number of accounts that you've reached, as well as a visual breakdown of reach for your followers compared to non-followers (people who've viewed your content but don't actively follow your profile). You also see a visual breakdown of your reach sorted by content type, as well as your top posts, stories, IGTV videos, reels and Instagram Live videos sorted by reach.

  Underneath, you also see your account's *impressions* (how many times your posts were seen) and insights on your account activity, such as profile visits. If you have any *action buttons* (such as call or email) on your profile, you also see the number of taps on that button. For example, you can see data on website taps, email button taps, business address taps and call button taps.

- » **Content interactions:** When you tap on this metric, you can see a detailed breakdown of your post, story, IGTV video, reel and live video content interactions. These include likes, comments, saves, shares, replies and other actions on your content. You can also see your top posts, stories, IGTV videos, reels and live videos sorted by interactions.

- » **Total followers:** When you tap on this metric, you can discover more about trends across your followers when you have at least 100 followers. These insights include *growth* (how many followers you've gained or lost), the top locations of your followers, their age range and the times they're most active on Instagram.

- » **Content you've shared:** This section showcases the content you've posted and boosted across your feed, stories and IGTV for your selected preset or custom time frame within the past 90 days. If you want to see all of the posts, stories, IGTV videos, reels and live videos on your account, you can tap under each content type to go to the media library. Here, you can view and filter all your content by media type, reach, interactions and time frame.

TIP

You can adjust the period of time you'd like to check within the last 90 days.

You can also tap on View Insights under individual posts, IGTV videos and reels, or swipe up on your stories and Instagram Live videos to view insights specific to that piece of content, including:

- » **Interactions:** This section displays what actions people take when they engage with your account.

>> **Discovery:** This section keeps track of how many people see your content and where they find it.

>> **Ad:** This section provides more information on your post if it's been *boosted* (turned into a paid ad — you can elect to boost posts if you think they're performing well or might look good as an ad).

Adding Instagram Shopping in Shopify

Using the Facebook sales channel, you can sell your products on Instagram using the Instagram Shopping feature. *Instagram Shopping* creates a shop on your business's Instagram profile and allows you to tag your products on posts and stories. Followers can click View Shop on your Instagram profile to view all your products in Instagram, and they can also click on View on Website to go to your website and make a purchase.

When a customer clicks on a product and then buys it, the referral is marked as 'Instagram' on the order page in Shopify, so you can track how powerful your Instagram Shop is.

TIP

Before you add Instagram Shopping, make sure that you have a Facebook Business page and that your Instagram profile is a business or creator account (also known as a professional account). If you have a normal Instagram profile already for your business, then you can swap it to a business or creator account — simply open your profile in Instagram, tap on the hamburger icon, then tap on Settings → Account → Switch to a Professional Account. Select a category for your business, and then connect your Facebook Business page when prompted.

If you have added the Facebook sales channel to your Shopify admin, click on this to reach the Facebook Overview page, where you can select Sell Your Products on Instagram from the list of options you see when you click on Sales Channels → Facebook from your Shopify admin. Click on Set Up to begin setting up Instagram Shopping for your store. When prompted, connect the required Facebook accounts to the Facebook sales channel (if you haven't already), review and accept the terms and conditions, and click on Request Approval. It can take 24–48 hours for your request to be approved.

Adding products to Instagram Shopping

After your request for approval has been accepted, you can log into your Instagram account, go to the Settings section, tap on Business → Shopping, and then confirm your Facebook account (I realize this is confusing, now that Facebook owns Instagram!). Select the product catalogue that you want to connect to Instagram (you should only see one which is your main product catalogue from

Shopify), which will be synced to Instagram via the Facebook Channel in Shopify, and then click on Done.

TIP

When you make a product available to the Facebook sales channel, it'll be available to all the features that you have set up in the Facebook channel — so Facebook Ads, Facebook Shop, Instagram Shopping, and so on. For example, if you have both Facebook Shop and Instagram Shopping set up in your Facebook sales channel, and you make a product available to the Facebook sales channel, then the product becomes available to both Facebook Shop and Instagram Shopping.

If you want to hide products from the Facebook channel (for example, you may have products in your Shopify store that are exclusive to another sales channel, such as Amazon, or you might want to hide products that are discounted or don't sell well), follow these steps:

1. **From your Shopify admin, go to Products → Collections.**

2. **Click on the name of the product that you want to hide from Facebook.**

   The Product Details page appears.

3. **On the Product Availability section of the Product Details page, click on Manage.**

   The Manage Sales Channels Availability dialogue box appears.

4. **Uncheck Facebook, and then click Done.**

5. **Click on Save.**

TikTok

TikTok is one of the world's fastest-growing social platforms, with hundreds of millions of active users and, from February 2020 to February 2021, installs across Shopify's social commerce channels increased by 76 per cent.

TikTok is used by users to upload short-form videos, from 15 seconds to three minutes long. Users often post pranks and entertaining videos in a light-hearted fashion. TikTok is a fast-growing channel for ecommerce businesses who cater to younger audiences, mainly for its large organic reach. I haven't seen amazing conversion results for the channel yet; however, for free, large-scale reach, it's a great channel for creative types who can put out clever content.

In 2021, Shopify and TikTok teamed up to bring product links to Shopify merchants, which can be used to tag products in organic TikTok posts in a similar way to Instagram. The TikTok community can choose to shop directly from the merchant's storefront or click on a tagged product in a merchant's TikTok video, which takes them to the online store to complete checkout or find out more about the product.

At the time of writing, this tool is in pilot mode in the United States and the UK, with selected merchants in Canada also trying it out. Additional regions will be rolled out over time. To find out more about Shopify's TikTok integration, go to `apps.shopify.com/tiktok`.

Pinterest

If you've ever renovated your house, studied architecture, looked for a new hairstyle idea or wanted some inspiration for anything creative, the chances are you've stumbled across Pinterest. *Pinterest* is an image-sharing social platform that allows users to share their own images of certain things, and pin other people's images to their own boards.

TIP

Naturally, this presents online retailers with an opportunity to present their products to potential customers. I've worked with online retailers who sell furniture and rugs who have done particularly well with quite a small spend on Pinterest. If you're planning to sell something in the creative homewares sphere of products, then Pinterest could be a nice organic channel for you.

Shopify has a Pinterest app that allows businesses to post their product photos to Pinterest, and then turn them into shoppable 'pins'. The Pinterest app on Shopify includes some great features, such as product tag installation, which makes products shoppable in a similar way to Instagram and Facebook. It also offers automatic daily updating of products and an ads-buying interface if you decide you would like to try some paid Pinterest marketing.

For Shopify store owners, the app provides a very simple way to get set up on Pinterest. The app automatically creates a connection between the Shopify store and Pinterest, with no developer required.

Shopify's Pinterest app prompts you to connect to your Pinterest account, and allows merchants to deploy a tag on their website, upload their product catalogue and quickly publish products in the form of pins. A Shop tab also appears on a business's profile as an additional way for their products to be discovered by Pinterest users.

To add the Pinterest sales channel, visit the Sales Channels section of your Shopify admin, and in the box that appears, select the green + icon next to the Pinterest logo. Follow the prompts to connect your Pinterest account to Shopify.

Snapchat

Although not considered a mainstream marketing channel for most ecommerce businesses, Snapchat can play a part for certain businesses if their research indicates that their target audience is using the channel. *Snapchat* is a social media channel popular among younger demographics. It is used as a tool to post short images or videos that disappear after a certain period of time. The platform was designed to encourage users to post spontaneous content in a person-to-person format. It's since evolved and is a popular tool for making avatars — for example, turning a young face into that of an older person, or turning a person into a cartoon character.

I haven't seen many ecommerce businesses use Snapchat as a mainstream channel, although if your content is clever it can get reasonable reach. However, Instagram — and to a lesser degree, TikTok — appear to have taken place of preference for broadcasting images and videos to followers.

The Shopify App Store has a Snapchat app that is mostly geared towards creating Snapchat ads directly from Shopify.

Linking Your Social Media Profiles

It's commonplace for a website to have links to its social media accounts on the homepage, usually in the footer, so it's a good idea to set that feature up in your new store so that customers can find out more about your business, particularly if it's a new venture.

Several of the free Shopify themes come with the ability to link your social media accounts via social media platforms, for example:

>> Brooklyn

>> Simple

>> Supply

>> Venture

TIP

When you're choosing a theme, don't forget to search for key features in the theme store to find your ideal theme — for example, search for 'social media' to view themes that have features geared towards using social media channels. Chapter 4 talks in more detail about the key considerations when it comes to choosing your store's Shopify theme.

Tapping In to Influencer Marketing

The term *influencer* broadly refers to anyone who uses their profile to sell or bring awareness to products or brands. Technically, the concept of an influencer has been around for hundreds of years; however, in the context of this book and in modern marketing, when I refer to an influencer I am talking about a social media influencer.

A *social media influencer* makes money by being paid to post content across social media platforms (mainly Instagram) that shows certain products they claim to use. Alternatively, influencers can be paid dependent on their performance — for example, they may get paid a percentage of the sales that they refer to a website.

TIP

Although influencers are generally considered to be a paid marketing channel (unlike the rest of this chapter, which deals exclusively in free, or organic, social channels), or they are at least gifted products to try, influencers are generally managed by the social media team in an ecommerce business.

There are varying levels of influencer:

>> **Mega:** 1 million or more followers

>> **Macro:** 500,000–1 million followers

>> **Mid-tier:** 50,000–500,000 followers

>> **Micro:** 10,000–50,000 followers

>> **Nano:** 1,000–10,000 followers

The chances are you won't have the budget to use Kim Kardashian to promote your new business, so beginners should focus on Nano and Micro influencers initially to keep costs low. Nano and Micro influencers are often everyday people who have developed moderately decent follower numbers based on their actual content and opinion, not just their celebrity following. Using influential people in your target demographic is a marketing tactic as old as time, and you too can successfully adapt this strategy to grow your business, particularly if your target market has a propensity to use social media (especially Instagram).

Most brands that I see working with influencers do not know how to correctly attribute sales to influencers, because influencers do not show up as referring sales or traffic sources in Shopify Analytics or Google Analytics, or any other generic tracking platform. You can ask influencers to show you the insights on their posts of your products — for instance, how many users interacted with the post — however, it's preferable to be able to quantify any marketing spend based on the revenue it generates.

Some platforms out there allow you to give an influencer an affiliate link to use in their posts. An *affiliate link* is a URL that shows up within a platform and can measure the traffic and revenue generated by people who click on that link. Two apps that do this are GrowthHero Affiliate Marketing and High Scale Influencer App, both available in the Shopify App Store. For more on affiliate marketing, turn to the nearby sidebar 'Finding good affiliates'.

Another way to simply track the impact of using influencers to promote your products or brand is to record the change in daily sales and website visits with and without influencer activity. For example, if your store makes $500 a day in sales, and one day you decide to pay an influencer $500 to post for your brand and sales remain at $500, with no increase in your traffic (you can check Shopify's Analytics to monitor changes in sales and traffic), then the chances are that post has had no financial impact on your business.

So, what does it cost to use an influencer to promote your business? According to an article on Instagram influencer marketing on the Shopify blog, you can expect to pay (US$):

>> **Nano influencers:** $10–$100 per post

>> **Micro influencers:** $100–$500 per post

>> **Mid-tier influencers:** $500–$5K per post

>> **Macro influencers:** $5K–10K per post

>> **Mega influencers:** $10K+ per post

TIP

You can use platforms like Grin and Upfluence to find and engage with Influencers that are suitable for your business or products.

REMEMBER

Influencer marketing is a channel that you should consider as part of your marketing channel mix, just be careful not to allocate too much money to influencers too soon, knowing that attribution of sales can be tricky. A balanced approach to marketing is always safest, pausing to reflect on which channels have succeeded for you in the past (use the Marketing Overview section of your Shopify admin to check on the success of your marketing efforts).

FINDING GOOD AFFILIATES

Affiliate marketing is when an online store partners up with another website or individual, such as a content creator or blogger, a shopping comparison site, or a discount code site, in order to gain sales. Affiliate marketing usually works commercially, via an online store that pays a commission to a website (or sometimes an influencer) who has referred a sale for a product or service.

In an ideal world (and in the early days of affiliate marketing), the process was pretty simple. A skillful writer or blogger could create a website about a certain category, for example video games, and write great reviews about games that might link back to an online store where the reader can buy the game. The online store would then literally post a cheque to the blogger for 5–10% of the value of the sale (or whatever the agreed commission rate was) if the reader went on to make a purchase after clicking on the link to their website from the blogger's review. These days, the sales are tracked through third parties such as Rakuten and Commission Factory, which can be used to pair online stores with affiliates, and to track sales and facilitate commission payments.

Discounting sites dominate affiliate strategies. Coupon websites such as Honey offer discount codes on your favorite websites and are often using an affiliate model to generate sales while making a sales commission. It can be a slippery slope for online retailers, as many of the customers that are referred from discounting sites may have intended to purchase from them anyway, but because the customer tried their luck finding a discount code first on the affiliate site before making their purchase, the retailer may have to absorb both the extra discount and the cost of a commission.

Not all affiliates are discounters — some airlines offer frequent flyer points that can be used on airline online stores, and this works on an affiliate model.

My advice would be to try and work with affiliates who produce genuinely relevant content that attracts quality traffic and customers. Be careful as to how many discount-type affiliates you work with, unless of course discounting is part of your value proposition.

6

The Part of Tens

Discover ten helpful apps that make it even easier to run a successful and growing business.

Fine tune your customer and user experience.

Get ready to go live with your online store.

Chapter **18**

Ten Helpful Apps for Your Shopify Store

'm excited about this chapter, as I get to share some of my favorite apps that I've used to help build Shopify businesses collectively turning over more than $500 million per year. I should clarify here that when I'm talking about Shopify apps, I don't mean an app owned or created by Shopify — I mean anything that is available in the Shopify App Store or has a Shopify integration.

This chapter gives you insights into the apps and integrations that some of the world's best ecommerce businesses are using — and the good news is you can use them too (without having to go through years of trial and error).

Part of the reason I love Shopify, and its many apps, is that I would have paid tens of thousands of dollars for these sorts of features when I started my ecommerce career, and you can have many of them for less than the cost of a good dinner. Using these apps, in conjunction with a good business plan and great products, is giving you every chance to succeed in your Shopify journey.

I hope you enjoy exploring this list that I've compiled over many years of using Shopify. I've tried to include a little something for every part of the ecommerce stack, from shipping and reviews through to customer service. So, sit back and relax as you browse what I think of as 'the Shopify Integrations A-Team'.

Gorgias: Customer Service

The customer always comes first, so it's only right that Gorgias occupies the number-one spot in my list. I've used most of the big customer service platforms available, and Gorgias continues to come out on top for me.

REMEMBER

Shopify Inbox is a great way to get up and running and offer good customer service, but Gorgias goes a little deeper into your customer service analytics and integrations.

Gorgias was founded in Paris in 2015 by Romain Lapeyre and Alex Plugaru, and it launched on Shopify in 2017. Gorgias works with online retailers of all sizes, with its sweet spot being merchants who are turning over between $100,000 and $200 million a year.

Gorgias is so simple to use and it integrates seamlessly with Shopify. You can connect to your customer service email servers and start pulling in new and old emails within minutes of set-up. There's no need for lengthy onboarding sessions — who has time for that!

The integration with Shopify is key, and because it's set up so well, you're able to update Shopify orders directly from Gorgias! For example, if a customer emails you to ask for a refund or update a shipping address, you don't need to log in to Shopify — you can perform both of these actions directly from inside Gorgias. You can even create and send a draft order from inside Gorgias, which is really powerful for a customer service agent hoping to make a sale while they're advising a customer.

Turn to Chapter 7 for more on customer service. You can find out more about Gorgias at gorgias.com.

Okendo: Product Reviews

Okendo is the best standalone platform for product reviews that I've come across. It plays nicely with some of the other apps that I recommend, and it has become a staple in my Shopify tech stack.

I like Okendo because it's super simple to get going, it's reasonably priced and you can start generating a positive return on investment from day one. Okendo gathers product reviews from customers who've made a purchase, including text, photo and video reviews, all of which can be displayed on your website and turned into Google or Facebook ads.

Some of Okendo's other features include capturing product attributes, such as comfort level and size, which can help customers make decisions that help them with their purchase decision — for example, allowing customers to leave reviews that indicate whether a pair of shoes runs small, large or true to size.

TIP

Okendo also works well with the email marketing app Klaviyo, which is another one of my favorites (see the next section). You can use Okendo to gather valuable customer data that you can use to create segments in Klaviyo — or to send personal, one-to-one emails rather than generic mass mailings.

Okendo does so much more than just collect reviews, which makes it an ideal app for a Shopify store that's ready to get serious. By adding Okendo to your Shopify store, you can create a pretty slick on-site experience that helps lift your conversion rate.

Chapter 8 considers the importance of product reviews. Okendo is available in the Shopify App Store, and you can find out more about Okendo at okendo.io.

Klaviyo: Email Marketing

Email is one of the most profitable marketing channels for an online business. Klaviyo is an email marketing platform that is used to send marketing emails and automations, such as abandoned cart emails. Klaviyo stores all your customer data, using it to send better, more personal forms of communication — as opposed to sending all customers the same marketing content.

Klaviyo has taken online retail by storm in the last five years or so, particularly for Shopify merchants. It is easy to set up, so you can send great emails without the need for expensive expert designers or marketers — it's what I call a DIY platform because it's so easy to use. Klaviyo gets to know your customers' past behaviors, and it applies this knowledge to show them the products or categories they're most interested in across your marketing emails and SMS messages.

The beauty of Klaviyo is that it offers highly sophisticated personalization, which is so popular in ecommerce these days. For example, if I visit a site and sign up to its newsletter because I love that site's sneakers, then I don't want to see emails that keep sending me baseball caps — I want to see the sneakers that I like. Showing me the sneakers that I like is simply going to increase the chances that I will make a purchase.

TIP

Klaviyo not only integrates with Shopify, but also with a number of other great apps, including some of the others in my top ten, such as Okendo and Gorgias. When you start working with apps that all 'talk' to each other, it forms a really nice tech stack and can unlock extra features and benefits, such as being able to pull customer order data from Gorgias into Klaviyo.

Klaviyo's pricing scales up depending on your email list size, so as your subscriber numbers increase, your Klaviyo fee increases.

Chapter 10 covers personalization in more detail. Find out more about Klaviyo at `klaviyo.com`.

Glew: Data and Business Intelligence

I've put Glew in my top ten because I use it almost every single day. Glew is a BI (business intelligence) platform that brings your business data together in one beautifully clean user interface. Glew has made sophisticated BI accessible to everyone, including ecommerce start-ups.

Data is useful when it's used to provide actionable insights, and Glew does exactly that. For example, Glew can provide information for your marketing campaigns by segmenting out different groups of customers, from high spenders to customer who shop sale items, or customers who have lapsed to those about to lapse.

TIP

If you're ever preparing to acquire investors for your business, or even to sell it, Glew is a valuable source of the typical data that investors look for. Taking the time to learn how to use Glew's features is going to hold your business in good stead when it comes to knowing your numbers inside out.

Pricing starts on a free account, which gives you 20 key metrics — perfect for a beginner who's eager to develop their analytical skills. You can scale up from there to other plans, but the Starter plan is a great tool to add to your ecommerce armory from day one.

You can read more about Glew and my thoughts on the platform here: `https:// go.glew.io/paul-waddy`.

Oberlo: Dropshipping

You might consider Oberlo a controversial inclusion in my top ten, given I don't talk a lot about my love for dropshipping in this book, and Oberlo is strictly an app for dropshippers. However, creating a dropshipping online store in Shopify is a great, low-risk way of cutting your teeth in ecommerce.

When I first used Oberlo it blew my mind. Owned by Shopify, Oberlo is an app that bolts on to your Shopify store and allows you to add products from AliExpress directly into your Shopify store at the click of a button — it even imports product descriptions, images and prices. You can edit the product descriptions to better match your brand or tone of voice, as well as set pricing rules — for example, you might add 20 per cent to the AliExpress price so that the price adjusts automatically to a 20 per cent profit margin. You can even round the pricing to the nearest dollar, or manually change it if you think some products may attract more or less than 20 per cent on top of the cost price.

TIP

Using Oberlo serves as a great way to familiarize yourself with the basics of an online store without having to spend any money on inventory.

If you think dropshipping is a path you might like to take, I recommend Oberlo as a great tool to streamline the entire process. Pricing starts with a free plan, and there's a great browser extension for Chrome users that allows you to identify products in AliExpress and quickly add them to your Shopify store.

To find out more about dropshipping, turn to Chapter 3 or check out my book *Selling Online For Dummies*. Oberlo can be found in the Shopify App Store.

PushOwl: Web Push Notifications

Web push notifications are those little marketing boxes that appear when you're using your mobile device that remind you of sales, new arrivals and general news from your favorite brands. With over 1,800 reviews in the Shopify App Store, web push notifications app PushOwl is a marketing gem and I love it — so do other customers, it seems, as it has a rare five-star rating.

PushOwl works across desktop and mobile and can be used to promote new arrivals, promotions or flash sales, or even abandoned cart reminders. You can also send tracking updates, 'back in stock' alerts and discount codes via web push notifications.

In my experience, PushOwl subscribers grow at a faster rate than email subscribers because, by default, many users tend to accept web push notifications as it just relies on the click of a button — there's no email address or phone number required.

WARNING

Your message tends to cut straight to the user, bypassing any spam filters your email marketing may encounter. Don't abuse the trust though — I advise using apps like PushOwl sparingly, such as for back in stock, sale and new arrival notifications. Over-sending can be a little intrusive.

PushOwl has a clean dashboard that reports clearly on revenue you've made, and I always see it generate a positive return — especially on the free plan! Plans scale in an affordable manner as your subscribers grow, so you only pay more when your success increases.

PushOwl is available in the Shopify App Store, or find out more at pushowl.com.

Back in Stock: Customer Alerts

The purpose of a back in stock app is to allow customers to enter their email or phone number under a sold-out product so they can be notified when that item comes back into stock. On popular out of stock products, I have seen some companies make tens of thousands of dollars in one day using this app. You can try several different back in stock apps through Shopify, but the one I recommend is simply called Back in Stock: Customer Alerts.

TIP

Back in Stock: Customer Alerts works at the variant level, so even if only one size or color of a pair of jeans has sold out and the other sizes and colors are still in stock, a customer can sign up to be notified when the variant they want (the size or color, for example) is back in stock.

Back in Stock: Customer Alerts integrates with Klaviyo, so you can design your 'back in stock' emails to look like the rest of your email marketing. You can also create Facebook Ads to notify customers when an item is back in stock.

This app is super simple to set up and use and is a guaranteed money-maker if you're constantly selling out of great products. Like most of the apps I am including, it has a free plan and then scales up as you grow the number of notifications you need to send.

Find the Back in Stock: Customer Alerts app in the Shopify App Store.

Foursixty: Shoppable Instagram and User-Generated Content

There's a fair chance you're going to use Instagram to promote your business, and invite influencers to use or wear your products. Or, if you love what your customers are doing with your products, you might want to encourage them to share their images on Instagram. Foursixty is a nifty app that allows you to import such images to your website.

Foursixty turns your Instagram posts and user-generated content into collections in your store that a customer can click on and buy. I think Foursixty is a great low-cost investment that can help drive conversions and sales even in the early days, plus it helps you create content without having to spend big money on photographers and models, making it a good start-up tool.

TIP

An added bonus of Foursixty is that it allows you to track influencers who are posting your products, so you can see which influencer is driving the most engagement. You can also see which customers or influencers are organically posting about you, which allows you to reach out to them to ask about establishing a partnership.

Foursixty integrates with many other useful apps, including two of my favorites, Okendo (so you can combine Instagram content with customer reviews) and Klaviyo (which allows you to use user-generated content and your Instagram feed in emails).

Foursixty is a must if your store trades in fashion, beauty or similar creative products.

User-generated content is explored further in Chapter 8. To find out more about Foursixty, visit foursixty.com.

ReferralCandy: Referrals

In your early days as an ecommerce entrepreneur, unless you're taking on capital investment, there's a good chance you're boot-strapping your business, so you need to watch every penny and spend your money on areas where you're going to get good bang for your buck. Referrals are as old as time, and a great, cheap way to get more customers.

ReferralCandy allows you to create a referral program for your store's customers, who are rewarded with cash, discounts or custom gifts — which as you can imagine is a powerful incentive to make a referral. ReferralCandy allows you to nudge your loyal customers to refer your brand at various points throughout their user experience journey.

TIP

To push the program's success, you can offer both the referrer and the person being referred an incentive, such as '$10 for you, $10 for them', so both parties get something out of the exchange.

ReferralCandy is extremely low maintenance. Most of the work is done for you via automations and sequences. You can also clearly track your referrals and how much revenue they've made for you.

ReferralCandy integrates easily with Shopify and can be found at referralcandy. com or in the Shopify App Store. It offers an initial free trial before you commit to a monthly plan.

For more on referral and loyalty programs, turn to Chapter 8.

Plug in SEO: Search Engine Optimization

Eventually, you'll want your *organic* (free) traffic to take over from your paid media (in terms of where your traffic is coming from), which is going to make your business more profitable.

Using a search engine optimization (SEO) agency or contractor can cost anywhere from $500 a month to $20,000 a month, depending on what is involved and the size of your business. So, anything you can do to keep SEO in-house when you're starting out is a good thing, as it's money kept in your pocket to invest in other things, such as a wider product range.

The Plug in SEO app is made by the same people as the Back in Stock: Customer Alerts app, and I like it because it's easy to use, it's affordable and it works.

Plug in SEO makes many of your SEO-related tasks a whole lot easier. For example, it offers you templates for editing meta titles and descriptions in bulk and it detects broken links. It even has a keyword suggestion tool, which is great for your new store.

TIP

Plug in SEO has great customer support, which comes in handy with SEO as it is a pretty technical job. It provides great training videos to help you get started, and it's automating a lot of the work that an agency would charge you for — in fact, many SEO agencies use Plug in SEO!

Plug in SEO is available in the Shopify App Store. It has a free plan and an affordable monthly paid plan. For more on SEO, turn to Chapter 16.

Chapter **19**

Ten Ways to Improve the Customer and User Experience

The X factors — customer experience and user experience (which you may see referred to as CX and UX) are two of the most important things you need to focus on to succeed with your online business.

Customer experience involves every touchpoint a customer has with your business, from the time they first visit your online store to the moment they receive their order. In the early days of ecommerce, many physical (or 'brick and mortar') retailers used to say that online stores couldn't compete with physical stores because they couldn't match the overall customer experience provided when a customer enters a store. It's up to you to prove them wrong by utilizing all the tools at your disposal to provide a great customer experience.

User experience refers to the on-site experience — in other words, how the customer uses your website. It's true that a good user experience is just one part of the overall customer experience, but I focus on it here because nailing your site's user experience can bring more sales through your virtual door.

In this chapter, I share a list of go-to customer and user experience checks you can regularly perform to ensure that your customers are having a pain-free shopping experience, which helps to keep conversion rates healthy. Part 3 goes in-depth on customer and user experience if you need to remind yourself of the essentials.

Check Your Page Load Speed

Also known as the average load time of a page on your website, your *page load speed* is the time it takes in seconds for a page to load on your website. A poor average load time often correlates to a low conversion rate, so if you see your conversion rate suddenly dip, it's a good idea to check your page load speed. In addition, Google now ranks faster stores higher in its search engine results.

So what is a good average load time for a web page on an online store? You can find articles online that suggest aiming for less than two seconds is ideal, however I don't remember the last time I saw a website load a page that fast. If your average page loads in less than four seconds, I think that's okay.

Shopify ranks your site speed a little differently by providing a score out of 100, which is recalibrated each day using Google's Lighthouse performance metrics. The higher the number the better, with the score system using other similar online stores as a benchmark.

TIP

To check your site speed ranking in Shopify, go to your Shopify admin → Reports → Analytics → Behavior → Online Store Speed, and you'll see your store speed score at the top of the page.

As with anything technical, you can always hire a Shopify expert to help you out (experts.shopify.com), but you can also take action in your store to help improve your site speed:

>> Remove any apps you aren't using.

>> Consider using a theme that's optimized for performance, such as Shopify's Dawn, which is free.

>> Large image and video files can slow down your site, so try and keep the sizes and formats within reasonable limits.

TIP

Try and use *system fonts* on your theme (fonts that are already installed on most of your users' computers), otherwise your users' computers may need to download the fonts your sites uses — which can take time.

Optimize Your Site for Mobile

A website doesn't just translate by itself from desktop to mobile — both versions require proper design consideration when you're building your store, so pay equal time to both.

Make the effort to change things that aren't looking great on a mobile device before launching — this is known as optimizing for mobile, or having a mobile-optimized site. Most online stores that I work with receive more than 50 per cent of their visits from mobile users, so it's important to design your store with a friendly mobile user experience in mind.

TIP

Shopify allows you to preview your site in both desktop and mobile view while you're building it, so be sure to check the mobile view from time to time.

To check and adjust your website design in mobile view, follow these steps:

1. **From your Shopify admin, go to Online Store → Themes.**

2. **Find the theme that you want to edit and click on Customize.**

   Make any changes you require.

3. **Click on the Mobile icon to see the changes from a mobile device perspective.**

Fix Broken Links

Broken links are links or URLs that lead to a page that doesn't exist, typically resulting in an 'Error 404 Page Not Found' message. Broken links can occur for a variety of reasons — maybe it links to a collection page or product that no longer exists (perhaps the product has sold out, so you removed it from view), or a URL has changed, and you forgot to redirect the old URL to the new one.

Google sees broken links as a sign of a website that has been neglected or is of lower quality, and so it punishes such websites with poor search engine rankings, which may damage the search engine optimization (SEO) work that you've done. A broken link also provides a poor user experience and can lead a customer to *bounce* (leave your online store) — it may even make them question whether your website is trustworthy.

Regularly check for broken links so you can redirect site visitors to a working link — or at least to a similar page, product or collection, or your homepage.

There's an app I use for checking and redirecting broken links — Broken Link 404/301 Redirect by Giraffly (available in the Shopify App Store). It has a free plan and you can have a broken link report sent to your email each day. You can even use the app to bulk edit or redirect broken links!

Include a Search Function

One of your key objectives as an online retailer is to bring your customer to a product they're likely to buy, in as few clicks as possible. Website visitors who use the search feature on a website have a higher conversion rate than those who don't, so it's important to ensure that you have a reliable and helpful search feature.

An effective search function is an important part of a good user experience, especially if you have lots of products and variants on your store. Online shoppers can be impatient and will rarely scroll past the first page of a collection.

Try and use a Shopify theme that has the search feature inbuilt. If your desired theme doesn't show it in the demo, reach out to the theme's support team to ask if it can be added.

Failing that, you can also use an app to insert a search bar into a theme, such as the Smart Search Bar and Filters app by Rapid Search (available in the Shopify App Store). I like this app as it is compatible with every Shopify theme. It also has some nice features, such as 'typo tolerance', and a predictive search function than auto-completes when a customer starts to type. If a customer doesn't know what to type, they'll be shown a drop-down list of your store's most popular products. It has a free plan, and it's an app I recommend you check out as part of your overall user experience strategy.

When it comes to search:

>> Speed is key.

>> Allow for typos.

>> Ensure it's easy to use on a mobile device.

Test your search function as a customer would — if you don't get the results you're looking for, you need to fix your search function.

Use AB Testing as Your Business Grows

AB testing (also known as *split testing*) is when you show different groups or segments of visitors (usually two) two different designs or functionalities on your website, with the intention of determining which one drives more clicks, revenue or results.

The purpose of AB testing is to constantly work on your website's user experience by putting data behind any ideas that you have to increase key metrics, such as conversion rate. You can also use AB testing in your email marketing or on marketing platforms, such as Facebook Ads.

Look at AB testing when your business starts to get bigger, because it can be a little technical and costly to get started, and you're not likely to see useful results in your early days of trading. When you are ready to AB test, you may find a good solution in the Shopify App Store, although I tend to use VWO or Google Optimize (which are not available in the Shopify App Store, but they both work well with Shopify websites).

Give Little Unexpected Extras

Also known by its acronym, GLUE, surprising and delighting customers is a nice way to build a great customer experience. It's cheap, easy and impactful to adopt a GLUE strategy, so it's a winning approach for ecommerce beginners.

The belief behind adopting a GLUE strategy is that going above and beyond for your customer, over-delivering, or exceeding their expectations is likely to result in a favorable response, whether that be a repeat visit, a referral to a friend or general brand goodwill.

EXAMPLE

A good GLUE strategy that has people talking is Australian company Adore Beauty's tradition of giving away a Tim Tam (an Australian chocolate biscuit) with every order. People know Adore Beauty as the Tim Tam company now!

Something you could try is sending a handwritten note with every order, from you the founder, because little things go a long way and can help you stand out from the crowd. Chapter 10 provides more suggestions of ways you can give little unexpected extras to wow your customers.

Offer a Personalized Experience

Personalization is a buzzword in ecommerce, and it's helpful for online retailers get to know their customers as well as they can.

Getting personal with a customer comes in two forms in ecommerce:

1. The onsite experience, which impacts the user experience
2. The offsite experience, which impacts the customer experience

Examples of how you can personalize the customer experience are everywhere in ecommerce, from adding first names into your email marketing to using Smart Shopping in your Google Ads to show customers the products they've already been browsing. You can even use your customer service software to recognize when your most valuable customers (your 'VIPs') call or email, so you can talk to them like they're a regular.

The way you treat your customers is entirely within your control and forms part of your customer service (refer to Chapter 7); however, if you'd like to enter into some form of onsite personalization, you can use artificial intelligence (AI) to show customers the products they're most interested in.

Chapter 10 dives deeper into personalizing your online store using apps, many of which are available in the Shopify App Store.

Create Surveys to Help You Understand Your Customers

I've said it before and I'll say it again — online businesses often think they know who their customers are, but the truth is they rarely know them at all. However, one sure-fire way to get to know your customers is to find out more about them — and surveys are a great tool for that.

TIP

Tools like SurveyMonkey and Typeform are great for surveying customers to find out what drives them and what they think of your business.

TIP

When surveying your customers, here are some good questions to ask (aside from the obvious ones, such as age and gender):

>> **When buying from us, what other brands did you consider?**

This identifies your competitors.

>> **Do you consider your purchases from us to be:**

- Very expensive
- Expensive
- About right
- Cheap
- Very cheap

This identifies whether your pricing is too expensive, too cheap or just right.

>> **When you think of our brand, what is one word that comes to mind?**

You can leave the space for the answer open-ended and see what customers say, or provide a multiple choice selection, such as 'classy', 'cheap', 'quality', 'casual' and so on.

>> **Who is your number one follow on Instagram?**

This helps to identify the type of marketing you should engage in, plus it highlights potential influencer partnerships.

Surveying your customers is about gathering actionable insights — you need to be able to sit down and review the responses, and take away meaningful actions. Surveys are not for raising your eyebrows at — if you can't action the results in a meaningful way, they're not very useful. Chapter 9 offers more advice about understanding your customers through surveys.

Get to Know How Your Customers Behave

Understanding your customers' behavior is something that every good UX specialist tries to do. If you know how your customers behave when they're on your site, you can look to improve the user experience to match their behaviors. For example, if 70 per cent of visitors to your homepage are bouncing, you can know that the homepage is not appealing for some reason.

It's a good idea to get familiar with some of the tools you can utilize within and outside of Shopify to examine your customers' behaviors. Your go-to reports in Shopify are your Behavior reports, which you can access via your Shopify admin → Analytics → Reports → Behavior.

TIP

Try using my two favorite Shopify reports on customer behavior to improve your customer experience:

1. **Top Online Searches:** This report shows you the most commonly searched phrases or keywords on your store. You can use this to make sure your product offering matches your top search results. For example, if your number-one search term is 'black sneakers' and you only have one style of black sneaker and six styles of white sneaker, you may need to think about buying more black sneakers.

2. **Online Store Conversion Over Time:** This report charts your conversion rate on a line chart, with the ability to change the dates and group results by Hour, Day, Week, Month, Hour of Day and Day of Week. You can use this to see if there is a particular moment in time when your conversion rate increased or decreased, and think about what happened on that hour, day, week or month that may have caused this outcome. For example, if your conversion rate began to drop on a certain day, maybe you launched a new app on your site that is having a detrimental impact on your conversion rate. Conversion rate is a key indicator as to whether users are enjoying their experience on your site.

Use Logistics as a Point of Difference

Logistics is more than just a means to an end when it comes to sending out your customer orders; it's one of the key parts of a customer's overall experience. Amazon has been the industry leader for years, using fast delivery as a way to grow its business. In my experience, when an online store offers fast delivery, conversion rates increase in comparison to stores with slower delivery times.

To ensure your Shopify store is optimizing the logistics experience for your customers, consider:

>> **Speed:** Ensure you're using reputable shipping carriers that deliver quickly to your target regions. I suggest using Shopify Shipping if it's available in your country, as the shipping partners are world class.

>> **Price:** If your margins allow it, consider offering free shipping on orders above a certain value. One strategy is to offer free shipping just above your average order value (AOV), or just above the average selling price (ASP) of one of your products, in the hopes of encouraging customers to order a second unit.

>> **Tracking:** One of the most common reasons for a customer to email an online store after they've placed an order is to ask where their order is, so don't forget to add tracking to your orders when you're fulfilling them so that your customers are updated. As you grow, platforms like Starshipit are great for automating tracking for your orders.

Customers care about how quickly they can receive their orders, and how clearly tracking and order updates are communicated to them, so it's important that your store offers a competitive logistics solution. Chapters 6 and 13 talk more about shipping and logistics.

Chapter **20**

Ten Ways to Prepare to Go Live

I n any business, it's important to go into it with your eyes wide open. Just because things may start slow, it doesn't mean they'll always be slow. I can't tell you the number of businesses that I have worked with that started from the humblest of beginnings, sometimes losing money, to eventually become house-hold names turning over tens, if not hundreds, of millions of dollars.

In this, my final chapter, I talk about managing your expectations and preparing to go live with your online store. I remind you of some important checks you need to make so you're sure you've covered all your bases. I also show you how to push the button and make your store live, setting it off into the wilderness that is cyberspace.

Failing to plan is planning to fail!

REMEMBER

Pop Quiz: Are You Sure You're Ready?

Take the time to make sure you're as comfortable as you can be with all the topics in this book. After all, it's your hard-earned money, sweat and sometimes tears that are at stake here — and so often, the difference between succeeding or not is down to the planning and research you commit to the project, which can be even more important than choosing the right product(s).

So, here's a little quiz to see if you're ready:

1. What does AOV stand for, what does it measure and where can you check it?

2. What does CVR stand for, what does it measure and where can you check it?

3. How can you measure if your customers are being provided with a great customer experience?

4. Can you accurately sum up the problem that your online store's products are solving for a customer?

5. If you're running ads on Facebook and Instagram, what do ROAS and CPO stand for?

Answers:

1. Average order value (AOV) is your total sales for a given period of time (such as one day, one week or one month) divided by the total number of orders in the same period. It measures how much on average a customer spends with your store per order. You can check your AOV at any time in your Shopify admin by going to Analytics, then Dashboards.

2. Conversion rate (CVR) is the number of orders your online store receives during a certain time period, divided by the number of visits your store receives during the same period, expressed as a percentage. If you don't know your conversion rate, it's almost impossible to succeed, as you won't know how effective your marketing channels are. There's no rule around what the right conversion rate is — it differs by industry and product, but a conversion rate of less than 2 per cent is on the low side. You should be careful not to throw too much money into traffic that doesn't convert — you're likely to incur a loss. You can check your CVR by going to your Shopify admin → Analytics → Dashboards.

3. Surveys certainly help. There are many ways to survey customers, but the NPS (Net Promoter Score) is regarded as a universal benchmark of overall customer experience as it factors in the entire customer journey. Check in the Shopify App Store for tools to monitor your NPS. Turn to Chapter 7 for more on measuring customer experience.

4. Honestly, there's no real answer here! If you think you're able to sum up the problem your products are solving, and your products give you that 'aha!' moment where you know you've nailed it, you're on the right track. Pitch your product idea to family and friends, and ask them to honestly critique it. A good product is more than half the battle in ecommerce. Find your product niche, invest in it, and nail it.

5. ROAS stands for Return on Ad Spend, and CPO stands for Cost Per Order. The ROAS measures the sales you've made versus the amount spent on the ad. The CPO tells you the dollar amount you've paid to get each order. CPO and ROAS are both important metrics to understand before spending any money on ads (Chapter 16 looks at these metrics and ad spend in more detail).

The Price Must Be Right!

Check, double check and triple check the pricing you've decided on for your products.

REMEMBER

As a rule, if you're sourcing products directly from a manufacturer or creating your own brand (as opposed to buying from brands and re-selling) then you should be aiming for 70 per cent profit margin on the product — sometimes called the mark-up. This allows you enough wiggle room for marketing, wages, promotional activities and any other costs of running your business.

REMEMBER

The *profit (or product) margin*, or mark-up, is the profit you make before any costs of sales are considered, factoring in only the cost price of your product and the sales price you are selling at. Your *gross margin* factors in your cost of sales (such as shipping costs and merchant fees), not just the product costs.

If you're buying and reselling the products of established brands, a gross profit margin of 45–50 per cent can work, but remember that the lower your gross margin, the less you can spend on your operating expenses, including marketing expenditure, so the rule may change to 40 per cent gross margin, where 20 per cent covers operating expenses, leaving a 20 per cent net profit.

If you're still unsure about how to price your products or check your margin, I suggest re-reading Chapter 14, as you won't be able to make good decisions on where to spend your money without understanding the profit that each product generates.

TIP

After you go live, you can check your profit margin in the Profit by Product report (refer to Chapter 11 for more on this). If you see anything with too low a profit, consider increasing the price or removing it from your product range after it sells out.

Manage Your Expectations

Humans are curious things, online shoppers even more so. The average customer browses a website multiple times before eventually deciding to purchase. It's totally reasonable to expect that a customer won't make a purchase on their first day visiting your online store, and so your first day can be very slow.

So, before you panic and decide to pack it in, remember that it's important to manage your expectations. In your business plan, you may assume that you'll have very little organic (free) traffic at first, as you'll have no word of mouth and no SEO traction — both of these things take time to generate.

EXAMPLE

Imagine you're aiming for a conversion rate of 1.5 per cent (which is on the low side, but it's always best to budget cautiously). If you're relying heavily on paid media at first, you may be paying $1 to generate each click through to your website (an estimate, but probably not too far off the money). If you spent $1,000 for the week on a combination of Facebook Ads and Google Ads, your efforts may have driven 1,000 visitors to your website — add in another 200 'free' visitors from your email database and your social media pages, and you have a total of 1,200 visitors. If these visitors convert at 1.5 per cent, you calculate your order number as follows:

$$1,200 \times 1.5 = 18 \text{ orders}$$

If your AOV (average order value) is $100, that's $1,800 in sales! However, if you subtract tax at 10 per cent you're left with $1,620, and if you subtract the cost of goods sold (COGS) for your products, assuming a product margin of 65 per cent (65 per cent of $1,620 is $1,053, which gives you a COGS figure of $567), you're left with $1,053 in net sales — a profit! But profit or not, it's not enough to pay your wages, your rent or yourself!

This example highlights three important points:

1. **Don't depend heavily on paid media.** You want a product than generates buzz and gets people talking; that way, you're likely to get more free traffic and generate revenue from organic sources. If you're targeting a product that's not unique, or that other big retailers are selling, it's going to be harder to get that organic traffic, and more expensive to try and outrank bigger businesses on keywords in your search engine marketing.

REMEMBER

Paying for more traffic to a low-converting website is a recipe for losing money. Scale your marketing spend up when your conversion rate rises to a profitable level.

2. **Be patient.** Amazon took ten years to turn a profit; you can get there much faster if you're clever. In my experience, you can generate a good income within a year if you do things properly. Plenty of my clients have started a small business and turned it into a fully fledged, successful online store within their first 12 months.

3. **Be prepared.** Make sure your business plan tells you how much money you need to breathe life into your new venture, and try and avoid going into your new business half-baked. Planning is the key!

TIP

I recommend holding three months' worth of your forecasted operating expenses in ready cash — if your business model predicts a *cash burn* (the amount of money a business spends and loses until it becomes profitable — because new businesses often initially spend money to penetrate a market before they become profitable), then you'll be comfortable that you have the cash to weather the storm. For example, if your forecast requires your business to spend $10,000 per month for three months, then always hold $30,000 in the bank. This takes the pressure off when sales are slow to begin with.

REMEMBER

Be prepared to play the long game — one year at least. If you're prepared to go for a year with minimal expectations, I feel confident that if you follow the guiding principles of the book, you can make it a roaring success.

You Can't Be All Things to All People

You don't need to sell every product in the world, and you don't need to compete with every Tom, Dick or Bezos in the world to sell a product. Do your research, find a product and look out for the 'aha!' moment that suggests your product is a good one.

TIP

Don't be afraid to pivot. If your product isn't working, there's no point in throwing good money after bad; your job is to keep on top of product trends and constantly try to match supply to demand.

The same applies when you're finding an audience to sell to. Who you want your customer to be, and who they really are, can be two very different things.

REMEMBER

You're not selling to an identical twin version of yourself, so research the heck out of your customer, find out what motivates them, and show them the products that they want to buy, not the products you wish they would buy. When you strip back ecommerce to its roots, it's simply providing products and services to people who need or want them. The chapters in Part 3 provide guidance on getting to know your customer and making their shopping experience a positive one.

TIP

Also, know your own strengths and weaknesses. You can't be good at everything, so use the Shopify Experts marketplace when you need to. Being thrifty has merit, but not at the expense of quality.

There's an App for That!

The Shopify App Store is your friend, so make sure you use it. When I started out in ecommerce all those years ago, unless you were a developer, the features that apps can now bring you were unheard of!

TIP

Browsing the Shopify App Store, or asking other Shopify merchants what good new apps they've seen, is one of my favorite things to do in Shopify. I find something new every time!

In Chapter 18 I share my top ten favorite Shopify apps. See if any of these apps can help you along your ecommerce journey.

Believe the Hype (Phase)

At least a month before you launch your store, you should be launching a 'hype phase', which is when you start building momentum so that when your store eventually goes live, you have as much organic traction as possible.

A *hype phase* can include drip-feeding content across your socials, collecting as many email addresses as possible, and simply spreading the word through friends, family and anyone who will listen.

It always surprises me when someone opens an online store and doesn't shout it from the rooftops. You need to do that!

Chapters 15, 16 and 17 take you through marketing your store so you can build a buzz around your products.

Not Too Heavy, Not Too Light: Getting Ordering Just Right

Getting your product mix and inventory levels right can be the difference between a raging success and a fizzling failure. Before you go live, take a look at your product mix alongside that of your nearest competitor. If your competitor is selling something similar but has ten, 20 or 30 times the range size, you're going to find it very difficult to take a customer away from them — which is essentially what you're trying to do.

The fewer products you have in your product range, the less likely you are to make a sale due to the lack of options. The way to combat this is to invest properly in inventory and make sure you're holding just as much variety as your genuine competitors. I'm not talking about department stores with millions of visits each day, but medium-sized competitors who you know your target market shops with, and who you know to be successful — or at least popular.

TIP

Don't skimp on product — going into a new online business with three varieties of socks, T-shirts or backpacks is unlikely to be a life-changer for you, so get busy sourcing products!

On the inventory front, don't bend to the whim of pushy suppliers. Order what is right for you and try not to be tempted into reaching supplier MOQs (minimum order quantities) that you know aren't possible.

TIP

If you're selling apparel, make sure you know what sizes or variants are most popular. If you sell out of your bestselling sizes but have too much of the other sizes, the chances are you won't have enough money generated from profits to repeat an order of the best sizes only, which puts a huge strain on your cash resources. What's the point of reordering your best sizes if all your profits are tied up in the less popular sizes on your shelves?

Chapter 11 tackles inventory in more detail.

Shopify Reports to Watch

One of the great assets that Shopify provides its sellers is its suite of reporting and analytics tools that can be found in the Shopify admin (go to Analytics → Reports).

Here are my top three reports to keep an eye on:

>> **Sales:** Who doesn't love a Sales report? Shopify has a range of out-of-the-box sales reports sitting under the Sales menu of the Reports section. This is a great place for your bookkeeper to come and do their end-of-month financials, or to simply check how sales are progressing from month to month, week to week, or day to day.

TIP

For extra insight on sales, click into the Sales Over Time report.

>> **Profit by Product:** Given I've gone on and on about protecting your profit margin, it seems only fitting to include this profit margin report in my top three! Use this report to ensure your profit margins remain on track.

The Profit by Product report relies on you having input your cost prices when you created products. It then calculates your profit margin, so that you can check if your actual profit margin is the same as what you had planned. I cover this report in detail in Chapter 11.

>> **ABC Analysis by Product:** I'm a big believer in analyzing inventory as a means to grow your business. Knowing your ABC inventory status is imperative for determining whether or not your buying and replenishment is satisfactory.

The ABC Analysis by Product report gives your inventory a grade based on the sales that those products drive. I cover this report in detail in Chapter 11.

Last-Minute Checks Before You Go Live

As you round the final bend, ready to launch your Shopify store into cyberspace, give your store a last-minute once-over.

Here's a checklist to tick off:

>> Have you connected your domain to your Shopify store? If not, turn to Chapter 2.

>> Have you registered all your social media accounts, including Facebook, Instagram, Twitter, TikTok, Snapchat and Pinterest? If not, turn to Chapter 17.

>> Have you got a plan to beef up your product reviews? A lonely looking product page with zero reviews is having the opposite of the desired result. Ask your family and friends to try your products, and then, if they're happy to, leave you reviews when you go live, detailing their genuine experience and thoughts on your product. Part 3 is all about the customer, and Chapter 8 dives deeper into reviews.

>> Have you placed a test order? Go through your website and place a test order or three. Ask your friends to do the same, with a fresh set of eyes, and look out for anything that doesn't work as it should. It's better to fix these things before you send traffic to your online store.

To place a test order, enable test mode by following the below steps:

1. **From your Shopify admin, go to Settings → Payments.**

2. **In the Shopify Payments section, click on Edit.**

3. **Check Use Test Mode.**

4. **Click on Save.**

After you place your test order, turn off test mode following the same instructions.

REMEMBER

>> Within two clicks from your homepage, can you locate the following pages?

- About Us

- Shipping Info

- Returns Policy

- All your product categories

If not, turn to chapters 4 and 5 and adjust your menus.

>> Are your product descriptions optimized for SEO and addressing the problem your product solves for a potential customer? It's important to get the basics right from the start, and the quality of your product descriptions are a key influence on your customer's decision-making progress. If you haven't nailed your product descriptions, turn to chapters 5 and 16.

>> Have you set an intended target for any paid ads you may be doing, such as Facebook Ads? How will you measure the success of your campaigns after the first week?

REMEMBER

How much a business can spend on things like paid media goes back to its business's marketing plan, and how to measure the impact of your marketing channels is an essential part of knowing whether or not your marketing is working. If you're not sure how to measure the impact of your marketing campaigns, turn to Part 5.

>> Have you got live chat turned on? Live chat is a great, cheap way to see what your early visitors think of you.

REMEMBER

As an ecommerce business owner, never stop asking questions of your customers and getting to know them better. If you haven't turned on live chat, turn to Chapter 7.

>> Have you familiarized yourself with Shopify's Help Centre pages and support? They're full of useful information and tips.

>> Have you managed your own expectations? Launching your Shopify store is an incredibly fun and fulfilling experience, so enjoy it and don't let a few slow days get you down. Many of the best businesses I work with had zero sale days for weeks at the start.

REMEMBER

Expecting high sales from day one almost never happens — it's usually a slow and steady build.

Ready, Set, Go: Time to Go Live!

If you've tested, prodded and poked your Shopify store, and then tested it some more, and you're confident that it's ready to go live, then it's time to remove the password from your online store, which then publishes your store to real visitors.

REMEMBER

The password you need to remove here is not the same password that you use to login to Shopify; instead, it's the password that you have the option to set up to keep your site private until you're ready to launch. Pre-launch, nobody can see your website unless they have the password — which is useful when you're in the designing and building phase. Refer to Chapter 2 for how to set up this password.

To remove the password from your store, follow these steps:

1. **From your Shopify admin, go to Online Store → Preferences.**

   The Preferences page appears.

2. **In the Password Protection section, uncheck the Enable Password option.**

3. **Click on Save.**

Congratulations, you're now a Shopify merchant!

REMEMBER

It takes time to be the next Jeff Bezos, so don't be too hard on yourself. A successful online retailer is a patient person, so enjoy the ride and don't forget to tell me how you go! I get a real thrill from seeing people succeed on Shopify, so I'd love to hear about your online stores when they go live.

Until then, crawl till you can walk, walk till you can jog, and jog till you can sprint. However fast or slow you go, keep moving forward because will always beats skill.

Index

Numbers

1% principle, 193
3D models, 95

A

AB testing (split testing), 200–202, 393
ABC analysis by product, 245–246
About Us page, 147
accordion menus, 63–64
activating products, 107
active product availability, 239
address verification service (AVS) checks, 262
admin panel, 25–32
  Analytics page, 27–30
  Apps page, 30
  Customers page, 27
  Home page, 26–27
  Marketing page, 30
  Orders page, 27
  Products page, 27
  Sales channels page, 30–31
  settings, 32
Advanced Shopify, 17
advertising, 333–362
  email marketing, 357–362
  Facebook Marketing, 334–343
  Google Ads, 343–350
  search engine optimisation (SEO), 350–357
affiliate marketing, 377, 378
AI (artificial intelligence), 107
Alibaba.com website, 37
alternative payment providers, 136–137
alternative text, 354–355
Amazon, 39
Analytics page, 27–30, 195–197
analytics tools, 195–197
announcement bar, 69
AOV (average order value), 27, 28
application programming interfaces (APIs), 18, 49

apps, 381–388
  Back in Stock: Customer Alerts, 386
  for digital products, 34
  Foursixty, 486–487
  Glew, 384
  Gorgias, 382
  Klaviyo, 383–384
  Oberlo, 384–385
  Okendo, 382–383
  Plug in SEO, 388
  PushOwl, 385–386
  ReferralCandy, 387–388
  using fulfillment service with, 279–280
Apps page, 30, 104
AR (augmented reality), 95
archiving orders, 251–252
  automatic archiving, 252
  manual archiving, 251–252
artificial intelligence (AI), 107
at-risk customers, 177, 182–183
audience building ads, 337–342
augmented reality (AR), 95
automated collections, 82, 87
automatic archiving, 252
automatic fulfillment, 275
automatic payments, 251
availability status, 239
average order value (AOV), 27, 28
AVS (address verification service) checks, 262

B

B2B (business to business) sales, 43–44
B2C (business to consumer) sales, 42–43
back end developers, 56–57
Back in Stock: Customer Alerts app, 386
backend orders, 253–254
banners
  adding extra, 73
  personalization of, 208–209

barcodes, 99, 235

Basic Shopify, 16

bestsellers, 211–212

black hat dropshipping, 45

blog posts, Sales channels page, 31

bounce rate, 57

broken links, 198–199, 391–392

business extensions, 46

business intelligence, 384

business registration number, 135

business to business (B2B) sales, 43–44

business to consumer (B2C) sales, 42–43

Buy Now button, 17

C

carriers, 116, 117

cash-positive business, 47

channel mix, 323

chargebacks, 141–142

chatbots, 150–151

CLTV (customer lifetime value), 158, 169–172, 274

coding, 56–57

COGS (cost of goods sold), 242–243

collections, 72, 81–107

  activating products, 107

  adding new products to store, 90–106

    adding initial inventory quantity, 98–99

    adding media to products, 94–97

    adding product description, 93–94

    adding variants, 100–102

    creating new product in Shopify, 91–93

    final adjustments, 103–106

    pricing products, 97–98

    selecting shipping options, 99–100

  adding to menu, 89–90

  creating, 82–86

  merchandising, 106–107

  using product tags, 86–89

communication with customers, 146–154

  about orders, 258

  clear policies and product information, 146–148

  customer service channels, 149–154

    chatbots, 150–151

    email, 149–150

    live chat, 150

    phone, 151–152

    Shopify Inbox, 153–154

    social media, SMS, WhatsApp, 152–153

community forums, 20

Compare At price, 97–98, 298–300

confirming orders, 248–249

Contact page, 148

content, social media, 364

conversion rate (CVR), 27, 28

conversions, 256, 322

cost of goods sold (COGS), 242–243

credit card processing fees, 16

CSAT (customer satisfaction) surveys, 160

CSS platforms, 149–150

currency

  personalization by, 212–213

  setting up multiple currencies in Shopify Payments, 138–139

custom fulfillment service, 277–279

customer experience, 145–219

  communicating with customers, 146–154

    clear policies and product information, 146–148

    customer service channels, 149–154

  customer reports, 177–187

    customizing, 184–187

    using in Shopify, 177–184

  customer satisfaction (CSAT) surveys, 160

  Gorgias app, 382

  improving, 389–397

  key performance indicators (KPIs), 154–155

  loyalty programs, 169–174

    customer lifetime value (CLTV), 169–172

    referral programs, 172–174

  making friends with customers, 12

  maximizing, 155–160

  monitoring customer behavior, 320

  personalization, 203–219

    creating personalized shopping experience, 204–206

    gift cards, 213–217

    giving little unexpected extras (GLUE), 218–219

    of store, 206–213

  researching, 403–404

  reviews, 162–168

    free offsite review platforms, 168

    offsite customer reviews, 164–166

    onsite product reviews, 163–164

    selecting platform for, 166–168

user experience (UX), 189–202
  AB testing, 200–202
  improving, 193–200
  overview, 190–193
  user-generated content, 174–177
customer lifetime value (CLTV), 158, 169–172, 274
customer reports, 177–187
  customizing, 184–187
  using in Shopify, 177–184
customer satisfaction (CSAT) surveys, 160
Customers page, 27
customs declaration form, 284–286
CVC code, 262
CVR (conversion rate), 27, 28
CX. *See* customer experience

D

D2C (direct to consumer) sales, 41–42
Dashboards, Analytics page, 27
data intelligence, 384
data-led buying, 38
defectors, 177
delivering orders, 12–13
demand, 37
description, product, 93–94
design, inventory, 237–238
detractors, 158–159
device analyses, 199
digital marketing, 13–14, 317–332
  building marketing plan, 318–324
  implementing marketing campaigns and automations, 324–332
  overview, 318
digital products, 33–34
direct to consumer (D2C) sales, 41–42
discounts, 301–315
  creating codes for, 302–310
    buy X get Y discount codes, 307–310
    percentage or fixed amount discount codes, 303–307
  free shipping, 311–312
  shortcuts for, 312–315
DNS (domain name system), 22
domain name, 21–22
domains, Sales channels page, 31
draft orders, 253–254

draft product availability, 239
drop-down menus, 63
dropline menus, 64
dropshipping, 44–48, 277
  comparing different kinds of, 45–46
  Oberlo, 384–385
  pros and cons of, 47
  on Shopify, 47–48
dynamic banners, 208–209
dynamic retargeting ads, 342–343
dynamic shipping rates, 115

E

eBay, 50
ecommerce, 7–14, 20–21
  delivering orders, 12–13
  digital marketing, 13–14
  going live, 14
  making friends with customers, 12
  managing stock levels, 12–13
  overview, 8
  planning for success, 10–11
  rise of social media in, 364–365
  Shopify
    overview, 9–10
    setting up store, 11–12
economies of scale, 113
editing orders, 257–258
EDM (electronic direct mail), 27, 357
email
  as customer service channel, 149–150
  email hosting, 22
  marketing
    Klaviyo, 383–384
    overview, 357–362
engagement levels, 369
Etsy.com website, 37
experts, hiring, 20, 390
express shipping, 115–117

F

Facebook, 366–368
Facebook Marketing, 334–343
  audience building ads, 337–342
  dynamic retargeting ads, 342–343

Facebook Marketplace, 49
Facebook Messenger, 152, 367–368
Facebook Shop, 366–367
FAQs (frequently asked questions) page, 146–147
favicon, 76
Featured Collections option, 72
first response times, 154
fixed amount discount codes, 303–307
flash sales, 311, 321
flat rate shipping, 114–115, 125
flyout menus, 63
focus groups, 198
followers, 376
footer, 74
Foursixty, 486–487
fraud, 139–142, 262–265
    fraud analysis indicators, 262–264
    handling, 264–265
    investigating suspicious orders, 139–141
    processing chargebacks, 141–142
free shipping
    discounts for, 311–312
    paid shipping vs., 110–115
free trial, 15–16, 22–23
frequently asked questions (FAQs) page, 146–147
front end developers, 56
fulfilling orders, 251, 267–289
    automatic fulfillment, 275
    customs declaration form, 284–286
    local pickup, 287–289
    manual fulfillment, 268–275
    packing slips, 286–287
    shipping labels, 280–284
    using fulfillment service, 276–280
full stack developers, 57

G

gift cards, 213–217
    issuing, 214–215
    for purchase, 215–217
gift with purchase, 219
giving little unexpected extras (GLUE), 218–219, 393–394
Glew, 384
going live, 14, 399–408
    browsing Shopify App Store, 404
    checking prices, 401

checklist, 406–408
launching hype phase, 404
managing expectations, 402–403
ordering and inventory amounts, 405
pop quiz, 399–401
removing password, 408
researching customers, 403–404
watching Shopify reports, 405–406
Google Ads, 343–350
Google Analytics, 194, 320, 322
Google Reviews, 164–166
Google Smart Shopping campaign, 348–350
Google Trends, 38–39, 351
Gorgias app, 382
gross profit, 242–243
gross profit margin, 110–114, 294
guided selling, 210–211

H

H1 header, 356
hamburger menus, 64
handwritten notes, 218, 394
headers, 67–69, 89
homepage, store, 26–27, 62–76
    adjusting theme settings, 74–76
    menu, 63–64
    styling, 64–74
hype phase, 404

I

ICE score methodology, 207–208
images
    alternative text, 354–355
    image gallery, 73–74
    with text, 71
    text columns with, 71–72
IMSs (inventory management systems), 99, 224–226
influencer marketing, 376–377
information ecology, 191–192
initial inventory quantity (stock on hand (SOH)), 98–99
Instagram, 368–373, 386–387
Instagram Insights, 370–372
Instagram Shopping, 372
internal search, 200
international sales, 17, 100, 116–117

interviews, 198
inventory, 223–246
    before going live, 405
    initial inventory quantity, 98–99
    inventory management systems (IMSs), 224–226
    inventory reports, 243–246
    listing across sales channels, 238–241
    purchase order (PO), 227–234
    storing, 234–238
    tracking stock movement, 242–243
inventory management systems (IMSs), 99, 224–226
IP addresses, 140, 263

J

Jaded Pixel, 9

K

key performance indicators (KPIs), 154–155
keywords, 351–356
Klaviyo, 383–384

L

label printers, 281
landed cost price, 98, 111
landed stock, 230
language, 212–213
Launch Engineer, 18
launching hype phase, 404
layout, inventory, 237–238
licenses, 33
linking scoial media profiles, 375
Liquid template language, 57
live chat, 150
Live View, Analytics page, 28
local pickup, 287–289
location-based sizing, 213
locations, inventory, 236–237
logistics, 396–397
loyalty programs, 169–174
    customer lifetime value (CLTV), 169–172
    referral programs, 172–174
LoyaltyLion, 173–174

M

machine learning, 205–206
Made-in-China.com website, 37
mail order shopping, 44
manual archiving, 251–252
manual collections, 82–83
manual fulfillment, 268–275
manual payments, 250
marketing automations, 324–332
marketing campaigns, 324–332
Marketing page, 30
marketing plan, 318–324
    creating marketing channel plan, 323
    knowing customer behavior, 320
    marketing strategy, 320–321
    measuring success, 321–322
    reviewing performance, 323–324
    unique value proposition, 319–320
media, adding to products, 94–97
mega menus, 64
menus
    adding collections to, 89–90
    creating, 79
merchandising, 106–107
meta descriptions, 352–354
metrics, 28–29
mining data, 176
mobile version, 391
Morville, Peter, 191–192

N

navigation, Sales channels page, 31
net profit margin, 294–296
Net Promoter Score (NPS), 158
net sales, 243

O

Oberlo, 48, 384–385
observation tests, 197–198
offsite customer reviews, 164–166
Okendo, 168, 382–383
omnichannel retailers, 32, 45, 225
one touch tickets, 155

1% principle, 193
O'Neil, Tom, 193
online marketplaces, 48–51
online resources
  AB testing platforms, 202
  digital platforms, 37
  dropshipping, 48
  free offsite review platforms, 168
  label printers, 281
  marketplaces available on Shopify, 50–51
  support services, 19–20
online sales channels, 41–44
  business to business (B2B) sales, 43–44
  business to consumer (B2C) sales, 42–43
  direct to consumer (D2C) sales, 41–42
Online Store section, 105–106
onsite product reviews, 163–164
orders, 247–265
  creating draft orders, 253–254
  fraud, checking for, 262–265
    fraud analysis indicators, 262–264
    handling, 264–265
  fulfilling, 267–289
    automatic fulfillment, 275
    customs declaration form, 284–286
    local pickup, 287–289
    manual fulfillment, 268–275
    packing slips, 286–287
    shipping labels, 280–284
    using fulfillment service, 276–280
  inventory levels and, 405
  managing, 255–261
  receiving and confirming, 248–249
  stages of online order, 249–252
Orders page, 27
organic sales, 21
organic social media, 363
Organization section, 104
outbound freight costs, 111
overselling, 244

P

package types, 121–123
packing slips, 286–287
page load speed, 198–199, 390–391
pages, 31, 76–78

paid media, 318
paid shipping, 110–115
pallet racking, 236
Pareto principle, 245
partial orders, 271–275
passives, 158–159
passwords, 24–25, 408
payment gateways, 134
payment processing, 133–139, 249–251
  alternative payment providers, 136–137
  automatic payments, 251
  manual payments, 250
  setting up multiple currencies in Shopify Payments, 138–139
  setting up third-party payment provider, 139
  Shopify Payments, 134–136
  Shopify Payouts, 137
'people also bought' feature, 210
percentage discount codes, 303–307
personalization, 203–219
  creating personalized shopping experience, 204–206
  gift cards, 213–217
  giving little unexpected extras (GLUE), 218–219
  improving customer experience (CX), 394
  of store, 206–213
phone, 151–152
Pinterest, 374
plans, 15–19
  Advanced Shopify, 17
  Basic Shopify, 16
  regular Shopify, 16–17
  Shopify Plus, 17–19
Plug in SEO app, 388
PO. *See* purchase order (PO)
policies, 146–148
preferences, Sales channels page, 32
price-based shipping rates, 125–126
pricing products, 97–98
print on demand, 46
product creation model, 46
product recommendation engines, 209
Product Reviews (Shopify), 166
Product Status section, 103
product-based shipping, 125
products, 35–51. *See also* collections
  adding new products to store, 90–106
  adding to Instagram Shopping, 372–373

checking prices, 401
customer service and, 146–148
dropshipping, 44–48
  comparing different kinds of, 45–46
  pros and cons of, 47
  on Shopify, 47–48
including tax in product price, 133
online sales channels, 41–44
  business to business (B2B) sales, 43–44
  business to consumer (B2C) sales, 42–43
  direct to consumer (D2C) sales, 41–42
pricing, 294–296
quizzes and guided selling, 210–211
selling on online marketplaces, 48–51
sourcing right products to sell, 36–41
  checking trending products in Shopify, 40–41
  locating products to sell, 36–37
  tools to check for trending products, 37–40
Products page, 27
profiles, shipping, 120–129
  adjusting default package type, 121–123
  rates and, 124–129
profit margin, 294–296
promoters, 158–159
promotions, 296–298, 358. See also discounts
purchase order, 227–234
  creating, 228–229
  receiving, 229–234
PushOwl, 385–386

Q

quality control check, 229

R

real time shipping rates, 115
receiving orders, 248–249
recordings, 190–191
referral programs, 172–174
  LoyaltyLion, 173–174
  ReferralCandy, 174, 387–388
  Yotpo Loyalty, 174
ReferralCandy, 174, 387–388
refunding customers, 259–260
repeat customer rate, 29
replenishment, 244–245

Reports, Analytics page, 28, 177–187, 405–406
reselling, 46
resolution time, 155
RET (rolled edge type) shelving, 236
return on ad spend (ROAS), 322
returns, 260–261
reviews, 162–168
  free offsite review platforms, 168
  offsite customer reviews, 164–166
  Okendo, 382–383
  onsite product reviews, 163–164
  selecting platform for, 166–168
Reviews.IO, 167
RFM metrics, 172
ROAS (return on ad spend), 322
rolled edge type (RET) shelving, 236
Rosenfeld, Louis, 191–192

S

sales and marketing, 293–378
  advertising, 333–362
    email marketing, 357–362
    Facebook Marketing, 334–343
    Google Ads, 343–350
    search engine optimisation (SEO), 350–357
  Compare At price, 298–300
  digital marketing, 317–332
    building marketing plan, 318–324
    implementing marketing campaigns and automations, 324–332
    overview, 318
  discounts, 301–315
    creating codes for, 302–310
    free shipping, 311–312
    shortcuts for, 312–315
  metrics for, 28–29
  by POS location, 29
  preparing to run sales and promotions, 296–298
  pricing products, 294–296
  social media, 363–378
    affiliate marketing, 378
    influencer marketing, 376–377
    linking profiles, 375
    marketing channels, 365–375
    rise of in ecommerce, 364–365

sales channels, 104
  listing inventory across, 238–241
    making products available to, 239–241
    product availability status, 239
  page navigation, 30–31
    blog posts, 31
    domains, 31
    navigation, 31
    pages, 31
    preferences, 32
    themes, 31
search engine optimisation (SEO), 350–357
  broken links and, 392
  keywords, 351–356
  Plug in SEO app, 388
  SEO-friendly store, 356–357
search function, 200, 392–393
Selling Online For Dummies (Lundquist), 18
sell-through, 245
SFN (Shopify Fulfillment Network), 286
shareable discount link, 312–313
shelving equipment, 236
shipping, 99–100, 109–129
  express shipping vs. standard shipping, 115–117
  free shipping vs. paid shipping, 110–115
    dynamic (real time) shipping rates, 115
    flat rate shipping, 114–115
    gross profit margin, 110–114
  printing labels, 280–284
  profiles for, 120–129
    adjusting default package type, 121–123
    rates and, 124–129
  Shopify Shipping, 117–119
shipping aggregators, 115
Shopify, 15–34
  choosing plan, 15–19
    Advanced Shopify, 17
    Basic Shopify, 16
    regular Shopify, 16–17
    Shopify Plus, 17–19
  domain name, 21–22
  Google sales channel in, 344–348
  navigating admin panel, 25–32
    Analytics page, 27–30
    Apps page, 30

    Customers page, 27
    Home page, 26–27
    Marketing page, 30
    Orders page, 27
    Products page, 27
    Sales channels page, 30–31
    settings, 32
  overview, 9–10
  selling digital products, 33–34
  setting up store, 11–12
  Shopify POS, 32–33
  signing up, 22–25
  support services, 19–21
Shopify Analytics, 194
Shopify App Store, 404
Shopify Compass, 20
Shopify Email app, 359–362
Shopify Fulfillment Network (SFN), 286
Shopify Inbox, 153–154
Shopify integration, 279
Shopify Liquid, 18
Shopify Lite, 17
Shopify Payments
  setting up, 134–136
  setting up multiple currencies in, 138–139
Shopify Payouts, 137
Shopify Plus, 17–19
Shopify POS, 32–33, 226
Shopify Shipping, 117–119, 282–284
signing up, 22–25
SKU (stock-keeping unit) code, 99, 235
SMS (short message service), 152–153, 357
Snapchat, 375
social media, 363–378
  adding social media icons to homepage, 76
  affiliate marketing, 378
  as customer service channel, 152–153
  influencer marketing, 376–377
  linking profiles, 375
  marketing channels, 365–375
    Facebook, 366–368
    Instagram, 368–373
    Pinterest, 374
    Snapchat, 375
    TikTok, 373–374

rise of in ecommerce, 364–365

shareable discount link, 312–313

user-generated content on, 176

social proof, 65

SOH (stock on hand), 98–99, 230

split menus, 64

split testing (AB testing), 200–202, 393

standard shipping, 115–117

static banners, 208

stock levels, 12–13

stock on hand (SOH), 98–99, 230

stock-keeping unit (SKU) code, 99, 235

Stocky, 226–227

store, Shopify, 55–107

adding pages, 76–78

collections, 81–107

activating products, 107

adding new products to store, 90–106

adding to menu, 89–90

creating, 82–86

merchandising, 106–107

using product tags, 86–89

creating menu items, 79

fraud prevention, 139–142

investigating suspicious orders, 139–141

processing chargebacks, 141–142

going live, 399–408

homepage, 62–76

adjusting theme settings, 74–76

menu, 63–64

styling, 64–74

making content SEO-friendly, 356–357

payment processing, 133–139

alternative payment providers, 136–137

setting up multiple currencies in Shopify Payments, 138–139

setting up third-party payment provider, 139

Shopify Payments, 134–136

Shopify Payouts, 137

personalization of, 206–213

setting up, 11–12

shipping options, 109–129

express shipping vs. standard shipping, 115–117

free shipping vs. paid shipping, 110–115

profiles for, 120–129

Shopify Shipping, 117–119

tax rates, 129–133

including tax in product price, 133

setting up tax collection, 130–133

themes, 59–62

web development and coding, 56–57

website architecture, 57–59

storing inventory, 234–238

layout and design, 237–238

locations, 236–237

shelving equipment, 236

subscribers, 357–358

supply, 37

support services, 19–21

surveys, 197–198, 395

suspicious orders, 139–141

T

tags, 86–89, 105

tax rates, 129–133

including tax in product price, 133

setting up tax collection, 130–133

testimonials, 73

themes, store, 31, 59–62

adding, 60–61

choosing, 60

customizing, 62

publishing, 61–62

social media and, 375

third-party payment providers, 139

3D models, 95

TikTok, 373–374

Timeline section, 256–257

title tags, 352–354

top landing pages, 29

tracking

orders, 274, 397

stock movement, 242–243

trade shows, 36

traffic source, 29

Transfers function, 230–232

trending products

checking in Shopify, 40–41

tools to check for, 37–40

Trustpilot, 167

typography, 75

U

unique value proposition, 319–320
Urchin Tracking Modules (UTMs), 29, 322
usability tests, 197–198
user experience honeycomb, 192
user experience (UX), 189–202
  AB testing, 200–202
  improving, 193–200
  overview, 190–193
user research, 194–198
user-generated content, 174–177, 386–387
users, 12
UTMs (Urchin Tracking Modules), 29, 322

V

variants, 87, 100–102, 299, 386
VAT (value-added tax), 132
vendors, 104
video, personalized, 219
voiding shipping labels, 283–284

W

warehouse management system (WMS), 99
web development, 56–57
web hosting, 21–22
web push notifications, 385–386
website architecture, 57–59
weights, 100
WhatsApp, 152–153
white hat dropshipping, 45–46
wholesale trade, 41
WMS (warehouse management system), 99

Y

Yotpo, 167
Yotpo Loyalty, 174

Z

Zalora, 49
zones, shipping, 126
zoom feature, 96

About the Author

Paul Waddy is a passionate online retailer who has built, bought and advised online retail businesses across the world. Paul's primary focus is to help people improve their lives using the vehicle of ecommerce, with the help of the Shopify platform.

Paul was born in Sydney, Australia, and attended school at Redfield College. After leaving school, Paul worked in various jobs, before starting a men's footwear business in 2007, which he owned for ten years. He derived most of its sales via online channels, which started Paul's love affair with all things relating to selling online.

After rounding out his practical experience by completing an MBA, Paul moved into ecommerce advisory work (through his business, Paul Waddy Advisory), and he now advises many online retailers, including several he has invested in. Paul is also the co-founder of Ecom Nation, a digital marketing agency created to build and scale online businesses; the founder of learnecommerce.com.au, a resource for people to learn ecommerce through an online course Paul has created; and the co-founder of the Tippy toothbrush, a sustainable toothbrush aimed at reducing landfill.

Paul lives in Sydney with his wife and three daughters, and his dog. Feel free to get in touch with Paul at paulwaddy.com, or follow him on LinkedIn for free ecommerce insights.

Dedication

For my mum, Caroline, and my grandparents, Paul and Rosheen — thank you for everything.

Acknowledgements

Far more goes into writing a book than I'd ever imagined, and I couldn't have done it without a great team — thanks to the John Wiley editorial team, especially Kerry Laundon, Ingrid Bond, and the publishing and marketing team, in particular Lucy Raymond.

I'd like to acknowledge all the team at our digital marketing agency Ecom Nation, especially my co-founders Mal Chia and Andrew Sabatino, world-class experts in their respective fields.

I'd like to thank all my corporate advisory clients, and my students at learnecommerce.com.au, who have been pivotal in giving me exposure to many different businesses and products.

Last but not least, I'd like to thank my family: my wife and kids, for being so patient during the writing of this book, and for giving me many entertaining writing breaks; and my dog Archie — my co-author. My inspiration for staying up late writing this book came from my mum and my grandparents, so this is for you.

Publisher's Acknowledgements

Some of the people who helped bring this book to market include the following:

Acquisitions, Editorial and Media Development

Project Editor: Tamilmani Varadharaj

Editorial Manager: Ingrid Bond

Acquisitions Editor: Lucy Raymond

Copy Editor: Kerry Laundon

Production

Proofreader: Susan Hobbs

Indexer: Estalita Slivoskey

The author and publisher would like to thank the following copyright holders, organisations and individuals for their permission to reproduce copyright material in this book:

›› Cover image: © AnnaStills/Shutterstock

›› Screen captures from Shopify used with permission. © Shopify Inc. Shopify is not affiliated with John Wiley & Sons Australia, Ltd in any manner. Shopify has not approved or otherwise endorsed this Publication and its contents.

Every effort has been made to trace the ownership of copyright material. Information that will enable the publisher to rectify any error or omission in subsequent editions will be welcome. In such cases, please contact the Permissions Section of John Wiley & Sons Australia, Ltd.